AF520047

KNOWLEDGE SOCIETIES AND LIBRARIES

Papers in honour of Prof. A.A.N. Raju

Edited By

N. Laxman Rao
S. Sudarshan Rao
T. V. Prafulla Chandra

Ess Ess Publications

4837/24, Ansari Road, Darya Ganj,
New Delhi-110002
✆ : 23260807, 23201533
Fax : 23274173
E-mail: essess@del3.vsnl.net.in

© Editors

First Published 2004

ISBN : 81-7000-353-9

Price: Rs.1075/

All rights reserved. No part of this publication may be reproduced, stored in a retrieval system, or transmitted in any form or by any means, electronic, mechanical, photocopying, recording or otherwise, without the prior permission of Ess Ess Publications.

Published by:

Ess Ess Publications

4837/24, Ansari Road, Darya Ganj,
New Delhi - 110 002
Phone : 23260807
Fax : 23274173
E-mail : essess@del3.vsnl.net.in

Laser Typesetting:

Mukesh Graphics

L-2/8, DDA Market,
Mangolepuri, New Delhi
Ph. : 27924405

Printed at :

Mehra Offset Press, Delhi.

Prof. A.A.N. Raju

Contents

Introduction

Knowledge Society is an Enlightened Society and the present day society is being described as Information Society or Knowledge Society. In Knowledge Society, learning, understanding, creativity and ideas value to everything. To create Knowledge Society, there is a need to collect, preserve and provide access to World's information resources with the help of network of information resources or libraries, which promote world of ideas and creativity. In this Society, the information / knowledge plays a vital role in managing all the resources such as human, material, machines and capital to compete both at local and international levels in various respects.

Knowledge, ideas, innovations, adaptability and creativity stand as the foundations of the economy of nations. The progress, prosperity and sustainability of societies and nations of the world are dependent on the availability, access and adaptability of appropriate knowledge and information as solutions to the specific problems of the nations. The fast changing modern World is mainly dependent on information / knowledge to survive and sustain in the competitive environment.

In this context, the knowledge and information management, and information dissemination or transfer to the society is of great importance and it is more so for the developing societies like India.

As a result of which the importance for information / knowledge organization and dissemination / transfer of World's Information Sources have gained greater importance. The knowledge workers / information processors, organizers, disseminators have been extensively using the computer and communication technologies to provide customized, user friendly and quality information products and services than the earlier times. The present work is an attempt to focus such issues that are concerned involved with the Library & Information Centers and the Knowledge Society.

Prof. A. A. N. Raju is well known in the LIS profession in Andhra Pradesh in particular and India in general. Having served in many capacities such as Faculty Member, Professor, Head, Chairman, BOS in Library & Information Science and Dean, Faculty of Social Sciences of a prestigious University, viz. Osmania University for more than three decades. He contributed 13 books and 50 articles with which he could carve a place for himself on the map of Indian Librarianship. He was also associated with professional bodies as a Life Member and also Office Bearer.

The present Festschrift *"Knowledge Societies and Libraries"* is the outcome of the expression of respect and regard to Prof. A. A. N. Raju by his professional colleagues, well-wishers and students.

This volume contains 44 original articles written by LIS professionals of rich experience. These articles are arranged in ten broad sections covering areas of current concern to the libraries and information centers including schools of Library Science.

Section-I contains 5 articles dealing with the themes such as *Right to information, Information Services to Academics and Researchers, Information pricing, Information gathering habits of scientists and the role of librarian in the Information World / Knowledge Society.*

Section-II deals with Information Technology and Internet. Seven articles are presented in this section. They deal with the *Use of IT and Electronic media in modern day libraries, searching the web, Internet Services and Hypertext.*

Section-III contains three articles on *Library Automation and Computerized Circulation System.*

In Section-IV, there are four articles and they deal with *Natural Language Interface, Design of a Micro-Schedule,*

Structural relations in Colon Classification and hierarchical retrieval in library classification.

Section-V contains three articles, which deal with *Non-book material their preservation methods and use in the present day libraries.*

Section-VI contains six articles, which deal with the *quality aspects of libraries and library services. The articles in this section cover the issues such as TQM in LICs, Quality Information Services in the changing IT environment in LICs, Human Resource Planning in academic libraries, Sustainable manpower development including the intrinsic of information management.*

Section-VII contains three articles which cover the areas such as *Electronic Information Sources in digital libraries, growth pattern and scietometrric studies of literature / information.*

Section-VIII has 4 articles dealing with public and rural libraries in India. The issues covered under this section include *public library movement, public library collections and services, and transforming rural public libraries into Rural Information Centers by using IT.*

Section-IX has three articles and they deal with academic libraries in India. The specific areas dealt in this Section are: *Teacher Training College Libraries, University Libraries including the Open University Library and their Student Support Services.*

Section-X, the last section of the Volume contains six articles. *They deal with various aspects of LIS Education and Research, such as Curriculum Design and Specialization in LIS Education, Research in LIS, Continuing Education Programs in LIS including LIS as a Profession.*

The contents of the Volume are on the thrust areas of Library & Information Science and they are directly related to the library and information professionals of the Information Society.

Therefore, the present volume is expected to be of immense value to the modern day information professionals such as librarians, Information Managers, students and faculty members of different LIS Schools.

— The Editors

Acknowledgements

We are grateful to Prof. A. A. N. Raju for accepting our proposal to bring out a Festschrift Volume in his honor covering various issues of the Library & Information Science field that are of relevance to the present day Information Society. We sincerely acknowledge our thanks the LIS Professionals who have contributed their expertise and knowledge in the form of articles for this work. Many professional colleagues have helped us by extending their support and advise in the course of bringing out this publication. We acknowledge their support with thanks.

Our thanks to Mr. S. Yadagiri, Research Scholar in Library & Information Science, Osmania University and Librarian, Center for Indian Ocean Studies, O.U. has been helpful to us in comparing the proofs of the work.

We thank Mr. Madhusudan, Office Secretary, Dept. of Library & Information Science for extending his timely secretarial assistance in the course of preparation of the work.

Our sincere thanks go to Mr. Sumit Sethi of M/s Ess Ess Publications, New Delhi, who could firmly stand by us in our difficulties in the publication of the book and also for bringing out this document in a befitting manner to honor Prof. Raju.

— The Editors

Contributors

1. Dr. U.K. Agarwal,
   Assistant Librarian,
   College of Commerce & Management Studies,
   M.L. Sukhadia University,
   Udaipur 313001.

2. Mrs. S. Ally Sornam,
   Head, Dept. of Library & Information Science,
   Bishop Heber College,
   Tiruchirapalli (Tamil Nadu).

3. Dr. (Mrs) Amrit Pal,
   Senior Lecturer,
   Dept. of Library & Information Science,
   Guru Nanak Dev University,
   Amritsar.

4. Mr. M. Anjaiah,
   Coordinator, SDLCE,
   Kakatiya University,
   Warangal.

5. Mr. T. Ashok Babu,
   Scientist, RCI,
   D.R.D.L.,
   Kanchanbagh,
   Hyderabad 500058.

6. Ms. A. Bagavathi,
Research Scholar,
Dept. of Library & Information Science,
University of Madras,
Chennai 600005.

7. Prof. A.K. Baradol,
Professor & Chairman,
Dept. of Library & Information Science,
Mangalore University,
Mangalagangotri 574199.
(Karnataka).

8. Dr. P. Barua,
Professor,
Dept. of Library & Information Science,
University of Burdwan,
Golapbag,
Burdwan 713104. (West Bengal).

9. Mrs. Bharari Tubachi,
Library Assistant,
Agricultural University,
Dharwad.

10. Ms. Chaya Devi,
Research Scholar (SRF),
Dept. of Library & Information Science,
Andhra University,
Visakhapatnam 530003.

1. Mr. Cholin, (Scientist-B),
INFLIBNET Centre,
Near, Gujarat University Guest House,
P.B. 4116;
Navrangpura,
Ahmedabad 380009.

12. Dr. Dinesh K. Gupta,
Assistant Professor,
Dept. of Library & Information Science,
Faculty Wing,
Kota Open University,
Kota 324010.

13. Mr. Basavaraj Kademani,
Scientific Officer-D,
Library & Information Services Division,
Bhabha Atomic Research Centre,
Mumbai 400085.

14. Mr. V.L. Kalyane,
Turning Point Centre,
2:2, C5-29, Sector-5, Konkan Bhavan,
Navi Mumbai 400614.

15. Dr. M. Kanakachary,
Assistant Librarian,
Central Institute of English & Foreign
Languages,
Hyderabad 500007.

16. Mr. S.G. Karakun
Librarian
College
Gulbarga.

17. Dr. C.R. Karisiddappa,
Professor & Chairman,
Dept. of Library & Information Science,
Karnatak University,
Dharwad 580003.

18. Dr. A. Lakshmana Moorthy,
Scientist-E,
DRDL, Kanchanbagh,
Hyderabad.

19. Dr. B.S. Maheswarappa,
Professor & Chairman,
Dept. of Library & Information Science,
Gulbarga University,
Gulbarga 585106.

20. Prof. Manorama Srinath,
Dept. of Library & Information Science,
University of Madras,
Chennai 600005.

21. Dr. S.S. Pal,
Dept. of Library & Information Science,
Panjab University,
Chandigarh 160014.

22. Prof. T. Rajagopal,
Dept. of Library & Information Science,
S.V. University,
Tirupati 517502.

23. Mr. L.S. Ramaiah,
Former Librarian,
Ramesh Mohan Library,
Central Institute of English and Foreign Languages,
Hyderabad 500007.

24. Prof. B. Raman Nair,
University Librarian,
Kerala Agricultural University,
Trichur 680654.

25. Mr. A. Ramasamy,
Librarian,
YMCA College of Physical Education,
Nandanam,
Chennai 600035

26. Mr. L.S.R.C.V. Ramesh,
Type-II, Qr. No. 23,
ANGR Agricultural University Campus,
Rajendranagar,
Hyderabad 500030.

27. Dr. B. Ramesh Babu,
Associate Professor,
Dept. of Library & Information Science,
University of Madras,
Chennai 600005

28. Dr. R.K. Rout,
Professor,
Dept. of Library & Information Science,
Sambalpur University,
Sambalpur (Orissa).

29. Prof. S.L. Sangam,
Dept. of Library & Information Science,
Karnatak University,
Dharwad 580003.

30. Ms. Sangita Behera,
Librarian,
Kalahandi Training College,
Bhawanipatna,
Dist: Kalahandi (Orissa).

31. Mr. T.R.B. Sarma,
Deputy Librarian,
Institute for Social and Economic Change (ISEC),
Nagarbavi, P.O.
Bangalore 560072.

32. Prof. M.P. Satija,
Dept. of Library & Information Science.
Guru Nanak Dev University,
Amritsar 143005

33. Mr. Sunil Kumar Satpathy,
Librarian,
D.B. College,
Bhatli 768030
Dist. Bargarh (Orissa).

34. Prof. N.R. Satyanarayana,
Professor,
Dept. of Library & Information Science,
University of Lucknow,
Lucknow.

35. Prof. S. Seetharama,
17, Varadarajulu Naidu Road,
Egmore,
Chennai 600008.

36. Dr. P. Soma Raju,
Professor,
Dept. of Library & Information Science,
Andhra University,
Visakhapatnam 530003.

37. Dr. K. Somasekhara Rao,
Associate Professor,
Dept. of Library & Information Science,
Andhra University,
Visakhapatnam 530003.

38. Dr. (Mrs) Sonal Singh,
Head, School of Studies in LIS,
Vikram University,
Ujjain 456010, (M.P.).

39. Dr. M.S. Subramanian,
Dept. of Library & Information Science,
University of Madras,
Chennai 600054

40. Dr. S. Sudarshan Rao,
Associate Professor & Chairman, BOS
Dept. of Library & Information Science,
Osmania University,
Hyderabad 500007.

41. Dr. Surendra Singh,
Head, Dept. of Library & Information Science,
Sandipani P.G. College,
Ujjain 456010, (M.P.).

42. Mr. Suresh Jange,
Assistant Librarian,
Gulbarga University Library,
Gulbarga 585106

43. Dr. P.G. Tadasad,
Dept. of Library & Information Science,
Gulbarga University,
Gulbarga 585106.

44. Dr. Urmila A. Thaker,
Reader,
Dept. of Library & Information Science,
Sardar Patel University,
Vallabh Vidyanagar 388120, Gujarat.

45. Dr. R.S.R. Varalaxmi,
Dept. of Library & Information Science,
Andhra University,
Visakhapatnam 530003.

46. Dr. K. Veeranjaneyulu,
Assistant Librarian,
Central Library,
Agricultural University,
Rajendranagar,
Hyderabad 500309.

47. Dr. Velaga Venkatappaiah,
Former Librarian,
Dept. of Public Libraries,
Government of Andhra Pradesh,
4-22-25, Ithanagar,
Tenali. 522201

48. Dr. P. Venkata Ramana,
Assistant Librarian,
School of Planning and Architecture,
JNTU, Masab Tank,
Hyderabad 500028.

49. Mrs. J. Vijaya Kumari,
Associate Professor,
Dept. of Library & Information Science,
Andhra University,
Visakhapatnam 530003.

50. Dr. V. Vishwa Mohan,
Associate Professor,
Dept. of Library & Information Science,
Osmania University,
Hyderabad 500007.

51. Prof. P.L. Vishweshwar Rao,
Dept. of Communication & Journalism,
Osmania University,
Hyderabad 500007.

52. Dr. S.D. Vyas,
Librarian,
Banasthali Vidyapith,
Banasthali 304022.

53. Dr. J. Yadagiri Reddy,
Associate Professor & Head,
Dept. of Library & Information Science,
Osmania University,
Hyderabad 500007.

Prof. A. A. N. Raju : A Profile

Addepalli Appala Narasimha Raju was born on 1st July, 1938 at Bobbili. He had his schooling at the esteemed Govinda Chandra Dev High School at Rayagad, Orissa. After completing his 10th Standard in 1957, he shifted to Hyderabad in the year 1959. He pursued his higher education at Osmania University. He completed his PUC in the year 1960, Certificate Course in Library Science in 1962, B.A. (1963), Dip.Lib.Sc. (1964), M.Lib.Sc. from Banaras Hindu University, Varanasai in 1966, M.A. (History) 1967, Ph.D. (1987), and Diploma in Distance Education (1992) from IGNOU, New Delhi.

Raju is a self-made man, after passing his 10th standard he worked as a Clerk at the Bobbili Agricultural Cooperative Marketing Society during 1957-59. In 1959 after shifting to Hyderabad he joined Andhra Pradesh Academy of Music and Drama (Andhra Pradesh Sangeeta Nataka Akademy) as clerk. While continuing in employment he continued his studies. He obtained a Certificate in Library Science and with the blessings and help of Professor Birduraju Rama Raju and Sri Kodati Narayana Rao, he joined the Hyderabad City Grandhalaya Samstha as Grade III Librarian. Thus his career in the field of Library Science was started. During 1964-66 he worked as Deputy Librarian in the Andhra Pradesh Public Library System. In 1966 he joined Osmania University Library as Library Assistant and after two years i.e. in 1968 he moved to teaching profession by joining the Department of Library & Information Science, Osmania University as Lecturer. He was promoted as Reader in the year 1972 and as a Professor in September 1983. He worked for 30 long years as a Teacher and retired on June 30th 1998 as Dean, Faculty of Social Sciences, Osmania University.

PERSONALITY:

Prof. Raju is one of the model teachers and is known for his punctuality. He served the Dept. of Library & Information

Science as Head & Chairman, Board of Studies for about 20 years. Most of the students used to feel that he is a teacher without any personal feelings. But he used to work for the students' cause and used to make all the efforts to solve their problems. He was immensely rule minded and impartial.

He is a specialist in Library Classification. His contributions include schedules for Indology as supplement for the Dewey Decimal Classification Scheme. He prepared practical guidebooks for the use of classification schemes such as DDC, UDC and CC. He is also a regular contributor for Grandhalaya Sarwaswamu, a professional journal in Telugu. Apart from Library Classification his areas of specialization are Public Library System, Information Systems etc. He has made significant contribution to the literature of Library & Information Science. He has contributed about twenty-three books and one hundred and twenty five research articles in LIS.

RESEARCH PROJECTS UNDERTAKEN:

1. College Library Survey Research Project

Undertaken during the years 1973-75. This project relates to the survey of the conditions of college libraries under the jurisdiction of Osmania University. The objective of this survey was to obtain necessary statistical data on various aspects of College Libraries.

2. Study of Indian Information Sources in Social Sciences

Undertaken during the academic year 1980-81 with the objectives to study the institutions involved in social science research; and prepare a list of Indian Source Materials in the field of Social Sciences.

3. Access to Documentary Heritage in Select Libraries in South India (under UGC Emeritus Fellowship Program, 1999-2001)

In this Project the study was made on the accessibility of documentary heritage in 34 very old and prominent libraries in South India.

SEMINARS/WORKSHOPS, etc. ORGANIZED AND ATTENDED:

Prof. Raju was responsible for organizing seven seminars in addition to nine refresher courses. He also attended 57 Conferences / Seminars / Workshops at International, National, Regional and Local levels.

1. Attended UNISIST / FID / IFLA International School and Workshop for Teachers in Information Science, held during 7th May to 1st June, 1979 at Graz and Lindabrunn, Austria, under Unesco's Fellowship Programme.
2. Attended First International ISKO Conference on Tools for Knowledge Organisation and Human Interface organised by International Society for Knowledge Organisation held at Darmstadt, Germany from 14-17 August 1990.

RESEARCH WORK LEADING TO Ph.D. DEGREE:

Research work entitled "Library Movement in Coastal Andhra and Telangana 1900-1956: A Study in Comparison with select case studies". The study deals with genesis and development of library movement in Coastal Andhra and Telangana regions of Andhra Pradesh. It is a thorough, exhaustive and an authoritative study on the subject.

PROJECT WORKS & DISSERTATIONS SUPERVISED:

Prof. Raju guided the Ph.D. Scholars in LIS and five Ph.Ds were awarded and one candidate is still working for Ph.D. He supervised 17 Dissertations of MLISc Students.

CONTRIBUTION TO CURRICULUM DEVELOPMENT:

He had contributed for curriculum development in the Department of Library and Information Science at Osmania University. His contribution includes designing and updating of syllabi for BLISc, MLISc and M.Phil. Every attempt had been made to blend the traditional and modern topics. He had also contributed in designing the syllabi of several other Universities both within and outside the State. He implemented the

University's concept of preparation of detailed teaching programme based on the syllabi for each paper in BLISc / MLISc Courses.

CONTRIBUTION TO PROFESSIONAL GROWTH:

He is associated with Indian Library Association (ILA, New Delhi), Indian Association of Special Libraries and Information Centres (IASLIC, Calcutta), Indian Association of Teachers in Library and Information Science (IATLIS), Andhra Pradesh Library Association (APLA, Vijayawada) and other professional bodies. He was also a Member of the UGC Panel on Library and Information Science for two consecutive terms.

He made all the efforts along with Sri B. P. Shenoy to start MLISc Programme for the first time in Andhra Pradesh at the Osmania University in 1978. Further, he also took initiative to start Ph.D. programme at the Department of Library and Information Science, Osmania University in 1988. This provided research facilities to scholars in this region.

He has actively participated in the distance education programmes (BLISc and MLISc) of Dr. B. R. Ambedkar Open University and IGNOU in various capacities such as resource person for curriculum design, course editor and course writer.

AWARDS:

1. He was awarded IATLIS-Motiwale Best LIS Teacher Award for 1995 instituted by the Indian Association of Teachers of Library and Information Science (IATLIS).
2. UGC Emeritus Fellowship 1999-2001.

PUBLICATIONS:

Books in English:

1. *Documentary Heritage of Indian Libraries.* New Delhi, Ess Ess Publications, 20023.
2. *Objective Question Bank for Library and Information Science Ability Tests.* New Delhi; Ess Ess Publications, 2002.

3. *Colon Classification: Theory and Practice; A Self-Instructional Manual* New Delhi; Ess Ess Publications, 2001.

4. *Handbook of Pseudonymous Authors in Telugu.* 2nd Edn. Hyderabad, 2001. The Author.

5. *Information Systems and Programmes.* Hyderabad, Dr. B.R. Ambedkar Open Univ. (MLISC course Material) 1999. Editor.

6. *Fifty Years of Library and Information Science Education in India.* Hyderabad, Suchithritha Graphics, 1997. Editor.

7. *Information Technology and Its Impact on Library and Information Science Education and Library Management.* Editor Delhi: Delta Publishing House, 1997. Editor's

8. *Universe of Knowledge: Its Development and Structure.* New Delhi: Ess Ess Publications, 1997. Editor.

9. *Dewey Decimal Classification (DDC-20): Theory and Practice: A Self-Instructional Manual.* Madras: T.R. Publications, 1995.

10. *New Vistas in Library and Information Science: Prof. G.V.S.L. Narasimha Raju Festschrift.* New Delhi: Vikas, 1995. Editor.

11. *37th Andhra Pradesh Library Conference on "Contemporary Issues in the Field of Library Science", May 19-21, 1995, Department of Library and Information Science, Sri Krishnadevaraya University, Anantapur.* Vijayawada: Andhra Pradesh Library Association, 1995. Editor.

12. *Universal Decimal Classification (IME, 1985): Self Instructional Course Material.* Madras: University of Madras, 1995.

13. *Academic Libraries: Role in the National Development.* Madras: T.R. Publications, 1993. Editor.

14. *Universal Decimal Classification (IME, 1985): A Practical and Self-Instructional Manual.* Madras: T.R. Publications, 1991.

15. *Library Classification—DDC & CC (Practice).* New Delhi: IGNOU, 1989. Editor

16. *Library Classification (Theory).* New Delhi: IGNOU, 1989. Course Writer.

17. *History of Library Movement in Andhra Pradesh.* Delhi: Ajanta, 1988.

18. *Hyderabad City Grandhalaya Samstha Silver Jubilee (1961-1986): Souvenir.* 1986. Editor.

19. *Library Classification (Theory).* Hyderabad: A.P. Open University, 1985. Editor and Course Writer. Revised Edition, 1993. Editor. (B.L.I.Sc. Course)

20. *Decimal, Universal Decimal and Colon Classification: A Study in Comparison.* Delhi: Ajanta Publications, 1984.

Books in Telugu:

21. *Sampradimpu Samachara Sevalu, Aadharalu.* (Reference and Information Sources and Services.) Hyderabad: Telugu Akademi, 2001. Editor.

22. *Grandhalaya Vargikarana Prayoga Dipika.* (Library Classification Practice: Colon Classification.) Hyderabad: Telugu Akademi, 1991.

23. *Grandhalaya Vargikarana Siddantam.* (Library Classification Theory.) Hyderabad: Telugu Akademi, 1987.

I : 1

Right to Information : A Fundamental Right in a Democracy

P.L. Vishweshwar Rao

INTRODUCTION

The characteristics of a democracy are freedom of the people in thought, word and deed; a government that rules with the consent of the people and the openness of the administration which is of the people by the people and for the people. These three pillars support a democracy and further it. Any curtailment or abridgement of any of these would dilute the spirit of democracy. And yet we have been practising a highly diluted form of democracy for the past fifty years, restricting the right of the people for a transparent and an accountable administration. While no doubt our infant democracy tottered quite a few times, missing a step or two and gradually learning to gain balance, especially in ensuring freedom to the people and in giving ourselves a government of our choice, we have lagged behind in giving ourselves an administration that functions with least secrecy, one whose all decisions and actions are open to public scrutiny and critical assessment. The administration has remained shrouded in the secrecy of rules, accountable to nobody, not even to itself. This secretive functioning of administration is a hangover of colonial practices which saw people as subjects rather than masters. The movement for the right of information is a struggle of the people to regain their rightful position, that of masters, of which they were usurped by a devious bureaucracy and a corrupt political system.

RIGHT TO INFORMATION

Right to information is basic to the functioning of a democracy. The right to seek and collect information from government and from all individuals and institutions using public power and public resources is implicit in the right to free speech and expression. Without the requisite information, it is not possible to form an 'informed opinion'. This right applies to information not only from the government and the public authorities, but also information from all individuals and institutions which use public power and resources including private individuals, companies and corporations. They are accountable to the people for the misuse of the power and the funds. The functioning of a true democracy must be transparent since one of the essentials of democracy is the accountability to the people of all the managers of its affairs for their day to day acts of omission and commission. The accountability is not possible in the absence of the transparency of the functioning. Some restrictions of the right may be essential and reasonable in the interest of the security and integrity of the State, friendly relations with the other States, public order, the need to protect internal notings and communications or trade and business secrets. However these places of confidentiality need to be critically scrutinised. The burden should be on the authorities to prove the grounds on which the secrecy of the relevant information is claimed.

Often, even in countries with hoary traditions of freedom and democracy, authorities use grounds of national security, internal order, public interests and others as convenient excuses to stonewall enquiries into the functioning of government departments, public organisations and private corporations. The right to information should be mandatory for a free press and effective functioning of democracy. The information sought must further be available to the applicant at a reasonable cost.

Otherwise the right given by such legislation would be virtually defeated in practice.

THE BEGINNINGS OF THE MOVEMENT TO KNOW

In 1990, a mass-based organisation called the Mazdoor Kisan Shakti Sanghatan started working with the very poor in Bhim Tehsil of Rajasthan, one of the most backward regions of one of the most backward states of India.

The struggle of Mazdoor Kisan Shakti Sanghatan (MKSS) for the right of the rural poor to know how the development programmes meant for them were being implemented began as a struggle for minimum wages which climaxed in the poor wanting information regarding how many of them were benefited by development programmes and how many cheated out of their wages, land and houses by a corrupt bureaucracy. During its work with the very poor, MKSS discovered that minimum wages were being very widely denied in the region. When it intervened to obtain the legal minimum wage, the government made all out efforts to block its efforts. At one place, Dadi Rapat, particular care was taken to ensure that there was no laxity on the part of the workers, but still they were sanctioned much less than the minimum wage rate. In another incident when peaceful MKSS activists were sitting on a hunger strike in Bhimown, the administration sent eight vans of policemen to break up the protest.

This resistance of the government to a basic legal right of the poor to obtain minimum wage declared by the same government motivated the MKSS to get more information on the extent to which the resources meant for the poor were being stolen by corrupt bureaucrats and politicians. This led to a series of "jan sunwais" or public hearings in 1994-95 in which local people, officials, elected representatives, media persons and eminent citizens were invited to hear details of how government funds meant for the poor were actually used. Shocking stories came out of how people who were not even living in villages at that time had been shown as receiving wages on the muster rolls. People who were not aware of land deals had been shown as beneficiaries of concessional sale of land, and how fraudulent companies had been created to corner a large share of rural development funds without actually supplying the materials or doing any work. It was a littany of misappropriation of funds meant to provide a livelihood to the poor through rural employment schemes and others. Works were left incomplete as the budgeted amount was squeezed out. School buildings with no roof, dispensaries with no walls, dams left incomplete and community centres with no doors and windows... the story was familiar.

Corruption was nothing new. There is no one in the villages in Rajasthan who does not think that the village officials are petty thieves. So what was to be achieved by jan sunwais? By reading the details of the bills and vouchers and names of people, they made it very personal. The audience reacted with rage at the brazenness of the officials and their elected leaders. The impact was electrifying. Several other public hearings were organized from December, 1994 to April, 1995 in the same region. With every public hearing, village officials and politicians, in spite of polite invitations from the MKSS, stayed away and proclaimed their guilt by their silence and absence. Poor people came by the hundreds to listen in eerie silence to accounts of embezzlement of public funds. The collective rage and anger was enough to make one engineer of the State Electricity Board return in public Rs. 15,000 he has extracted from a poor farmer, the one and only instance of money ever being returned in Rajasthan because of public pressure and humiliation. From these historical jan sunwais emerged two demands of the people: one, any citizen from the village should have the right to make photocopies of all bills, vouchers and muster rolls on payment for any work done by the Government in their village, and two, that the embezzled and misappropriated funds should be recovered from the village officials and politicians, their property attached and publicly auctioned and that the money recovered should be spent in the same village. While the government said the issue was really a non-issue and that all such information was readily available at the Block level, the Union of Gram Sevaks, the village level development officials, in January, 1995, threatened to go on a strike if the government acceded to the MKSS demand. As the movement got wide publicity and support from prominent public figures and journalists, the Rajasthan Chief Minister Shri Bhairon Singh Shekhawat in a historic announcement on the floor of the State Assembly, in April, 1995 declared that citizens had the right to information, and on payment anyone could demand and receive details of expenditure on work done over the past 15 years in their villages and all the documents could be photocopied as evidence should they want to use it in future. However, even after one year this historic promise was not fulfilled. When in April, 1996, MKSS launched an indefinite hunger strike in Beawar town, the government came out with a G.O. that fell far below the promise made by the Chief Minister. The order made no mention of the right to photocopy documents but allowed for "inspection" and hand-written details which made certification impossible. In a state where literacy is the lowest in the entire country, the G.O. was more an insult than a sleight of hand by a bureaucracy intent on saving its hide. The MKSS refused to budge and there was an outpouring of support from the people of Beawar. They offered free accommodation, food and free printing of pamphlets to the MKSS volunteers. The dharna continued for 40 days and spread to Jaipur too. It was called off after the government appointed a sub-committee to study the practical aspects of providing photocopies and certified copies of its records on development budget and expenditure. The committee, headed by the State's additional Chief Secretary, submitted its report to the Chief Minister in August, 1996 and it has not been accepted nor made public because the government felt the recommendations were impractical and therefore difficult to implement.

Mr. Shekhawat proudly announced at the Chief Ministers Conference held in new Delhi on May 24, 1997 that it was now possible in Rajasthan to obtain information about irregularities committed in the execution of works, sanctions of purchase of materials whereas the fact is that no such arrangement or system has yet been evolved. The Chief Minister once again baulked from making good his promise. The Chief Minister has formed yet another cabinet sub-committee under the chairmanship of the Deputy Chief Minister, Mr. Hari Shankar Bhabhra. Veteran journalist Kuldip Nayar who has taken an active role in this movement says, "The Chief Minister Bhairon Singh Shekhawat, I have come to believe, does not want the account books examined. It seems a big chunk of the allocated funds has been siphoned off. But the matter should not be allowed to rest here. The Center gives Rajasthan Rs. 750 crores annually for rural development. The State allocations are in addition. The CBI should enquire how the allocations have been used. Both politicians and bureaucrats may be pocketing money meant for building roads, schools and health centers. What distresses me is that if Mr. Shekhawat, considered a comparatively clean chief minister, can throw dust in the eyes of people, what about other States? A central legislation on the subject will be welcome but what punishment should be meted out to Mr. Shekhawat for making false promises." ("The Right to know", The Hindu, June 15, 1997).

THE SPREAD OF THE MOVEMENT

The Right to Information spread throughout the country in a few years after Beawar started it. The implications of the denial of information for the country as a whole were grave and in an era of looting of the state and national exchequers by a nexus of politicians, bureaucrats and industrialists, it seemed more relevant if not essential than ever before.

Several NGOs took inspiration from the movement and replicated it in their own areas. For instance, in Tehri Garhwal region of Uttar Pradesh citizens of Bhilangana Block backed by a local NGO, Chetana Andolan, made a demand similar to the one made in Beawar: how were the development funds earmarked and used?

From the arid Beawar Village in Bhim Tehsil of Rajasthan to the Chamiyala village in foothills of Himalayas in Uttar Pradesh, the stories of swindling the poor are similar. Only details vary. Similar is the brazenness of the system; its apathy, uniform. On March 1, 1997, activists of Chetana Andolan held a "Lok Adalat". Women gave up their daily chores to sit in the audience along with their infants and men took the day off from their toil. The "stories" they heard left them open-mouthed. They realised they had been cheated systematically out of roads, buildings, bridges, schools, canals, and most important their wages, which would have made a difference to most of them, poor as they are.

Chetana Andolan (The Movement for Awareness) stumbled upon the fraud accidentally. When some of their activists submitted a list of people needing employment to Bhilangana Block Development Officer they were told that under the Jawahar Rozgar Yojana and Employment Assurance Scheme, 700 employment cards had already been given in 12 villages in the Bhilangana Block. On verification, Chetana activists found that not a single villager had received the card nor was he even aware of the card. The movement took a crucial turn when Chetana volunteers stumbled upon the swindling of Rs. 2.5 lakhs sanctioned for development works in Dhansani village. Pressure tactics on the Gram Pradhan and the BDO bore fruit and the corrupt officials were forced to return the amount of Rs. 2.0 lakhs they had siphoned off.

The NGO, Chetana, started the movement mainly to ensure that the local people got adequately employed and did not have to migrate to the cities to seek employment. Also this movement was meat to ensure that the funds from the Jawahar Rozgar Yojana and Employment Assurance Scheme were available to the people instead of going into the pockets of corrupt officials. These officials would employ labour from outside Garhwal, from Nepal or Bihar, pay them little or no wages and pocket the rest. Development funds were going the same way.

Out of Rs. 1,88,000 earmarked for eight development projects in the region, Rs. 83,10,000 was siphoned off, according to a report prepared by Chetana. However, the affected have realised that activists and local citizens who were exposing the corrupt officials are themselves being dragged into the court on false and trumped up charges.

This success led to the declaration of a "war" on corrupt officials through Jan-Sunwais or Lok Adalats at block level During the Chamiyala "Khula Manch" (Open House), it was revealed that 95 percent of the public funds meant for development had been siphoned off by a coterie of middlemen and administrators. Six cases were taken up at the meeting and the findings were startling. Out of Rs. 20.43 lakhs sanctioned for roads, only Rs. 45,700 was actually spent on the work. Similar is the case of a four-km Nauli-Baroma road. An amount of Rs. 17 lakh was allegedly spent on it but there was no road other than in official records. According to Ganga Devi Rawat, the newly appointed Gram Pradhan, "The village development officer approached me to sign some paper to confirm that they have built the road. After checking all the documents, I realised they were taking money for the road which they never built". In another instance, a toli nayak of Kepars, Mr. Gajender Negi, who executed a project of an approach road in Kapars-Dhantha Kor, told the audience that while Rs. 75,000 was sanctioned for the work, only Rs. 14,000 was given to the workers. Similar is the case of Gana Samanedi contact road, where Rs. 75,000 were sanctioned but only Rs. 14,000 were paid to the labourers. "Forged signatures were signed on muster rolls", said Chandan Singh, a contractor of Gona village. The Gram Pradhan of Maikoth village, Mr. Prem Singh revealed that a 16-km canal in Maikoth was built 20 years ago and since then they have been spending money every year to repair the canal. The irony was that water was been available in the canal after it was built. Even though government functionaries were absent the odds were loaded against them. The villagers, armed with evidence, proved that rural development has remained only on paper. Dhoom Singh Lagheri of Pedagaon pointed out that Rs. 1,20,000 had been sanctioned for developing a dam forest reserve area of over 10 hectares in his village but in reality less than three hectares have been converted into reserve area. Records show money has gone into the hands of Range Officer and the Forest Guard but the work has not been done, he said. The villagers of Bhilangana Block, in Tehri district, have already succeeded in partial cleansing of the system by ousting 35 of the 92 gram panchayats, who were found guilty of misappropriation of funds during the panchayat elections in November, 1996.

The MKSS campaign on the right to information regarding development expenditure has faced the most organised opposition from Panchayat authorities in Jawaja block of Ajmer district in Rajasthan. It has received unstinted support from the Panchayat of Thana in Bhilwar district. Experience in these Panchayat illustrates the growing importance citizens attached to right to such information; the use of such information to control corruption, to reach an informed understanding about norms and priorities of development works, and finally to show how transparent systems of functioning can lead to more efficient systems of democratic governance.

Thana Panchayat elected an activist of the MKSS, Ladu Singh, as Sarpanch in February 1995. He was elected without spending any money on his campaign as he had been put up as a people's candidate.

Ladu Singh had been involved with the Right to Information campaign of the MKSS. The first thing he did upon taking charge was to provide open access to all citizens to all panchayat documents. He also said that all future works would be executed in a completely transparent manner and any citizen would have the right to obtain a photocopy of any document upon paying the cost.

In April 1995 the Panchayat of Thana and the MKSS jointly organised a public hearing on development information. The hearing was the first real public audit of the expenditure that the people of the area had participated in, and it brought home to them the critical importance of access to such information. A comparative study of the functioning of Thana Panchayat with Rawatmal and Badkochra Panchayats in Jawaja block showed up interesting findings.

In Badkochra Panchayat, 14 out of 22 works executed were evaluated partially due to lack of time, according to a document. (The Right to Know, The Right to Live: People's struggle in Rajasthan and the Right to Information, MKSS, July, 1996).

Out of the 16 works examined (in the years 1993 to 1995), there has been roughly 30 percent fraud established already, amounting to Rs. 1,67,775. Some works like repair work of the Bhairu Kheda road billed at Rs. 3,200, repair work of Bhuria Kheda Khurd Talab billed at Rs. 3,000, repair work of Khatela Talab billed at Rs. 3,180, social forestry work of Rs. 4,786 were concocted. The work of Ratna Talab feeder undertaken in 1995 had Rs. 45,075 in false material bills. Out of a total expenditure of Rs. 99,918, a sum of Rs. 69,205 was shown as material expenditure. Many works were billed at higher material ratios and they were approved by the block office.

The newly elected representatives of the Thana Panchayat held a jan sunwai soon after the Rajasthan Chief Minister announced in the State Assembly that ordinary people and elected representatives would have access to all records related to development works. The hearing was conducted by Sarpanch Ladu Singh. Despite having a constitutional mandate of being a representative of the people and an executive head, the Chief Minister's announcement and the order issued by the District Collector to the Block Office, he still had difficulty in getting hold of the past five years records which were to be presented at the hearing. It was only with the persistent efforts of the MKSS that the Block Office agreed to part with some information on the night before the hearing. Why was audited information not being made available despite orders of a Collector? What was the fear of the bureaucracy? Why the resistance to part with information even to elected representatives? The reasons were clearly revealed in the hearing in Thana. For the first time government officials were present in this hearing. The Gram Sewak and Junior Engineer were pointedly asked by a few villagers who came on stage about the bribes they had taken from them as beneficiaries of a programme. The people exposed the false bills and vouchers of material bought that were on record for the various construction works executed in the village in the previous years. Even government employees like the school teacher, the dispensary chaparasi and the patwari did not fear the consequences and openly validated the facts showing the misuse and misappropriation of development funds in the presence of the Block Development Officer.

Most interesting was the debate on the so-called "adjustments". The justification given by the officials for the now documented instances of corruption was that norms of labour material ratio set by the government had to be met and therefore records were being fudged. It took the people only a single testiomony to expose the fallacy of the argument. As the speaker pointed out, the false bills pertained to material, and such falsification would only further destroy the laid down norms.

The Gram Sewak when cornered, quietly conceded that 'adjustments' were made to pilfer money and that he had been party to the fraud. He offered to return whatever he had taken. In all the hearings a popular demand had been made that money stolen from the village by any individual be promptly returned.

The Commissioner of Bilaspur in Madhya Pradesh Mr. Harsh Mandar was so impressed with the MKSS movement that he passed orders that information regarding the issuance of rations through public distribution system outlets be made available to citizens on demand. This initiative, begun on October 2, 1996, is reported to be highly successful, checking diversion of the commodities from the fair price shops to the black market. However, this experiment has not been appreciated by everybody in Madhya Pradesh. Although the Chief Minister Digvijay Singh promised to enact a right to information bill, it had been stalled both by politicians and bureaucrats. According to reports, the Singh Cabinet unanimously opposed the bill saying if "public affairs" are thrown open to public scrutiny, it would lead to anarchy. The Chief Minister has put it off saying his government would ascertain public opinion on the issue and organise a public debate on the nature and scope of the bill for the right to information. As a consequence of the Bilaspur initiative, the Madhya Pradesh Government had passed a State-wide order. In Bilaspur, Mr. Mandar has gone a step further, opening up records of the public works, transport, employment and pollution control departments. Although the impact is already evident, he admits that the levels of utilisation of the right are low because the people are not fully aware or motivated.

Role of Public Hearings

Jan Sunwai or public hearings has been practised, especially by environmental groups but it evolved into a forum to expose, to share information, a tool to organise people and even as a protest only during the last three years of the movement for the right to information.

Similar hearings have been held in different states on different subjects, from primary health to the working of coal mines but it must the admitted that nowhere it has been successful as in Rajasthan and Uttar Pradesh. However, there is no doubt that public hearing has emerged as a factor lending strength to the society, as a means of forcing governments and managements to be transparent, accountable and clean and as a powerful instrument of exposing the hitherto comouflaged, well-protected dishonesty of public servants, politicians and their stooges.

The jan sunwais were designed primarily to give people's voice a platform and to conduct a social audit on the misuse of development resources in their area. It emerged as a forum which attracted a diversity of participants with a convergence of interests between the poor, the middle class, and even those amongst the local opinion makers who were looking for support before they took a confrontational though legitimate stand. Prior to the hearings, extensive contact work was done by the MKSS workers to share information, identify issues, and motivate people to come. A pamphlet announcing the hearing, the issues and the venue was widely circulated before each hearing. Five village-based jan sunwais were held in the four districts of Rajasamand, Pali, Bhilwara and Ajmer in Rajasthan. The five hearings were organised in a radius of fifty square kilometres spilling over four districts. Four of the five public hearings were planned in a span of one month, interspersed with three citizens meeting in the neighbouring cities, so that they would have the impact of a campaign. They were organised in the period of December, 1994-January, 1995, just before the Panchayat Elections of the State so that the issues raised would influence the elections. In response to the popular demand by the people of one area in Bhilwara district, the fifth public hearing was organised in April, 1995 jointly with the newly elected representatives of a few panchayats. The effect of the hearings, the testimonies has been dramatic.

Five hundred to eight hundred people participated in each hearing. Fifty percent of the participants were women. It provided a forum to individual voices of poor men and women. In many cases these participants had knocked at every door to have their complaint sorted out. Their grievances were against the malfunctioning of a programme designed to empower them. Yet, the programme and its delivery system had no provisions to attend to their grievances. For many it was their first experience of speaking into the mike. The public hearings gave a collective identity to the participants. Every hearing had a good attendance of middle class residents of the village (including the State Government employees) who were not the direct beneficiaries of a government delivery programme. For the middle class corruption has always been an important issue. In the public hearings they demanded honesty and efficiency in the use of public money and thus the poor who are the immediate victims of the systematic syphoning off of development funds have found a sympathetic ear. The involvement of people from a cross section of rural society has been one of the most significant aspects of these hearings. People have spoken out, followed up and stuck their necks out thereby establishing that it is important for them to live by ethical values.

The effect of the hearings on the culprits has also been beyond all expectations. Several petty officials have returned money they stole; payments long 'forgotten' were made after three years; corrupt officials have had completed incomplete structures, and powerful sarpanches and officials have scurried to make sure there was no pilferage in their works. All this, with no official support or sanction to the hearings. These public hearings brought transparency, social audit, and accountability as demanded by the poor into their lives. These basic democratic rights, which have so far been discussed primarily in conference rooms, have been made relevant to ordinary lives. The people who have been involved in the public hearings have begun to feel their new found sense of power, both individually and collectively. The energy thus generated has brought alive democracy in villages. The public hearings have given us a glimpse of a collective monitoring of a system of governance, which is appropriate in a country that is beginning to find its feet, where most people are illiterate and unassertive.

THE RIGHT TO INFORMATION : AN ASSESSMENT

The movement for the right to information has been a unique experience. It is a grassroot level, people-driven, democratic, peaceful struggle that seeks to bring to the poor the fruits of freedom that have been denied to them for the past 50 years. Apart from the ritual exercising the right to vote, the right to information though truncated it is in some areas, is the only other democratic right that has empowered the poor, giving them a voice in decision-making, in asserting their right to know, so that their right to survive is not compromised by dishonest officials.

Information is power. It always has been so. Otherwise, the colonial rulers would not have enacted the Official Secrets Act, 1923, and a host of other laws to keep a tight lid on information, restricted its access and spread and manipulated it to further its interests. This control and manipulation of information by governments is practically universal, though it may vary in degree. Information, its selective use, its 'leak' at opportune times to gain maximum advantage for the government over its opponents, to protect its interests is part of a strategy of governments everywhere to stay in office, promote its interests and harm the opponents to the maximum extent possible.

The right to information or the right to know is the foundation on which the democratic edifice stands. An informed citizen who makes decisions based on a thorough understanding and knowledge of the administration can choose wisely when called upon periodically to vote. This understanding is possible when the government removes the shroudes under which it works. A citizen needs to know the functioning of the public institutions and officials who run them and political leaders who take decisions that affect the nation and its citizens. Thus, by right, a citizen is entitled to information relating to the government so that he can assess, question and thereby control those who act in his name and on his behalf. The right to know gives a powerful handle to the citizen to exercise control over his government by making it accountable to the people.

The right to information and the concept of an open government has been accorded constitutional status through a series of judgements of the Supreme Court and it has been argued that an amendment of the constitution can do no more than declare the right to information as a fundamental right.

The right to information and the need for an open government does not however mean that the access to information would be an absolute right, just as the right of freedom of speech and expression is not absolute. Areas where the government can be permitted to withhold access to information could include:

i. Internal relations and national security;

ii. Law enforcement and prevention of crime;

iii. Internal deliberations of the government;

iv. Information obtained in confidence from some source outside the government;

v. Information which, if disclosed, would violate the privacy of an individual;

vi. Information, particularly of an economic nature, which if disclosed, would confer an unfair advantage on some person or subject some person or government to an unfair disadvantage;

vii. Information which is covered by legal professional privilege, like communication between a legal adviser and his client;

viii. Information about scientific discoveries and inventions and improvements, essentially in the field of weaponry.

These categories are not all-inclusive and absolute, They should not serve as a an excuse to shield all information under them. While applying the yardstick of these categories, the overriding concern should be that of serving public interest without compromising national interest.

There has been an unprecedented resistance from the government to the right to information although, typically, political leaders have committed themselves to it when in the opposition, conveniently pushing it under the carpet once they came into power. Often political leaders have proclaimed their support to it even as they headed the government but failed to substantiate their commitment on the ground by making laws and rules that would wake for an open government. The instances of Rajasthan Chief Minister and the Madhya Pradesh Chief Minister are well known. The National Front Government headed by Mr. V.P. Singh had announced its intention to make the Right to Information a fundamental right. "Our government is committed to open session government, freedom of information and specifically, the right to seek receive and disseminate information is a basic right", he declared while inaugurating the 20th Conference of Ministers of Information and Cinematography at New Delhi on April 18, 1990. "In tune with our firm commitment for transparent functioning of our government, we propose to suitably amend the Official Secrets Act so that the people have increased access to information. While statutory changes are necessary, law by itself cannot ensure greater openness in government. Much of the current secrecy stems from the prevailing negative administrative culture. There is a need for a radical transformation in the attitude of those who are in possession of information relating to public interest. The States as well as the Centre can take steps to see that unnecessary blockage of information is avoided so as to promote public good".

The United Front of 14 political parties which came to power in 1996 included the right to information in its Common Minimum Programme. The programme of the United Front Government states specifically: "The Official Secrets Act will be reviewed and amended, keeping in tune with the need for openness and transparency in governance. A Bill on Freedom of Information will be introduced within six months to give the people access to information at all levels". The time limit is an improvement on the similar pledge made in 1989 but not fulfilled by the then National Front Government. But this time too, with the government uncertain about its future, it has not figured in the list of priorities of neither the Deve Gowda nor the Gujral governments. Such is their commitment to the right to information. The conference of chief ministers in May, 1997 reached a broad consensus in favour of a law for freedom of information. The Andhra Pradesh chief minister N. Chandrababu Naidu has promised that his government would pass a legislation on right to information without waiting for the outcome of the center's effort in this direction. The Press Council of India under the chairmanship of P.B. Sawant has drafted the right to information fill and the United Front Government has appointed a committee headed by consumer activist H.D.Shourie to study the draft (See Annexure for copy of the draft bill).

CONCLUSION

The fruits of a democratic system cannot reach the people, it will have no meaning beyond being a slogan without making a difference to their lives, if actions are taken by the rulers without their consent. A consent that is not based on information and knowledge has no sanctity nor can it be effective as a check on the government, Nor can the government hope to get the trust of a people who are not active and knowledgeable participants. A democracy means that the government be trusted by its people whom it governs. It cannot hide behind a veil of secrecy in the name of national interest to keep the people in the dark about its aims, decisions and the justification for the decisions leading to actions.

Corruption thrives in the dark corners of secrecy. Light and fresh air, in the form of right to Information, can drive it away. Most important, real empowerment of people can be possible only when they can question the government, sit in judgement over its actions, and based on information, act on it, A government which throws open its processes to public scrating is a good government. Openness is the very foundation of democracy. To give meaning and vibrancy to democracy, which we have been practising for 50 years, the people need to be strengthened and armed with the right of information.

RIGHT TO INFORMATION : HIGHLIGHTS

These are highlights of the proposed draft on the Right to Information which has been submitted to the Government of India. The draft was formulated by a group set up by the Govt. of India headed by consumer activist H.D.Shourie.

A bill to provide freedom to every citizen to secure access

to information under the control of public authorities, consistent with public interest, in order to promote openness, transparency and accountability in administration and in relation to matters connected therewith or incidental thereto.

Subject to the provisions of this Act, every citizen shall have the freedom to seek information from a public authority.

OBLIGATIONS ON PUBLIC AUTHORITIES

Every public authority shall be under a duty to maintain all its records, as per its operational requirements, duly catalogued and indexed and subject to the provisions of sections 9 and 10 (which deal with exemption from disclosure of information and Grounds for Refusal of Access in certain cases) grant access to information to any citizen requesting for such access.

Each public authority shall publish periodically, and keep updated, information indicating:

Particulars of its organisation, functions and responsibilities; description of its decision making processes in terms of procedures and powers and responsibilities of its officers and employees; norms for performance of activities such as prescribed periods for their processing and completion of physical and financial targets, etc., and the actual achievements with reference to such norms; classes of records under its control including the rules, regulations, instructions and list of manuals, etc., used by its employees for carrying out activities; the facilities provided for access to information; and the name, designation and other relevant particulars of the Public Information Officer to whom requests for information may be addressed.

It shall also be the duty of the concerned officers of a public authority to give reasons for decisions— whether administrative or adjudicative–to those affected and to disclose the relevant facts and analyses when major policies or decisions are announced.

APPOINTMENT OF PUBLIC INFORMATION OFFICERS

Every public authority shall appoint officers to be called Public Information Officers in its offices. It will also be the responsibility of Public Information Officers to deal with requests for access to information and to render reasonable assistance to requesters seeking access to information.

REQUESTS FOR ACCESS TO INFORMATION

A request under this Act shall be made to the appropriate public information officer in writing and shall specify, as clearly as possible, the particulars of the information, document or records to which access is being sought. Provided that where a requester cannot, for valid reasons, make a request in writing, the Public Information Officer may either accept an oral request or render reasonable assistance to the requester in making a written request.

DISPOSAL OF REQUESTS

Upon a request being made to him, the Public Information Officer shall provide access to information, where it is decided not to refuse such access, as expeditiously as possible and in any case within 30 days of the receipt of the request; provided that where it is not possible to provide access within 30 days, the period may be extended upto a maximum of another 30 days, for reasons to be recorded and communicated to the requester in writing.

Provided further that where it is decided to grant access to information on payment of any additional fee representing the cost of providing such access, the Public Information Officer shall send an intimation to the requester, accompanied by details of fees determined by him, requesting him to deposit the fees; and the period intervening between the dispatch of the said intimation and payment of fees shall be excluded for the purpose of calculating the period prescribed for grant of access to information.

DEEMED REFUSAL OF REQUEST

Where the decision on a request for access to information is not communicated to the requester within 30 days or within the extended period, the request shall be deemed to have been refused and the requester shall have the right to make a review application in accordance with the provisions of the Act.

EXEMPTION FROM DISCLOSURE OF INFORMATION

Information covered by any of the following categories shall be exempted from disclosure under the provisions of this Act:

Information of disclosure of which would prejudicially affect the sovereignty and integrity of India, security of the State, conduct of international relations, including information received in confidence from foreign government, their agencies or international organisations, etc.

GROUNDS FOR REFUSAL OF ACCESS IN CERTAIN CASES

A Public Information Officer may refuse access to information where :

The request is too general or is of such a nature that, having regard to the volume of information required to be retrieved or processed for fulfilling it, it would involve disproportionate diversion of the resource of a public authority or would adversely interfere with the functioning of such authority.

Provided that, where access is being refused on the ground that the request is too general, it would be the duty of the Public Information Officer to render help as far possible, to the requester to reframe his request in such a manner as may facilitate compliance with it; the request relates to information that is required by law or convention to be published at a particular time; or the request relates to information that is contained in published material available for sale.

FEE

The appropriate Government may prescribe the fees to be charged for access to information, which may include an application fee and such additional fees as may represent the cost of providing access.

Provided that the fees may be waited where the disclosure of information can be said to be in the larger public interest.

ANNEXURE

RIGHT TO INFORMATION: A DRAFT BY PRESS COUNCIL OF INDIA

Statement of Objects and Reasons

Article 19 (1) (a) of the Constitution guarantees the fundamental right to free speech and expression. The prerequisite for the effectuation of this right is knowledge and information. The absence of authentic information on matters of public interest discourages informed debate and encourages wild rumors and speculation and avoidable allegations against individuals and institutions.

Knowledge is power and information empowers the people both for individual and collective upliftment. It is therefore an essential input of socio-economic development and justice. For development of any kind, there has to be a two-way traffic of information between the agencies of development and the beneficiaries. Without the availability of information to each side, the development may be unreal, harmful and faulty and their implementation difficult, inefficient, and corrupt, The right to information is an essential part of the right to life, development and social justice itself.

In a democracy, it is the people who are the masters and those utilizing public resources and exercising public power their agents. The governance and the management of the affairs of the society has to be transparent to the people except that which needs to be kept confidential in the interest of the people themselves. The Act therefore seeks to effectuate the above objects.

A bill to make provision for securing the Right to Information.

Be it enacted by the Parliament in the Forty-Seventh year of the Republic of India as follows:

1. Short Title, Extent and Commencements

(1) This Act may be called the Right to Information Act, 1996

(2) It extends to the whole of India except Jammu and Kashmir.

(3) It shall come into force on such date as the Central Government may, by notification in the Official Gazette, appoint.

2. Definitions

Unless the Act in this context otherwise requires.

(i) Information means any fact relating to the affairs of the public body and includes any of the records relating to its affairs;

(ii) Right to Information means the right to be informed about the affairs of a public body and includes inspection, taking notes and extracts and receiving certified copies of the document;

(iii) Public body includes:

(a) State within the meaning of Article 12 of the Constitution of India.

(b) All public undertakings and non-statutory authorities; and

(c) A company, corporation, society, trust, firm or a cooperative society, whether owned or controlled by the government or by private individuals and institutions whose activities affect the public interest.

3. Right To Information

(i) Every citizen shall have a right to information from the public body;

(ii) It shall be the duty of the public body to maintain all records duly catalogued and indexed;

(iii) The public body shall be under a duty to make available to the person requesting information, the information sought for including such information as it is under an obligation to obtain and furnish and shall not withhold any information or limit its availability to the public except the information specified in section 4:

(iv) All individuals whether citizens or not shall have right to such information as affects their life and liberty.

4. Restrictions On Right To Information

The public body may, for reasons to be recorded in writing, withhold information:

(i) The disclosure or contents of which prejudicially affect the sovereignty and integrity of India; The security of the State and friendly relations with foreign States, Public order; Investigation of an offence or which leads to incitement to an offence;

(ii) Related to personal and medical information and other such information, The disclosure of which has no bearing on public affairs and would constitute a clear and unwarranted invasion of personal privacy:

(iii) Trade and commercial secrets protected by law. Provided that information which cannot be denied to the parliament or the State Legislature shall not be denied to a citizen.

5. Duty Cast On Certain Public Bodies

(i) Notwithstanding anything contained in this Act or any other law, It shall be the duty of the public body, As soon as possible and in any case before the commencement of the activity to be undertaken, to notify for the information of the general public and the person affected and to be affected by it, such matters within its knowledge and control as are vital to life, health and livelihood but not commonly known

(ii) It shall be mandatory for each custodial establishment such as a police lock-up, jail, mental asylum, remand houses, beggars home, etc., to appoint a visitors' Committee comprising of independent citizens which shall have full access to the custodial establishment at all hours of the day and night and to the records and inmates of such establishments.

6. Procedure For Supply Of Information

(i) A person desiring information from a public body shall prefer an application in this behalf to the head of the department/establishment/institution/body concerned.

(ii) The information shall be furnished within 30 days of application made for the purpose. In case, where the information relates to life and liberty of the individual, the information shall be supplied within 48 hours.

(iii) The information sought shall be supplied in writing either in English or Hindi or in the language of the State in which the informing authority is located.

(iv) If a copy of the document is asked, the fee of any charges for supplying it will not exceed the cost of making and supplying the document.

7. Penalty For Non-Supply Of Information

(i) Any individual responsible for providing any information as defined in earlier sections will be personally responsible for not furnishing the information.

(ii) If the information sought is not furnished within the time stipulated above, the person responsible for supplying the information shall be personally liable to pay penalty of Rs. 50/- for each day of delay.

(iii) Any individual who knowingly furnishes wrong, false, misleading or incomplete information shall be liable to be punished with a penalty which shall not be less than Rs. 1,000/- and up to a maximum of Rs.5,000/-

8. Refusal To Be Given In Writing

If the information is refused, the reason for such refusal shall be given in writing by the authority concerned.

9. Appeal

An appeal against refusal or failure to supply the information sought for or against inadequate or misleading information shall lie to the Principal Civil Judge of the Tehsil or of the District or of the city as the case may be where the informing authority is located. The appellate authority concerned shall dispose of the appeal within thirty days of its filing by a written order and giving reasons for its decision.

10. Protection Of Action Taken In Good Faith

No suit, prosecution or other legal proceeding shall lie against any individual or body for anything which is done or intended to be done in good faith in pursuance of this Act.

11. Act To Have Over-Riding Effect

The provisions of this Act and the rules made thereunder shall have effect notwithstanding inconsistent therewith contained in any other law for the time being in force.

12. Power To Make Rules

(i) The government may make rules regulating matters for which no provision has been made in the Act.

(ii) The rules so made shall be placed before the Parliament (Legislature in the case of the State) for its approval.

I : 2

Pricing of Information: Factors and Methods

S. Ally Sornam

Information is power – it is the essence of decision making, policy formulation and developmental activities at various levels. Information triggers research. Access to information at the right time saves wastage of resources. Advancements in IT have been greatly contributing to the evolution of Information Society. Hi–Tech inventions have entered into the portals of traditional Indian Libraries and have brought a sea change.

Information effects all people and all disciplines. But information by itself has no value unless it is properly packaged, communicated and used. Inter-disciplinary nature of research and advancement of technology created a newer bread of information users. One of the unique problems of information is its abundance. Recent development in micro electronics, artificial intelligence, voice synthesizer paved way for new Information products and Information services.

Collection, storage and retrieval of information involves cost. It begins with acquisition and ends with supply. All profit making organisations and some non-profit organisations face the problem of setting a price on their products or services.

WHAT IS PRICING ?

Price is the measure of value of any product. Price is the only element that produces revenue, other produce cost ?

Demand for the product largely sets a ceiling to the price.

The price normally covers the costs of producing, storing and distributing the product.

Information personnel does the same thing. They collect information from various sources. They package and distribute it in the suitable format.

Pricing is normally done for the following reasons :

* Survival
* Maximum Sales
* Maximum Profit
* Maximum Market Skimming
* Maximum Revenue
* Maximise Product Quality Leadership

Libraries and information centres in India are generally non- profit organisations. Libraries and information centres play the middle man role – they do not generate information but they supply information to the end user in such way that lead to further generation of information. Libraries and information agencies haven't yet put price tags for their products and services. But the factors mentioned below forces the libraries of today to price their products and services.

They are:

* Evergrowing, versatile demand information which necessitates long hours of search and continuous provision of funding to enhance.
* Limited and inadequate budgetary provisions within which the libraries must give their best.
* Appearance of new Telecom, Computer products in the market – their optimal use in information retrieval and dissemination.

FACTORS IN PRICING OF INFORMATION

The focus of attention in any good library or information center is its users. Any amount of information collected, meticulously stored and processed systematically looses its value if users are not its (central concept) meaning for existence.

Introduction of a new technology affects the library system in two ways – physical and psychological. The former goes with cost, location, equipment involved, techniques adopted, the latter has an effect on the behavior of end users for whom the products and services are made.

Hence the library and information professional must be careful to satisfy the following criteria:

* Identifying the user grouping, i.e., grouping of the services based on individual needs.
  (This can be done using demographic, socio economic and geographic variables)
* Studying the environment
  a. External Environment like social, political, technological.
  b. Operating Environment including the user profile, etc. (customer group served)

PRICING METHODS

After studying the above mentioned, the information professional can select any one of the pricing methods. These methods are mainly applied by profit making bodies. Libraries can adopt them with changes suitable to their environment.

a. **Mark Up Pricing:** Adding a standard mark up to the cost of the service or product (Information). This mark up pricing vary among different services. Bibliographies, SDI, CAS, Referral services may have a different pricing when compared to on–line access to information, CD–ROM usage etc.

b. **Perceived Value Pricing:** Here the user's perception of value acts as key to pricing. Price is set up to capture the perceived value in user's mind.

c. **Sealed Bid Pricing:** The price is based on expectation of how similar institutions will price information. And there is no rigid relation towards cost and demand in this method.

d. **Geographical Pricing:** This involves the organization's decision to price the services or products to users located in different parts of the country.

e. **Customer Segment Pricing:** Different user groups of libraries and information centers are charged different prices for the same product or service.

f. **Time Pricing:** Pricing varies with seasons, i.e., demand for specific information at a particular time.

CONCLUSION

Pricing of information will yield fruitful result only when the services and products are designed to satisfy the user needs. Users who are otherwise accustomed to free service may not appreciate fee based one in the beginning. But when information is sold in attractive packages justifying the price it adheres, the psychology of users will definitely change. This is time for libraries to shed of their image as a purely non-profit organizations, to that of a revenue generating institution, the goal of which is to serve the user effectively.

REFERENCES

1. S. Nagarajan and H.C. Jain, ed, *On – line information processing through mini and micro computers*, New Delhi: Badra Book Service, 1988.
2. Nagle (Thomas. T), *The strategy and tactics of pricing*. Englewood Cliffs, N.J. Prentice-Hall, 1987.
3. A. K. Phophalie, *Sales Management, Concept Principles and Practice*, New Delhi; Kanishka Publishers, 1997.

I : 3
Librarian – The Supremo of Information World

Sonal Singh
Surendra Singh

INTRODUCTION

Man with his tremendous capabilities of intellect, wisdom and mind has been mastering situations since his very inception. Man is an intelligent animal who gains and distributes knowledge. Knowledge is the result of human needs and human desires. Man's desire to know more and more about this world has led him from primitive superstitions to modern scientific knowledge. Man always comes in contact of new thoughts created by himself and others and with the development of such thoughts, knowledge develops. As thinking is a continuous process, development of knowledge is also continuous. Population pressure is accelerating the growth of knowledge. Today, knowledge is ever-growing, infinite, continuous and multidimensional.

The human society cannot survive without being fully familiar with all the past intellectual contributions of man as well as keeping himself up-to-date with the growing and ever adding knowledge in the domains of disciplines such as humanities, social sciences, sciences and technology. To overcome this endless complexity, modern man has discovered libraries. Today libraries have become the essential ingredients of a civilized society. Libraries are the storehouses of knowledge. They keep the knowledge safe by preserving it in an organized manner and provide it to the users according to their needs. Quick dissemination of knowledge is of prime importance. Knowledge is growing at a tremendous speed. And because of its ever-growing and multidimensional nature, proper organization of knowledge is very necessary for its easier, quicker and better use. Library provides information, inspiration and recreation for the enlightenment of the personality of the individual at the vital, spiritual and mental levels. Libraries help to inculcate virtues, social responsibilities and social duties amongst the readers and try to make them worthy citizens. Librarianship is an exalted profession which enhances the broadness of vision, increases the sphere of knowledge and the depth of friendship amongst human beings. The very essence of librarianship is to serve readers/users.

A teacher's field is limited only upto his subject and class-room teaching. But a librarian's field is unlimited. He is a teacher of teachers. He has to perform multidimensional duties and functions. A teacher's task is to provide formal education, which in no way is sufficient to build up a full bloomed personality of the students. Librarians provide real and informal education by providing material for extra reading.

The 'knowledge explosion' thrust forward the information explosion. The new technologies have accelerated the research and development and lead to information explosion. Libraries provide timely access to relevant information by collecting, storing and processing recorded information. Today, libraries are rightly known as information centres which increase national capabilities for innovative development and for making optimum use of local and international information resources. Thus, an efficient library and information system is of prime importance for any country wishing to achieve and sustain real independence.

The importance of information science in modern librarianship can hardly be over emphasized. Today's world is the world of mechanization and computerisation. The technological developments have dramatically changed the face of library profession. The aim is to facilitate free flow of information from all parts of the nation and from all countries of the world. The aim is to provide access to precise and reliable information – scientific, technical, commercial or other at the right time and to the right person in the form most conveniently usable by him, so that duplication of research may be avoided. Librarianship in modern times is undergoing significant changes in its outlook, functions, range and types of services and in its methods and techniques on one side, the development of technology and its application to storage, processing and dissemination of information, and on the other side, the fast growth of subjects with complex interdisciplinary character, and increasing demand for specific information have posed great challenges to information officers. Now, it is an established fact that library and information centers cannot be organized properly to provide optimum services to users unless they are headed by highly educated and professionally trained information officers.

INFORMATION OFFICER–THE SUPREME OF INFORMATION WORLD

The modern era of librarianship is an era of machine and method, which are operated by the human touch – man i.e. Librarian. The librarian is at the supreme position of this information era because human touch is necessarily required in information handling. This human touch of a librarian miraculously transforms even the insignificant pieces of information into the treasure of invaluable knowledge. This reminds us of the famous imaginary "Paras Stone" which just by its magic touch could transformation simple iron into the precious gold. From time immemorial, the people are in search of such a "Paras Stone" to make their own lives wealthy and comfortable. May be, the Lord Almighty has heard their prayers and sent the 'Librarian" as the "Paras Stone" of modern world.

Hence, the librarian naturally becomes the supremo of information world. The supremo i.e. informal person in overall authority. The supremo who plays a major role in making the research programmes effective, efficient and economical as he is well acquainted with information handling, information exchange behavior and information gathering habits. He also knows the information needs of the users. In the modern world of cables, cassettes and computers, it is impossible for the scientists and researchers to go through all the relevant literature available in their field of specialization without active participation of supremo. Thus, supremo is at the supreme position of modern information world.

He not only satisfies the demands of the existing thinkers and the seekers of truth but also tries to create and sustain users' interest. Information centers are the 'Intellectual service stations' where supremo understands the intellectual needs of the users and makes proper arrangements for meeting them adequately. Today, each and every individual of the community needs information in some form or other. Today, we all became information oriented consciously or unconsciously. Today, if we don't have information we will be in great difficulty. Information is a vast, dynamic and inexhaustible resource that effects all disciplines. Today information is an essential part of everyone's daily activities. Without information, we cannot expect development of society, country, personality. The supremo of information world stores, arranges and handles the information successfully, properly and systematically in an ordered way and provides it to the information seeker, pinpointedly, exhaustively and expeditiously. Thus, supremo is the active partner in information flow who can read the pulse of the user. Dynamic progress in the information environment is a challenge before information officers which forces them for continuing education for developing information handling competencies. Today librarian can no longer remain as traditional, static, linear contact between the readers and the documents. Today's librarian is the supremo of information world who is dynamic and capable of altering and moving in the communication channels of the networks, at any point in any direction. The heart of an information center is found in its leader (boss) and in skilled, imaginative, courageous, alert, enthusiastic information officer, with an ability to be constructive, creative, decisive, expressive and receptive and with a truly professional point of view.

Man is a decision maker and information is the vital source of decision making. Information is the power. It is a vitamin like source. It is a basic resource and link between a variety of intellectual and materialistic activities. Today, information is an essential part of everyone's daily activities. The information is vital to modern research in science and technology. The information is vital for the socio–economic progress of a country and it has become a vital raw material in our rapidly changing highly cost–oriented society.

Today, libraries are supposed to provide active information services. The maximum use with minimum cost and time is the motto of library service. Today, information officer plays a significant role in information handling and information transfer. He must be the master of traditional as well as modern library techniques so that he can select, evaluate and direct the material to the right user at the right time and in the form most useful to him. As a result of advances in communication technology, computer has become the essential part of information handling. But, it is a dead mass. Human touch is necessarily required. An information officer with an ability in handling computers, possessing knowledge of databases and knowledge of search strategies, and providing the ruler information to the society is responsible for the development and progress of nations in this electronic age of information.

CONCLUSION

Thus, the instant and continuous growth of modern information world demands for an efficient information officer who can act as an information consultant and who can handle electronic transmission, computer technology and telecommunications. Thus, librarian is the supremo of information world. The supremo, at whose finger tips dance the knowledge of the users' needs as well as the proper information that is to be made available to them. Thus, librarian – the supremo of information world becomes a bridge to join the demand and supply. We can't even imagine a modern world of mechanization computerization and other technological advances without its supremo– the librarian. May the Lord Almighty bless this supremo amongst us to serve our society.

I : 4

Information Gathering Habits of Biological and Physical Scientists in a University Environment in India: A Case Study of Karnatak University, Dharwad

B S Maheswarappa
S G Karkun

INTRODUCTION

The libraries are the repositories of information and the treasure houses of knowledge, they are non-profit making, service oriented organizations, exist to serve the users. One of the primary purposes of a library is to provide right information to the right user at the right time and in right form. This implies necessarily that the libraries have to plan, develop and organize their resources, services in such a way that it should facilitate easy retrieval of specific and relevant information with minimum effort and time. The libraries, if they want to provide effectively, the pin-pointed and exhaustive information services, means that they have to understand first, who are their users? What are their functional responsibilities? How much time they spend for each one of the functional responsibilities such as teaching, research and development and on other activities? How much time they spend in gathering and reading of information? What are the subject areas in which the users are interested? What is the nature of present research undertaken by the users, the different types of information required and gathered? For what purpose the information is gathered? How they gather and the methods that they follow for gathering of current and retrospective information? How the users search information and whether they search on their own or delegate the work to the information workers. What are the important primary and secondary journals used by the users? How the users gather information from the foreign language materials? What are the difficulties faced in gathering of information? Do the users consult the library catalogue and if yes, how far the different parts of a library catalogue are useful in gathering of information. Are our users aware of the information facilities/services available at the national and international level and if yes, how far their services are useful in gathering of information? How far the users are using the resources of libraries and library staff in gathering of information? How far they are successful in getting the information from the libraries and library staff? What are the information services that the users feel that they are most useful in gathering of information? These are certain questions for which the organizers of libraries have to find answers, if they want to provide effectively, the information services to the users that they serve. Therefore, a clear understanding of the users, their needs and requirements and gathering habits go a long way in the planning of a library, its resources and services.

A large majority of user studies have been reported from the western countries than from India. Sridhar while reviewing the status of user research in India states regretfully that " no single comprehensive user study has been reported in the country. Many piecemeal research works of varying qualities have possibly been done and only some of them have been published.

There are large number of theoretical and review types of papers reported by stressing the use of user studies, quoting the findings of the studies of either USA or UK..... Besides, there are a large number of master's degree theses submitted to various Indian universities of highly limited scope and utility." Further, Sridhar (2), clearly states, "the void in nature of user research in the country. User studies have been neglected both at local and national level by planners of information systems. The piecemeal studies have been mostly local studies of a particular aspect of user behavior". In view of the paucity and lack of in- depth studies relating to users of libraries in India, the present study has been taken up to determine and compare the information gathering habits of biological an physical scientists in a university environment in India.

OBJECTIVES OF THE STUDY

The primary objective of this study is to determine and compare the information gathering habits of biological and physical scientists in a university environment. The specific objectives of the study are to identify and compare the:

a) Time spent, types of information gathered and the purpose of gathering information;

b) Current awareness needs and the methods used in gathering of information;

c) Relative importance of information sources in gathering of information;

d) Searching methods used in gathering of information;

e) Gathering of information from foreign language publications and difficulties faced in gathering of information;

f) Use of library catalogue in gathering of information;

g) Use of libraries, library staff and success in gathering of information and

h) The information services most useful in gathering of

information among the biological and physical scientists in a university environment in India.

METHODOLOGY AND STUDY POPULATION

Methodology

User studies are useful in planning and organization of information resources and services in libraries and information centers. User forms an important component in any library. Understanding the users of information means half the battle in providing information services is over. Hence, now a days much emphasis has been given to studies relating to users. Various techniques have been evolved hitherto in the area of user studies, most of the techniques are not new, but they have been borrowed from other fields. The various techniques/methods employed in collection of data required for user studies are, viz., questionnaire, interview, observation, case study, query analysis, diary method, Delphi technique, pink card technique, critical incident technique, diffusion study technique, on–line information search assessment and publication studies. Each one of these methods or combination of two or more can be used in studying the users of information. The investigators have used the questionnaire method for collection of data. Accordingly a questionnaire was designed keeping in view the objectives of the study.

Study Population

The population selected for the present study consisted of members of faculty, research scholars, research/project assistants, and M. Phil students of the departments of botany, zoology, chemistry (includes biochemistry), physics and mathematics of Karnatak University, Dharwad. Out of the total 161 working scientists, the questionnaires were distributed personally to 156 scientists and out of which 149 scientists responded to our requests , with a response rate of 95%. The data collected through questionnaire was further tabulated, analyzed and the statistical tests such as chi-square (X^2), spear-man's rank correlation coefficient (P) were applied for results and discussion.

RESULTS AND DISCUSSION

Characteristics of Study Population

Majority of the population studied consisted of Research scholars (46.98%) and it was followed by Readers (30.37%), Lecturers (10.74%), Professors (4.03%), M. Phil students (4.03%). (vide Table-1). Among the biological and physical scientists, the majority of them consisted of research scholars. The percentage of readers and professors were relatively more in physical sciences than in biological sciences. Slightly less than half of the population consisted of biological scientists, while the rest of them (50.31%) were physical scientists. Among the biological scientists, the majority represented the subject zoology (21.47%), and it was followed by botany (19.47%) and biochemistry (8.72%). The majority of the scientists in the field of physical sciences were represented by the subject chemistry (22.14%), and it was followed by physics (17.44%) and mathematics (10.73%) (vide table-2). Thus, the population studied was a representative of biological and physical scientists. The majority of the scientists (55.70%) were post-graduates, while 41.61% were Ph.D. holders and the rest of them were M. Phil degree holders in their respective subjects (vide Table-3). Approximately, 39.18% of biological and 44% of the physical scientists were Ph.D. holders, while the M. Phil degree holders were relatively more among biological scientists than among physical scientists. More than half of the biological scientists (56.76%) and physical scientists (54.63%) were postgraduates.

Majority of the scientists studied consisted of males (83.22%) when compared to females (16.78%). The population consisted relatively more number of females in biological sciences (22.98%) than in physical sciences (10.66%) (vide table-4). The age group of majority of the scientists surveyed (37.58%) ranged between 25-30 years as the 46.98% of the total population studied comprised of the research scholars and it was followed by 31-35 years (11.40%), 46-50 years (11.40%), 41-45 years

(10.06%), 36-40 years (9.39%), less than 24 years (8.72%), 51-52 years (6.71%) and 56-60 years (4.69%) (vide Table-5). The biological scientists have an average age of 34.12 years, while it was slightly high (36.38 years) among the physical scientists. Approximately, about 40.93% of the total scientists, 51.35% of biological and 30.93% of physical scientists respectively, were not having any teaching experience. Nearly, 9.39% of scientists, 10.81% of biological and 8% of physical scientists were not having any research experience. About 87.91% of scientists, 86.48% of biological and 89.33% of physical scientists were also not having any administrative experience (vide Table-6). Thus, 59.07%, 90.61% and 12.09% of the scientists were respectively having an average of 14.42 years of teaching, 9.51 years of research and 4.39 years of administrative experience. Nearly 48.65%, 89.19% and 13.52% of biological scientists respectively, were having an average of 13.41 years of teaching, 9.51 years of research and 4 years of administrative experience, while the 77%, 92% and 10.67% of physical scientists respectively were having an average of 15.11 years of teaching, 10.68 years of research and 4 years of administrative experience. The physical scientists have put in more number of years in teaching, research and administrative experience than the biological scientists.

The foreign language knowledge and the reading and writing ability among the scientists as a whole and in biological and physical scientists in specific, was very poor (vide Table-7). The number of publications published by the scientists showed that 30.87% of scientists, 29.73% of biological and 32% of physical scientists were not having any journal articles to their credit. Approximately, 28.85% of scientists, 33.70% of biological and 24% of physical scientists were not having any conference/seminar papers to their credit. Nearly, 79.86% of scientists, 74.32% of biological and 85.34% of physical scientists were not having any review articles to their credit. About 83.22% of scientists, 82.43% of biological and 84% of physical scientists were not having any books to their credit. More than 87.91% of scientists, 85.13% of biological and 84% of physical scientist, were not having any book reviews to their credit. Thus, 69.13% of scientists, 70.27% of biological and 68% of physical scientists were having respectively an average of 18.43, 20.5 and 16.34 papers to their credit. Approximately, 71.15% of scientists, 66.22% of biological and 76% of physical scientists were having an average of 6.39, 4.94 and 5.89 seminar/conference papers to their credit. Slightly less than one-fourth (20.14%) of scientists, 26% of biological and 14.66% of physical scientists were having respectively 3.83, 4.31 and 3 reviews to their credit. Nearly 16.78% of scientists, 17.57% of biological and 16% of physical scientists respectively were having 3.8, 3 and 4.67 books to their credit, while 12.09% of scientists, 14.87% of biological and 9.33% of physical scientists respectively were having an average of 3 book reviews each to their credit (vide Table-8). Thus, biological scientists were having relatively more number of publications than the physical scientists. More than half of the scientists (64.42%) were regularly attending the seminars/ conferences/workshops, while 35.57% of them were not attending. Further, there was no significant difference as far as the proportion of scientists attending conferences/ seminars/ workshops among the biological (64.86%) and physical (64%) scientists ($X^2 = 0.0121$) in a university environment (vide Table-9).

The majority of the scientists studied (64.42%) have enrolled themselves as members of learned societies/professional associations and there was no significant difference as far as the membership enrollment to learned societies among the biological (63.51%) and physical (64.47%) scientists ($X^2 = 0.000013$) (vide Table-10). Of the total scientists studied, 45.63% of them were faculty members, out of which, 79.41% of the scientists, 82.14% of biological and 77.5% of physical scientists were guiding the research students leading to Ph.D (vide Table-11) and there was no significant difference as far as the guiding of research students among the biological and physical scientists ($X^2 = 1.69$). Majority of the scientists (40.26%), 39.18% of biological and 41.33% of physical scientists, where the nature of research undertaken was both basic and applied. Approximately 33.56% of scientists, 36.48% of biological and 30.67% physical scientists were involved in basic research, while 19.46% of scientists, 20.67% of biological and 18.67% of physical scientists were doing applied research (vide Table-12). There was no significant difference as far as the nature of research undertaken among the biological and physical scientists ($p = 1$) in a university environment.

Slightly more than half (59.06%) of the scientists, 60.81% of biological and 57.33% of physical scientists were not having personal library/collection of their own (vide Table-13).

Time Spent, Types of Information and Purpose of Gathering Information

The time spent per week on various activities by the biological and physical scientists is shown in Table-14. Approximately, 11.4% of scientists, 8.1% of biological and 13.65% of physical scientists were not spending their time for gathering of information, while 88.6% of scientists, 91.9% of biological and 85.34% of physical scientists respectively, have spent on an average 9.28, 9.54 and 8.86 hours per week for gathering of information. Approximately, 92.62% of scientists, 93.24% of biological and 92% of physical scientists respectively, have spent on an average of 13.45, 14.08 and 13.65 hours per week for reading of information. On an average the scientists were spending more time in reading than for gathering of information. Slightly less than 80% of scientists, 79.76% of biological and 77.34% of physical scientists respectively, have spent on an average of 26.37, 26.76 and 24.8 hours per week on R and D work. Thus, the majority of the biological and physical scientists were spending more time on R and D than for gathering and reading of information. More than half of the scientists (57.72%), 52.71% of biological and 62.66% of physical scientists respectively, have spent on an average of 13.17, 10.82 and 13 hours per week on teaching. Slightly less than half of the scientists (42.24%), 39.19% of biological and 45.34% of physical scientists respectively, on an average have spent 9.9, 9.37 and 10.35 hours per week for guiding the research students. Thus, the biological and physical scientists have spent on an average of 10 hours per day on various activities.

Three-fourth of the total scientists studied were gathering current information and it was followed by R & D (57.04%), procedural (41.61%), factual information (41.61%), bibliographical (28.18%), retrospective (23.48%), and conceptual information (18.12%) (vide Table-15), slightly less than three-fourth of the biological and physical scientists were gathering current information as it was required for keeping abreast of latest developments in their field of specialization and it was followed by R & D information. There was a fair agreement as far as the types of information gathered by the biological and physical scientists (P = 0.723) in a university environment.

Majority of the scientists (61.07%) opined that the purpose of gathering information was to avoid duplication of research and it was followed by designing of research project (58.38%), support theory (54.36%), identify the specific problem (53.38%), formulate hypothesis (33.55%), and for background reading (31.54%) (vide Table-16). There was a significant difference as far as the purpose of gathering of information among the biological and physical scientists (P = 0.49) in a university environment.

Current Awareness Needs and the Methods Used for Gathering Information

Slightly more than three-fourth of scientists (77.85%) were scanning abstracting and indexing journals for their current awareness purpose and it was followed by regular scanning of current issues of journals (75.83%), scanning of Current Contents (ISI) (41.61%), attending conferences, symposia, workshops (41.61%), personal communication (31.27%), through CAS provided by the National Center for Science Information (IISc, Bangalore) (27.51%), and through various in-house information services provided by the Karnatak university library, Dharwad (vide Table-17). There was a strong agreement as far as the methods used for gathering of information for current awareness among the biological and physical scientists (P = 0.79) in a university environment.

Relative Importance of Sources of Information in Gathering of Information

Abstracting and indexing journals were very useful sources of information used by the majority of the scientists (78.52%) and these were followed by research reports (65.15%), and primary journals (57.71%). Among the biological scientists, the abstracting and indexing journals (83.78%) were very useful sources of information for gathering of information and it was followed by research reports (68.91%), conference/ seminar papers (56.76%) and primary journals (54.05%). Among the physical scientists also the abstracting and indexing journals occupy the first rank as the sources of information for gathering information (73.33%), and these were followed by research reports (61.34%), primary journals (61.33%) and conference/ seminar papers (37.34%) (vide Table-18).

Theses and dissertations were moderately useful among the scientists (41.95%), and these were followed by books (53.69%) and reviews of progress (36.91%). Books were moderately useful (56.76%) among the biological scientists and these were followed by theses and dissertations (47.29%), and reviews of progress (44.59%). Books were moderately useful among the physical scientists and these were followed by theses and dissertations (36.67%). Guides to subject literature (67.78%), were not useful among the scientists and they were followed by handbooks and manuals (66.44%), standards and specifications (65.75%), directories (63.75%), patents (63.75%) and subject bibliographies. Guides to subject literature (62.16%), handbooks and manuals (62.16%), subject bibliographies (47.29%), directories (47.29%), standards and specifications (47.29%) and patents (39.19%) were not useful for the biological scientists for gathering of information. Patents (89.3%), standards and specifications (84%), directories (80%), guides to subject literature (13.34%), handbooks and manuals (70.67%), subject bibliographies (68%), theses and dissertations (68.67%), and reviews of progress were not useful among the physical scientists for gathering of information.

Mean ranking of sources for scientists fall in the following order: Abstracting and indexing journals, research reports, primary journals, conference/seminar papers, books, reviews of progress, theses and dissertations, patents, directories, guides to subject literature, standards and specifications, and handbooks and manuals.

Mean ranking of sources for biological scientists fall in the following order: Abstracting and indexing journals, research reports, conference/seminar papers, primary journals, books, reviews of progress, theses and dissertations, patents, directories, subject bibliographies, guides to subject literature, and handbooks and manuals.

Mean ranking of information sources for physical scientists fall in the following order: Abstracting and indexing journals, primary journals, research reports, standards and specifications, conference/seminar papers, books, reviews of progress, theses and dissertations, guides to subject literature, subject bibliographies, handbooks and manuals, directories and patents. There was no significant difference as far as the ranking of different sources of information for gathering of information among the biological and physical scientists (P = 0.73) in a university environment.

Literature Searching Undertaken, Delegation and Methods Used

The majority of the scientists (84.56%), 86.48% of

biological and 82.67% of physical scientists were searching the literature on their own for gathering of information (vide Table-20). There was a significant difference as far as the literature searching undertaken among the biological and physical scientists (X^2 = 0.416). Only 15.44% of the total scientists were not undertaking literature searching on their own. Out of which, 65.21% of the scientists, 60% of biological and 69.25% of physical scientists, delegating the literature searching to information workers and others were neither doing on their own nor interested to delegate the work to the information workers. There was no significant difference as far as the delegation of literature searching to information workers among the biological and physical scientists (X^2 = 0.21).

Slightly less than three-fourth of the scientists were searching the literature by consulting the contents pages in a periodical/book and it was followed by the literature cited at the end of review articles (62.69%), following the references given at the end each chapter (36.71%), by consulting the various indexes given at the end of each document and by consulting the subject bibliographies (vide Table-22). There remains statistically significant difference in the rankings of the methods used in literature searching among the biological and physical scientists (P = 0.676) in a university environment.

Foreign Language Materials, Difficulties Faced and Use of Library Catalogue

Slightly less than 70% of the scientists (69.79%), 68.92% of biological and 70.66% of physical scientists were not gathering information published in other languages other than English (vide Table-23). There was no significant difference as far as the gathering of information from the foreign language publications among the biological and physical scientists (X^2 = 0.053). In view of the poor knowledge and reading ability of foreign language/s among the scientists coupled with the lack of interest in gathering of information reported in foreign language publications, have all implications for the planning, development and organization of information resources and services in a university library environment in India.

The lack of abstracting and indexing journals (67.11%) was one of the major problems faced by the majority of the scientists in gathering of information from foreign language publications and it was followed by in decreasing order: lack of time (32.88%), lack of access to all the information (31.54%), location of the suitable sources (26.84%), lack of training in reading skills (23.84%), lack of specialized training in literature search technique (21.47%), and unfamiliarity of the sources of information (20.8%) (vide Table-24). There remains no statistically significant difference in the rankings of the difficulties faced in gathering of information among the biological and physical scientists (P = 0.72) in a university environment.

Majority of the scientists (81.2%), 73.33% of biological and 88.08% of physical scientists were using the library catalogue for gathering of information (vide Table-25). There was a significant difference as far as the use of library catalogue among the biological and physical scientists (X^2 = 4.56) in a university environment. Majority of the scientists (67.76%), half of the biological (56.36%) and slightly more than three-fourth of the physical scientists were using both author and title approaches in using the library catalogue (vide Table-26). The majority of the scientists, biological and physical scientists opined that the author catalogue is very useful when compared to title catalogue (vide Table-27). There is a perfect agreement between the rankings as far as the use of author Vs. title catalogue among the biological and physical scientists (P = 1) in a university environment.

Use of Libraries, Library Staff and Success in Gathering Information

More than half of the scientists, 55.38% of biological and

55.41% of physical scientists were visiting the Karnatak University Library, Dharwad more than four times in a month. Nearly about 35% of scientists, 39.18% of biological and 30.67% of physical scientists were visiting the library four times in a month, while 8.72% of scientists, 5.4% of biological and 12% of physical scientists were not visiting the library at all (vide Table-28). More than 60% of scientists, 58.1% of biological and 62.67% of physical scientists were mostly successful in gathering of information from the university library. There was no significant difference as far as the use of library and the library staff and their success in gathering information among the biological and physical scientists (X^2 = 0.323) in a university environment. Majority of the scientists (69.79%), 71.62% of biological and 68% of physical scientists were not using other libraries for gathering of information required for them (vide Table-29). The scientists ranging between 22-30% using other libraries once in a month and the percentage of scientists using other libraries twice in a month was quite insignificant. Majority of the scientists (92.61%), 90.54% of biological and 94.67% of physical scientists were not successful in gathering information from other libraries and there was no significant difference as far as the success in gathering of information from other libraries among the biological and physical scientists (X^2 = 0.927) in a university environment (vide Table-30). Slightly more than half of the scientists, half of the biological and physical scientists were mostly consulting the library staff in gathering of information (vide Table-31). More than half of the scientists (53.02%), 47.29% of biological and 58.67% of physical scientists were successful in gathering of information from the library staff (vide Table-32) and there was no significant difference as far as the use of the library staff (X^2 = 0.32) and success in gathering of information (X^2 = 1.9) among the biological and physical scientists in a university environment. Approximately, 65.77% of scientists, 64.86% of biological and 66.67% of physical scientists felt the need for user education in using the libraries and in gathering of information (vide Table-33).

Information Services Considered Useful for Gathering of Information

More than three-fourth of the scientists opined that they need in-house abstracting service and it was followed by other services in the decreasing order as follows: indexing services (69.12%), reprographic service (68.45%), translation service (66.44%), current awareness service (65.1%), reference service (54.36%), book lending service (48.99%), selective dissemination of information service (35.55%), literature search (30.87%), bibliographical services (21.47%), interlibrary loan (20.13%), digest service (12.75%), newspaper clipping service (11.4%), compilation of state of the art reports (8.72%), referral service (7.38%), and compilation of trend reports. There was a strong agreement as far as the different types of information services considered useful for gathering of information among the biological and physical scientists (P = 0.904) in a university environment (vide Table-34).

Summary of Findings and Conclusion

In summary, the following are the important findings of the study: The majority of the biological and physical scientists were spending more time for R and D work than for teaching, reading and gathering of information, with an average of 10 hours per week on various activities. Three-fourth of the scientists were gathering current information and it was followed by R and D, procedural, factual, bibliographical, retrospective and conceptual information. There was a fair agreement regarding the types of information gathered among the biological and physical scientists. Although the majority of the scientists mentioned that the purpose of gathering of information was to avoid duplication of research. but there was a significant difference as far as the purpose of gathering of information among the biological and physical scientists. There was a strong agreement regarding the methods used for gathering information for current awareness purpose among the biological and physical scientists. Both the biological and physical scientists were using variety of information sources and there was no significant difference as far as the rankings of different sources of information used for gathering of information among them. The majority of the scientists, biological and physical scientists were searching the literature on their own and there was no statistically significant difference, but there remains significant difference in the rankings of methods used in literature searching among the biological and physical scientists. Majority of the biological and physical scientists were not gathering information published in other languages other than English and there remains no statistically significant difference in the rankings of the difficulties faced in gathering of information among the biological and physical scientists. Although, the majority of the scientists in general and biological and physical scientists in particular, were using the library catalogue for gathering of information, but there was a significant difference in the use of library catalogue and majority of the scientists were using both the author and title approaches, and the majority opined that the author catalogue was very useful when compared to the title catalogue and perfect agreement between the rankings of the use of author Vs. title catalogue was found. There was no significant difference regarding the use of university library, library staff and success in gathering of information among the biological and physical scientists. Majority of the biological and physical scientists were not using other libraries. The majority were also not successful and there was no statistically significant difference concerning the success in gathering of information among the scientists. Nearly, half of the biological and physical scientists were mostly consulting the library staff, they were successful in gathering information and no significant difference exists as far as the use of library and success in gathering of information. Majority of the biological and physical scientists felt the need for systematic user education in using the libraries and in gathering of information. There was a strong agreement regarding the different types of information services considered useful for gathering information among the biological and physical scientists. The findings of the study have implications for the collection development and management and there, is an urgent need to educate the scientists in the use of libraries and in gathering of information in a university environment in India.

REFERENCES

1. Sridhar, M.S. *User Research : A Review of Information Behavioral Studies in Science and Technology*. Bangalore : Billion Infon Services. 1990. p. 35.
2. Ibid, p. 39

Table-1 : Designation wise distribution of biological and physical scientists in a university environment

Designations	*Biological Scientists*	*Physical Scientists*	*Total*
Professors	2 (2.70)	4 (5.33)	6 (4.03)
Readers	18 (24.32)	28 (37.34)	46 (30.87)
Research Scholars	37 (50.00)	33 (44.00)	70 (46.98)
Research/Project Assistants	5 (76.76)	–	5 (3.36)
M. Phil Students	4 (5.41)	2 (2.67)	6 (4.02)

Note: Figures in the parentheses indicate percentage.

Table-2 : Subject wise distribution of biological and physical scientists in university environment

Subject/s	*Number*	%
Biological sciences		
Botany	29	19.47
Biochemistry	13	8.72
Zoology	32	21.47
Physical Sciences		
Physics	26	17.44
Chemistry	33	22.14
Mathematics	16	10.7
Total	149	99.97

Table –3 : Qualification wise distribution of biological and physical scientists in a university Environment

Qualification/s	*Biological scientists*	*Physical scientists*	*Total*
Ph.D	29 (39.18)	33 (44.00)	62 (41.61)
M. Sc., M. Phil	3 (4.05)	1 (1.33)	4 (2.68)
M. Sc.	42 (56.76)	41 (54.67)	83 (55.70)
Total	74 (99.99)	75 (100)	149 (99.99)

Note: Figures in the parentheses indicate percentage.

Table-4 : Sex wise distribution of biological and physical scientists in a university environment

Sex	*Biological scientists*	*Physical scientists*	*Total*
Male	57 (77.02)	67 (89.33)	124 (83.22)
Female	17 (22.98)	8 (10.66)	25 (100.00)

Note: Figures in the parentheses indicate percentage

Table-5 : Age wise distribution of biological and physical scientists in a university environment

Age	*Biological scientists*	*Physical scientists*	*Total*
<24	5 (6.67)	8 (10.67)	13 (8.72)
25-30	34 (45.94)	22 (29.33)	56 (37.58)
31-35	10 (13.51)	7 (9.33)	17 (10.06)
36-40	6 (8.10)	8 (10.67)	14 (9.39)
41-45	8 (10.01)	7 (9.33)	15 (10.06)
46-50	5 (6.76)	12 (16.00)	17 (11.40)
51-55	3 (4.05)	7 (9.33)	10 (6.71)
56-60	3 (4.05)	4 (5.33)	7 (4.69)
Total	74 (99.98)	75 (99.99)	149 (99.96)
	@ = 34.12	@ = 37.38	

Note: Figures in the parentheses indicate percentage.

Table-7 : The Foreign language knowledge of biological and physical scientists in a university environment

Language(s)	Biological Scientists		Physical Scientists		Total	
	Read	Write	Read	Write	Read	Write
French	13 (17.56)	7 (9.46)	14 (18.67)	8 (10.12)	27 (18.12)	15 (10-.06)
German	15 (20.27)	10 (13.51)	13 (17.33)	6 (8.00)	28 (18.79)	10 (10.74)
Russian	5 (6.76)	3 (4.05)	11 (14.67)	7 (9.33)	16 (10.74)	10 (6.71)
Portuguese	1 (1.35)	1 (1.35)	1 (1.33)	1 (1.33)	2 (1.34)	2 (1.34)

Note: Figures in the parentheses indicate percentage.

Table-9 : Attendance of biological and physical scientists at the conferences/symposia/seminars/workshops

Response	***Biological Scientists***	***Physical Scientists***	***Total***
Yes	48	48	96
	(64.86)	(64.00)	(64.42)
No	26	27	53
	(35.13)	(36.00)	(35.57)
Total	74	75	149
	(99.99)	(100)	(99.99)

$X^2 = 0.0121$

Note: Figures in the parentheses indicate percentage.

Table-10 : Membership to learned societies/professional associations among biological and physical scientists in a university environment

Response	***Biological Scientists***	***Physical Scientists***	***Total***
Yes	47	49	96
	(63.51)	(65.33)	(64.42)
No	27	26	53
	(36.48)	(34.66)	(35.57)
Total	74	75	149
	(99.99)	(99.99)	(99.99)

Note: Figures in the parentheses indicate percentage.

Table-11 : Guidance of research students among the biological and physical scientists in a university environment

Response	*Biological Scientists*	*Physical Scientists*	*Total*
Yes	23	31	54
	(31.08)	(41.33)	(36.24)
No	51	44	95
	(68.91)	(58.66)	(63.75)
Total	74	75	149
	(99.99)	(99.99)	(99.99)

$X^2 = 1.69$

Note: Figures in the parentheses indicate percentage.

Table-12 : Nature of research undertaken by the biological and physical scientists in a university environment

Nature of Research	*Biological Scientists*	*Physical Scientists*	*Total*
Basic research	27	23	50
	(36.48)	(30.67)	(33.56)
Applied research	15	14	29
	(20.27)	(18.67)	(19.46)
Both	29	31	60
	(39.18)	(41.33)	(40.26)
No response	3	7	10
	(4.05)	(9.33)	(6.70)
Total	74	75	149
	(99.98)	(100)	(99.99)

P = 1

Note: Figures in the parentheses indicate percentage.

Table-13 : Information about the personal collection among the biological and physical scientists in a university environment

Response	*Biological Scientists*	*Physical Scientists*	*Total*
Yes	29	32	61
	(39.19)	(42.67)	(40.94)
No	45	43	88
	(60.81)	(57.33)	(59.06)

$X^2 = 0.19$

Note: Figures in the parentheses indicate percentage.

Table-15 : Type(s) of information gathered by the biological and physical scientists in a university environment

Type of Information	***Biological Scientists***	***Physical Scientists***	***Total***
R & D information	42	43	85
	(56.76)	(57.33)	(57.04)
Procedural information	26	36	62
	(35.13)	(48.00)	(41.61)
Factual information	26	36	62
	(35.13)	(48.00)	(41.61)
Conceptual information	11	16	27
	(14.86)	(21.33)	(18.12)
Biological information	32	10	42
	(43.24)	(13.33)	(28.18)
Current information	55	56	111
	(74.32)	(74.66)	(74.49)
Retrospective information	21	14	35
	(28.37)	(18.66)	(23.48)
Any other	1	1	2
	(1.35)	(1.35)	(1.35)

P = 0.723

Note: Figures in the parentheses indicate percentage.

Table-16 : Purpose of gathering of information among the biological and physical scientists in a university environment

Purpose of gathering of information	*Biological Scientists*	*Physical Scientists*	*Total*
To formulate hypotheses	21 (28.37)	29 (38.67)	50 (33.55)
To support the theory	42 (56.75)	39 (52.00)	81 (54.36)
To avoid duplication of research	50 (67.56)	41 (54.67)	91 (61.07)
To identify the specific problem	34 (45.94)	45 (60.00)	79 (53.02)
To design research project	40 (56.05)	47 (62.66)	87 (58.38)
For background reading	25 (33.72)	22 (29.34)	47 (31.54)
Any other	-	2 (67.67)	2 (1.76)

P = 0.49

Note: Figures in the parentheses indicate percentage.

Table-17 : Information gathering habits of biological and physical scientists for current awareness purpose

Method(s)	*Biological Scientists*	*Physical Scientists*	*Total*
Scanning of current issues of periodicals	56 (75.67)	57 (76.00)	113 (75.83)
Scanning of abstracting indexing journals	55 (74.32)	61 (81.34)	116 (77.85)
Scanning of current contents	53 (71.62)	51 (68.00)	104 (69.79)
By attending conference, symposia, workshops etc.	28 (37.83)	34 (45.34)	62 (41.61)
By going through critical reviews	31 (41.89)	17 (22.67)	48 (32.21)
By personal Communications	25 (33.78)	22 (29.34)	47 (31.54)
Through the CAS provided by NCSI, Bangalore	28 (37.84)	13 (17.34)	41 (27.51)
Through various in-house information services of KUL, Dharwad	5 (6.76)	4 (5.34)	9 (6.04)
Any other	5 (76.76)	–	5 (3.36)

Note: Figures in the parentheses indicate percentage.

Table-19 : Information sources used by the biological and physical scientists in a university environment for gathering of information: Mean use score and rank

Source(s)	***Biological Scientists Mean (rank)***	***Physical Scientists Mean (rank)***	***Total Mean (rank)***
Primary journals	1.36(4)	1.45(2)	1.40(3)
Abstracting and indexing journals	1.78(1)	1.62(1)	1.70(1)
Review of progress	1.17(6)	0.90(7)	1.04(6)
Books	1.29(5)	1.06(6)	1.18(5)
Patents	0.98(8)	0.14(13)	0.56(8)
Standards and specifications	0.74(10)	0.21(4)?	0.47(12)
Research reports	1.60(2)	1.40(3)	1.50(2)
Conference/seminar papers	1.37(3)	1.09(5)	1.23(4)
Theses and dissertations	1.12(7)	0.84(8)	0.97(7)
Directories	0.77(9)	0.24(12)	0.50(9)
Subject bibliographies	0.62(11)	0.36(10.5)	0.48(11)
Handbooks and manuals	0.54(13)	0.36(10.5)	0.44(13)
Guides to literature	0.60(12)	0.37(9)	0.49(10)

P = 0.73

Table-20 : Literature searching undertaken by the biological and physical scientists in a university environment

Response	***Biological Scientists***	***Physical Scientists***	***Total***
Yes	64 (86.48)	62 (82.67)	126 (84.56)
No	10 (13.51)	13 (17.33)	23 (15.44)
Total	74 (99.99)	75 (100)	149 (100)

$X^2 = 0.416$

Note: Figures in the parentheses indicate percentage.

Table-21 : Delegation of literature searching to information workers among the biological and physical scientists in a university environment

Response	***Biological Scientists***	***Physical Scientists***	***Total***
Yes	6 (60.00)	9 (69.23)	15 (65.21)
No	4 (40)	4 (30.77)	8 (34.78)
Total	10 (100)	13 (100)	23 (99.99)

$X^2 = 0.21$

Note: Figures in the parentheses indicate percentage.

Table-22 : Methods Techniques used in literature searching among the biological and physical scientists in a university environment

Methods/Techniques	*Biological Scientists*	*Physical Scientists*	*Total*
Following the references given at the end of each article/chapter in a book	37(54.81)	41(66.12)	78(61.90)
By consulting the various indexes given at the end of each document	24(37.50)	19(30.64)	43(34.12)
By consulting the contents pages in a periodical/book	49(76.56)	41(66.12)	90(71.42)
By consulting the subject bibliographies	19(29.68)	22(35.48)	41(32.53)
Following the literature cited at the end of review article	41(64.06)	38(61.29)	79(62.69)
By consulting the library catalogue	24(37.50)	21(33.87)	45(35.71)

P = 0.676

Note: Figures in the parentheses indicate percentage.

Table-23 : Gathering of information published in other languages other than English among the biological and physical scientists in a university environment

Response	*Biological Scientists*	*Physical Scientists*	*Total*
Yes	23	22	45
	(31.08)	(29.34)	(30.20)
No	51	53	104
	(68.92)	(70.66)	(69.79)
Total	74	75	149
	(100)	(100)	(99.99)
	$X^2 = 0.416$		

Note: Figures in the parentheses indicate percentage.

Table-24 : Difficulties faced in gathering of information among the biological and physical scientists in a university environment

Difficulties	*Biological Scientists*	*Physical Scientists*	*Total*
Lack of time	26 (35.13)	23 (30.67)	49 (32.88)
Lack of access to all the information	28 (37.83)	19 (25.34)	47 (30.54)
Lack of suitable abstracting and indexing journals	52 (70.27)	48 (64.00)	100 (67.11)
Locating suitable sources	22 (29.72)	18 (24.00)	40 (26.84)
Unfamiliarity with the various sources of information	12 (16.21)	19 (25.34)	31 (20.80)
Lack of specialized training in literature search techniques	6 (8.10)	9 (12.00)	15 (10.06)
Lack of training in reading skills	16 (21.62)	19 (25.34)	35 (23.48)
Too much of information	8 (10.81)	6 (8.00)	14 (3.39)

Note: Figures in the parentheses indicate percentage.

Table –25 : Use of library catalogue by the biological and physical scientists in a university environment

Response	***Biological Scientists***	***Physical Scientists***	***Total***
Yes	55 (74.33)	66 (88.00)	121 (81.20)
No	19 (25.67)	9 (12.00)	28 (18.29)
	$x^2 = 4.56$		

Note: Figures in the parentheses indicate percentage.

Table-26 : Approaches to library catalogue by the biological and physical scientists in a university environment

Approach	***Biological Scientists***	***Physical Scientists***	***Total***
Author	23 (41.81)	13 (19.70)	36 (29.75)
Title	1 (1.81)	2 (3.00)	3 (2.48)
Both	31 (56.36)	51 (77.27)	82 (67.76)

Note: Figures in the parentheses indicate percentage.

Table-27 : Frequency of visit to Karnatak University Library, Dharwad by the biological and physical scientists in a university environment

Frequency of visit	*Biological Scientists*	*Physical Scientists*	*Total*
Four times	29	23	52
	(39.18)	(30.67)	(34.89)
More than four times	41	43	84
	(55.40)	(57.33)	(56.38)
Not at all	4	9	13
	(5.4)	(12.00)	(8.72)
Total	74	75	149
	(99.98)	(100)	(99.99)

Note: Figures in the parentheses indicate percentage.

Table-28 : Success in gathering of information from Karnatak University Library, Dharwad among the biological and physical scientists

Response	***Biological Scientists***	***Physical Scientists***	***Total***
Mostly	43	47	90
	(58.10)	(62.67)	(60.40)
Seldom	31	28	59
	(41.89)	(37.33)	(39.59)
Total	74	75	149
	(99.99)	(100)	(99.99)

$X^2 = 0.323$

Note: Figures in the parentheses indicate percentage.

Table –29 : Use of other libraries in gathering of information among the biological and physical scientists in a university environment

Response	***Biological Scientists***	***Physical Scientists***	***Total***
Mostly	17 (22.97)	23 (30.67)	40 (26.84)
Seldom	4 (5.40)	1 (1.33)	5 (3.36)
Not at all	53 (71.62)	51 (68.00)	104 (69.79)
Total	74	75	149

Note: Figures in the parentheses indicate percentage.

Table-30 : Success in gathering of information from other libraries among the biological and physical scientists

Response	***Biological Scientists***	***Physical Scientists***	***Total***
Mostly	7 (9.46)	4 (5.33)	11 (7.38)
Seldom	67 (90.54)	71 (94.67)	138 (92.61)
Total	74 (100)	75 (100)	149 (99.99)

$X^2 = 0.927$

Note: Figures in the parentheses indicate percentage.

Table-31 : Use/Consultation of library staff in gathering of information among the biological and physical scientists in a university environment

Response	***Biological Scientists***	***Physical Scientists***	***Total***
Mostly	39 (52.70)	43 (57.33)	82 (55.03)
Seldom	35 (47.29)	32 (42.67)	67 (44.97)
Total	74 (99.99)	75 (100)	149 (100)

$X^2 = 0.32$

Note: Figures in the parentheses indicate percentage.

Table-32 : Success in gathering of information from the library staff among the biological and physical scientists in a university enviroment

Response	***Biological Scientists***	***Physical Scientists***	***Total***
Mostly	35 (47.29)	44 (58.67)	79 (53.02)
Seldom	39 (52.70)	31 (41.33)	70 (46.97)
Total	74 (99.99)	75 (100)	149 (99.99)

$X^2 = 1.9$

Note: Figures in the parentheses indicate percentage.

Table-33 : Need for user education among the biological and physical scientists in a university environment

Response	***Biological Scientists***	***Physical Scientists***	***Total***
Yes	48 (64.86)	50 (66.67)	98 (65.77)
No	26 (35.13)	25 (33.33)	51 (34.22)
Total	74 (99.99)	75 (100)	149 (99.9)

Note: Figures in the parentheses indicate percentage.

Table-34 : Information services considered useful for gathering of information by the biological and physical scientists in a university environment

Information services	***Biological Scientists***	***Physical Scientists***	***Total***
Book binding service	38 (51.35)	35 (46.67)	73 (48.99)
Current awareness service	45 (60.81)	52 (69.34)	97 (65.10)
Selective Dissemination of Information	21 (28.37)	29 (38.67)	50 (35.55)
Abstracting service	54 (72.97)	63 (84.00)	117 (78.52)
Indexing service	52 (70.27)	51 (68.07)	103 (69.12)
Bibliographical service	13 (17.56)	19 (25.34)	32 (21.47)

Information services	*Biological Scientists*	*Physical Scientists*	*Total*
Compilation of trend reports	6 (8.10)	3 (4.0)	9 (6.04)
Compilation of the state of the art report	9 (12.16)	4 (5.34)	13 (8.72)
Literature search	22 (29.72)	24 (32.00)	46 (30.87)
Translation service	45 (60.81)	54 (72.00)	99 (66.44)
Reprographic service	54 (72.97)	48 (64.00)	102 (68.45)
Digest service	12 (16.21)	7 (9.34)	19 (12.75)
Newspaper clipping service	4 (5.40)	13 (17.34)	17 (11.4)
Reference service	37 (50)	44 (58.66)	81 (54.36)
Inter–library loan service	12 (16.21)	18 (24.00)	30 (20.13)
Referral service	7 (9.45)	4 (5.33)	11 (7.38)

P = 0.904

Note: Figures in the parentheses indicate percentage

I : 5

Information Services for the Academicians and Researchers: A Comparative Study of UK, USA and India

V. Chaya Devi

The academic libraries have been focusing on developing and improving a number of programs from time to time to meet and exceed its user expectations. Most of the academic libraries are able to provide only traditional service such as lending, reference, interlibrary loan, photocopying etc., from its internal sources only. However, these services are inadequate and passive to satisfy the accelerating information needs of academic community, infact, the academic community demands access to nascent information which has a pivotal role in the completion of academic tasks. However, the emerging technological revolution has reshaped the way in which the academicians are using information for performing their tasks. "Libraries, especially academic and research Libraries have long been caught in the dilemma to encourage use, the electronic media has the potential to resolve this conflict"[1]. It is only the information technology which is capable of disseminating information to any academic user at remote sites and at the same time creating linkages among them to facilitate on –line database search, CD-ROM search and networking.

Further, the financial constraints have forced the academic libraries to find alternate methods to provide efficient services. Thus, the adoption of it has been recognized in all academic environments throughout the world as reported by Follet, Fielden and Coles Committee Reports of BLRDD, UK[2] to offer varied information services with limited grants and resources.

Technology has a major impact on the academic libraries and causing to rethink their positions on collections, budgets, building, staff and services.

According to Dempsey "The concern of academic libraries now is to offer access to their own and other libraries, catalogues, to CD-ROM services, to commercial on-line services and to various other local and remote network information resources"[3].

The technological developments such as packet switched transmission, extension of the frequency spectrum for satellite communications, optical cable transmission, coupled with disciplined evolution of software protocols have opened up opportunities to the academic and research libraries for new types of information access and delivery services including on-line database services, E-mail, videotext and computer conferencing etc. the recognition of all these services in performing of various academic and research tasks has caused for the initiation and development of academic networks in different countries throughout the world sharing of resources and services of various academic and research institutions existing through out the nation. Important among such type of networks are JANET (1984) of UK, OCLC and NREN of USA and INFLIBNET of India etc. These are some of the largest and wider geographical coverage networks that are accessible not only to that particular country but also to the other countries of the world through Internet connection.

SERVICES TO THE ACADEMICIANS OF U.K.

There has been a tremendous growth in the provision of services to the academic community in university libraries of U.K. since launching of the Joint Academic Network (JANET) in 1983. It has been supporting academic environment during last 17 years with a variety of services in supporting academic related tasks. Further, most of the universities having access to citation indexes on pertinent topics through JANET only. "A survey conducted by the information market observatory of the Commission of the European Communities indicated that the CD-ROM market has grown by 235 percent between 1988 and 1991. Moreover, on-line information retrieval has proved to be an extremely powerful tool in the academic libraries of U.K. Even the Internet based E-mail become common in U.K.'s academic community to replace more traditional methods of communication. (Gourd & Picot, 1986; Kovacs and Kovacs, 1991; Schaefermayer and Sewell, 1988)[6]. During the survey conducted, a classification of active www use in academic libraries of U.K. has been done. It identifies Greenwich, Keele, Loughborough, Surrey, York, Bath, Dardee, Edinburgh, Exeter, Leeds, Oxford (Redcliffe Science Library and Bodleian Library), Queen's Belfast, Sunderland, Warwick and West Winster university libraries contain homepage with local library information in HTML format and some HTTP links to external information[7]. In brief, in the university libraries of U.K., the following services are offered.

Along with the traditional services, the application of computer and communication technologies is facilitating the U.K. University Libraries to offer the following services:

01. E-mail
02. Fax
03. Electronic discussions
04. Teleconferencing
05. Bulletin Boards

06. Multimedia
07. CD-ROM networking: Reference. Document delivery, inter library loan
08. On-line search and information retrieval
09. Network based services
10. Computerized House-Keeping operations
11. JANET (1984):
    a. Multimedia
    b. Audio, video text and data
    c. Document delivery
    d. OPAC of university libraries
    e. Internet based services: E-mail, Hypertext, List servers (Bull information service)
    f. National Information services (NISs):
       - Information Gateway
       - Reference and Bibliographic services
       - News and current affairs
       - Subject oriented information services for disciplines
       - The IT and computing
       - For Higher education – Administrative & professional
    g. Bath information and Data Services (BIDS):
       - Access to bibliographic databases to academics & students
    h. Information networking over JANET (ISSC):
    i. Mail-base
    j. Campus information services
    k. The subject approach
    l. Indexes and abstracts

m. File-transferring services

n. Access to BLDSC and BLAISE

o. Access to CABI, SCOLCAP, BLCMP (tunded by OSTI)

ACADEMIC LIBRARY SERVICES IN THE UNIVERSITIES OF U.S.A.

In the academic world, the academic libraries of U.S.A. are the leaders of the library profession. The great land mark in the development of academic literatures in USA has started with the advent of National Research and Education Network (NREN) which is equivalent to Janet of U.K., supporting with the high performance of computer and communication facilities to increase dramatically the ability of researchers and educators to carry out the collaborative research and education activities regardless of physical location[10]. This non-profit public access system has been serving all the education institutions and libraries by making use of the internet services. Majority of the academic libraries of U.S.A. have put their collections on on-line and are searching for information through OCLC, BRS, SDC. DIALOG, ORBIT and RLG. The University of –Pennsylvania, one of the first academic libraries to begin offering on-line search services with SDC Lock-heed and the New York Times Information Bank[11]. The University of Chicago, Ohio state University and other big 10 Universities of U.S.A. are initially utilizing OCLC & RLG as major sources, for holding of information[12]. Further, most of the academic institution are highly interested in having access to the increasing rich information sources of internet with a dedication to create an electronic environment where they can publish, share and find information and build on line academic communities both locally and globally. A survey conducted at Murray State University has revealed that increasing availability of abstracting and indexing services on On-line and CD-ROM sources used for personal study and lesson preparation by both faculty and students has resulted in cancellation of the equivalent print subscription[13].

SERVICES OF U.S.A. ACADEMIC LIBRARIES

Besides the general services, the university libraries of U.S.A. have been offering the modern services mentioned below with the assistance of latest information technologies.

01. Audio-visual services
02. Computerized housekeeping operations[14]
03. On-line bibliographies[15]
04. On-line searching of BRS, SDC etc.[16]
05. Multimedia
06. E-mail
07. Fax
08. Teleconferencing
09. Internet based services:

    Hypertext

    E-mail, List servers
10. National Research and Education Network (NREN) based services.
11. OCLC:
    - a. Inter library loan service
    - b. OPAC
    - c. Document delivery services
    - d. Dial order service
    - e. Access to virtual resources
    - f. Intelligent gateway
    - g. Dialog based services:
        - i. E-mail
        - ii. Word-processing
        - iii. Bibliographical retrieval
        - iv. Post-processing and
        - v. Statistical analysis

h. Translation of cataloguing formats

i. Uploading and downloading with automatic format conversion between local and external Databases[17].

12. CD-ROM databases[18]

13. L A N[19]

SERVICES AVAILABLE TO THE ACADEMICIANS IN INDIA

Similar to JANET in U.K., NREN of U.S.A., in India, the Information and Library network (INFLIBNET) of University Grants Commission (UGC) has been serving academic community's information needs. As part of this programe, it has confined mainly to modernize all the Universities, colleges and R & D institutions some of which are identified as nodal points and to create a link among them with an aim to enable the academicians to have access to any type of resources available at the national level through catalogue based, Communication based, database and document delivery services of INFLIBNET, So far it has provided financial support to approximately 70 University libraries for modernization. The University libraries that have been identified as nodal points and received financial grant of 50 lakhs each for its modernization. The progressive stage has been prevailing in the University libraries during the process of the automation. So far, the partial implementation of the INFLIBNET program has resulted to brought out the following products and services.

01. On-line access

    I-net

    Dial-up access

02. E-mail access

03. Provision of contents with abstracts of periodicals in science and technology (COPSAT) a joint venture with NCSI (IISc, Bangalore)

04. Contents providing with abstracts of 25 journals on paper or 40 journals on floppy diskettes.

05. Offering of bibliographic information services based on
    a. 3,00,000 union catalogue of books
    b. 30,000 union catalogue of serials
    c. 65,000 union catalogue of theses
    d. 2,000 records of database experts
    e. 5,000 records of database of current serials

06. CD-ROM based information services

07. Development of ILMS (Integrated Library Management System) software for housekeeping operations. New SOUL (Software for University Libraries).

08. End-user interface programs for searching of various databases and Contents with abstracts of Periodical in Science and Technology (COPSAT).

09. Catalogue cards generation in AACR-II format.

10. Loading of structured text to CDS/ISIS database

11. Computerized networking using ERNET, I-Net, MCNET and GIAS (VSNL) facilities.

12. Conducting of training courses and workshops for library operational staff and executives[20].

In addition to the services and programms that are developed so far, the participating libraries and information centers of the INFLIBNET program has signed on memorandum of understandings for the following proposed plans and programs for the expansion during the coming years to speed up the progressive implementation of the program of the Center and to enable the Center to serve the entire academic community in a better and effective way.

01. It is proposed that the books, serials, theses that are added to the library collection, starting from April, 1998 need to be sent to the INFLIBNET center on monthly basis, as

and when they are entered and accessioned and processed before they are sent for circulation;

02. The experts database mad research projects should be updated and extended regularly in the following year. Further, in the case of Research projects the focus will be on the areas that are not covered by other organizations.
03. Starting from the year 1999, the Center would like to use the current serials data collected, for the purpose of rationalizing the periodical subscription atleast at the State levels.
04. Development of document delivery policy for the participating libraries over the Internet using the suitable software.
05. Proposal to set up a satellite based network having a minimum of one VSAT at each of the University.
06. On-line access to all the union databases not only to the participating universities but also to other libraries that have good network connections.
07. Provision of contents of periodicals in science and technology service will also be extended to the areas of humanities and social sciences and promoting the same to all the universities and colleges.
08. Making available the existing information services based on bibliographic databases received in the center, will be made available to all the academic institutions in the country.
09. The Center would like to establish closer interaction with some of the well-known networks such as JANET, OCLC, RLIN, WIN, and AARNET for the mutual exchange of information and their experiences.

However, during the current years major attention will be given to extend the following internet based services.

01. Creating a Center's web page and facilitate on-line search

to the union databases.

02. Link the useful sites such as Uncover, and Elsevier contents service etc., to have free access to the contents pages of large number of databases.
03. Starting-discussion forms on Internet by setting up a list server for librarians and other professionals.
04. Providing access to internet based electronic journals by establishing links through the Centre's home page.
05. Access to other useful information such as conferences, meetings and publications etc.
06. Create a gateway for intranet/Internet for getting the information using independent search engine.
07. Create a comprehensive catalogue of internet based information sources,
08. Publish INFLIBNET newsletter through webpage.
09. Bringing out a newsletter listing important announcements about internet sources and sites on a regular basis[21].

CONCLUSION

The plans and strategies of the INFLIBNET programme that are mentioned above has made it clear that the Information and Library Network Centre is gearing up to take all the necessary steps, initiatives, plans and programmes for the successful implementation of the programme to serve the academic and research community to an expected level. Though the Inflibnet programme has not yet reached to the stage of highly specialised and technology based services offered by tis counterparts in U.K. and U.S.A., it has been trying to touch high level user oriented services of academic and research community. The success of this programme is very much vital for the future of library and information networking in India. Even though it is having a wider geographical coverage and constraints in its full implementation, its mission is to improve the interactions among the academic and research libraries of the nation. Therefore, the plans and strategies that are proposed during the 9th plan period may help to bring the implementation process of the INFLIBNET programme to a major extent, which will then work in parallel to the services of JANET of U.K. and OCLC and NREN of U.S.A.

REFERENCES

1. Lewis (David, W). Inventing the electronic university college and research libraries. July 1988. P 291-303.
2. The Scientific, technical and medical information system in the UK. BLRDD report 6123. London, Royal Society, British Library and the Association of Learned and Professional Society Publishers. 1993. p 218.
3. Dempsey (Lorcan). The Future of library systems: Integrated or insulated. *In* John W. T. Smith *ed.*, Networking and the future of libraries. Proceedings of the UK. Office for Library Networking Conference, April 2-5 1992, London, Meckler.
4. Lambert (Jill). Managing CD-ROM services in academic libraries, *Journal of librarianship and information science*. 26 (1) March 1994. P. 23-28.
5. Lewis (Mike). Academic library case study. CD-ROM at the University of Sussex. CDROM in libraries : Management issues. Ed. By Terry Hanson and Joan Day. Bowker-Saur, London, 1994.
6. Kovacs (Diane K) and others, Scholarly E-conferences on the academic networks : How library and information professionals use them. *JASIS*. 46 (4) May 1995. P. 244-253.
7. Furner – Hines (Jonathan) and Willett (Peter). The use of the World Wide Web in UK Academic libraries. *Aslib proceedings*. 47 (1) Jan. 1995. P. 23-32.
8. Ibid.-3.
9. Smith (John W.T.), A Review of the use of networking and related technologies by the UK Academic Library and Information Sector, *IASLIC Bulletin*. 41(2). 19996 p. 49-70.
10. Keenan (Stella), Access to information networking and co-operation. *In* Librarianship and information work worldwide, 1993. Ed. by Maurice B. Line. Bowker Saur, London, 1993.
11. Gennaro (Richard de). Impact of on-line services on the academic library. The on-line revolution in libraries. Proceedings of the 1977 conference in Pittsburgh. Pennsylvania. Ed. By Allen Kent and Thomas J. Galvin. Marcel Dekker. New York, 1978.

12. Sanders (Nancy P) and Others. Automated collection analysis using the OCLC and RLG bibliographic databases. *College and Research Libraries*. July, 1988, p. 305.

13. Wall (Celia) and others. Hard copy versus on-line services: Results of a survey. *College and Research Libraries*. July. 1988. P. 305.

14. Sharma (R. N..). Academic libraries in the United States: An overview: *Herald of library science*. 18 (3) July, 1979. P. 281-277.

15. Ibid.

16. Ibid.

17. Burton (Hilary D.). Technology to provide excellence in information services. *Special libraries*. Winter 1987. P. 1-6.

18. Howden (Norman) and Dillard (John). Technology used in on-line searching. *Special libraries*. Fall 1991. P. 288-293.

19. Budd (John M.) and Williams (Karen A.). CD-ROM's in academic libraries: A survey. *College and research libraries*. Nov. 1993. P. 529-535.

20. IT applications in academic libraries in India: with emphasis on network services and information sharing. CALIBER-97 (Souvenir). Fourth National Convention on Automation of Libraries in Education and Research institutes, Thapar institute of Engg. & Technology, Patiala March 6-8, 1997.

21. Pramod Kumar and Kumbar (T. S.). INFLIBNET activities : status, plans and strategies for the future. Information Management in Academic and Research Libraries. Ed. By M. Mahapatra and others. CALIBER-98. INFLIBNET, Information and Library Network Centre, Ahmedabad.

II : 1
Hypertext

Manorama Srinath
A. Bagavathi

INTRODUCTION

The concept of hypertext and hypermedia has been popularized recently in the field of information techonology. Though these concepts appear to be of recent origin, their history can be traced back to the second world war, when Vennevar Bush developed 'Memex' system which was based on associative indexing.

Hypertext is a knowledge representation, composed of nodes of information connected by links. A node might contain text, data files, graphics, images, code, animation or a mixture of these,

Nodes can be arbitrarily large or small, but contain information, which is equivalent to the contents of a full page or a portion of a page. Links are associative paths between nodes or cross references. Links allow the creation of a conceptual web with complied interdependencies among nodes. Thus it is a framework for non- linear representations of knowledge. The users are able to navigate the complex web of nodes of information through the links or highlighted key terms.

To sum up, hypertext can broadly be defined as an external, extended temporal system in an electronic form, facilitating non-sequential reading and writing as well as providing phrase matching technique or key word.

A diagramatic illustration explaining the concept of hypertext is given in Fig. 1.

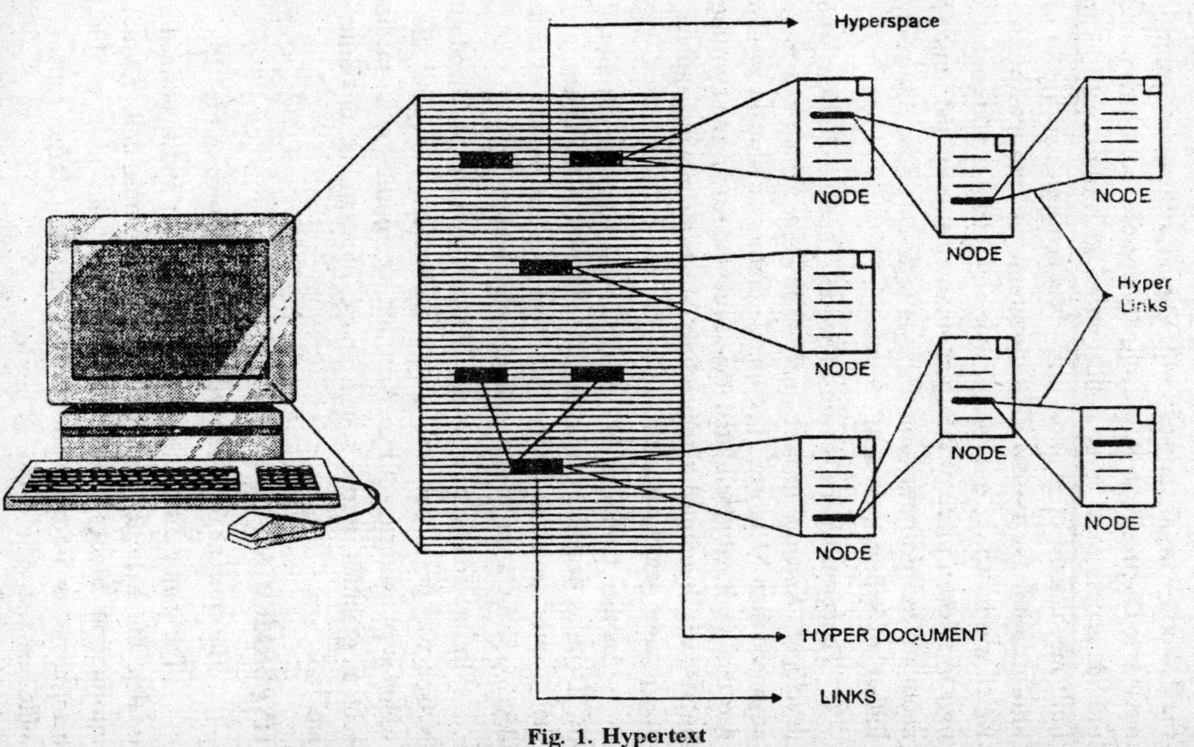

Fig. 1. Hypertext

HYPEREXT: ORIGIN AND DEVELOPMENT

The history of hypertext can be traced back to the days of the II World War, as early as 1945. Vannevar Bush, the scientific advisor to US president, Roosevelt, developed a tool which would provide access to a large collection of microfilms, with an in built mechanism of making links between any two pieces of information in the system. This invention was known as Memex which was based on 'associative indexing' and it would enable a user to select a piece of information automatically and jump to another piece of information. Bush is regarded as the 'Founding Father' of hypertext system.

The term hypertext was coined by Theodore Nelson, who developed 'Xanadu project' in 1960 in USA, which was more advanced than Memorex. The unique feature of Xanadu system was that it not only facilitated non-sequential reading and writing but it was a 'hypermedia' which linked texts along with graphics, video, audio, animation, etc.

Another landmark in this field was Augment introduced by Douglas Engelbert, who is better known as the inventor of the 'mouse' pointing device. Augment is a text writing system developed for a multi-user network environment.

In due course of time the 'Xanadu system' of Theodore Nelson was developed into a very sophisticated 'hypermedia' which is an extension of hypertext that incorporates other media such as graphics, stereo, sound, image, illustrations, animation, etc.

HYPERMEDIA

The concept of hypermedia has been shown in Fig. 2.

The major difference between hypertext and hypermedia is that the hypertext allows the user to link only textual information blocks, hypermedia enables the user to link heterogeneous information blocks. For this, large capacity multimedia storage device is needed.

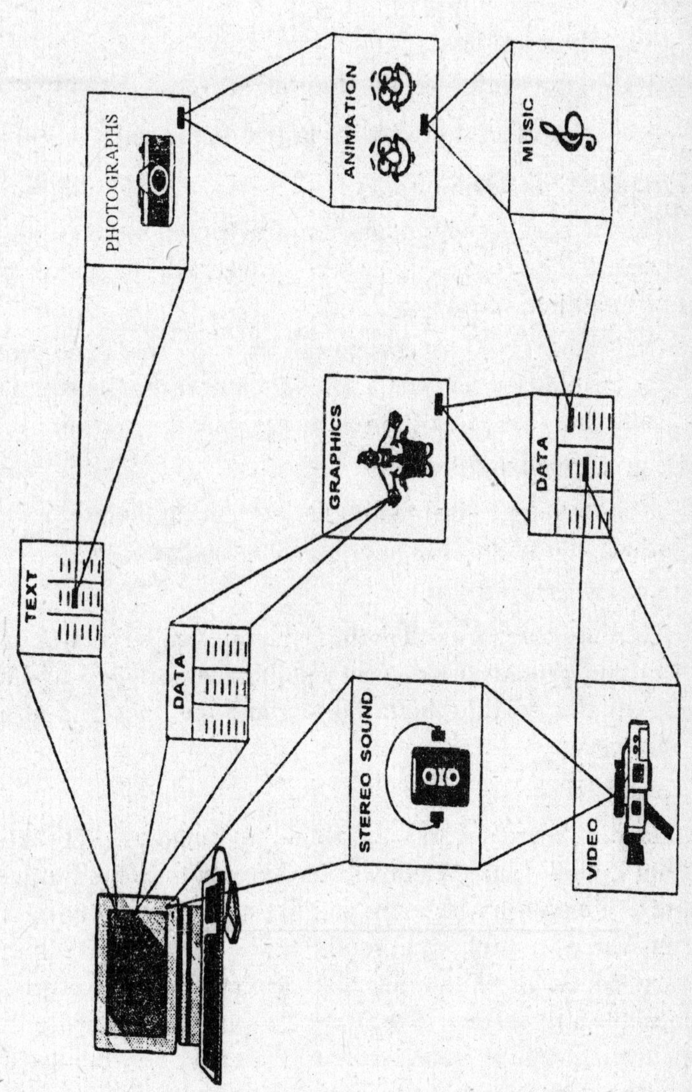

Fig. 2. Hypermedia

STRUCTURE OF HYPERTEXT

The structure of hypertext can be grouped under three categories:

a) A databases of text.

b) A semantic net which connects the text components.

c) A user interface software for browsing the text.

AUTHORING TOOLS

For the past decades a number of hypertext systems have been created. The type of hypertext systems can be generally grouped into three categories.

1. One category of systems comprises of a word processor for creating the text and a software for creating link or an authoring tool and a browser to navigate the system.

   e.g. Weapon and Netscape

2. In another type lined facility is 'in-built' in the processor which allows the user to browse the database.

   e.g. Hyper word

3. The third category is that the Hypertext can be created by writing programs using an application software which facilitates creating both the text and the links and also browsing.

   e.g. FoxPro

'Hyper Word' works in DOS environment. 'HTML Assistant' works in Windows environment and 'Guide-Hypertext' is a system which runs on Unix system. These systems are considered as authoring tools, which facilitate creating hypertext document. Authoring tools are specialised software which enable a researcher to create or design a new database in hypertext environment. Such authoring tools have been tabulated below along with their features and applications.

Table : Authoring Tools and their Applications Hypertext Systems

Developer	*Name of the system*	*Features & Application*
1. University of Maryland	Hyperties developed for IBMPC (1983)	It is used for browsing a text Eg: Hypertext hands on Disk!, a demonstration package which explains about the hypertext system.
2. Carnegi Melon University	KMS (Knowledge Management System (1985)	It is used for multi user network & electronic publishing.
3. Xerox Palo Alto Research Center	Hypercard (1987)	It is used for information analysis, task reading, categorization, interpretation, technical writing and creating bibliographic database.
4. Rada & Martin	MEDLINE (1987)	It is used to retrieve bibliographical citation by generating queries from the semantic net called MeSH.
5. Lotus Develop Corp.	SMARTEXT (1993)	This can be applied for several library uses.

Application of Hypertext for Educational Purposes

Colon Classification: A self – learning package in hypertext environment was designed by Geeta which serves as a teaching aid as well as a self-learning tool for library and information science students. The hypertext environment is created by writing programs in Foxpro windows platform.

Preparation of antirabies vaccine involves various complicated procedures. Hence , an expert system with hypertext facility was designed by Gayatri, which explains the procedure involved in the preparation of antirabies vaccine. This system was designed in Dos environment using VP shell.

V. Deepa designed an expert system, which was intended to be used as a self-learing tool for the choice of access points using AACR II rules. VP expert shell has been used to create the knowledge–based system, which is represented by using hypertext technique.

A self–instruction tool for CDS/ISIS package was designed by Sowmya Lakshmi, in the Department of Library and Information Science, University of Madras. The database was created in hypertext environment by using 'Hyper Word' which is a display oriented word processor, developed by Zarone Software Corporation.

CONCLUSION

Hypertext has been widely used as a browsing technique in CD-ROM and internet which indicates that it serves as a very effective information retrieval system compared to any other menu based retrieval system. Hypertext is a very effective self-instruction tool and it can also be used as a teaching aid.

II : 2

Searching the Web : An Evaluation of Search Engines

Suresh Jange
Basavaraj Kademani

INTRODUCTION

INTERNET is a borderless, barrierless and boundaryless information system providing a new dimension for information storage and retrieval. It contains not only books and journals but also raw scientific data, menus, meeting minutes, advertisements, video and audio recordings and transcripts of interactive conversations. Internet will not resemble a traditional library because its contents are widely dispersed than standard collections. Consequently, the Librarians' skills of classification must be complemented by computer professionalist's ability to automate the task of indexing and storing information led to the emergence of search engines. The ultimate objective of any information system including INTERNET is to provide maximum retrieval efficiency on the net. Search engines are the main retrieval tools for searching information on the web.

It is estimated that there are about 9,47,000 host computers on INTERNET (Network Wizards,1996). As per latest information, there are 2,20,00,000 current users on the INTERNET and every month 1,50,000 new users are joining it. As per the yahoo's collection, there are 88 web-search engines while in India there are 12 Indian-based search engines.

The rapid growth of World Wide Web is outpacing current attempts to search and organize it. New user interfaces may better offer. In this context, evaluation of performance of search engines is absolutely necessary to identify their strengths and weaknesses of an engine so that they can be put to better use. User-based evaluation and determination of user needs should be considered as a part of strategic planning process and an investment for the future for the development of network information service. Various studies have been conducted on performance of search engines between 1995 to 1997 with respect to their salient features like database size, scope, indexed field, search options, relevance of results, output ranking and updating of information.

The present study attempts to explore the role of search engines; their capabilities (both national and international search engines) and to review the various studies undertaken in order identify the areas which need to be explored further for searching the information on the web.

SURFING ON THE NET

World Wide Web is a very powerful navigation tool on the INTERNET and provides hypertext multimedia information system on the net. WWW links offer many advantages over the Gopher that can be embedded in text anywhere on the web.

To surf on the INTERNET, one must have web browsers i.e.,

1. Internet Explorer or
2. Netscape Navigator.

Netscape Navigator has succeeded in becoming the de-facto standard for browsers. INTERNET surfers can choose from multiple search directories to locate just about anything. These two browsers are most suitable for searching information under windows based environment.

SEARCH ENGINES

The world wide web is most widely used for information

on subject interest. INTERNET is a large repository of information and searching relevant information is like finding a needle in the haystack owing to the size of INTERNET, the amount of information and different methods of storage. To facilitate efficient searching of information on INTERNET, search engines have come to the rescue of users. Search engine is a software that enables searching through databases of HTML documents. The main objective of web based search engines are:

1. They are free, faster more timely than CD-ROMs.
2. Many times web site addresses change without notice; an INTERNET search engine is the best for finding latest information .

SALIENT FEATURES OF WEB-BASED SEARCH ENGINES: AN INTERNATIONAL PERSPECTIVE

Search engines are compared under broad categories i.e., individual search engines, subject directories and meet search engines with respect to salient features like data coverage, indexed field, search features, output ranging and updating.

SEARCH ENGINES : INDIAN CONTEXT

Now it's time to look at the status from a 'deshi' standpoint of various Indian specific search engines, which made the task of the Indian web surfer much easier. Leading search engines are compared with each other to evaluate their performance and weaknesses, using criteria like database size, scope, relevance of results, response time and output options (Table-2).

Although the performance of India's search engine like Khoj is popular and is known as India's Yahoo, but still the need to work with one or more of the popular global search engines was however inevitable. It was therefore resolved through IEEE's three days brain storming conference on INTERNET for India that –'think globally, then sort out the indigenous problems so that we could act locally, till we had our own unique stake in the world wide web.

Table-1 : Comparison of Global Search Engines

Features Engines	*Individual search Engines*	*Full text individual Lycos*	*www*	*Subject Altavista*	*Excite*	*Opentext*	*Web crawler*	*Infoseek*	*Yahoo*
Size	web page	20	3	30	50	20	0.16	0.80	1
1	(In millions)								
Database	URL	*	*	*	*	*	*	*	*
Coverage	FTP	*		*		*	*		*
	Usenet	*		*	*	*	*	*	*
	Web page	*		*		*	*		
	Image	*	*						
	Graphics	*		*					
Indexed	Full text								
Field	URL	*	*	*	*				
	Title	*	*	*		*	*	*	*
Search	Boolean	*	*	*	*	*	*	*	*
Features	Keyword	*	*	*	*	*	*	*	*
Updating	Daily	*	*	*	*	*	*	*	*
	Weekly	*	*	*	*	*	*	*	*
	Irregular	*							

Source : Web search engines: IW lab comparison chart (Venditto, 1996, p. 85)

Table-2 : Comparision of Indian Search Engines

Search engine	*URL*	*Scope*
Khoj	*http://www.khoj.com*	It is an India World presentation developed on the lines of YAHOO. Apart from search facilities, general areas are dealt & updated features like thought of the day, link of the day, recipe of the day, etc.
123India search	*http://www.india.com*	Like Khoj, it is India's first premier search engine, provides search and indexing facilities; online greeting service; personal directories; E-mail addresses, etc.
Agni	*http://www.indiawatch.com/agni*	India related information on arts, business, computers, education, entertainment, etc.
Khel	*http://www/khel.com*	Information on India's sports events.
Samachar	*http://www/samachar.com*	India related news.
Bawarchi	*http://www/bawarchi.com*	India's cookery information.
Manthan	*http://www/nio.org/manthan*	Oceanographic engine.

There are several studies carried out on search engines to identify their strengths and weaknesses and so also to provide a new direction for their improvement or newer user interfaces for a better approach especially due to rapid growth of world wide web being outpacing current attempts to search and organize it. On the basis of findings of the study, the effectiveness and efficiency of search engines are evaluated using criteria like database size, relevance ranking, searching capability, update of database, display of results, automatic truncation, etc. (Table 3)

1. Altavista

Altavista developed by Digital Research Lab gives access to largest web index; 30 million pages found on 2,25,000 servers and 3 million articles from 14,000 Usenet news groups. It is accessed over 12 million times per year. Vendetta (1996) found that it had most comprehensive results compared with others and the broad based full text indexing proved consistently reliable but relevance ranking was not most effective. Chuand Rosenthal (1995) and Lebedev (1996) reported that it had highest precision and recall while Chalapathi Rao and Raghuram (1997) report that Altavista is fast and equally good in performance.

2. Lycos

Lycos is very popular because it has caught highest attention in studies. The results show that it has largest and most powerful database and is good for searching obscure topics (Cutois, et. al. 1995, p. 21). While Lycos is relatively slow and inaccurate when compared to Altavista (Chalapathi Rao and Raghuram, 1997). Winship (1995) has found that it has higher recall but many duplications and is not stable when doing research. In the other study, Ding & Marchianini (1996) reported that Lycos has most duplicates and more invalid links in the database, eventhough it returns the most relevant results and has higher quality output.

3. Excite

It provides both web directory and web search engine. It is good in performance and the most accurate search engine (Chalapathi Rao and Raghuram, 1997). It is a complete search engine because it offers a directory, news and classified aids (Venditto, 1996).

4. Infoseek

Infoseek offers a quick way to find popular web pages and lets users to access newswire and magazines free of charge. It provides access to range of databases which includes full text articles from computer periodicals and abstracts from large range of subject databases and are normally chargeable. But its database size was limited and not comprehensive (Vendetta 1996, p. 80). It has best response time and comparable results with Lycos as top its precision (Leighton 1996, p. 4-6).

5. Yahoo

Yahoo is most popular search engine for faster results and one can narrow it to specific categories. It is hierarchical subject oriented guide which lists sites and arranges them into appropriate subject categories but it does not provide any original content but only references of sites that already exist. (Venugopal, S 1997, p. 137-139). Yahoo had lower recall but higher precision. (Winship, 1995)

6. Webcrawler

It has a friendly interface, quick response time and an up-to-date database but it does not seem be good for complex searches (Venditto 1996, p. 86).

7. Khoj

Khoj is a general purpose India-based search engine developed by Ravi Database Consultants (P) Ltd., Mumbai on the lines of Yahoo. It is not comprehensive but response time is good and accurate. Apart from search facility, it offers daily updated features. (Varun, UK 1997, p. 26)

Evaluation of Search Engines Based on Previous Studies

The evaluation of search engines based on already made studies is furnished in table-3 below :

Table-3

	Altavista	*Lycos*	*Excite*	*Infoseek*	*Yahoo*	*Web-crawler*	*Khoj*
Relevance							
Ranking	=+	–+ +	–	+	–	+ +	–
Precision	+ +	– + +		– +	+		=
Recall	+	+ +				–	
Response time	+	+ +	+	+	+	+	+
Validity of link		– +					=
Interface		+ +					
Complex search							
Update of data		+	+		+	–	=
Database size	+	+					
Duplication							
Comprehensiveness	+	+		–	–		=

\+ Good

= Medium

– Not good

IDEAL SEARCH ENGINE

It is evident from the previous studies that no single search engine tested had a perfect performance and could cover all the web browsers. But now the question arises as to what a search engine should be to constitute a comprehensive and ideal tool for information searching on the net. So a good and an ideal search engine features should include:

1. Search engine should contain comprehensive information on all broad areas with multimedia effect i.e. textual, image/video, audio and graphics.

2. To facilitate searching of information on different query it should be indexed on fields of full text, URL, title header and weighted word.
3. Search engine should provide a hierarchical subject oriented guide which lists sites and organize them into appropriate subject categories providing full text information. To achieve the same, it is advisable to utilize Dr. S R Ranganathan's Laws, principles and cannons of classification for developing and designing a hierarchical database to provide maximum access to users in time.
4. It should have quick response time and higher precision and recall.
5. It should act as a user friendly interface interacting with the other in a co-operative and flexible way that makes the underlying system transparent to users of the system.
6. The database should be of hypertextual nature which should perform good validation of link with less duplication links.
7. It should regularly up date the contents of the database.

CONCLUSION

There is hardly any doubt that the existing search engines have already become popular among users for searching information on the net. But as per the results of the previous studies undertaken on search engines reveals that no single search engine is comprehensive in nature and still requires the development of ideal and sophisticated search engine to satisfy all the users of the system. This sort of evaluation study in fact helps to identify the strengths and limitations of search engines so that it can be of greater help to the software developers for the development of a successful information retrieval interface and continued improvement for the existing tools. Further, there is a need to carry out in-depth study on end users, judgement and evaluation of effectiveness and efficiency of search engines and its relevance ranking at institute level, regional, national and international level.

REFERENCE

1. Chalapathi Rao and Raghuram. S. Internet for India. *IEEE seminar*, Hyderabad 1997.

2. Ch, H. T. & Rosenthal. M. Search engines for www : A comparative study and evaluation methodology. Proceedings of American Society for Information Science, 1996.

3. Courtois, M., et. al. Tools for searching the web : a performance evaluation. *Online*. Nov 1995, p. 15-32.

4. Dong, Xiiaying. Search engines on www and information retrieval from internet. *Online & CD-Rom review*, vol. 21 (1) 1997.

5. Ding, W & Marchoinni, G. A comparative study of web search service performance. Proceedings of American Society for Information Science, 1996.

6. Lebedev, A. Best search engines for finding scientific information in net. http://www.chem.msu.su/eng/comparision.html.

7. Varun, UK. RU on Internet. *Information Today & Tomorrow*, Vol. 16 (2), 1997.

8. Venditto, G. Search Engines Showdown: *In* Labs test seven internet search tools, Internet World, May 1996, p. 49-54.

9. Winship, I. R. WWW searching tools : an evaluation, *VINE, 99*, p. 49-54.

II : 3

IT Infrastructure and Use of Electronic Media in Indian Libraries

A. Lakshmana Moorthy
C. R. Karisiddappa

INTRODUCTION

This paper is based on a study for assessing the impact of electronic media on library and information centres in India. In order to find out the preparedness of the librarians, a questionnaire survey was conducted to collect data from librarians. The survey was aimed to analyse the existing scenario in the use of information infrastructure in the libraries in the country.

The Directory of R & D Institutions (DST, 1996) was used to prepare a list of institutions. Since use of electronic media requires certain minimum infrastructure, which in turn depends upon financial position of the library, S & T organisations, universities and institutions of national importance were selected. Further, it has been found that not all institutions have their own libraries and some laboratories/complexes house more than one institution but share resources of a common library; some laboratories do not have their own library and depend on other libraries. A final list of 344 institutions was prepared. The questionnaire was mailed to the libraries of these institutions with a covering letter. In all 153 responses were received –89 of them (59%) in response to the first mailing and 64 (41%) for the two reminders. The response accounts for 44.5% in agreement with the observations made by Goode and Hatt (1952) and Miller and Erdos (1970) compares well with the responses received from mail surveys in social sciences (Table-1).

Table-1: Break-up of response to the questionnaire

Organisation	***Questionnaires***		***Response***
	Mailed (%)	***Responded (%)***	***Rate (%)***
DAE	10(2.9)	7(4.6)	70
DRDO	42(12.2)	23(15)	54.8
ICAR*	50(14.6)	26(17)	52
ICMR	15(4.3)	8(5.2)	53.3
ISRO	9(2.6)	5(3.3)	55.6
S&T**	40(11.6)	18(11.8)	45
Universities***	178(51.8)	66(43.1)	27
Total(N)	344(100)	153(100)	44.5

* 6 Questionnaires were returned by postal authorities;

** Includes institutions from Council of Scientific and Industrial Research (CSIR) and Department of Science and Technology (DST);

*** Includes deemed universities and institutions of national importance.

Of the 153 responses received, 78 libraries are in government sector, 69 belong to autonomous institutions, and 6 did not answer (DNA). While 72 libraries are attached to R & D institutions, 70 libraries are academic in nature, and 3 are from other types of organisations with 8 not answering the questionnaire.

INFRASTRUCTURE AND USE OF IT

Some 13 questions with a number of supplementary questions were included in this section. Two questions were included to elicit information on the hardware and software availability and usage: four questions on the library automation, database development and networking activities; three questions on the use of electronic/digital media including subscription of CD-ROM databases; one question on on-line searching of foreign databases; two questions on on-line electronic journals; and one question to find out the infrastructure for dissemination of information including accessing electronic information resources over internet.

Use of Computers

The respondents were asked if they are using computers and if so, what type of hardware and software, including application software. It is partly an open-ended question with space to record information about these items (other than what has been included in the questionnaire). They were also asked as to how long the computers and other IT equipment were being used and the software details, etc. Analysis of data reveals that while 13 (8.5%) did not answer the question, as many as 115 (75.3%) are using computers in library work. Only 25 (16.3%) are not yet using, among which a few recorded that they are in the process of acquiring computers. Of the 115 who are using computers, 30 (19.6%) are using between 1 and 2 years, 18 (11.8%) are using between 2 and 5 years, and a majority, i.e. 67 (43.2%) are using computers for more than 5 years. This shows that use of computers in libraries is on the increase and in a couple of years, computers would penetrate all the libraries.

With respect to hardware availability, 23 (15%) did not answer the question and a further 17 (11.1%) indicated that they have no computers. Among the remaining libraries which possessed computers, as many as 10 (6.8%) have 10 or more computers with one having as many as 28 computers. A majority (44, i.e., 28.7%) have a single computer each and 81 (52.9%) have computers ranging 1 to 4. There are 29 (14.5%) libraries, which have computers ranging between 5-9. Minicomputers are held by 8 (5.3%) libraries. 22 (14.4%) libraries have workstations of which 12 (7.8%) have one each, and 3 (2%) libraries have varying number (5, 8 and 16) of workstations. Apple mackintosh computers are not popular in Indian Libraries. Only four libraries are having one Mac each. In all 47 (31.4%) libraries are possessing laser printers; while 40 (26.1%). Of them have one each, 6 have two printers each and one has four laser printers. In the case of CD-ROM drives, 77 (50.4%) libraries have installed among which a majority of 50 (32.7%) have one CD drive each, while 13 have two drives each, 7 with three drives each. One library has 16 CD-ROM drives and another 13 drives. This shows that a majority of the libraries have the infrastructure to use CD-ROM databases. However a little over a third of the libraries (57) possess modems; 37 (24.2%) of them one each, 15 (9.8%) with two each with two libraries possessing 10 modems each. This indicates the low penetration of telecommunication infrastructure. As regards to the use of computer and communication infrastructure for information dissemination, a majority of the responding libraries (43.2%, 66) are using computers for more than 5 years, while about one-fifth (19.6%, 30) are using between 1-2 years. Among the respondents, a majority are involved in library automation and using Fax for more than 5 years while in the case of using on-line searching of international databases, CD-ROM databases and internet, those using between 1-2 years are more.

Library Automation Software

There are a number of library automation software packages in use in India. Many of these packages were the result of the efforts of institutions, which owing to the specific requirements and the nature of routines and services developed them in different programming languages. Lack of coordination amongst these libraries, multiplicity of formats used and absence of a national agency to coordinate/direct such efforts are other notable reasons. Thus, those libraries that have resources were able to develop automation software in-house; others outsource experience through contracts. During this time, initially the MINISIS and later the CDS/ISIS, promoted by UNESCO and distributed by NISSAT in India, has found some users. Mainly because of its free availability and the training imparted by NISSAT over a period of time, its users have grown. In the late 1980s and the early 1990s, many private firms and public sector units have shown interest and a few packages have been developed. The Libsys package is one such software package, which is popular among the high-end, integrated library automation software.

The questionnaire listed 19 different software packages and an open column to specify any other package used. The response was encouraging. Although there were 45 (29.3%) libraries not using any library automation software, the remaining 108 (70.7%) libraries were using some 16 different types of automation software packages. There were 21 (13.7%) libraries using in-house developed software, a majority of which again would be dissimilar from each other. Some of the libraries are using more than one software package resulting in 133 instances of usage of some software package. Out of the 108 libraries which use library automation software package, a majority of these libraries were using CDS/ISIS (including one instance of MINISIS). In all, 65 libraries (accounting for about 60.2 percent) are using CDS/ISIS, out of which 30 are from universities and 35 from other instances. Coupled with the 35 libraries which use this software (most of them are common) for database purposes, CDS/ISIS becomes the most popular software package in use in Indian libraries. This is on expected lines due to the reasons explained earlier. Libsys software is a distant second with 23 (21.3%) libraries, 8 of them from universities using the software. Suchika, the library automation software package developed by DESIDOC with 9 (8.3%) libraries, Basisplus promoted by National Informatics Centre with 5 (4.6%) libraries, Sanjay and SLIM with 4 (3.7%) libraries each, and LIBRIS with 3 (2.8%) libraries are the other software packages. There are 8 other software packages each being used by one library. There are about 11 libraries who did not identify the software package developed in-house by them.

Of the 153 libraries majority (52.3%) have purchased the software while 21 (13.7%) reported to have developed the library automation software in-house. Of the 52 (34%) libraries which did not reply to this question whether the software package is developed in-house or purchased, some might have got the package free of charge. This is the case of CDS/ISIS initially as well as the Suchika software developed by DESIDOC which is freely distributed to other DRDO laboratories/establishments. The respondents were also requested to answer the various housekeeping operations covered by the software. Cataloguing is the most widely computerised routine with 85 (78.7%); this is closely followed by circulation with 57 (52.8%), acquisition with 55 (50.9%), serials control with 54 (50%), OPAC with 46 (42.6%) budgeting with 42 (38.9%), and classification with 28 (25.9%) other house keeping operations like current journal content service, etc. are provided by 16 (14.8%) libraries only (Table-2).

Table-2 : Use of library automation software in libraries (n=108)

Software package*	***No. of libraries (%)***
CDS/ISIS (including MINISIS)	65(60.2)
Libsys	23(21.3)
Suchika	9(8.3)
Basis plus	5(4.6)
Sanjay	4(3.7)
SLIM	4(3.7)
LIBRIS	3(2.8)
Others**	8(7.4)
Modules covered	
Cataloguing	85(78.7)
Circulation	57(52.8)
Acquisition	55(50.9)

*Software package**	*No. of libraries (%)*
Serials control	54(50)
OPAC	46(42.6)
Budgeting	42(38.9)
Classification	28(25.9)
Others	16(14.8)

* Some libraries use more than one software package;

** Includes dBase, ILIS, LIBINF, LIBMAN, Lib soft, LIS, LMS and MCAIRS.

Use of E-media

CD-ROM databases form an important component of the e-media. So, three questions including six supplementary questions were included to elicit information from libraries. There are 65 (43.1%) libraries which are subscribing to CD-ROM databases; 29 of them provide CD-ROM based information service of which 20 provide on a daily basis, 1 on weekly basis, and 8 on monthly basis. A question on the number users of CD-ROM databases was included which was answered by 39 libraries; the users range from 3 to 999. The number of CD titles subscribed received response from 55 libraries. Of these, 12 libraries subscribe to one title each and 14 libraries subscribe to two titles each. On the whole, there are 44 libraries which subscribe to less than 10 titles each, another 8 libraries subscribe between 10 and 20 titles, and 3 subscribe more than 30 titles each. One academic library in the agricultural science field holds as many as 70 CD-ROM databases. When a break-up of bibliographic and full-text databases was considered, only 40 and 19 libraries respectively responded. With respect to bibliographic databases, 32 libraries subscribe between 1 and 8 CD-ROM titles each with 8 libraries subscribing to 10 and more (maximum 17). In the case of full-text databases, only 16 libraries are subscribing between 1 and 8 CD-ROM titles each; another 3 libraries are subscribing to more than 10 titles each including one library subscribing as many as 53

A question was included on the broad areas of coverage of CD-ROM databases. Science and technology titles are being subscribed by 39 (25.5%) libraries, followed by engineering (22, 14.4%), social sciences (19, 12.4%), reference works (17, 11.2%), medical sciences (10, 6.6%), and others (13, 8.5%). Although 19 libraries are subscribing to full-text journals on CD-ROM, except one library, none of them provided the list of titles subscribed by them. However, except two, others have rated the use of the full-text journals satisfactory. A majority of the libraries search CD-ROM databases up to 5 times per day, with almost an equal number of them searching between 10-20 times a day. In general, the overall use of CD-ROM databases is more than satisfactory (Table 3).

Table-3 : Use of CD-ROM databases (n = 65)

Use of CD-ROMs	*No. of libraries (%)*
Databases subscribed	
1-5	36 (55.4)
6-10	8 (12.3)
11-15	4 (6.1)
>16	7 (10.8)
*DNA	10 (15.4)
Databases subscribed (Subject-wise)	
S&T	39 (60.0)
Engineering	22 (33.8)
Social sciences	19 (29.2)
Reference works	17 (26.1)
Medical sciences	10 (15.4)
Others	13 (20)
Use of all databases	
Very heavy	8 (12.2)
Heavy	7 (10.8)
Satisfactory	46 (70.8)
Not satisfactory	4 (6.1)

*DNA = did not answer

Use of On-line/Electronic Journals

The number of electronic and online journals as well as the volume of digital information is steadily growing. More and more libraries are embracing electronic journals and slowly marching towards using on-line journals which provide a number of advantages. To find out whether the library heads are aware of the on-line and electronic journals and if they are willing to subscribe to on-line journals, two open questions were included in the questionnaire. The respondents were requested to record their opinions against the two questions.

As regards the opinion about the usefulness of the on-line/ electronic journals, 49 (32%) have recorded response. Among these, as many as 16 have expressed that they have no experience/ not aware of them or those on-line journals are not being used in their library and so they cannot comment on the question. Others (33) opined that on-line journals are very much useful for library users as well as staff; they facilitate on-line bibliographic searches; they save space, time and cost; they are easy to access and store; they do not mutilate and have no aging problem; they facilitate faster provision of information, Boolean searches and narrowing/widening of search scope to satisfy user's multifarious demands; they allow real-time accessing by multiple users in LAN environment and downloading; and they are up to date and are easy to maintain.

In response to the question if they are subscribing or willing to subscribe, almost a half (74, 48.3%) replied affirmatively, while a little over one-fifth of them (34, 22.3%) replied in the negative, and 45 (29.4%) did not reply. This question also included a supplementary requesting the respondents to record the reasons for their (both positive and negative) replies. As many as 64 have provided their comments which again reflect the advantages of the on-line journals as well as the concerns and issues involved in accessing them. Those who responded positively felt that currency, speed, saving shelf space, reduced subscription and maintenance costs, ability to access latest information instantaneously, access beyond office hours, quicker publication and delivery of issues, absence of binding and related costs, multiuser access from individual terminals including saving of user search time, browsing of related articles/journals, etc., as the reasons for their willingness to subscribe on-line journals. As many as 20 respondents expressed relief as the problem of missing or loss of issues in transit/post, which is a primary concern of print media, will be avoided. In the long run, some felt subscribing to on-line journals would prove economical. Those who are subscribing to CD-ROM databases are willing to migrate to on-line journals to satisfy the demands of their research users.

As regards why they are unwilling to subscribe on-line journals, respondents expressed inadequate computer literacy among users and library staff in fully utilising the on-line journals, non-availability of a separate telephone line for library, inadequacy of library budget, browsing difficulties, the expenses related to taking hard copy of articles, lack of training for users/ readers who are not conversant with IT and computers, and the need for extensive hardware to satisfy large number of users particularly in university environment.

The respondents also expressed many concerns. These include users' preference to print versions and their reluctance to digital versions due to reasons such as aesthetics and reading at their convenience; the time taken to replace the print version; the narrow bandwidth of internet and the unreliable and poor telecommunication infrastructure; the inordinate delay to get telephone connection; lack of reliable usage of on-line journals; and frequent power failures and software problems. A few expressed that caution is needed as the time is not ripe for usage of electronic journals. A couple of respondents emphasised the need to evaluate the on-line journals. Thus the replies to the utility of on-line journals reflect the advantages as well as issues and concerns of the library heads, staff and users. Other concerns of respondents are the high initial cost for infrastructure.

higher costs (vis-a-vis printed versions) of on-line journals, unreliable telecommunication links making sending even e-mails difficult, and lack of networking and Internet connectivity (IP addresses). The present communication tariffs are not affordable to many libraries especially for those in the cities where DOT DSNL nodes are not available, thus making the on-line subscription and communication charges more than the subscription charges of printed journals. The constraints of archiving and back volume consultation were also raised by some respondents.

Infrastructure for Information Dissemination

Out of the 153 respondents, only 37 (24.2%) libraries possess direct telephones showing the inadequacy of communication infrastructure in libraries. An overwhelming 118 (77.2%) possess and use telex while 62 (40.5%) use fax, 77 (50.3%) e-mail and a mere 13 (8.6%) use Internet home page for information dissemination (Table 4).

Fax: Though fax has become a major facility for dissemination of information, Indian libraries are not able to use them because of lack of direct telephone lines and other constraints. Although 62 libraries are "possessing" fax, only half (31) of them are using it for dissemination of information. A majority (13) send between 1 and 5 pages per day, 9 libraries send 10 pages each per day, and 2 disseminate 15 pages each per day. There are 7 libraries which are major resource centres sending 25 or more pages by fax per day. Of these. 4 libraries fax 25 pages per day, 2 libraries send at the rate of 50 pages per day, and one library sends as much as 70 pages per day. There are 28 libraries, which receive information by fax. Here too, 13 libraries receive between 1 and 5 pages each per day, 6 receive 10 pages each per day, and two libraries receive 15 pages each per day. Again there are 7 libraries receiving 25 and more number of pages each per day with 3 receiving 30 pages each per day, 2 receive 40 pages each, and one receives as many as 45 pages per day.

Table 4: Use of IT infrastructure for information dissemination (N=153)

Facility	*Duration of using in years (%)*			*Total (%)*
	1-2	*3-5*	*>5*	
Computers	31 (20.3)	18 (11.8)	66 (43.2)	115 (75.3)
Automation	25 (16.3)	16 (10.5)	41 (26.8)	82 (53.6)
On-line search	17 (11.1)	12 (7.8)	15 (9.9)	44 (28.8)
Fax	18 (11.8)	10 (6.5)	23 (15)	51 (33.3)
E-mail	41 (26.8)	21 (13.7)	7 (4.6)	69 (45)
CD-search	28 (18.3)	25 (16.3)	19 (12.6)	72 (47.2)
Internet	27 (17.6)	10 (6.5)	1 (0.7)	38 (24.8)

E-mail : Of the 77 respondents who use e-mail for dissemination of information, 73 use it for correspondence followed by 36 for document ordering, 26 for transmitting digital information to remote users, 24 for paper submission, 7 for surveys, and 3 for other purposes. This compares well with other studies (for example Babu and Gopalakrishnan, 1998 and Kogannurmath and Jange, 1999) which too found that over 90 per cent of the use of e-mail is for correspondence. As regards the utility of e-mail service by users, 52 rated it satisfactory followed by heavy use (15) and very heavy use (3). However, as many as 7 are not satisfied with e-mail use by their users.

Internet : One question was asked to find out the various uses of Internet. E-mail is the major facility used by all the 38 libraries having Internet connectivity while 27 use it for searching databases, 24 for file transfer and 21 for current events and news. Internet is also being used for downloading software (by 13), bulletin board services (12), special interest groups (10), listservs (9), on-line shopping (1) and for other purposes (2). Although 13 libraries use Internet home page for dissemination of information only 5 libraries have their own home page on Internet.

Digital Libraries

The developments in the mass storage, computers and communications technologies have resulted in many projects and initiatives for the creation and establishment of digital libraries (DLs). In view of this, as many as four questions were included to elicit information from the respondents on the impact of DLs on the Indian library and information centres. One open question and three structured questions were given. These questions were intended to know the awareness of the librarians on the impact of DLs on library system and functions. A majority (82, 53.6%) has answered the question with 77 finding positive impact on libraries while 2 replied in negative and 3 expressed that they cannot comment as they are not aware of the DLs. Many of the advantages have been recorded by some of the 77 respondents who found positive impact of DLs. As on-line electronic journals are a sub-set of DLs, many of the advantages are common. Some of the opinions expressed with respect to DLs include:

(a) They improve efficiency, productivity, accuracy and flexibility and allow the librarian to attend more innovative jobs.

(b) For serving users with current S&T information in no time on their desktops.

(c) For scanning large information resources to provide exhaustive information at a faster pace.

(d) It is an historical inevitability for libraries to serve user community.

(e) They have great potential for information handling activities and will change global information scenario.

(f) Libraries are in transition and are accepting DLs as a reality.

On the negative side people felt that there will be no cost savings; only those who are engaged in research only will benefit from them; masses will not be interested in DLs; and that the developments will not reach remote places early.

Impact on Library System

The respondents were requested to answer the impact of DLs on library system as a whole and on library functions. The analysis of the data shows that a majority of the librarians are of the opinion that DLs have a positive impact on libraries. This question got response from 73 to 81 per cent of the total respondents; more than 20-30 per cent responded to the previous question which elicited their view, in general, on the impact of DLs on libraries. This shows that a clear majority (ranging from 55 to 77 %) of the respondents are aware of the various issues and concerns of the electronic media and DLs. More than three-fourths of the respondents 116 (75.8%) visualise positive role of DLs on library professionals in providing services and 106 (69.3%) view that DLs improve the productivity of library professionals. Almost an equal number (117, 76.5%) feel the positive effect of DLs in meeting the multifarious demands of users and 94 (61.4%) are of the opinion that these will result in positive library-user relationship. A maximum number of 118 (77.1%) are of the view that DLs would improve the quality of services and 109 (71.2%) feel that there would be positive impact on the quantum of qualitative information provided to users. These are reflected again in the positive impact of DLs on the use of library material (103, 67.3%) and the image of the library (104, 68%). Only 84 (54.9%) viewed positive impact of DLs on socio-cultural aspects of libraries and users. The lower response to the socio-cultural impact and the library-user relation ship in the digital era could be attributed to the fact that very little research has been done on these aspects and so the respondents are not able to have a clear idea. This is also reflected in the answers related to the copyright and legal issues.

Impact on Library Functions

The respondents were requested to choose appropriate answer whether DLs would improve or do not improve or have no effect on various functions of the library. Again the response to the various supplementaries ranged from 60 to 79 per cent.

The respondents had no doubt that the library services would improve in the DL environment with 121 (79%) responding so. However, 31 (20.3%) felt that DLs would have no effect on the library services. There was similar response of improved user satisfaction (116, 75.8%), meeting users' needs (114, 74.5%), library services (116, 75.8%), and also library image (104, 68%). However, only 92 (60.1%) felt that positive impacts on library use with 15 each (9.8%) responding that DLs would not improve or have no effect on library functions (Table 5).

Table 5: Impact of digital libraries (N=153)

Facet	*No. of libraries (%)*			
	Improve	*Don't improve*	*No effect*	*DNA**
Library services	121(79)	1(0.7)	31(20.3)	—
User satisfaction	116(75.8)	1(0.7)	4(2.6)	32(20.9)
Meeting users' needs	114(74.5)	2(1.3)	5(3.3)	32(20.9)
Library use	92(60.1)	15(9.8)	15(9.8)	31(20.3)
Library services	116(75.8)	2(1.3)	2(1.3)	33(21.6)
Library image	104(68.0)	4(2.6)	7(4.6)	38(24.8)

* DNA = did not answer

It has been reported in the literature that the digital and virtual libraries would have a negative effect on library user interaction, which would result in psychological barriers between librarians and users. A majority of respondents do not agree (88, 57.5%) that the DLs will have negative effect on library-user interaction, while 19 (12.5%) agree with it and 13 (8.5%) do not know if it is so. The library without walls was expected to allow users directly access information, minimising the intermediary role of the librarian. Also, this was reported to result in psychological effect on librarians. However, 67 (43.8%) of the respondents to the study do not feel so, while 16 (10.5%) agreed with it and 34 (22.2%) do not know about it. However, a majority of the respondents (60, 39.2%) agree that the electronic/digital information will have negative effect with respect to copyright, legal and ethical issues, while an equal number do not agree or do not know.

Acknowledgements

The authors are thankful to Dr Mohinder Singh, Director, DESIDOC, for extending facilities and giving permission for publishing this paper. They are also thankful to Smt. K. Shailaja Reddy for her secretarial assistance in preparing the paper.

REFERENCES

1. India, Dept. of Science and Technology. *The Directory of R & D Institutions 1996*. New Delhi, Department of Science and Technology, 1996.
2. Goode, W. and Hatt, P. *Methods of social research*. New York, McGraw Hill, 1952.
3. Miller, D and Erdos, P. *Handbook of research design and social measurement*, Ed. 2. New York, David Mckay, 1970.
4. Babu, D. Ramesh and Gopalakrishnan, S. Internet : A survey of its use in Chennai. ***In*** *Towards the New Information Society of Tomorrow : Innovations, Challenges and Impact. Papers presented at the 49th FID Conference and Congress, New Delhi, 11-17 October 1998*. N.M. Malwad, *et. al.* (Eds). New Delhi. INSDOC, 1998. pp. 1.9-1.13. FID Publication No. 719.
5. Kogannurmath, M.M. and Jange, Suresh. Use of internet by social science research scholars : A study, ***In*** *CALIBER-99 : Academic libraries in Internet era. Papers presented in the Sixth National Convention for the Automation of Libraries in Education and Research, 18-20 February 1999, Nagpur*. Ahmedabad, INFLIBNET Centre, 1999. pp. 239-245.

II : 4

Internet Services for Libraries

T. Ashok Babu

"The fundamental choice : either become an agent of the change, or become obsolete."

INTRODUCTION

The internet is one of the most important and complex innovations of the mankind. It is a network of networks. Physically, the internet is a number of computers connected to each other talking a common language or protocol known as TCP/IP (Transmission Control Protocol/Internet Protocol). It is the largest and most complete tool for information exchange for the global population. It serves as a good encyclopaedia giving detailed information on a wide variety of subjects. Presently, it is possible to access about 40,000 networks all over the world through the Internet.

HISTORY OF THE INTERNET

During 1969, the US Department of Defence, through there Advanced Research Project Agency (ARPA), conducted an experiment. This is a pocket switched network over telephone lines. Out of this initial network Advanced Research Project Agency Network (ARPANET), one of the early forerunners of internet was born. During 1970's, the ARPA developed a set of rules called protocols that helped in connecting different networks having different host computers. The number of networks connected to ARPANET continued to grow over the years. In 1982, ARPANET joined with MILNET (the Military Network) and few others and it is said that the Internets thus formed from this consolidation of networks. As per the latest information available, there are 2,20,00,000 current users on the internet, and every month 1,50,000 new users are joining it. It is estimated that by the end of the year 2000, there will be 10 crore users and 10 lakh hosts in the Internet.

INDIAN SCENARIO

In India, the network offering on-line services on the internet are:

1. Educational and Research Network (ERNET)
2. SOFTNET of Software Technology Parks of India (STPI)
3. National Informatics Center Network (NICNET) and
4. Videsh Sanchar Nigam Limited (VSNL)

ERNET : It was started in India in November, 1986 and is offering internet services to the academic and research community since 1989.

SOFTNET : It started offering internet services apart from point to point links from 1993.

NICNET: It is offering Internet services since 1994. It is a viable gateway to internet in the country. With more than 700 micro earth station nodes all over the country, it has the widest reach in the country.

VSNL : Since August 1995, the internet connections are provided by Videsh Sanchar Nigam Limited (VSNL) for commercial use. VSNL offers 'shel' or terminal dial up and 'TCP/IP' type of connections. As per the latest announcement by VSNL, the charges for 'shel' type of accounts will be Rs. 5000 per year or 500 hours whichever is earlier for all categories of dialup users. But this type of account cannot download graphics. The service for the students, to be priced at a concessional rate of Rs. 500 per year with a maximum two hours, is expected to be launched shortly, VSNL's internet access mode was commissioned at

Mumbai connecting to internet node at USA via satellite and to the internet node in Europe via submarine cable providing diversity and highly reliable network connectivity. At present, VSNL commissioned remote Internet access nodes in 10 cities and this will be expanded to 10 more cities very soon, Currently VSNL has approximately 1300 users all over India.

To get more technical assistance and expertise about the Internet connections one can contact: Internet Consortium India, 59/9 Kalkaji, New Delhi-110 019.

INTERNET SERVICES

There are basically four things we can do on the Internet:

1. Communication
2. Document or file transfer
3. Interactive browsing
4. Bulletin boards

Corresponding to these activities, there are four basic tools;

1. **E-Mail**–Electronic message exchange.
2. **FTP (File Transfer Protocol)**–Moving electronic documents, images, sounds, etc.
3. **TELNET**–Accessing another computer system's databases or archives.
4. **USENET** – Global bulletin board service.

In addition to the above, in recent years some new tools have emerged that expanded these four basic activities.

1. **World Wide Web (WWW)**–a hypertext interface to information on the internet.
2. **Gopher** –an information browser that lets us retrieve what we find.
3. **Veronica**–an enhancement to gopher that searches many gophers databases.
4. **WAIS**–a powerful tool for searching some large databases.

5. **Archie**–a simple but effective mechanism for searching FTP archives.

We can discuss the above services in detail.

E-mail : It is the most commonly used application on the Internet. The main attraction of E-mail lies in its sped; it is much more powerful than paper mail (or "snail-mail"). With the E-mail, we can send and receive anything we use or create on computer, words, documents, programs, photos, images and sounds. It is much cheaper than other modes of communication services.

FTP (File Transfer Protocol) : This facilitates transfer of files over the Internet . The complete process involves transfer of the file from one host to another. FTP has become popular and most widely used tool because of the number of anonymous FTP servers available.

Telnet : Telnet is one of the major Internet applications. It is a the tool that delivers you to the front door of other networks. Through telnet we can browse library card catalogs, search for papers or journals of interest. Telnet allows one to log on to another system and use various services available on that host computer.

USENET : Usenet is conceptually a huge bulletin board system. This allows us to send messages to a specific person or group. Network news lets one send messages on an electronic bulletin board for any one to see. Both E-mail and news groups are extremely useful Internet tools.

ADVANCED APPLICATIONS

These application provide the users with advanced facilities. Some of these applications are mentioned in the following sections.

Archie : Archie is the companion software tool to FTP (file transfer protocol). The archie program searches a constantly updated index of FTP sites, file names and descriptions. Archie system helps us to find information located anywhere on the internet.

Gopher : Gopher is a software tool that connects a variety of computers and information data and information databases on the Internet and displays them as a series of menu item. Gopher servers accept simple query and send the clients a document or a list of documents.

Veronica : Veronica ("Very Common Rodent-Oriented Network Index to Computerized Achives") is the companion tool to Gopher. It is a search tool that allows one to quickly scan gopher for particular files and directories. It is a program that one can access through gopher.

WAIS : The Wide Area Information System (WAIS) is a full-text indexing software that is used to index large text files, documents and periodicals.

World Wide Web (WWW) : It is a client-server based distributed hypertext multimedia, an information system on the Internet. It was originally developed at the European Particle Physics Laboratory (CERN), Geneva. It has now become the most popular navigation tool on the Internet. Just as one can access Gopher space through a gopher server or client, one can access the www through 'browser'.

NEEDS OF LIBRARIES TO ACCESS THE INTERNET

There are at least five reasons why the users require to access information centres and libraries through the Internet

1. To get help for publishing their information.
2. To get help for locating information (online services and catalogues).
3. To get help in determining the quality of various information resources.
4. For delivery of documents.
5. Full text documents and information are also available via internet.

Following are some of the possibilities for exploiting the Internet or Intranet for publishing and delivery of information to the users.

1. E-mail can be used for delivering information to the users. It could be used for the preparation of the list of additions, CAS/SDI bulletins and for updating databases.
2. Internet can be used for preparing electronic news and for reporting new resources, services, etc.
3. It is useful for maintaining up to date information about library services, collection, staff, etc.
4. It is useful for providing access to databases, OPAC, current contents, etc.
5. It is useful for preparing union catalogues.
6. It is also useful for database indexing and searching.

With the use of internet, the role of library has highly revolutionized. The user who had geographic limitations can now have access to information available anywhere in the world.

INTERNET VISION BY 2000

According to the latest paper from STPI, in the year 2000, the Internet will:

- have more than 100 million connected hosts.
- have more than one million connected networks.
- have traffic which exceeds voice telephony.
- be available worldwide.
- support thousands of different applications.
- reshape institutional, business, financial and political boundaries.
- become part of every communicative and collaborative aspect of our lives.

CONCLUSION

Although many libraries have access to the Internet, radical changes in library and information services have yet to appear. There is a tendency to put new wine into old bottle, that is to add network access to traditional bibliographic information services while the librarian jealously guards his role as intermediary Library services must center now on user needs and wishes.

REFERENCES

1. Cedeno, Nanny. The Internet tool kit. New Delhi, BPB publications, 1996,
2. Folk, Bennett: The Internet-basic reference from A To Z. Ed. 2. New Delhi, BPB publications, 1996.
3. Indira Subbaram. J: Internet in a nutshell. *DESIDOC Bulletin of Information Technology* 16 (3) 1996: 3 –10.
4. Radriguez, MVR and Ferrante, A.J.: Information Technology for the 21st century: Managing the change. Boston, CM publications, 1996.
5. Stewart, Barbare: Internet advantages for the technical services librarian. *DESIDOC Bulletin of information Technology*, 1996.

II : 5

Internet: A Boon Or A Bane For Librarians

N. R. Satyanarayana

AN INTRODUCTION TO INTERNET

The practice and provision of library and information services the world over is being greatly influenced by the advent of on-line public access catalogues, on-line information services and the development of CD-ROM databases. These technological innovations have also found their way into the library and information arena. The development of networks, networking and internet–working are the most prominent examples for this.

The internet is a network of networks spread all over the world. Thus it is a conglomeration of smaller networks from different countries of the world. It permits electronic mail, remote login and file transfer between computers on the networks. Each country has at least one backbone network. Other networks in that country are connected to that backbone network.

In other words, Internet is another telecommunication network. Majority of the connections for the internet run on standard telephone lines. Thus it is changing the ways in which people communicate. It is changing the very publishing model. Researchers from all corners of the earth are finding that their work thrives in a networked environment, immediate access to the work of colleagues and a virtual library of millions of volumes and thousands of papers afford them the ability to incorporate a huge mount of knowledge hitherto unthinkable. People from all walks of life in different countries use the internet for exchanging messages, carry on real time chatting, play games, sell goods and services, advertise products, download software, search for useful and usable information and do many more things. Work groups can now conduct interactive conferences with each other regardless of physical location. The possibilities are endless.

INTERNET: HISTORY

In the year 1969, the US Defence Department has created an experimental network, using packet switching technology called ARPANET (Advanced Research Project Agency Network). The beginning of ARPANET is considered as the beginning of internet. The fears of cold-war, perhaps the fear of a nuclear attack of the early sixties, motivated the research for the creation of network which would ensure the survival. Information is usually transmitted in fragments which were re-assembled at the receiving end. This facilitates the security of the data to avoid its misuse and mishandling by undesired elements. In other words, in event of one host fails in the network, or get bombed out the communication should be routed to the unaffected areas and thus keep the network alive, was perhaps the principle underlining the creation of internet. Subsequently, ARPANET allowed other bodies to be linked to this network by using the TCP/IP (Transmission Control Protocol/ Internet Protocol) suit, which was developed in the 1970s. In the early eighties other computer networks were also connected to the ARPANET creating an inter-network. The technological development such as evolution of component network, increasing transmission speed, improved protocols had their influence on this network. As the word internet came to refer to any interconnection of computer network, the largest such network became to be known as the internet. With the fading of the fear of cold war in the 1980s, other federal agencies took interest in this network. The National Science Foundation took a major role in the development of the internet with the creation of its network called NSFNET. The NSF's interest was in developing this for remote connection to super-computer. After taking over the responsibility and control of this backbone network, NSF could help many research projects in distinct fields to benefit from the computing power of super computer.

Internet provided a means for the super computing centres to maximise the use of the machine by scheduling different projects in different times in such a manner that researchers are not required to be present at the site of the super computers. In the year 1990, ARPANET was officially dismantled. By that time NSFnet and many other TCP/IP networks have already become major traffic carriers. Subsequently, the internet itself continued to grow. Now, in the internet one can communicate with around ten million hosts worldwide, a population which is being doubled in every year. Thus, internet is now a loose network of millions of computers at thousands of sites around the world the communication among each of these sites is done through a common language. TCP/IP is that common language. It is a loose network because there is no central authority controlling the network. At the moment, internet is accessed by about 77 countries, connects nearly 50,000 networks with almost twenty million people around the would as its users. The five million computer strength of the internet today is expected to grow up to one hundred million machines by the end of the century. No one person or group runs the internet. Voluntary organizations like INSDOC (internet society), IAB (Internet Architecture Board) and IETF (Internet Engineering Task Force) hold on-line discussions to create standards for the internet connectivity. Similarly, no one pays for it, but at the same time it is not free. Some service providers on the internet are non-government funded agencies like UUNET, PSI, etc. These commercial operators have inter-connected their backbones to form CIE (Commercial Internet Exchange).

THE WAY INTERNET OPERATES

The key to the treasure of internet is the transmission control protocol (TCP) of its network. The TCP/IP is actually a set of protocols developed to allow computers to share resources across another computer in the network. Today, TCP/IP is the most successful mechanism for networking of computers. TCP breaks the message into datagrams, reassembles them at the other end, resends anything that get lost, and puts things back in the right order. IP is responsible for sending individual datagram. Every IP datagram contains the source address and the destination address so that each datagram can be delivered independently. TCP module contains the necessary logic to provide a reliable circuit. Thus by employing TCP/IP one can contact computers of different platforms and different networking functions such as e-mail, remote login and file transfer by using client-server architecture. The client-server approach involves two programmes, viz., the client and the server. The client programe is the one with which users interact on their local internet connected computer. The server programme located on the remote computer interacts and responds to the client.

ACCESS TO INTERNET

Many of us are aware that internet is a great source for information. But very few of us know how hard it could be to find the required information. There are people who often comment that internet is used only for e-mail services, groping the dark and thus wasting their time in this process, one is frustrated and utterly disappointed. Thus they virtually loose themselves in the vast amount of information they gather from the internet. In order to get the best out of internet, all we need is patience. Understanding the skills and techniques to use the internet. The limitations of internet are only the user's ability to explore the resources. The internet has wide connectivity and allows communication among thousands of machines irrespective of their make and their operating system. To communicate, computers need a communicative language. TCP/IP is that communicative language through which all computers on internet communicate among themselves. This concept is as simple as two people talking to each other with the help of mutual language.

that is TCP/IP. The protocol is essentially a set of rules by which the communication takes place between users on the network.

Every computer on internet has an address. Initially numerics were used to express the address. Since human beings better remember the alphabetic sequence rather than a numeric sequence, Canonic (overall alphabetic) sequences were introduced later on. This address is called IP address. Since an individual connects to the internet through a computer, individuals have user names on specific machines. Thus, internet syntax for person's address is the user's name followed by @ symbol, followed by the computer's internet address.

In the later half of 1980s and early 1990s, the only option for access to internet was through a kind of leased or dedicated telecommunication line connection. However, with the introduction of individual dial-up accounts, access provision to internet is being increased tremendously.

INFORMATION SERVICES OF INTERNET

The popularity of internet centres round its communication capabilities. The communities that constitute the topical discussion groups for internet are the library and the information professionals. The most significant feature of internet is the information resources available on internet. These information resources are available through many connectivity tools such as TELNET, FTP, GOPHER, WWW, etc. which transfer information from a remote computer back to a local computer.

TELNET

Telnet is an internet application tool for getting connected to a remote machine. It is a programme. Telnet is the main internet protocol for login connection with a remote machine. Telnet is a utility which will allow one user to log on to another system and gives the user an opportunity to be on one computer system and work on another which may be thousands of miles away. Telnet is used to access a lot of public services including library catalogues and other kind of databases. Many universities like

Colorado Alliance of Research Libraries (CARL), Boston University, Stanford University and public libraries like Library of Congress made their library catalogues available for the internet user. CARL offers a number of library databases including searches of government periodicals, book reviews, indices for current articles and access to other library databases.

One of the interesting databases is science and technology information system (STIS). For searching the databases, Telnet to STIS, NST and login as "public". The STIS is maintained by NSF and provides access to many NSF applications. The full text publication can be searched online and copied.

FILE TRANSFER PROTOCOL (FTP)

In internet, FTP is used to move files between computers. Files can be graphics, software, datafile and text file. Any useful data found on any of the sites can be downloaded by using simple commands. Like telnet, FTP also requires an account on both the local and remote computer. As the internet grew in size resulting increase in the number of files and sites, a need was identified for providing certain files and programmes to everyone and certain files as anonymous login. An ordinary internet user needs password to achieve access to the freely available files, whereas for having access to anonymous as the login and guest as the password. Subsequently, the practice has been modified and internet user now use their e-mail address as a password. In other words, FTP requires specific address to the machine with which file has changes to take place. The command on Net for FTPing is: % ftp remote machine–name.

Here begins the FTP programme and connects to the named computer. The identity of the person demanding access is asked for. Usually this is a login name or a password. If there is no password security on a system only the login name may be asked. After the remote system has accepted the stated login name, the file transfer can be done. FTP prints ftp to prompt further command. It can transfer files in both directions. The get and put files have the following syntax:

ftp get source-file destination- file

ftp put source-file destination- file

For file transfer one needs to know the exact name of the file that is to be transferred and also where it is located. This needs browsing for the file. The basic commands to get file listing is "is" and "dir". The syntax for the command being:

ftp dir directory – name local –file – name

ftp is directory – name local –file –name

Both the commands list the files in the given directory on the remote machine, putting their output into a local file. Both the arguments in the syntax structure are optional; the "is" command gives a simplified listing of file names with additional information. The "dir" commands produce more complete information. The output of this command looks just like a full directory listing on the remote system. For multiple transfer of files by which a group of files may be transferred, "mget" and "mput" commands are used. The syntax for this being:

ftp mput list of source files

ftp mget list of source files

The file transfer usually requires the user identity to be specified and also asks for a password, However, anonymous ftp allows users who do not have a login or a password to access certain machines. There are some restrictions, though anonymous ftp allows to get files only and does not allow installation of new files or modification of files that already exist.

FINDING THE AVAILABLE FILES IN INTERNET

Internet is a decentralized system where thousands of computers support distinct databases, with discrete search interfaces. Therefore, there is no bibliographical control over the various information sources available. One of the greatest difficulties with the internet is to find out the available files in internet. For finding appropriate information one needs to involve and explore broad range of possible resources. It is like a library of books without a catalogue. However few finding tools have been developed for this purpose such as Archie, Wais, Netfind, etc.

Archie is a database system developed by few students of McGill university. Archie servers are available all over the world. One can ask Archie to find a file via telnet or e-mail. Archie helps in locating a file from any of the thousands of anonymous FTP sites, if the name of the file is known.

E-MAIL

Electronic mail, more popularly known as e-mail, is perhaps the most popular use of the net. E-mail is actually combining the advantage of writing with that of immediate communication through telephone. In other words, it is an electronic correspondence next only to normal conversation. Thus e-mail is the fastest way of communicating. With no wastage of time in dictating, typing, copying , and distributing further more, it allows people to write back and forth without any delay in time. The ability to communicate with the help of computers, to and from some of the most distant areas of the world, demonstrates the viability and usefulness of internet.

Besides sending personal message to people overseas, one can use internet E-mail to request software, files and information from a number of sources. Full range of internet services can be harnessed using e-mail facility in the following way:

Ftp by using E-mail to ftp mail@sunsite.unc.edu

Message:Open ftp. microsoft.com get/index.

Ext'

ARCHIE by using e-mail to archie@archie.un/edn

Many organisations who have only e-mail use this facility for file transfers for getting softwares.

MAILING LISTS (LISTSERVE)

In the year 1983, Eric Thomos designed a software with the name of listserve for electronic conference management. With the creation of this software, electronic conferences are taking place over the internet. In addition to this basic function, Listserve software also helps in taking a single message and sending it to all subscribers. Thus functions such as subscribing, unsubcribing, checking to use who is subscribed and retrieving information about the conference are all automated. This is often termed as mailing lists because subscribers to a particular list can post message to all other subscribers by simply sending one message to the listserve address, which will automatically be forwarded to all members.

For example, you can subscribe to: library science forum of Indian Institute of Science, Bangalore, India by sending e-mail to:

listserve@ncsi.iisc.ernet.in

with the message : subscribe LIS-FORUM your name

For cancellation send the message:

Unsubscribe your name

If you subscribe to too many mailing lists at a time, your mail box can become a big mess and it is worse when your system is down for a couple of days, or if you go on a vacation.

NETWORK NEWS (NEWS GROUPS)

Another related network is Usenet. It is also known as network news or news groups. In fact, Usenet is not actually a network, but it is a set of voluntary rules for passing and maintaining news groups, which are nothing but conferences. In Usenet a site usually receives a certain number of thousands of news groups. A user at the site can choose which group to read,. In other words, it is like a meeting place where people gather to meet their friends and keep abreast of latest trends in their field of interest or express whatever is on their mind. The transmission of Usenet news is purely co-operative out of goodwill and news is distributed everywhere. The news groups are arranged in several hierarchies, for example:

Comp: Topics of internet to both computer professionals and hobbyists.

Misc: Subject groups include fitness, job hunting, law, and investment.

Sci: Discussion relating to research in sciences.

News: Groups concerned a with the news, network group maintenance and software

K12 : Educational topics

BULLETIN BOARD SERVICE (BBS)

BBS is an electronic message system for reading and posting messages. It is usually comprised of small group of users who have a common interest, distributed to some geographical area. BBSs are not very expensive and sometimes free to callers. Subscribers reach bulletin boards via telephone lines. BBSs provide e-mail services as well as chatting forums on special subjects of interest to the individual. Now a days several BBSs are available on internet.

BBS is similar to news-groups. It contains programms documents, graphics, sound or video clips, etc. If it can be put in a computer file, it can be attached to a file. Most of what is found on a BBS can be downloaded. Members send (upload) information files to BBS also. Exchange of "personal mail" is also another feature of BBS. FAO, NATIS, DDA, DOE are some of the examples of BBS.

GOPHER

The need for the wide information system wherein many colleges and universities and general community could have access led to the development of the gopher protocol in order to link such a CWIS to internet resources. The University of Minnesota developed a suitable software named as Gopher. It is a way of accessing what you want without having to know where it is. This is like browsing the remote library card catalogue and automatically getting the wanted material. When we want something we like, we can read and access it through the Gopher without knowing the domain names, address, changing paradigms, etc.

Although each Gopher site uses its own organization for materials in its domain, Gopher menus are like a directory listing the information sources. In case the user does not find everything desired on Gopher, it allows the user to pass electronically to the next Gopher library and check there.

WORLD WIDE WEB (WWW)

More recently the internet was totally reshaped by the world wide web software. WWW allows the user to experience sights and sound in an innovative style through graphical user interfaces. The earlier tools for locating relevant information on internet such as TELNET, FTP, GOPHER, etc., have been merged, thus allowing access to internet through a single interface, i.e., WWW.

There are three main concepts that characterise the WWW:

1. URL (Uniform Resource Locator) specifies the protocol and location for information retrieval.
2. The Hypertext Transfer Protocol (HTTP) specifies how hypertext documents are transferred through the internet on the WWW.
3. The Hypertext Markup Language (HTML) contains rules for document publishing on the WWW. HTML contains the text and structure of the document, pictures and links to other internet sites and locations.

A "Home page" is the first page or the introduction page of a set of related information put up on the net. It is easy to set up a home page using several tools available for this purpose. The home page acts as powerful advertisement for your products/services. The number of home pages on the WWW was around 25 million in 1985 and it is likely to be 200 million by 1999.

VENDORS FOR INTERNET

With the rapid expansion of information resources, a number of online database vendors are allowing connectivity through internet. Most of these vendors use different data gathering mechanism and search mechanism. The interface and availability of tools with these vendors change from month to month. These vendors use the regular telecommunication systems which is the cheapest. The search output can be sent directly to user's e-mail address.

The charges mostly depend on connect time and document charges. All these commercial services require prior arrangement for becoming a valid user by obtaining a USER ID and a password from the concerned vendors. The following are some of the vendors:

KNIGHT-RIDER INFORMATION SERVICE PROVIDER

They are the largest commercial database vendors. Most of the databases are full text including many major newspapers, patents, etc. Accessing via internet cuts the communication charges to $4.20 per hour. It can be accessed by the command:

Telnet dialog.com

or http:www:krinfo.com

BIBLIOGRAPHIC RESEARCH SERVICE (BRS)

CD plus Technologies offer access through BRS to databases of medical and scientific collection. Access is via internet and charges are $ 5 per hour.

DATA STAR

Data Star is an online information service with heavy emphasis on European trade and business data. It is now owned by Knight-Rider. It can be accessed by the command:

telnet reserve.rs.ch

Access charges via internet are $3 an hour.

STN

STN is a database available online to the scientists, particularly chemists and engineers. It is a joint effort of several scientific organisations including Chemical Abstract Service of American Chemical Society. It can be accessed by the command:

telnet stane. ca.org.

Access via internet is $5 an hour.

HARDWARE AND SOFTWARE REQUIREMENTS FOR INTERNET

In order to get connected to internet, one needs a PC, at least a 486, a phone line and a modem on the hardware side. One also needs a subscription for internet connection from an internet service provider. Some special software is also required. While any PC will do to get hooked on to internet, in practice, a good high speed 486, machine with 4 to 8 MB RAM, 16" color VGA display and a modem of 14.4 kbps with error correction and compression are necessary. To print pictures after downloading, a good laser printer or inkjet is also needed.

As far as software is concerned, besides TCP/IP stacks, internet program for terminal connectivity like procomm, browsers like Netscape, Lynx etc. are also needed. Recently introduced windows operating system comes as an internet OS as it has inbuilt software for all internet needs.

The operating system provides complete information highway access solution and navigation is possible through the internet with easy to use graphical interfaces. It gives an automatic dial-up connection to internet services via any SLIP enabled provider. It includes web explorer, gopher, telnet, ftp, new searcher, e-mail and TCP/IP dial capabilities. It will enable the user to travel in the information highway fast lane, with high speed modem support.

NETSCAPE

Netscape is a software browser that helps user to navigate the world wide web. Installing and configuring is easy compared with other web browsers. Netscape's capability includes display of images with the text on pages as you download them, whereas other web browsers require downloading of all the images on a page before you start reading it and if you see a link you want to follow, you can check on it and connect to the next page with Netscape you just select, copy and paste. The evolution version is free and can be downloaded from Netscape's web site. Netscape enjoys an eighty percent share on the web browser market.

INTERNET AND ITS APPLICATION TO LIBRARIES

Inernet is undoubtedly a growing technological phenomena. It is a source of electronic information. Further it is a flourishing medium for communication. Because of these reasons internet is influencing the practice of librarianship throughout the world. The technological changes are constantly influencing the libraries and their services. In the few years internet even became a hot topic at conferences and in library literature. It is changing the way in which libraries and information personnel communicate. As a matter of fact, access to the networked information resource offers a supplement to the collection of the libraries. Librarians working in the technical services interact with vendors in a number of new ways in order to face the issue of cataloguing the net resources. The electronic publishing on internet is affecting the documentation of such resources leading to complexities in citation.

INTER-LIBRARY COMMUNICATION

As in the case of other professions, library and information professionals have found internet as an excellent medium for networking. In the beginning, internet was populated primarily by academic librarians. Slowly internet access has been expanded from beyond the research and academic sphere to a greater number of public libraries and even school libraries.

With the growth in quantity of networked information resources, the internet can become an adjacent collection to a library with internet access. With the shift from ownership to access that is occurring in many libraries, these remote resources can be especially valuable.

Hundreds of internet accessible library OPACs are a tremendous resource. Especially for patrons or librarians without ready access to search a bibliographic utility the growing number of foreign libraries with an internet accessible OPAC increases the options beyond even the scope of the bibliographic utilities. Many of the databases available can be accessed free of cost. There are databases on almost any subject, like agriculture, nutrition, geography, Hamradio, etc. Most useful of these databases are perhaps the Online Public Access Catalogues (OPACs) of the different academic libraries, most of which are now available on the net. Access to OPACs means that one can browse through the libraries sitting at a terminal to check the collection of the libraries for literature available on a given topic. The Library of Congress databases, LOCIS, Harvard Library databases. Yale Library databases are only a few to name which are available through the TELNET facility.

CATALOGUING AND THE INTERNET

Even though the changes and opportunities have been profound in the area of information retrieval aspect, a number of opportunities are there in the area of technical services in libraries such as classification and cataloguing. Librarians can communicate with vendors by e-mail and cataloguers can post cataloguing questions to a list such as AUTOCAT where other cataloguers including some from the Library of Congress may provide the answers. Classifiers and catalogers can also check MARC records in many of the available OPACs on Internet. In fact, they can search the LC catalog directly in order to get their required answer.

DOCUMENTATION AND THE INTERNET

If needed, internet resources begin to be considered as a part of the collection. If so then the necessity of documentation and citation of networked resources becomes more important.

More recently attempts are being made to prepare models for citing networked information resources in the form of classic style sheets. The National Library of Medicine Recommended Formats for bibliographic citation was one of the first attempts to address the problem of documentation of networked information resources.

INTERNET ACCESS IN INDIA

In India, access to internet for libraries is possible through ERNET, VSNL, and NICNET (RENNIC).

ERNET

The Education and Research Network (ERNET) implemented by Department of Electronics (DOE) has over 400 organisations connected within India and neighbouring countries. These institutions are mainly academic and research organizations, non-governmental organizations and to a limited extent private and international organizations. ERNET is supported by several backbone sites, covering DOE (New Delhi), IIT (Madras), IISc (Bangalore), INTECH (Chandigarh), VECC (Calcutta), IUCCA (Pune), NCST (Bombay) and University of Hyderabad, which enable organizations located at different geographical locations to access various services of internet. One can opt to any one of the nearest backbone sites to get the connectivity. There are three categories of connectivity, which are primarily based on tariff ranging form Rs.5,000 to Rs.5,00,000 per annum.

VSNL

Videsh Sanchar Nigam Limited (VSNL) offers full range of utilities in three options for access to Gateway Internet Access Service (GIAS):

1. *Using dialup access to GIAS Host.*
2. *TCP/IP Account* : VSNL provides direct TCP/IP connection on dial up or leased basis to GIAS system and access through online to all services of the internet.

3. *Packet Switched Network Access* : VSNL provides access via GPSS using D.Net, RABNN and HVNnet. GIAS tariff ranges from Rs.500 (only for students), Rs.5000 (with quota of 250 hours) to Rs.25,000 depending upon the option of services.

NICNET

The National Informatics Centre (NICNET) supported by the Planning Commission connects 700 earth station, with links to all district headquarters and a number of public sector undertakings. NICNET has become an important network facilitating decision making in the government.

NICNET offers electronic mail facilities only to research and educational networks (RENNIC) with a nominal annual subscription of Rs.1000 for registration. NICNET also offers services for the public (a tariff not yet advertised). The highlight of their service is their Management Information for Rural Development scheme. Medical Literature and Analysis and Retrieval Systems (MEDLARS) and National Library of Medicine (NLM) information for patient care is being provided within an hour of receiving the request.

Softlink Services

The Software Technology Park (STP) is another scheme of DOE. It deals with export of computer software using data communication links or in the form of physical media including export of professional services. Speeds upto 64 kbps and 128 kbps are offered. This is suitable for organisations having high bandwidth for implementing various networking protocols. Their subscription rate is Rs.5 lakhs irrespective of number of hours of usage and volume of data. This scheme does not fall in the scope of library activity.

The subscribers of any of the above service providers may opt for full range of internet utilities via I-Net, RABMN and HVNet, either by using dial-up line or leased line.

Private Internet E-mail Providers

Besides the above governmental agencies, there are number of private e-mail service providers in the country who help reach internet e-mail address. BI infotech, DART, DATApro, UUNET, CMC, Sprint/RPG and ICNET are some such companies. Libraries can get low cost internet e-mail connection for a fee ranging from about Rs.3000 to about Rs.15000 per year.

Internet and Its Future

The degree to which the internet succeeds as a communication media will determine how libraries and librarians will interact with the network in the future. One trend that can be seen is that libraries have been key players in bringing local internet access to their patrons and their community. The Seattle Public Library offers internet access within the library and was the first public library to offer patrons access to the internet from their home computers. Bibliographic utilities are discovering that they are uniquely positioned to offer internet access to libraries.

While many praise the freely available resources on the internet and suggest that such free communication and connection tools can reinvigorate democracy and produce a greater involvement in society in general, it is too often forgotten that "free" access to the internet is completely dependent upon access to a computer. Libraries' traditional role of providing free access to information may indeed propel them into providing free access to the internet. Very few other public institutions are in a position to be able to provide such a service. Even a small library could have a large percentage of information in books that is not available on the internet. Even so, the internet is often referred to as an electronic library or the virtual library of the future.

The internet has become a major part of librarianship. Librarians from all types of libraries and from all sides of the globe have actively used the net for professional communication. The connection tools often access to significant information resources, and the publishing industries and library have begun to find more and more ways to use this newly rediscovered technology to become more efficient and reach a broader audience. The way in which the internet will continue to impact the practice of librarianship will depend to a large degree upon the way in which the network develops and affects society, commerce, the government and all other library patrons.

CONCLUSION

The internet provides access to literally thousands of information sources on a variety of topics. Now a days with the advent of multinationals and global competition every profit conscious and service oriented agency has virtually reached a new level of intense activity. The pressures include sinking budgets, escalating information, increasing production cost, demand for quality and customer service. Thus, the business world and industrial society is in an age of hyper competition. The internet which has brought new revolution in information transmission communication is seen as a boon for the survival of business and industry in this highly competitive world. Common man in general also gets tremendously benefited from the effective use of information technology. The librarians and information professionals have a vital role to play in bridging the information gap between the "information-haves and information-have-nots".

Libraries striving to collect enough information sources to satisfy the needs of their clientele can be rest assured that with internet assisting them, they can cater to most of their demands, by making use of one or the other of internet's various services. But internet comes with its share of idiosyncrasies. The problems while surfing the internet relate to communication and computers. Other problems such as router-problem, different formats for addresses, etc., are also there. A few of them can be reckoned with but as one gets used to the working of the internet and its services, perhaps, one can make the better use of it.

REFERENCES

1. Aptagiri (Devika V). Information Super Highway : The Internet. *ILA Bulletin*. Vol. 31. 1996; pp 80-83.
2. Brij (Rusi). Let's go surfing the internet. *Computer Today*. Vol. 11. Jan. 1995; pp 160-3.
3. Cheng, Fab-chen. Internet Agents : Spiders, Wanderers, Brokers and Bots. New Riders Publishing, 1996.
4. Chitnis, Atul. The Internet is here. *PC Quest*, September, 1995.
5. Gilster, Paul. Finding it on the Internet; *The Internet Managing Guide to Search Tools and Techniques*. Ed. 2. New York : John Wiley, 1996.
6. Net Genesis Corporation: Build a World Wide Web; Plan, Programme and Manage Internet Connection for Your Company. New York: John Wiley, 1996.
7. Levine (John R) and Baroudi (Carol). *The Internet for Dummies*. Ed. 2, New Delhi, Pustak Mahal, 1994.
8. Net News. *Personal Computer World*. January 1995. P. 504.
9. Notess, Greg R. *The Internet-Encyclopaedia of Library and Information Science*. Vol. 59. Pp 236-265.
10. Vipul, Ved Prakash. The internet protocols. *PC quest*, February 1996. P 29-130.
11. Subbaram, Indira. Internet in a nutshell. *DESIDOC Bulletin of Information Technology*. Vol. 16. 1996 : pp 3-10.

II : 6

Role of Information Technology in Accessing Agricultural Information

L. S. R. C. V. Ramesh

"Libraries and information centres should not be made as a shrine for worship. They should grow as a delivery room for birth of new ideas."

(Socrates and Augustin Birrell)

INTRODUCTION

The Western world is probably over supplied with agricultural information and its use is just limited when compared with what can be paid for and what people can absorb. The amount of free information is becoming less and less, unless it is promoting a new product, and the system as a whole is self-regulating but in a rather cumbersome way. The need is for services which pick out the needles from the stacks of irrelevance.

Information technology now impinges on virtually every aspect of society and has developed dramatically.

In all areas of science, information technology is now of intrinsic importance, both as a research tool and as a medium in facilitating the information transfer. In the following sections such trends and developments which are particularly relevant to the transfer of scientific information are discussed.

THE VALUE OF INFORMATION

A farmer confronted with a crop pest of which he has no previous experience has to decide whether to:

* Ignore it and hope it will go away;
* Try what seems best and then hope for the best;
* Try, on the basis of what is known to others, to limit the likely damage and the resultant loss of crop or food.

If he decides on the last course, he may:

* Consult a neighbouring farmer;
* Call in an official or commercial adviser;
* Refer to published leaflets or handbooks if he is literate or in a developed society, he consults one of the teletext advisory services accessible online or on his own personal computer.

One or more of these sources of information should enable the farmer to identify the pest asses the risk and determine the best course of action.

On some occasions, perhaps because of changes in agricultural practice or climate, a pest may become more prevalent or appear on a new crop and information sources tried are of no help. Recourse is then made to an expert; either directly or indirectly through an intermediary, (perhaps an information officer or librarian). The expert will, if necessary, turn to his sources of information.

* Personal contacts:
* Departmental library or other local sources of data;
* Distant libraries and databanks.

These may be sufficient for him to make recommendations, or be so meagre that he feels he may have to conduct some research himself. In the latter case, he turns again to his information sources to determine who is working on similar problems and to obtain an in-depth review of what has already been done. From this he can assess what priority the problem should receive and what resources would be needed to implement a research programme, which is then put to the research planner and possibly even a policy-maker for decision.

This simple scenario highlights the central place of information in problem solving and research planning in the field of crop protection. It is typical of the situation in agriculture and rural development as a whole. Tragically, in institutional budgets, access to formal sources of information so often is the last item to be augmented and the first to get the axe in any period of budgetary constraint. Access to the right information at the right time can save time and money, and, when this is viewed globally, is clearly a matter of great importance.

USERS AND THEIR INFORMATION SOURCES

The different categories of users have overlapping sources of information. Broadly, researchers use primary journals, reports, news-letters, bibliographic databases and their associated photocopy services, reviews, books, directories, data collections, etc. The other categories of users turn to consolidated or didactic information in the form of mini-reviews and digests, extension leaflets, product literature, films, radio and TV. All users have their own more or less extensive networks of personal contacts (known at the research level as the invisible college), some have a 'gate-keeper', someone who is the informal focal point for a particular subject area and who is willing to offer or answer questions. Gate-keepers are often a point of access to valuable and old information stored in people's memories or buried industry archives which are otherwise overlooked.

• The amount of literature and other data sources in the field of agriculture worldwide is huge: probably in the order of 15,000 current scientific periodicals, 10,000 books per annum and an unknown quantity of informally or formally published leaflets and reports. About 15 years ago, the total number of individual items was estimated at a quarter of a million per year, by now it is probably more but it is as good a figure as any to bear in mind. No single library in the world can hold all these materials.

In the least developed countries, libraries now have virtually no current periodicals other than donations and exchanges or those on free circulation, such as product and trade items. In the better-off countries, locally published periodicals generally contain scientific material of local interest and there is much extension and advisory material produced on conventional literary lines.

BIBLIOGRAPHIC DATABASES

To help the researcher (and to a less extent the advisory worker and policy-maker) find the literature he wants, regardless of language or country of publication, there have been developed a number of bibliographic services with worldwide coverage which record the title and bibliographic details of each item and which may include an abstract of the content. The best known and most comprehensive are CAB International's range of abstract journals and the CAB ABSTRACTS database (135,000 records/year), the NAL's Agricola database and the printed Bibliography of Agriculture derived from it (70,000 records/year), and FAO's printed AGRINDEX and AGRIS database (110,000 records/year).

The CABI services, with their uniquely informative abstracts and detailed indexes, are required to be financially self-supporting and are priced accordingly. AGRICOLA, now with no abstracts and focusing more on USA material, is funded by the US Federal Government. AGRIS is a co-operative system. Each country is responsible for sending its own input (on average 10 percent abstracts) into the centralised database which is itself funded by FAO. AGRIS and AGRICOLA are becoming more complementary in terms of coverage, but they do overlap to a significant extent with the CABI service which stands apart in terms of information content and reliability. The CABI services are generally the preferred option if the money is available to pay for them.

Further the 'big three' bibliographic databases, such as BIOSIS (Biosis Reviews, Biological Abstracts and Biological Abstracts/RRM), the American Chemical Society (Chemical Abstracts) and IFIS (Food Science and Technology Abstracts) have some material of interest to agriculturists while they are primarily oriented to different disciplines. Technical advances in telecommunications have made this information publicly available via online vendors such as DIALOG to individual customer's terminals, either on the screen or 'downloaded' onto a microcomputer. Users without these facilities can apply direct to the database producers for special outputs, retrospective or current, which are supplied on computer printout or floppy disc.

DOCUMENT DELIVERY

The bibliographic databases indicate user about the availability of information, i.e., their surrogates accordingly, much use is made of document delivery services by asking for a copy of an item of interest having identified. FAO has encouraged the formation of AGLINET, a network of co-operating libraries mainly in the Third World, which will exchange photocopies. Various agencies are now established to ensure payment to the copyright holder for multiple photocopies.

DIRECTORIES AND DATABANKS

Good quality reference books are mainly the preserve of developed countries. Among these, books, directories and data tables are important sources of information which cover anything from current agricultural research programmes (CRIS in the U.S.A., AGREP for Europe and CARIS for developing countries, all of them funded operation) through the properties of pesticides, nutrient content of feeds, to statistics on employment, production and climate. Some of these services are also available in machine-readable (digitised) form for access by computer where they are usually referred to as databases or databanks.

INFORMATION TECHNOLOGY AS A MEDIUM FOR INFORMATION TRANSFER

The extension of the basic computer technology includes new and powerful peripheral devices and the development of the computer as a resource for the storage, management and retrieval of information in all of its manifestations.

The combination of these factors has led to the information technology of today, providing vastly more powerful and flexible hardware, and more powerful and sophisticated software than the earlier generations of computer systems.

COMPUTING TECHNOLOGY

This development across the range of computers contributed to the transfer of scientific information at all levels. The 'providers' of information such as the major publishers of secondary publication have the facilities to support the storage, management and delivery of very large volumes of data. As an example, the CABI database of abstracts of publications in agriculture now contains over two million records, requiring about 3,000 million characters of computer storage. The computing power and disk storage capacity needed to manage this kind of volume of information would not have been available 15 years ago.

PRINTING TECHNOLOGY

The invention and subsequent rapid development of laser printing technology has been one of the most exciting and in many ways one of the most important new components of technology for information transfer.

An important extension of this, again made possible only through the power of laser printer, is the relatively recent emergence of desktop publishing. DTP, as it is known, provides more extensive and more sophisticated features than conventional word processing systems, enabling the production of document of a quality which has previously been available only to commercial publishers.

TELECOMMUNICATIONS

Telecommunications today refer to the transmission of a variety of traffic using many different kinds of communication media. The traffic may include voice, television, telex, facsimile, and computer-generated data, and the media can be cables, optical fibres or satellite transmission.

In parallel with, and aided by, developments in computing, telecommunications technology has advanced to the point where international communication is technically possible from and to any point on the globe.

At the same time, a new technology of Local Area Networking (or LAN) has emerged allowing a range of devices from microcomputers to mainframes to be interconnected. The LAN typically comprises low-cost cabling connecting computing devices in a building or office environment and enabling these to communicate with one another and to share resources such as printers and magnetic disk storage systems.

OPTICAL DISK STORAGE

Laser technology has also opened the way to possibly the most exciting new medium for information storage and dissemination, that of optical storage. Of the several approaches to the medium, the CD-ROM (Compact Disk Read-Only Memory) has emerged as the most efficient and cost-effective. Using basically the same technology as applied to audio compact disks for the consumer market, CD-ROM provides the capability to create and distribute very large databases at low cost for use on microcomputers.

A single disk can contain upto 600 million characters of information at the present time and as the technology develops this storage density will increase rapidly.

EXPERT SYSTEMS

These are a special class of softwares applicable to a wide range of problems and providing the means of using the computer to transfer the knowledge of experts to the end-user. The user communicates with the expert system through a question/answer dialogue which can be tailored to particular requirements and environments.

The development of this kind of software, coupled with the increasing availability of low-cost microcomputers, provides a new potential for distributing expert knowledge in a readily-usable form direct to those who need it. The technique is already widely used in such diverse areas as medical diagnoses, commercial accounting and (increasingly) in agricultural research, extension and farming.

INFORMATION TECHNOLOGY IN DEVELOPING COUNTRIES

The major trends in information technology will be relevant to the storage and dissemination of scientific information. The various combinations of these provide powerful new opportunities to the international agricultural community and, importantly, to the developing world.

Developed countries have had relatively easy and cost-effective access to the major sources of scientific information since the early 1970s when the development of computer databases began and as information retrieval services became available.

There has subsequently been a proliferation of databases and an extension of their availability through online service providers. Telecommunication facilities have also advanced to such an extent that there are few barriers to international communications.

Further, the scope and size of the databases increase continuously so that information in virtually every scientific discipline is now available to anyone with the resources (technical and financial) to access them.

The early hope and assumption was that improved telecommunication would bring these resources to scientists in developing countries. In practice, many of these countries do not yet have reliable communications and in any case the costs of use of the services put them beyond the reach of many institutions.

There is, however, now real potential for a breakthrough in improving the dissemination of scientific information in developing countries provided by the kinds of technology referred to earlier and based on the microcomputer.

INDIAN SCENARIO

In a developing country like India the problems are similar but exacerbated by the general lack of resources. In the worst situation, there is no hard currency to purchase foreign information sources, equipment and materials or training; libraries are under-funded and under-utilized and staff demotivated.

There are undoubtedly constraints and information technology itself will not overcome the basic problems of shortages of skilled staff, the lack of well developed information infrastructures or the lack of awareness of senior levels of the intrinsic importance of information. There will also be the continuing difficulty of the costs of acquiring and maintaining the hardware, software and databases needed. Consequently there will be no dramatic change overnight but there will inevitably be a progressive improvement in the availability of information as the trend continues towards cheaper and more powerful microcomputers and as they become an accepted and essential tool in the research and extension field.

CD-ROM

This technology provides the best potential for enabling developing countries to obtain access to the large scientific databases which are otherwise only available in printed form or through commercial vendors providing online information retrieval services.

There are a number of significant advantages: the hardware

is simple to use and relatively cheap; the software is designed for ease of use, requiring minimal training; the costs of use are predictable and containable. All these aspects are in direct contrast to the use of online systems, which are designed for use by trained information professionals and are difficult and expensive to use. An important factor is that the facilities can be made available directly to the 'end-users', that is scientists in the laboratory or field station without the need either for telecommunications or for trained information experts.

The problem of cost remains unless and until CD-ROM databases are used in substantial numbers; the costs of production will not be recovered and the unit cost will be significant in real terms. It will inevitably be necessary for institutions in many developing countries to obtain sponsorship for the costs of subscription to CD-ROM databases.

ELECTRONIC PUBLISHING

Similarly, where the expertise and infrastructure exist, information technology presents new opportunities to developing country like India to prepare high-quality publications without the need to use expensive commercial services.

At one extreme, the combination of microcomputer, word processing software and laser printer can produce good-quality 'simple' documents. At the other, sophisticated desktop publishing systems can be used to prepare publications of the highest quality, including text, graphics and illustrations.

There is undoubtedly scope for developing countries to generate new publishing outlets for their scientific work at affordable cost.

CONCLUSION

Of all the new developments in information technology, the expert systems have the most potential to deliver information and knowledge beyond the agricultural research community and into the realm of the extension workers and even to the farm managers.

There is an increasing number of initiatives directed at using this kind of technology for the diagnosis and treatment of problems of crop protection These are based on the encapsulated knowledge of experts in particular fields and provide powerful aids to diagnosis symptoms of pest attacks leading to guidance on methods of treatment. They allow knowledge be transferred directly to where it is needed and many are directed at the situation of the Extension Officer providing advice in direct consultation with the farmer or farm manager who has the problem.

It is not difficult to envisage all the components of information technology being used in an agricultural research and extension institution in a developing country like India.

While there are undoubtedly barriers for developing countries not the least of which will be the costs, the potential for using advanced information technology is undeniable and undoubtedly opens up new vistas for the transfer of scientific information. The costs are still high but are reducing steadily. However, the cost-benefits are high when we are prepared to place a value on the benefits of access to information. The real significance of the microcomputer revolution is that it will allow information and information processing systems to be delivered directly to users, to a large extent bypassing the need for sophisticated information infrastructures which do not exist and which are difficult to sustain in many developing countries.

REFERENCES

1. H. Alan. *Technology transfer and communication*. (Paris; UNESCO, 1984)
2. Albert H Moseman, Ed. "Agricultural sciences for the developing nations." *A symposium presented at the Cleveland Meeting of the American Associations for Advancement of Science on 29 and 30 Dec. 1963*.
3. L. J. Haravu. "Strategies for the adoption of New Information Technologies in Indian Libraries." *A paper presented in CALIBER-1995 National Convention on Information Access through Networks held during 10-12 Feb. 1995, University of Hyderabad.*

4. John Metcalfe and Jim Gelmore. "Information Technology in Agricultural Development", *In : Developing World Agriculture* : (Groovenor Press International. 1994).

5. V. A. Kamath. "Evolution of information technoiogy--an overview." *ASMIC* 23 Sept. - Nov. 1984. 13-15.

6. Khem Singh Gill, G. S. Dhalwal and B. S. Hansra. Changing scenario of Indian Agriculture, New Delhi (Commonwealth Publishers, 1993) 374-379.

7. U. R. Radhakrishnan "The new business choices" *Dataquest 12.30* (1-15 July 1995) : 89-103.

8. A. S. Sandhu. Text book on Agricultural communication: Process and Methods. Oxford & IBH Publishing Co. Pvt. Ltd., New Delhi, 1993. 151-152 pp.

9. M. S. Swaminathan. Information technology : a dialogue. (Madras: Macmillan, 1993) 21-28

10. Peter Zorkoczy. Information Technology, (New York : Knowledge Industry, 1982) 3 p.

II : 7
INTERNET–Its Various Facets

P. Soma Raju

INTRODUCTION

The impact of modern technology on the society is tremendous. It is particularly so in the case of computer and communication technologies as they are practically changing the pace of human activity in each and every field of work. Such a modern technology is enabling us to do things in a much more faster, better and efficient way when compared to manual methods.

The field of Library and Information Science is not an exception to the above phenomena. Computers are facilitating to consolidate huge amount of information/data in an organised way and to retrieve any piece of information from that chunk, when required. The communication technology is enabling us to interact with any one on the globe, interface any database, transfer files and browse remote databases, irrespective of their geographical location on the globe, in a fast way. Internet is one of such a communication network system, fast developing for the last one decade.

ORIGIN AND GROWTH OF INTERNET:

Internet was originated as a 'Communication network' in a limited environment of US Army in mid 1960's. It was started as 'Advanced Research Project Agency (ARPANET) by the Department of Defence as an experimental packet switching network. Its main task was to link research contractors working in the field, for exchange of data, information and research results. Later, its use was extended to other Govt. laboratories, academic institutions, industrial organisations and commercial applications. However, such a use was in low profile in 1970's.

In 1980, the National Science Foundation of US has modified the above network to connect to super computers working at that time and it has then emerged as internet. Later many organisations began to join in this network from within and outside the country also. Thus by the end of 1980, the membership of internet has increased in an unexpected manner. The growth of computers connected with the Internet is as follows:

1970	: 100	
1981	: 213	
1987	: 10,000	
1989	: 80,000	
1991	: 3,76,000	
1992	: 7,27,000	
1994	: 20,00,000	(2 millions)
1996	: 3,00,00,000	(3 crores).

Now it became a world wide high speed communication network and there is an upsurge in the number of internet users in the world.

SALIENT FEATURES OF INTERNET

Internet is a bunch of computers connected together and talking communicating with each other. It is a sort of connecting a small road at house to a highway road. It is a network of networks, several millions of computers all over the world are connected to networks. In this system, if a computer has an access to one of those, it can have the access to all of them that are in the Internet.

Further, it is a peer-to-peer network. That means any computer on the network from a tiny lap-top to a super computer are in principle equal and can contact to any other in the network Any computer attached to the network can offer services to any other computer, whether it is a PC or super computer. Therefore, what the internet does is to deliver information/data from one place to another.

Now a days, all the hot topics are available on the internet. New kinds of information is gushing in world wide web (www) like a hurricane wind across the world. The amount of information that goes to the usenet is something in the order of 140 megabytes per day.

INTERNET INFRASTRUCTURE

The minimum equipment required to work with internet are as follows :

1. Personal computer (P.C.);
2. MODEM to convert messages from digital to analog and vice versa;
3. Telephone lines–Leased or subscribed;
4. Serial Line Internet Protocol (SLIP)/ Point-to Point Protocol (PPP) software;
5. Count on service.

Of course, there are different ways to get connection of internet now a days, but it depends on the communication facilities that are available to a given place. Internet providers fall under two categories as shown below:

(a) Shell system; and

(b) SLIP system.

In Shell system, the users PC is not really on the Internet, but it is connected to a service provider's computer which is connected to the internet. There are number of such service providers such as 'The World' 'America Online' 'Delphi' etc. They run internet applications using 'Telnet and FTP software.

whereas in the SLIP (Serial Line Internet protocol system) the user's PC becomes a part of the Internet. The network applications can run on his own computer using TELNET and FTP. In fact, the FTP can also supply to others, if one is interested.

USE OF INTERNET

Computers on the network are called as Hosts. They are identified by name and numbers. The numbers are written in four parts much as 140.186.81.2 and each is separated by a dot. The names are written in two or more parts like xuxa.iece.com. Every machine on the Internet has a number. The connection between the names and numbers is flexible. A single name can refer to several hosts, which is useful for a service with multiple machines.

NAVIGATIONAL TOOLS

There are number of navigational tools such as Gopher, www, Archie, Veronica, etc., to locate, identify and retrieve information stored in various Host databases on the internet.

Gopher software is used to have access to information available on Internet. WWW (world wide web) is most popular service to share the information among researchers. Archie is used for file transfer from one computer to another on the Internet. Veronica is a net-wide index to computer Archie. WAIS (Wide Area Information System) allows search for multiple databases located in the remote site. It gives the information through search terms. NSnet connects over 6,000 networks, comprising thousands of computers which are considered as global information sources.

TCP/IP (Transmission Control Protocol/Internet Protocol) is a low level data communication method on the Internet which controls the information traffic. The user can join hands with any other on the globe using TCP/IP. Similarly the Telnet, an internet protocol, connects remote computers (Remote Login).

INTERNET SERVICES

The following are some of the major services for which internet could be used:

1. E-mail service on the internet is being extensively used by many organisations throughout the world;
2. File transfer from one computer to another can be done on the internet. The FTP programme defines and describes how to move files from one computer to another;
3. The user can get information on any topic such as sports, commerce, trade, etc. on the Internet by using 'Usenet' programme; and
4. Besides other services like access to online system, availability of journals on the electronic format and list serves for discussion and professional matters are also available on the Internet.

INTERNET IN INDIA

Videsh Sanchar Nigam Ltd. (VSNL), Mumbai, a Government of India undertaking, has a near monopoly and helps monopolistic control over Gateway Access Internet Service (GAIS). The other internet service providers (ISPs) are Education and Research network (ERNET), National Informatics Centre Network (NICNET), New Delhi. DELNET has also an access to Internet since 1994 for getting E-mail service. The NICNET is bringing www services from January 14, 1995, which provides an access to world of information. It is also providing multimedia access to its users through Ku-Based Info-Highway through their nodes. The users of Internet in India are increasing year after year.

CONCLUSION

Information is considered as a basic need of the society. We are living in an information-based society. 'Right to have an access to information' is the modern slogan.

World is rich in information. Internet is assuming the role of Information Super Highway (ISH) facilitating for the easy transfer of information from one place to another, sharing the total wealth of information available on the globe for the prosperity of mankind. Internet may play a significant role in the distribution of knowledge for the welfare of the human society in the times to come.

REFERENCE

1. Levine, John R. Advanced Internet for Dummies. IDG Books, Complex Computer Pubs, New Delhi, 1995.

III : 1

Automation of Academic Libraries : Problems and Issues

C. R. Karisiddappa
V. S. Cholin

INTRODUCTION

Information Technology has revolutionized the information handling activities in the research and academic libraries during the past few years. The information services of academic libraries have been largely affected by the rapid changes in the information technology. The increased availability of information in electronic form, education/training activities in the country increased demand from the users for want of information in a limited period have focussed the application of new technology in the academic libraries. This resulted in the use of computers in the libraries. In order to create an advanced information society for the future, the use of sophisticated computer systems for the control and management of information has important implications for thinking about information in general and about its storing, processing, and dissemination in particular.

Library automation means the use of computers in the routine and important services of a library. The operations of library get quantum jump with the introduction of computers. The retrieval of information becomes much faster and accurate. Application of computers saves lot of labour and time, speeds up operations, increase, all round productivity. Ability to store and recall information when needed are the advantages of computers.

NEED FOR AUTOMATION

The automation of libraries in a developing country like India is a matter of serious consideration because the difficulties experienced in transfer of technology is seen as one of the crucial factors in dissemination of information. Information is both fugitive and a truly international resource, available to those equipped to receive and absorb it. The great demand for information both by individuals and the society and widespread availability of computers coupled with decreasing cost has enabled the building of large computerized information systems. The application of new information technology ensures that useful information will be made available to users effectively at faster speed and saves valuable time of the users.

Factors Considered for Computerizing Library

1. Computers are extremely fast processing information and magnetic media and have enormous potential to reduce storage space.
2. Computerized databases can be accessed in interactive mode and most often they are user-friendly.
3. Bibliographies on different subjects may be generated with multiple copies.
4. Human errors are minimized for day to day operations which helps for better utilization of human efficiency.

AUTOMATION : INDIAN SCENARIO

Automation activities in academic libraries in India steadily picked up with the support from INFLIBNET (Information and Library Network) Programme of UGC. NISSAT and other similar agencies combined with increased awareness of IT. Academic librarians are being given training on use of e-mail, CD-ROMs LAN, machine readable catalogues, etc. This change in academic libraries is due to a rapidly changing telecommunication and technological environment. Many metropolitan networks exists in the country: DELNET for Delhi libraries, CALIBNET for Calcutta libraries, ADINET for Ahmedabad libraries and BOMNET for libraries in Mumbai. They are slowly emerging with a purpose to bring change in the academic libraries.

INFLIBNET was established in 1991 by UGC for modernization of libraries and information centres in the country using computer and communication technology. Main aim of this centre is to offer speedy and efficient services to users all over the country through a well-articulated and versatile computerised information network. University Grants Commission (UGC) has funded 69 universities through INFLIBNET for procurement of computer hardware and software, establishment of communication facility at individual libraries, recurring expenditure to support computer/communication facilities, salary of one computer expert for five years and for conversion of retrospective data. Besides this, UGC has also provided funds for remaining 65 Universities a minimum grant to purchase computer with modem and telephone facility for getting access to national and international databases and INTERNET facilities. Many college libraries in the country have been provided grants for automation.

INFLIBNET is primarily concerned with the following activities

1. Standards and formats for data capturing
2. Development of databases
3. Conducting regular training courses
4. Onsite training support to university libraries
5. Organizing national conventions
6. Developing software for participating libraries
7. Networking facilities to libraries
8. Establishment of subject forums

Considerable progress is achieved under this programme to create computer awareness among the libraries and to modernize the service facilities.

AUTOMATION OF ACADEMIC LIBRARIES : PROBLEMS

Successful implementation of automation programme requires team efforts with higher degree of cooperation and coordination between library staff and IT experts. Librarians, depending upon the levels at which they are working, require to know certain computer skills including selection of hardware software design and development of databases, ability to upgrade systems, skill related to use of INTERNET and use of CD-ROM database tools, etc. Following are the problems encountered in the introduction of automation in academic libraries.

Retrospective Conversion

Retrospective conversion of a library collection is a major component of the automation process. It is time consuming, laborious and expensive but essential to begin computerized services.

Retrospective conversion means a process of creating database of library collection in a machine readable form which allows end-user to search and retrieve relevant information required. Factors considered for retrospective conversion are identified as

- Availability of funds
- Time limit for retrospective conversion
- Selection of hardware and software
- Training
- Role of national information systems

In Indian situation, funds may be arranged by the sponsoring institution of the library or the funding body. Universities are normally funded by UGC for this activity and college libraries may take help from authorities concerned and also from UGC. It is known that UGC in its grant for computerization of university libraries has also provide, necessary guidance for use of funds for retrospective conversion.

Depending on the number of records, time limit may be fixed, for example, a collection of not more than 50,000 records may take one year duration maximum to complete the task. Similarly depending upon the funds and number of records time limit may be fixed. However, proper care must be taken in order to create authenticated records and must be according to certain standards which must be acceptable by national information systems.

Increasing dependence on computers prompts us to think of proper hardware and software within the limited funds. Selection of software for retrospective conversion is very important step. There are several software programs available for creating database of different library materials. It is suggested that CDS/ISIS, an information storage and retrieval package for libraries, serves the purpose of creating databases because of its retrieval efficiency, storage efficiency, user friendliness and variable fields and variable field length.

Training of library professionals in order to create machine readable catalogue is essential. Several organizations such as NISSAT, INFLIBNET, INSDOC and DRTC are conducting regular training programmes for the professionals.

It is understood that the main task of INFLIBNET is to create an integrated information system. It is also noticed that several institutions have done tremendous effort in bringing out their library catalogue in machine readable form. Like OCLC and LC, INFLIBNET may take care of creating standard national database of books, journals, thesis, etc. from participating libraries and distribute it to the libraries. This database can act as tool for retrospective conversion for them and saves lot of time. Most of the academic libraries have common records and it is hoped that more than 70 percent of retrospective conversion can be achieved through this. Necessary software for searching and downloading of records will help the libraries in retrospective conversion.

TRAINING

Training is required for the staff to handle the automated systems. Training conducted in small groups with emphasis on hands-on experience will help the library professionals to implement automation activities. It is also advisable that all the permanent staff who will be using computer system are trained apart from detailed training for limited staff at various levels. Availability of trained manpower is very important for the success of automation programme. Existing staff in most of the academic libraries are not exposed to computers or computerized operations of libraries. Several organizations provide training in this area and the prominent among them are INFLIBNET centre of UGC, NISSAT, DRTC and INSDOC,

DATABASE DEVELOPMENT

Designing the database is a highly complex operation. This activity should be flexible enough to meet the requirements of the maximum number of users. Design should also anticipate to a certain extent the future requirements and make provision for them. The process of database development involves following steps.

1. Identification of data elements to describe the bibliographical data elements
2. Standardization of identified data elements.
3. Standardization of data input.
4. Standardization of software for data entry and processing which includes data representation in the standard format acceptable internationally for the purpose of compatibility and exchange with similar international databases.

The first step in the database creation is identification of data elements. Depending upon the type of database, the data elements (data fields) are to be identified. The data elements are to be standardized and a data input sheet may be prepared with those data elements. Once the data input sheet is prepared it is essential to identify the software package for inputting the data. Rendering the data such as author(s), title, etc. should be as per the rules prescribed by AACR-2. Several packages such as dBase, CDS/ISIS etc., may be used for inputting the data. However, it is essential to mention here that CDS/ISIS may be used for data capturing and storage as it supports the retrieval efficiency, storage efficiency, user friendliness, data representation in ISO-2709 format, support of LAN and Unix platforms and several other advantages over other packages. The database may be created using CDS/ISIS with the standard data elements and finally the data may be entered into the database.

SOFTWARE AND HARDWARE

Library automation requires hardware, operating systems, application software and trained and motivated library staff to handle the systems. Selection of hardware and software depend upon the present and future needs of the library and needs proper planning and appropriate decision. All possible aspects of library operations need to be analysed while deciding the system configuration and software selection. Before any computer system is installed in the library, a formal study is undertaken to ascertain feasibility of new systems. It is often desirable that the members of the committee may visit other libraries operating computer-based system. Help may also be taken from local, regional, and national information systems. In this regard, organisations like INFLIBNET help by providing system configuration details.

Once the computers are purchased in the library, the selection of application software is the most important component of library automation. Various in–house developed software as well as commercial software packages are available. It is essential on the part of librarian to decide whether to purchase a commercial software or develop in-house. Fully developed and tested software needs to be preferred in case of immediate implementation of the automation activities. Some of the well-known library packages available are:

1. ILMS (Integrated Library Management Software from Inflibnet)
2. LIBSYS
3. LIBRIS
4. OASIS
5. SANJAY
6. TECHLIB-PLUS BASIS PLUS
7. WILISYS
8. CDS/ISIS etc.

AUTOMATION OF ACADEMIC LIBRARIES : ISSUES

Standards and Formats

Need for standards to facilitate information handling has long been a subject of concern for the information community. Standards are essential to ensure compatibility for interconnection of libraries and information centers and to promote efficiency and effectiveness in easy transfer of information among the libraries. A detailed study has been undertaken by INFLIBNET at the national level by setting up a committee on standards and has finalised standards for different library materials such as books, theses, serials for creation of databases by the academic libraries. These standards are mainly based on the Common Communication Format and adapted for use. The different types of standards required for creation and maintenance of machine readable bibliographic databases are:

Standards for bibliographic record format

Standard codes for cataloguing

Standards for character set

In addition to these, it would be helpful if uniform practices are adopted for subject representation in the bibliographic records such as classification codes, subject descriptors/subject headings, etc.

Resource Sharing

UGC and the respective state governments are spending huge amounts every year on acquiring new library resources, which include substantial expenditure on foreign journals. Even then the libraries are unable to provide latest information to the research and academic community. Many libraries are forced to discontinue subscriptions to various titles due to ever-increasing cost of journals, high foreign exchange rates and limited financial provision This is adversely affecting the quality of education and research. At the same time there is considerable duplication of investments in library holdings. There is no hope to live or survive. in this age of competition unless all our academics, researchers and scholars are brought into an environment where all the latest thoughts and developments are made available to them precisely and speedily. It is neither feasible nor possible to equip all the libraries with required books/journals and other information material to be self-sufficient. It is therefore imperative to evolve a mechanism for sharing of resources and adopt methods based on modern information technology for meeting the requirements. Keeping pace with changing information technologies has necessitated rapid enhancement and modification of services. The challenge is to provide services that take care of the unmet needs of user to make library cooperation cost effective and to achieve overall economy.

Resource sharing is a sort of implied agreement amongst participating libraries wherein each participant is willing to spare its resources to other members and in turn has a privileged to share resources of its partners as and when need arises. Main objectives of resources sharing can be listed as follows.

1. Cooperative acquisition of library materials to avoid unnecessary duplication of costly materials.

2. Maximizing the accessibility to information and availability of materials and service at the minimum cost .
3. Extending the resources and services of the member libraries to a wide category of users.

It is estimated that the total holdings in the universities as well as in the institutions is over 150 lakhs and the annual in take of books itself is 9 lakhs and of periodicals is 1.1 lakhs by spending enormous amount. The Indian libraries are on the threshold of 21st century and they have to prepare themselves to accept the challenge of sharing of resources for providing full range of services to the scholars.

Cooperative Acquisition and Cooperative Cataloguing

Effective participation and active support of libraries by sending their holdings for creation of union database will enable the cooperative acquisition. Proper mechanism needs to be devised and should be acceptable for participating libraries in the network for the purpose. Cooperative collection development helps in the rationalization of acquisitions in the libraries, especially in the case of foreign periodicals. This ultimately helps to save money which can be spent for acquiring new information sources to fulfill the requirements of user community. Shared cataloguing and classification through networking can reduce financial burden on the library. This requires monitoring and support from institutions like INFLIBNET at the national level. In the study conducted at INFLIBNET based on its union catalogue of serials of 64 universities, data was divided into two regions, namely north-east-central and south–west regions. It was found that 80% of the journals covered in the union databases are available in the first 10 university libraries in each region and rest have duplicate titles of varying number. When these 10 universities in each region work together as document resource centres, the remaining libraries need not procure the journals covered in those libraries. They can spend the same amount towards the subscription of other new journals and in turn can be part of document delivery centres.

Networking

India is endowed with number of talented people whose contributions to the pursuit of knowledge is well known. But their need for creation of adequate information infrastructure to have access to latest information is undisputed. Networking allows these people to work together and some thing excellent can be expected as an output. With the ability to connect computers, it has become possible to access information resources of others. This has given a new definition to the concept of sharing of resources. Using various services available, it has become possible to communicate between libraries–not only within a city but also outside. Use of e-mail services has made it very convenient to send and receive messages, operate inter-library loan service, and transfer data or document. This service has also opened up many discussion groups like LIS forum and different subject expert groups for continuous interaction.

The application networks in India are INFLIBNET, DELNET, CALIBNET, etc. Each of these networks not only has the capability to communicate between the members but also the facility to link up with external networks for wider access to information. In this direction, the initiative taken by the INFLIBNET in providing VSAT connections to university libraries is laudable.

VSAT (Very Small Aperture Terminal) assures the capability of overcoming the limitations of the present networking arrangement. It is proposed to provide satellite-based network facilities by providing one VSAT to each university which will help academics and students all over the universities for easy access to information . This envisages a very vide accessibility of its resources, facilities and services to information users distributed all over the country.

Library automation primary refers to the use of computers to perform most of the traditional library operations such as acquisition, cataloguing, circulation and serials control. Some of the related fields such as information retrieval, automatic indexing and abstracting, automatic textual analysis., etc., do not fall under this purview. We can broadly classify the automation activity into two major categories:

1. Library house-keeping operations
2. Information handling

Apart from library house-keeping operations, computers are also used for information handling activities such as abstracting and indexing services, contents page service, current awareness service, SDI services, etc. The use of CD-ROM has changed the ways in which information searches have been provided earlier. It is now possible to scan a large amount of data at the same time. Options are also available for selecting information output, citations with abstracts, full text based references. Access to CD-ROM databases through a network is now a normal feature.

CONCLUSION

The information needs of an individual will not change much but technology is bringing new methods of information storage, retrieval and dissemination. The acceptance of any new methods mainly depends on the convenience in terms of efforts required by the individual in using the facility, the comprehensiveness and the cost involved in it. Behind every technological advance there is a provider, whose role is to store, organize and disseminate the information using IT. The need for an information professional who accesses, assimilates, reformulates and then packages information in a form to suit the end user is essential if meaningful outcomes are to be achieved.

Library automation in the present context refers not only to the house-keeping operations but also to the services based on the CD-ROM databases, e-mail, INTERNET services which are essential to the academic libraries. Looking at the recent developments in computer and communication technologies and the country's growing interest in investing money and expertise,

III : 2
Computerization of Circulation System : A Program Proposal

U.K. Agarwal

INTRODUCTION

A library popularly called People's University is a repository to the human knowledge meant for preservation of the past human experiences and knowledge for the posterity. In its role in the society and specially in the education system, this component is perhaps the most important one without which the whole system and society would be left paralysed. Obviously, it is our ethical duty to develop an official circulation system and maintain an efficient circulation system,

Functions :

The circulation section has the following functions.

1. Maintaining all the records relating to users of the library in handing admissions and cancellation of membership.
2. Maintaining all the records about the loan of books including inter-library loan, overdues, and collection of overdues.
3. Charging and discharging work.
4. All the work connected with the reservation of books

RESPONSIVE CHARGING SYSTEM

An efficient system should be responsive to the following nature of queries:

(i) Who has borrowed a particular volume on loan? When it is due?

(ii) Which and how many books subject-wise have been loaned on any date.

(iii) Which books are due on any date?

(iv) How many books were returned on any date?

VARIETY OF CHARGING SYSTEM

Following are few charging systems in use:

1. Ledger system
2. Dummy system
3. Indicator system
4. Browne system
5. Newark system
6. Computerised charging system (proposed programme)

CHOICE OF A CHARGING SYSTEM

The functioning of a library is driven by Five Laws of Library Science devised by Dr. S.R. Ranganathan. Two of them combined together to grow a need for the acceptance of computerised charging-discharging system. These are:

1. Books are for use and
2. Save the time of user/staff

The facility, i.e., Loan Privilege, gives meaning to the First Law and culminates the maximum use of the books by maximum number of users.

Long queues are found at counter during peak hours which is against the Fourth Law. Therefore, charging system chosen should be the one which takes least possible time in issue and return of books. It should also be economical in terms of staff, money and materials.

THE PROPOSED SYSTEM

The computerised system is meant to automate the circulation work to create the database, to update, to control the issue and return statistics and to satisfy the expected queries that users may require. The facilities of any proposed system are mentioned in the following paragraphs.

The proposed project has been written by using COBOL language and dbase III+ package separately. The COBOL (ANSI-74) creates the compatibility with both Unix environment as well as DOS environment, since there would be required only a minor change in the programme to make it compatible by the MS-COBOL compiler. Otherwise the batch processing of dot prompt commands of dbase III+ package would serve the purpose. The benefit of using MS-COBOL version would be that the care has been taken to avoid the state of memory overflow at every stage of the source programme.

WORKING

In a typical computerised system, there would not by any need to affix the book-jacket or leaves on the book nor would be the need to issue separate reader tickets, trays to keep them. However, Registers can be maintained for the security of some important data that would require a little pen and pencil work. The programme is supposed to be run by all the counters of the circulation section, viz. Issue counter, Return counter, Query counter and Registration counter. The working of object programme has following salient features:

(i) It can be started by one person only who is responsible for the security of the data of this section. A procedure or password to begin the working is introduced for the purpose.

(ii) No person of one counter can do the job of another counter except the query counter. This is because such overlaps usually lead to the malpractice.

(iii) Even a novice to the computer can handle the programme specially while querying the database. Also there are instructions specified in each MENU of the programme that helps the users of the programme to know exactly what the programme is expecting to be done and/or what went wrong after such doing.

(iv) Database can handle the statistics only in one floppy of capacity of 1.44 mb.

(v) The programme can handle the stack capacity of about one million books and 99 × 9999 users in total.

(vi) With every query, it produces a report file that can immediately be printed as hard copy of sorted records.

(vii) The programme maintains the history of how many times they have run on the system.

THE PROGRAMME CONSTRAINTS:

The programme constraints are actually the presumed suppositions regarding the project that was inevitable because want of time has caused some tentativeness of the working. These are as follows:

1. This is a MENU driven programme that does not fit for large libraries.

2. Search for books by first appearing author's last name is possible only and no search can made by the rest of the author's name if any .

   Despite various constraints, the computerisation is expected to make library circulation service most efficient.

3. No thesauri search is included in the programme. Thus while querying by the topic list, the users have to guess the nearest topic provided by the MENU-LIST.

4. There are stages where no operator is supposed to commit mistakes. Hence there is a programme that asks the authority to be checked by means of re-entering the password at this stage. The time saving elements withdraw the scene in this case.

5. It undertakes the job of circulation section only and does not support the activities of the reference section or the accounts section, though the overdue charge is calculated and may be levied by using this programme.

ROUTINE

The routine of the programme is that master controller will be logged in the areas specified where he starts the programme by entering the main password and also logs in the separate area with distinct ownership and runs the programme as above.

The main menu waits the concerned operators to come and go into the subroutine while the programme running at the different ownership area will be used by the users of the library for querying. After each query, if users want the hard copy, it is supposed to make a request to the concerned operator, who then would print the result.

SPECIAL FEATURES

The programme has following special features

For Updating Information

1. After every entry all the files are updated and closed immediately by the programme to provide the latest position on the other counter.
2. The 'Return' subroutine eliminates the record concerned but important information such as to who it was issued earlier is maintained by the STACK-FILE (the main database for the book).
3. For above such information, there are introduced a lot of confirmation tests that are fast enough to save the time.
4. Though minimum key operations are tried to maintain, the same is ignored if the operation is supposed to change the important content of database.

USER'S MANUAL

This section gives the necessary operations required to be known to run the programme.

For Master Controller

The entry password is "xvnz88".

Entering this password asks whether file initialization is necessary or not.

(i) If running the programme for the first time or not is the question and operator should take due care because it creates all the files new and afresh.

(ii) Since the issue is so important it is required that issue. Return as far as possible, the registration counter should never opt "y" or "y" for use of the programme and should confirm it.

Caution

Master controller is expected to

1. Enter the password.
2. Opt "y" for programme use if the new database is about to be created either afresh or removing the old one. Else he should opt "n" and should confirm it by "y" option and then only he should leave the terminal.

III : 3

Library Automation Circulation System (L.A.C.S.)

K. Somasekhara Rao

INTRODUCTION

The activities in Circulation system are most repetitive, thereby the application of computers in these activities attained importance. The circulation control systems are designed to store and manipulate three types of information:

1. Information about the material being borrowed. This includes accession number, call number, author, title, publisher, etc..
2. Information about the borrower. This includes borrower's name, identification no., department to which he/she belongs to, etc..
3. Information about the loan itself. This includes the data of borrowing, due date, number of days of borrow, fines, etc..

A centralised collection of data is called as database. Collection of related data items of entities having the same attributes may be referred to as a database. Database system is a general software which is mainly used for data storage and retrieval, etc.. This software serves as a base for application development.

Circulation database design

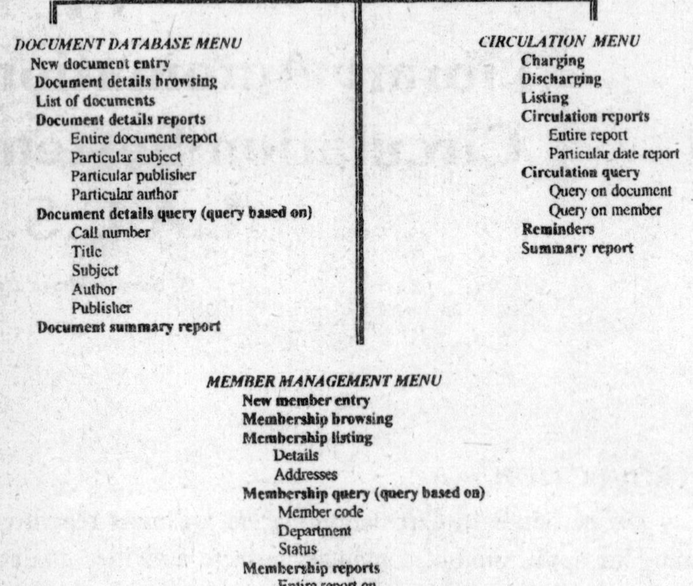

The database is designed as shown in the chart. Out of the available packages the Fox Pro 2.6 version is selected to develop and design the program for circulation system. This package can be executed by library professionals with minimum knowledge on computers and is suitable to college and university library circulation system.

After getting the system into Fox Pro 2.6 mode, type **"DO LMENU"** to execute the package. The entire package is divided into 3 menus namely Document Database Menu, Member Management Menu and Circulation Menu. By entering required number, the respective menu will be opened. The Document management menu is further divided into 1. New document entry. 2. Document details browsing, 3. List of document records, 4.

Document details reports, 5. Document details query, and 6. Document summary report.

DOCUMENT MANAGEMENT MENU

The new document entry consists of 22 fields which are sufficient to answer queries from users and to attend the administrative activities of circulation section. In document details browsing menu, each record can be viewed and edited if necessary. The list of document records menu is in a tabular form giving the details such as author, title, call number and accession number. The document which is to be viewed and edited can be accessed by entering its call number. The next menu is list of document details reports menu and similar to the earlier mentioned browsing menu, but editing of documents is not possible. The purpose of this menu is viewing the database in a tabular form continuously. The document details reports menu is designed into 3 types, 1. Entire document report, 2. Particular subject report, 3. Particular publisher report. The entire document report is further developed based on books code, subject wise report, publisher wise report. In book code report, documents acquired in the library is displayed according to call number, thereby we come to know the number of documents acquired on particular subject or specific subject, so also the subject wise report and publisher wise report. These menus carry all the necessary bibliographical details to answer various administrative queries. All these reports can be viewed on the screen beside print form.

The document details query menu is designed based on call number, document title, subject, author. In all these menus help facility is provided to select a particular call number, particular document title, particular subject, particular author and particular publisher. The query based on call number is properly executed, the details of that book appears on the screen as in the same way in new document entry. The query based on subject gives us the documents available with the following details in a tabular form, call no., author, title and accession no.. In the same way the other queries can be executed. The document summary report provides information of the total number of documents, total reference documents, total other documents, total documents available, total documents lost, reference documents available, other documents available, documents issued, documents for issue, number of authors, number of publishers, number of subjects, total cost of documents and documents can be added to database still.

MEMBER MANAGEMENT MENU

The Member management menu is divided into 6 further menus namely, 1. New member entry, 2. Membership browsing, 3. Membership listing, 4. Membership query, 5. Membership reports and 6. Summary report. To enter particulars of the borrower in new member entry menu, the status of the member is to be entered first, then the other details of the borrower such as name, father's name, sex, address, etc. By default the system gives the number of books entitled for a borrower according to their status. To incorporate changes into a particular borrower record, the browsing database menu should be opened. The member listing menu is developed in two modes—details of the member and addresses of the members. The details menu gives information of members, code no., member name, department, sex, date of joining, date of expiry (membership cease). In the address menu, the code number, door number, street, city, state and phone number are provided. In either of these menus the members are arranged according to their status. The membership query menu is designed on member code wise, department wise and status wise. In all these menus help menu is provided for easy access. By entering the correct code number of the borrower the screen displays the particulars of that borrower as it done in new member entry menu. In department wise query menu, the screen displays the particulars of members of that department, code no., member name, status, sex, deposit, no. of books of borrowers. Query based on status too provides information in a tabular form. The member database reports menu is designed into two modes, entire report and particular report. The entire report is further divided into member code wise, department wise and status wise, whereas particular report, department wise, status wise and expiry date wise. The member code report carries the following information of the registered borrowers, code no., name, status, date of joining, ceased date of member, amount deposited, number of books allowed to borrow and sex. The entire report on department wise carries the information of the borrowers as is in earlier menu. The entire report on status wise includes code no., name of the borrower, department, date of joining, ceased date, amount deposited, sex and books entitled to borrow. The members in each group are arranged alphabetically. The particular report on department wise provides information more or less same as in the earlier menus. The basic difference between the entire and particular is that in the entire report information of members is given on all departments whereas in particular report information is department wise or status wise. Reports can be generated period wise where the system asks us to enter from date and to date. The summary report menu gives the total number of borrowers, sex wise, status wise. At the bottom of the screen, the system displays the number of borrowers that can be accommodated further.

CIRCULATION MENU

The Document Circulation Menu is divided into seven menus, as 1. Charging, 2. Discharging, 3. Listing, 4. Circulation Reports, 5. Circulation Query, 6. Reminders and 7. Summary Report. The purpose of charging menu is to issue books to users. To issue a book the member code is to be entered and then call number of the book. The system by default displays the date of issue. A facility is made available to know how many books are entitled for a particular borrower and the books already issued so far. Therefore, we can easily tell the user regarding the number of books that can be issued further. To issue a particular book the system displays only the books that are available in database for issue and it does not display the reference books, books already issued and books lost in the database. If we try to issue more number of books than a borrower is entitled, the system displays a sorry message as "can't issue any more books". Before issuing a book the system asks us "Do you want to issue the book or not" if yes is pressed book will be issued and another message appears on the screen as "Do you want to issue any more books". To take back books from users discharging menu should be opened. The required member code is to be entered and the screen displays the number of books so far issued to that user in tabular form giving circulation code number, call number and date of issue. By entering circulation code number, discharging process is activated. The system asks us to make sure "whether the book is returned yes or no". If we press yes by default the system calculates fine per day 0-10 ps. for overdue books. The listing menu provides information in tabular form, member code, call number and issue date. The advantage of this menu is to know the books due to library and with whom. The circulation reports is divided into two types as today's report and particular period report. Today's report provides us member code, call number, date of issue and date of return. The chief advantage is to know how many books are issued on a particular day with necessary information. In the same way reports can be generated between two dates.

The circulation query menu attains great importance as it attends crucial and fundamental queries in circulation system. This menu is of two types – query on books and query on member. Inquiry on book menu, the call number of questioned book should be entered. Once the system accepts the call number, displays the particulars of documents, particularly its availability. At the bottom a message appears to view the details of that book further. If yes option is exercised it gives full details as "to whom document is issued, the date of issue and date of return". To open member query submenu, member code should be entered. The system display the books already issued in tabular form. At the bottom a warning message appears for ceased borrowership.

In circulation section sending reminders to overdue documents is one of the important activity. The reminders menu display the details of overdue documents in tabular form. This menu gives member code, call number of the document and issued date. The activities of document circulation menu completes with circulation summary menu. This report gives day wise, week wise and total transactions. The advantage of this report is one can easily understand the number of books issued, return and due to library periodically. At the bottom the system displays the number of circulation records that can be added and it depends on computer storage memory.

REFERENCES

1. Ashok Jambhekar and Neelam Mehta. Online Circulation System : V.S.L. Experience. *Library Science* 28, December, 1991, pp. 160-166.
2. Gaddagimath, R.B. and Parvathamma, N. Design and development of indigenous databases : Strategy and problems. CALIBER-97, 6-8 March, 1997, pp. 54-58.
3. Gull, C.D. Automated Circulation Systems. Information Science and Automation Division of the A.L.A. , San Francisco, California, 1967, 22-24 June, pp. 138-148.
4. Palaniyandy, M.V. and Ravichandra Rao, I.K. Automated Circulation Control System *Library Science* 29, December, 1992, pp. 183-189.
5. Veena Sharma. Automation of Library Procedures in Nagpur University. CALIBER-97, 6- March, 1997, pp. 19-21.

```
**LBOOK.PRG
*MENU FOR MASTERING BOOK MANAGEMENT MENU.
*CALLED FROM LIBRARY MANAGEMENT SYSTEM MAIN MENU.
*,,--...SET UP LOOP FOR PRESENTING MENU.
MCHOICE=0
DO WHILE MCHOICE # 7
.................
......................
TEXT
    1. NEW DOCUMENTS ENTRY.
    2. DOCUMENT DETAILS BROWSING.
    3. LIST OF DOCUMENT RECORDS.
    4. DOCUMENT DETAILS REPORTS.
    5. DOCUMENT DETAILS QUERY.
    6. DOCUMENT SUMMARY REPORT.
    7. RETURN TO MAIN MENU.
ENDTEXT
@ 23,1 SAY "ENTER YOUR CHOICE (1-7) :" GET MCHOICE PICT "9" RANGE 1.7
READ
.................
.....................
WHEN DONE, RETURN TO MAIN MENU.
CLEAR
RETURN
```

LMOUERY.PRG

```
**PROGRAMME TO ANSWER QUERY ON MEMBER:
    SET SCOR OFF
    USE MEMBER
    QCHOICE = 0
```

```
DO WHILE QCHOICE # 4
................
@ 4,0 SAY ULINE
TEXT
            QUERY BASED ON.....
        1. MEMBER CODE
        2. DEPARTMENT
        3. STATUS
        4. RETURN
ENDTEXT
@ 23,1 SAY "ENTER YOUR CHOICE (1-4):" GET QCHOICE
PICT "9":
RANGE 1,4
..............
CLEAR
RETURN_
```

<u>LBQUEC.PRG</u>**

*—— TO ACCEPT THE MEMBER CODE, FOR WHICH QUERY IS REQUIRED.

```
................
@ 19,13 SAY "ENTER THE CALL NUMBER.. " GET TCODE
READ
USE MEMBER
INDEX ON MCODE TO MEMBER
TCODE=UPPER(TCODE)
SEEK TCODE
   IF FOUNDC)
CLEAR
@ 2, 25 SAY "DOCUMENT QUERY - MEMBER CODE"
@ 5,  5 SAY "MEMBER CODE :"
@ 5, 20 GET MEMBER->MCODE
..................
```

```
....................
@ 18. 3 TO 22. 75   DOUBLE
SET COLO TO W+
@ 20, 20 SAY "END OF QUERY BASED ON MEMBER
CODE." WAIT " "
        SET COLO TO W+
        @ 19, 12 SAY "NO MEMBER EXISTS WITH THIS
        CODE."
        WAIT " "
        SET COLO TO
ENDIF
```

****LCLIST**

```
* TO LIST THE CIRCULATION RECORDS.
* CALLED FROM LCCIR.PRG.
        USE MASTER
        INDEX ON MCODE TO MASTER
        CLEAR
R=5
C=5
GO TOP
DO WHILE .NOT. EOF()
IF CSTAT-''NOT RETURNED"
................

..................
@ C, 68 GET MASTER->DISSUE
SKIP
R=R+1
C=C+1
ENDIF (R>21)
ENDIF (R<21)
....................
```

```
SET COLO TO
WAIT " "

**LCREP.PRG
*MENU FOR MASTERING CIRCULATION DETAILS REPORTS.
*CALLED FROM CIRCULATION MANAGEMENT MENU.
*-------SET UP LOOP FOR PRESENTING REPORTS SUB-
MENU.
USE MASTER.DBF
.......................
INDEX ON MCODE TO MASTER
@ 4,0 SAYULINE
TEXT
        1. TODAY'S CIRCULATION REPORT.
        2. PARTICULAR PERIOD REPORT.
        3. RETURN TO SUB-MENU.
ENDTEXT
@ 23,1 SAY "ENTER YOUR CHOICE (1-3) :" GET
CRCHOICE PICT "9" RANGE 1,3
................
        @ 21,10 SAY "ENTER ENDING PERIOD DATE :" GET
        TDATE PICT "(S)Z99/99/99"
        READ
REPO FORM CIR FOR ((DISSUE>=TTDATE .AND.
DISSUE<=TDATE) .OR. (DRETURN>=TTDATE
.AND.DRETURN<=TDATE)) &PRINTER

ENDCASE
*------- IF REPORT NOT GOING TO PRINTER.
..................
WAIT "Press any key to return to the reports menu..."
ENDIF
.....................
```

```
ENDDO(WHILE RCHOICE # 3)
*-------- WHEN DONE, RETURN TO MAIN MENU.
CLEAR
RETURN
```

IV : 1
Natural Language Interface to Database

M.S. Subramanian

NATURAL LANGUAGE

Natural language may be conceived of as "the system of vocal and written symbols used by human beings to communicate their thoughts and feelings". It is a system of units reliable in some sensory medium, only certain combinations of which have meaning by convention and hence can be used for interpersonal communication.

The most striking organisational feelings of language is that it permits the construction of our indefinite number of vehicles of communication (sentences) out of finite stock of elements (words).

Rules of Language

In the use of language as medium of communication, a potentially infinite variety of sentences are constructed according to systematic rules that dictate hard words may be combined into sentences. Such rules are of two sorts:-

a) Syntactic rules

b) Semantic rules

The syntactic rules determine to which connectives are permissible. Thus the grammar of a particular language sequences the words while the semantic rules specify the way in which the meaning of a large construction (phrase or sentence) is derived from the meanings and organisation (syntax) of the constituent words. Thus a language must be construed as a system of types, a system consisting of the formal, abstract elements of sound, grammar and lexicon, and distinct from any particular concrete instance of those types.

Natural Language in the Indexing System

Since natural language, especially, English language is being internationally used for global communication, it is easily and quickly adoptable for indexing concepts. Many indexing systems like uniterm indexing, KWIC, KWOC, KWAC, KWWC, etc. have been developed and used in the field of information storage and retrieval.

NATURAL LANGUAGE INTERFACE TO DATABASE

Natural language interface relates to the processing of natural language to the ability of computers to understand the language humans use in normal discourses.

Natural Language Processing (NLP) can be applied to several areas such as machine translations, text scanning and intelligent indexing, text generation for standardized reports etc., voice recognition to allow speech interaction with computers, tools for developing NLP systems for specific applications and for interfaces to databases. It has been statistically determined that nearly 40% of all NLP systems are used as interface to data bases.

Parsers to Overcome Ambiguity

The central problem in our NLP system is the transformation of a potentially ambiguous input phrase into an unambiguous form that can be used internally by a computer system. This transposition from a potentially ambiguous phrase to the internal representation is called parsing.

In NLP, parsing is a process of combining symbols of a phrase into a group that can be replaced by another, more general in use. This new symbol can, in turn, be combined into another group, and so on, until an allowable structure evolves.

Types of Parsers

For the purpose of NLP interface to computerized data base, five types of parsers have been evolved as given below:-

1. Pattern matching based
2. Grammar based
3. Semantic based
4. Knowledge based and
5. Neural network based

The first two parsers take into account the structure and syntactic aspect of a particular language, say English language. The semantic sensitive parser for an interface is based on SQL (Structured Query Language).

Any Database Management System (DBMS) must provide the user with a data access language. SQL is one such language which works with relational databases. However, like any other structured language, SQL suffers from inherent drawback such as it is syntax specific and difficult to master. Moreover, for a man who is not conversant with the language, it would not be possible to use this data access language. Thus a natural language interface is developed to help him access the data base and simultaneously shield him from the peculiarities and formalities of the underlying structures.

Features for Incorporation into NLI

The features to be incorporated into any useful Natural Language Interface should be

1) Domain independence (transportability)
2) Partition handling and
3) Access of heterogeneous system

The simplest form of NLI is around a specific database having a fixed structure. But updating of such interfaces proves to be enormously difficult and time consuming. Moreover, the interface restricts the users to a few predetermined ways of querying. One such approach is to base the interface on a set of menus to cover every aspect of a possible query. On the other hand interfaces of the present day are made transportable i.e. they can be adopted to a number of databases with ease.

NLI IMPLEMENTATION TO SQL

Having discussed the general aspect of NLI, let us now look at the implementation of it to structured query language (SQL) using semantic sensitive parser.

To have an insight into such a system, we must understand the concepts on which such a system is built. The primary concepts can be classified as:

1. Density of coverage and tolerance
2. Series information
3. Navigation of database

Density of Coverage

The English language is inherently very ambiguous due to synonymous and homonymous terms and the context of their usage. For example, in the following two identical statements, the meanings are different.

(i) Mani told Prasad that he (Mani) has lost his (Mani's) bag.

(ii) Mani told Prasad that he (Mani) had lost his (Prasad's) bag.

Thus the system should be tolerant to queries which are reworded slightly but still convey the same meaning. In case of unresolved ambiguities, the system should resort to dialogue with the user to classify the exact import of the query. Thus the system should be able to process all the numerous ways of putting across the same query.

Series Information

A set of words which convey a specific meaning in an input is referred to as a phrase. Phrases are the most entities in any natural language programme. In case of semantic sensitive parser based programmes they assume greater importance because the meaning conveyed by the phrases has to be taken into account. In case of transportable interfaces, the database expert is the one who builds the domains specific information into a knowledge base which is then used by the NLI to answer queries.

One way of describing the field of a domain is the significant word set technique. In this technique each field is completely and uniquely described by a set of significant words which capture the meaning too, for example

PCODE = (project, code)

PGVIDE = (project, Guide, Name)

Thus if we identify a group of these significant words in the query, it can be easily mapped onto the relevant field name. However, care must be taken to accommodate variations in the manner in which these words occur. Ambiguity occurs when we identify a set of words in the input which happens to be a subset of two or more SWS's.

Navigation of Databases

As stated already the Natural Language Interface should be as independent domain as feasible. To enable this, we depend on the user to build a knowledge base about the domain to which the interface is being applied with assistance from the programme. Once the knowledge base has been built, it is easy to formulate rules to navigate the database.

FUNCTIONING OF A TYPICAL NLI

The following chart indicates the functioning of a Natural Language Interface:

Following are the few simplified rules to navigate the database.

(i) Identifying the CONDITION Clauses

All fields appearing on the left or right of a constant are

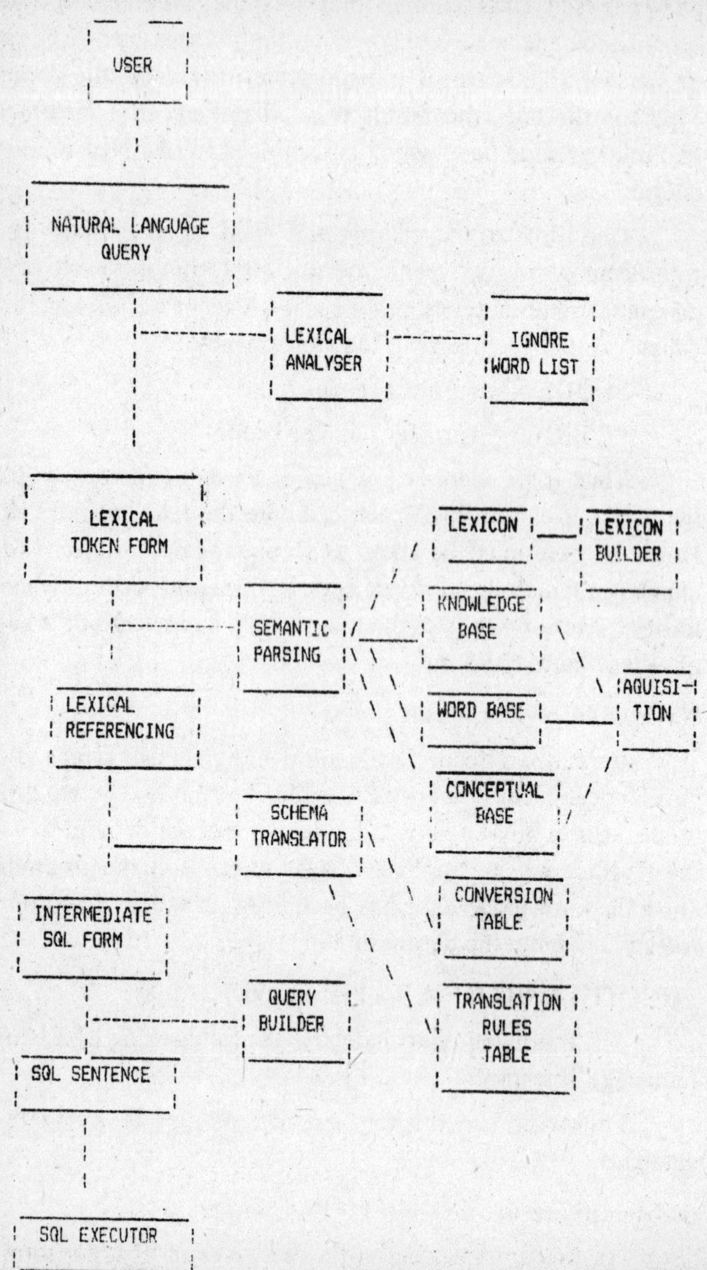
USER
NATURAL LANGUAGE QUERY
LEXICAL ANALYSER
IGNORE WORD LIST
LEXICAL TOKEN FORM
LEXICON
LEXICON BUILDER
SEMANTIC PARSING
KNOWLEDGE BASE
AQUISI-TION
LEXICAL REFERENCING
WORD BASE
CONCEPTUAL BASE
SCHEMA TRANSLATOR
CONVERSION TABLE
INTERMEDIATE SQL FORM
QUERY BUILDER
TRANSLATION RULES TABLE
SQL SENTENCE
SQL EXECUTOR

assumed to be a constituent of the CONDITION clause. Example:

(condition clause) If the door is knocked.	(constant) it will be opened	(field appearing at left side of constant)
(Constant) It will be opened,	(Condition clauses) if the door is knocked	(field appearing at right side constant)

(ii) Identifying the TARGET Fields

All fields not belonging to the CONDITION clause are said to be target fields.

(iii) Links

If we operate on more than one relation at a time, then we can use the linking information provided in the knowledge base to execute a JOIN on relations.

(iv) Query Building

For the purpose of building the structured query language, a typical query processing model is to be developed. The translation of an input query unto an SQL equivalent is due in two major steps namely:-

1. A semantic sensitive parser which dissects the English query into a list of tokens along with their related information which is called the logical representation.
2. Scheme translation which takes the logical form and generates the relevant SQL statement. It is at this shape of translation that we use translation rules which have been developed from linguistic principles. These translation rules are applied recursively on the input token until an acceptable intermediate form is generated (i.e. the translations can no longer be applied on them).

We then identify the relations which must be assessed to get the data required. Finally we use a query Builder to convert this intermediate form into a proper and executable SQL statement which can then be executed by the SQL executor.

CONCLUSION

Those who like to interface to database may like to adopt their natural language to set queries. Since natural language has many pitfalls, it cannot be, as it is, adopted to access database,

Hence any database management system (DBMS) must provide the user with a data access language. Structured query language is one such language which works with relational database using a semantic sensitive parser, To have an insight into such a system, concepts like density of coverage and tolerance, series information navigation of the database and query and query building etc., have been highlighted to construct a typical Natural Language Interface system for database.

REFERENCES

1. Adiba, M. and Lindsay, B.G. : Database Snapshots. 6th ed. VLDB, Montreal, 1980,
2. Ceri, S and Pelagatti, G.: Correctness of Query Extension Strategies in Distributed Databases. ACM-TODS, 1983.
3. Finkelstein, S. : Common Expression Analysis in Database Applications. ACM-SIGMOD, 1982.
4. King, J.J. : QUIST : A System for Semantic Query Optimisation in Relational Databases. Seventh VLDB, 1982.
5. Tsichristzis. D.C. and Lochovsky, F.H. Database Management Systems. Academic Press, 1977.
6. Ullman, J. D.: Principles of Data bases Systems. 2nd ed. Computer Science Press, 1983.
7. Wong, E : Retrieving Dispersed Data from SDD - 1: A System for Distributed Satabase. Berkeley workshop on distributed data management and computer networks, 1977.

IV : 2

Micro Schedule On Physical Education : A Panoramic View

A. Ramasamy
B. Ramesh Babu

INTRODUCTION

The fundamental technique adopted for the organisation of knowledge in libraries is "Classification". Unless books and other reading materials are classified, the full use of library resources becomes difficult and sometimes impossible. The history of library classification reveals that schemes for classification have evolved from purely enumerative to the freely/faceted, analytico-synthetic scheme. New and newer inter-disciplinary and intradisciplinary subjects are coming up. In order to organise such knowledge effectively an analytico-synthetic scheme of classification can be much helpful. Dr. S. R. Ranganathan has contributed much in this direction by bringing out Colon Classification (CC) as a universal faceted classification scheme. Colon Classification has a great deal of potential for the specificity that led to the design and development of depth schedules for various micro subjects.

PHYSICAL EDUCATION AS AN ACADEMIC DISCIPLINE

Franklin Henry defines an academic discipline as "an organised body of knowledge collectively embraced in a formal course of learning. Physical Education is a field of action of rules and of persons. It has been developed systematically as an academic subject. It possesses the following characteristics to qualify as an academic discipline.

1. a sound theoretical basis.
2. a scientific basis
3. sensitive tools of measurement.
4. areas of relationship and differences with other fields of knowledge.
5. an integrated body of knowledge (Curriculum)
6. specific methodology of teaching.
7. unique and specific objectives and purposes different from other fields of study.
8. personnel and facility[2].

Meaning and Purposes of Physical Education

Physical Education is a way of education through physical activities which are selected and carried on with full regard to values in human growth, developments and behaviour because it is a phase of the total educational programme. Physical Education aims for the same general goal that gives purpose to all the other learning experiences of the school – the all – rounded development of all children and youth as responsible citizens in our democratic society.

Physical Education provides a wealth of experience which along with other opportunities in the curriculum are particularly important in helping each child and youth to:

1. Develop and maintain maximum efficiency.
2. Develop useful skills.
3. Conduct himself in socially acceptable ways.
4. Enjoy wholesome recreation.
5. Select, organize and guide activities, suited to the needs, capacities and interests of everyone taking part.

Today the field of Physical Education is composed of specialisations in exercise physiology, motor learning, sports history, many other allied areas. There is an emphasis in study and research other than usual physical training. There exists natural relationship between social sciences, biological sciences and engineering subjects. It is an interdisciplinary subject and borrowed a number of concepts and ideas from other subjects. The following diagram[4] portraits the interdisciplinary nature of the subject of Physical Education.

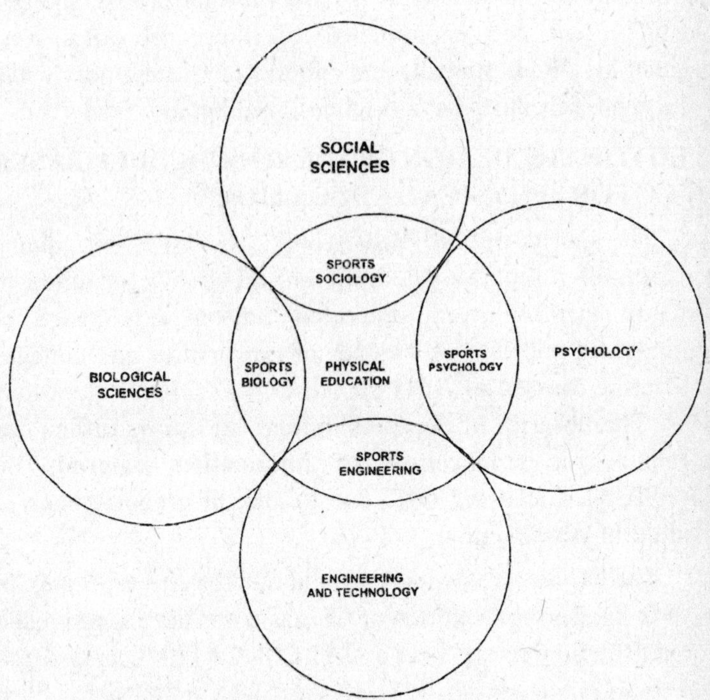

Diagram : Interdisciplinary Nature of Physical Education

To quote John Cheffores and Tom Evaul: "If human movement is the discipline that incorporates a body of knowledge about the human beings in motion, then Physical Education is a profession that applies that knowledge."[5]

Micro Schedules Developed based on CC : An Overview

The work of the designing depth version of the CC schedules has been started at DRTC in sixties. During 1963 to 1967, about 50 (Fifty) depth schedules were designed. During 1967 to 1973, 71 depth schedules were designed[6]. Since 80's design of depth schedule in DRTC has not gained much momentum, and in fact it is almost nil in recent years due to reasons not known. As reported in the **FID Report** No. 14 it was found that a total of 122 depth schedules have been developed. While many are published in the DRTC publications and few schedules remained unpublished, all these schedules were designed by DRTC students and editions of CC and nearly half of the depth schedules have been designed based on the 7 Ed.

NEED FOR THE DESIGN OF MICRO SCHEDULE BASED ON CC FOR "PHYSICAL EDUCATION"

The subject of "PHYSICAL EDUCATION" is gaining the status of a separate academic discipline. The quantum of literature that is being generated reflects a plethora of agglomerated subjects. A number of universities and colleges are offering courses on "PHYSICAL EDUCATION" at various levels. The libraries of these institutions are facing difficulties in the proper organisation of information materials on "PHYSICAL EDUCATION" due to lack of a comprehensive schedule of classification.

The CC has been widely used in the libraries especially in South India. The sixth edition of CC has not made any provision to organise materials on "PHYSICAL EDUCATION" in its depth level. In CC sixth edition "PHYSICAL EDUCATION" has been listed as one of the energy isolates of the Main Class "T" Education. Sports and Games have been listed as one of the canonical classes of the Main Class "M" Useful Arts. Thus there is a gap in the presentation of the related isolates under two different Main Classes. In the review of literature on micro schedules, it was found that no attempt has been made towards the design and development of micro schedule for "PHYSICAL EDUCATION". All these factors have contributed to undertake this research. This paper is based on the research work being carried out currently.

OBJECTIVES

The Main Objectives of this Micro Schedules are:

i. To trace the genesis and development of "PHYSICAL EDUCATION" as an academic discipline.

ii. To investigate and scan the micro and macro literature on "PHYSICAL EDUCATION", and to identify the isolates ideas.

iii. To design and develop the micro schedule on "PHYSICAL EDUCATION" based on Colon Classification, Ed 6.

iv. To test the micro schedule, thus designed, in order to ascertain the efficiency of the scheme.

DESIGN AND DEVELOPMENT

Depth schedule for any subject is warranted when classifier finds very difficult with the existing scheme to assign the notation. In such cases, depth schedule becomes inevitable. When Colon Classification (Ed 6) was designed by Dr. S. R. Ranganathan, the subject "Physical Education" was considered as one of the Energy isolates in Main Class [T] Education. Other sports and games were accommodated in the Main Class "MY" useful arts. Physical Education and Sports integrated discipline should not be diversified. It should be treated under one banner "PHYSICAL EDUCATION AND SPORTS & GAMES". The basic class MY has been chosen for representing the subject Physical Education and Sports and Games.

The notational system of CC and principles of classification enunciated by Dr. S. R. Ranganathan have been considered in the design of micro schedule. Literature on "PHYSICAL EDUCATION" at micro and macro level has been investigated and scanned very thoroughly.

The various concepts, isolates, ideas and terms in the subject have been selected and grouped under various sports and games as quasi isolates based on Wall-Picture Principle, Cow-Calf Principle and Whole-Organ Principle.

The facet formula mentioned in the CC sixth edition for the Main Class "T" Education has been adopted for this purpose with some additions.

Table 1 Presents the categorisation of isolate ideas and their quantum.

Table No. 1 : Categorisation of Isolate Ideas and their Quantum

Category	Facet Description	No. of Isolates	Cumulative Total
[P]	Personality	2418	2418
[2P]	Second Level Personality	31	2449
[M]	Matter	304	2753
[E] cum [2P]	Energy cum Second Round Personality	80	2833
[2P2]	Second Round Second Level Personality	121	2954
[2E] cum [3P]	Second Round Energy and Third Round Personality	13	2967
Specials		17	2974
Systems		14	2988

MICRO SCHEDULE ON "PHYSICAL EDUCATION"

Physical Education is an integral part of the General Education. Sports and Games were enumerated under "MY". Hence "MY" has been given to the BC Physical Education.

Facet Formula

MY [P], [P2]: [M] : [E] cum [2P], [2P2] : [2E] cum [3P]

MY	Basic Class	Physical Education
[P]	Personality Facet	Sports and Games
[P2]	Second Level Personality Facet	Educand same as in [P] of Main Class "T" Education
[M]	Matter Facet	Play Fields, Equipments and other materials
[E] cum [2P]	Energy cum Second Round Personality Facet	Problem and Action
[2P2]	Second Round Second Level Personality Facet	Methods
[2E] cum [3P]	Second Round Energy and Third Round Personality	Handling of [E]

After the arrangement of isolate ideas logically, an alphabetical index with numerals and alphabets has been compiled for the isolates enumerated in the micro schedule.

MAJOR AREAS IN PHYSICAL EDUCATION

Physical Education is the field of study which is partly theoretical and partly practical oriented discipline. It is identified as one of the academic and teaching disciplines. It tends to grow in terms of quantum of literature, which lead to have emerged new disciplines more and more. Major areas in Physical Education are determined and identified.

A brief outline of the Basic Class "MY" with respective facets along with notation is presented below:

Foci in [P]

1. Indigenous Sports
2. Calisthenics
3. Tumbling, Gymnastics, Pyramids, and Ropes and Hoops

4. Track and Field Events (Athletics)
5. Team Sports
6. Stick and Ball Sports
7. Racquet and Ball Sports
8. Bat and Ball Sports

91 Paddle Ring and Ball Sports
92 Racing Sports
93 Target Sports
94 Combat Sports (Martial Arts and Self Defence)
95 Weight Training, Training Methods, Body Building. Power Lifting and Fitness.
96 Water Sports
97 Minor Games and Sports, Recreational, Passtime and Social Games and Sports
98 Dances and Rhythmic Activities
981 Indoor Games and Sports
9A Systems
9B Specials

Foci in [P2]

Same as [P] in "T" Education

Foci in [M]

1. Stadium
2. Play field
3. Boxing Ring
4. Gymnastics equipments
5. Track and Field equipments
6. Stick

6 A Club
6 B Racquet

6 C Bat
6 D Stumps
6 E Wicket
6 F Paddle
6 G Net
6 H Ball
6 J Bow
6 K Arrow
6 M Antena
6 N Protecting equipments
6 P Pads
6 Q Guards
6 R Gloves
6 S Goal Keeper's equipments
6 T Stop Watch
7 Saddle
8 Weight lifting equipments
91 Cycles
92 Posts
92 A Sports Costumes
92 B Snickers
92 C Boots
92 D Shoes
92 E Canvas
92 F Socks
92 G Hat
92 H Cap
92 J Sunglass
92 K Cowboy dress

Foci in [E] cum [2P]

1	Nomenclature
2	Curriculum
3	Teaching Technique

Foci in [2P2]. Same as [2P2] in "T" Education

31	Coaching Technique
32	Training Technique
33	Playing Technique
34	Officiating Technique
35	Layout
37	Marking
3 A	Student's work
3 B	Educational Measurement

Foci in [2P2]. Same as 5 [E] of "T" Education

4	Sports Pathology
41	Foul Play
42	Environment
5	Physiological factors
6	Psychological factors
7	Developmental factors
8	Management

Foci in [2E] cum [3P] for 41 of [E]

5	Preventive step
6	Therapeutics for 42 of [E]
7	Repairing
8	Maintenance
9	Alternative Power Supply

Specials

MY 9A Specials

MY 9B	Integrated discipline
MY 9C	Cinematography
MY 9D	Movement Education
MY 9E	Sports Kinesiology
MY 9F	Sports Biomechanics
MY 9G	Anthropometry
MY 9H	Kine Anthropometry
MY 9J	Special Physical Education/Adapted Physical Education
MY 9K	Sports Engineering
MY 9M	Tableau
MY 9N	Aerospace Sports
MY 9P	Ballooning, Gliding, Skii, Air Jumping
MY 9Q	Falconry
MY 9R	Adventurous Sports

Systems

MY A	Systems by (C.D.)
MYJ	Commenius (Subject teaching)
MYL	Rousseau's School
MYL2	Kant's School
MYL5	Pestalozzi's School
MYL6	Fitchte's School
MYL7	Herbert's School
MYL8	Froebel's Kindergarten
MYL9	Mann's School
MYM	Manual Training
MYN	Plantoon School
MYNI	Montessori School
MYN3	Basic, Wardha

Physical Education books were classified and arranged according to increasing concreteness followed in the arrangement in the book shelf as follows :

Worked out examples

1. Lokesh Thani. Rules of Games and Sports Delhi : Sports Publication, 1998.

   Class No.: MYe

2. Lokesh Thani. Dictionary of Physical Education and sports science. Delhi : Sports Publications, 1997.

   Class No.: MYk

3. M. Ardle, William D, et.al. Exercise physiology Ed 3 Lea & Febiger " Philadelphia, 1991.

   Class No. : MY2 (L:3)

4. Gothi, Ekta. Teaching and Coaching Athletics : Delhi : Sports Publication, 1997.

   Class No.: MY4:3oj31

5. Yogaraj Thani, Teaching and Coaching Basketball : Delhi : Sports Publication, 1977.

   Class No.: MY52:3oj31

6. Scott M Gladys Scott. Kinesiology (Analysis of Human Motion) Delhi 1998.

   Class No.: MY4E

7. Doll-Deeper G, et.al Ed. Adapted Physical Activity : An Interdisciplinary Approach. New York Springer Vertag 1990.

   Class No.: MY9JojB

8. Officiating and Coaching. Jalandhar : Parkashu Brothers, 1984.

   Class No.: MY:34oj31

9. Krumhansl Bernic and opportunities in Physical Therapy. Lincolnwood, Illinois : VGM Career Horizones, 1988.

   Class No.: MY:41:6a

10. Chakraborty Sanuran, Sports management. Delhi : Sports Publication, 1998.

Class No.: MY:8

CONCLUSION

The Micro Schedule on "PHYSICAL EDUCATION' thus designed and developed can be regarded as a unique one which has been prepared on the basis of the guidelines and flexibility provided by CC Ed 6 itself. It helps the librarians and the users in the field of "PHYSICAL EDUCATION". It would also influence the existing classification schemes, especially analytico - synthetic classification schemes, in the design and development of schedules. It may also offer vistas and avenues to undertake similar research in the design and development of micro schedules for other subjects.

REFERENCES

1. Geroge R. Colfer et.al (1986), Contemporary Physical Education. Dubuque, Iowa : Wm. C. Brown Publisher, p.326.
2. Charles A Bucher, (1960). Foundations of Physical Education, Ed 3. St. Louis : The C.V. Mostry Co. p.27.
3. W. K. Streit and Simon A. Mc. Neely, "A platform for Physical Education" **Journal of the American Association for Health Physical Education and Recreation.** Vol zl:3 (1950).
4. V. Krishnamurthy and N. Parameshwara Ram (1990). Educational Dimensions of Physical Education. Ed 2; New Delhi : Sterling, p.18.
5. John Cheffores and Tom Evaul (1978). Introduction to Physical Education : Concepts of Human Movement. Englewood Cliffs N.J.: Prentice Hall, Inc.; p. xii.
6. M.A. Gopinath, Classification Research (India). 1968-1973 Classification Research (Committee on -). FID/CR Report No. 14, Bangalore : DRTC 1975, H.

IV : 3

Growth of Knowledge and Structural Relations in Ranganathan's Colon Classification

M.P. Satija

INTRODUCTION

S. R. Ranganathan (1892-1972) first conceived Colon Classification (CC) in 1924 in Europe to develop a composite classification to move beyond the monolithic and only hierarchic structure of the Dewey Decimal Classification which was first published in 1876. Ranganathan experienced that the DDC had become a defunct tool to cope up with the 20th century knowledge which had grown multidimensional. Classification is a tool to map the universe of knowledge and also represents its structure at a given time. Ranganathan's CC excels in this endeavour. Fran Miksa has rightly pointed out that "there is virtually no area of Ranganathan's work and personal life in which this quest for discovering the inner or essential order behind the visible world is absent."[1]

In the days earlier to the printing press (ca. mid 15th century) upto the Industrial revolution (Ca. mid 19th century) the growth of knowledge was slow and boundaries between subjects were clear. Main classes consisted of much broader areas (e.g. ten main classes of Dewey) and the structure of knowledge was simple. With the coming of industrialization, democracy and the universalization of education, the growth of knowledge took a brisk pace. End of World War-I (1914-1919) further accelerated the rate of growth. Specialization of knowledge became a natural necessity. Now we are amidst an information revolution which threatens to engulf us. Ranganathan perceived this acute proliferation of knowledge while designing his system of classification and later continued his studies of knowledge growth to mould his system accordingly.

SUBJECTS AND THEIR KINDS

Ranganathan defines a subject as an organized, systematized and coherent body of ideas whose length and breadth fall within the comprehension of a normal scholar[2]. A subject is independent of its length of treatment in a document. It could fill a multi-volume encyclopaedia or could be confined to a small journal article or to even less than that. Further three kinds of subjects are recognised by him:

Basic subjects

Compound subjects

Complex subjects

Obviously these terms from chemistry very easily fit into the situation.

Basic subjects are coherent chunks of knowledge without any ramification or focus. These are only postulated by the classificationists keeping in view the socio-academic conditions. Their number and boundaries change with time. In the 7th edition (1987) of the CC there are broadly two types of basic subjects.[3] These for want of better terminology are named as:

1. Main basic subjects
2. Non-main basic subjects

Main basic subjects have been divided into following kinds on the basis of their modes of formation:

S.No.	*Kind*	*Examples*
1.	Traditional main classes	Physics, Law, Literature
2.	Fused basic subjects	Biochemistry, Medical Jurisprudence, Geopolitics
3.	Distilled basic subjects	Research Methodology, Management Science.
4.	Agglomerate basic subjects	Social Sciences, Behavioral Sciences, Bio-sciences.
5.	Subject bundles	Deep-sea Sciences, Space Missions, Polar Expeditions.

Non-main basic subjects are also know as compound basic subjects[4] as these are some restricted areas of studies of a main class as a whole. These are of four types.

S.No.	*Kind*	*Examples*
1.	Systems basic subjects	Allopathy system of medicine, Homeopathy system, Marxist economy
2.	Specials basic subjects	Child medicine, Sports medicine
3.	Environment basic subjects	Tropical medicine, Space medicine
4.	Canonical basic subjects	Arithmetic, Algebra, Geometry in mathematics; Heat, Light Electricity in Physics

Basic subjects form the nucleus of compound and basic subjects.

Compound Subjects

These are formed adding one or more isolate facets to a basic subject.[5] For example, agriculture of wheat; or agriculture of wheat in India, all are compound subjects. Number of such subjects is virtually infinite.

Complex Subjects

These are formed by the interaction of two or more different basic or compound subjects taken usually from different disciplines. These two phased subjects are usually interdisciplinary. Ranganathan in the latest version has recognised six types of phase relations.[6]

MODES OF FORMATION OF SUBJECTS

D.W. Langridge aptly says that modes of formation of subjects represent a topology of relations and act as guiding ideas in recognising and formulating relations among concepts constituting a subject[7]. Ranganathan in order to study the nature and structure of knowledge discovered the modes of formation of subjects. These modes of formation naturally have some innate effect on the structure of the subjects. "Obviously the mode of formation of subjects leaves its impress on the structure of the subject"- to quote Ranganathan[8]. These modes can be divided into three kinds depending upon the kind of subjects they produce[9].

1. Specialization mode
2. Interdisciplinary mode
3. Multi-disciplinary mode

To represent diagrammatically

Modes of Formation of Subjects

↓

Specialization Subjects	**Interdisciplinary Subjects**	**Multi-disciplinary Subjects**
Fission	Loose-Assemblage	Distillation
Dissection	Fusion	Agglomeration
Denudation		Subject Bundles
Lamination		

Fissioned subjects are cohesive and have unitary structures formed by fragmentation of relatively bigger chunks of knowledge.

Dissection is slicing a subject into equally ranked subdivisions, i.e., forming an array of coordinate classes. Dividing the earth into continents is the process of dissection. When dissection is applied repeatedly on a single entity it becomes denudation. Earth-Europe –Western Europe-France is the process of denudation. It is like peeling off the layers and layers of an onion. The result is a chain of class. Dissection and denudation are relative processes.

Lamination is the process of producing compound subjects by placing laminae of isolate(s) on a basic subject. For example, agriculture of wheat, agriculture in India, and agriculture of wheat in India are all compound subjects formed by lamination. The number of compound subject in the universe of knowledge is virtually infinite. Lamination, though a very old mode, is still the predominant one of the formation of subjects. In comparison to basic subjects these are specializations, i.e., subjects of far greater intention than the basic ones.

Since the World War-II interdisciplinary subjects have emerged as an antidote to the specialization which had reached morbid dimensions.

Loose Assemblage and **Fusion** are first and the last stages of formulation of interdisciplinary subjects. Loosely assembled interdisciplinary subjects are complex subjects such as psychology for nurses; law for social workers; or statistics for librarians. Two different subjects across disciplines brought together on ad hoc relationship solidifies irreversibly into a new subject, the result is Fusion. Biochemistry, nuclear medical jurisprudence are basic subjects formed by fusion. Analogous to cross breeding such subjects are emerging fast.

During the last year of his life in association with his school men at the Documentation Research and Training Center, Bangalore, Ranganathan isolated three more modes of formation of subjects. All these are Multi-disciplinary modes. In the multi-disciplinary mode the trend of inter-disciplinary subjects goes further. In such subject the view is made through many conceptual sets.[10] Agglomeration is a cluster of neighborly subjects having a generic name. Some examples are: Natural science, physical science, bioscience, medical sciences. These are formed either by the affinity of their subject contents or by a common research methodology. Their dissection leads to main classes. Distilled subjects are seemingly, unitary subjects formed through distilling matured feedback of experience across many subjects. Its examples are research methodology, management science and

Careerology. Subject bundles are loosely assembled multi-disciplinary mission oriented grossly practical subjects. Some examples are ocean science, space science, and Antarctica expedition, Sinology, West Asia studies, International agency projects fall in this category.

These are the latest subjects emerging as a result of multi-disciplinary team research what D. J. Solla price called "Big Science".

The scale of the progressive cohesiveness or integration of subjects as given by Iyer is modified to make it more comprehensive.[11]

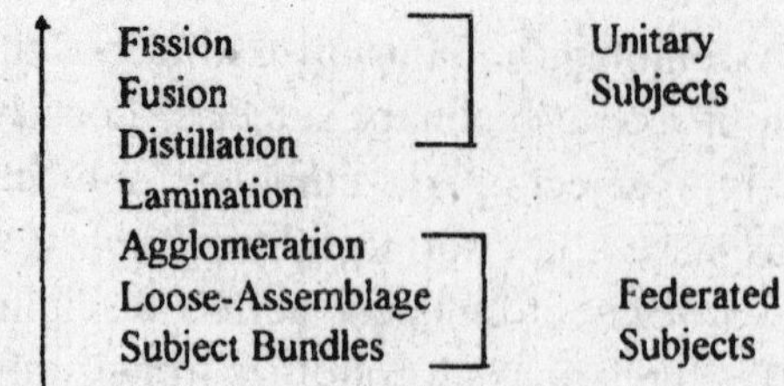

The scale shows the increasing order of internal cohesiveness

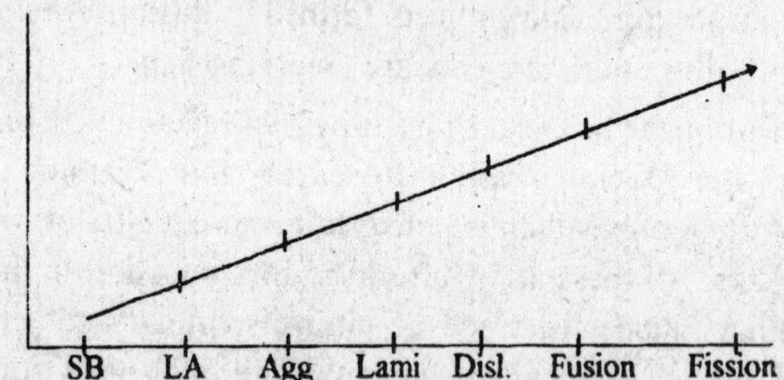

ORDER OF BASIC SUBJECTS

Ranganathan lay, much emphasis on the arrangement of basic subjects in his C.C. For him essence of library classification lies in a helpful sequence. The CC provides objective solutions to unravel the web of intricate relations in knowledge and represents them in some linear form. It has been explicitly stated that CC has two roots, one root feeds from the Vedic culture of

India. But the predominantly influential ideas and methods are from the current western thoughts; Vedic division of knowledge only adds it own colour and flavour.[12] Ranganathan's first division is into traditional disciplines, which Ranganathan arranges in the order of their evolution as studies, viz.

Science and Technology

Humanities

Social Sciences

Social Sciences are the latest academic discipline, whereas science and technology were studies of even the primitive man.

Within each discipline, the CC has an order based on objectively stated principles. Sciences (including technology) denoted by the alphabets A/M, have been arranged in the order of increasing concreteness: B Mathematics is the most abstract of the sciences while M Useful Arts (which includes crafts and applied technologies) is the most concrete in the group. Within this arrangement the theory and practice alternate: theory always preceding practice or its applications. For example, B Mathematics precedes C Physics; which in turn precedes D Engineering. E Chemistry precedes chemical technology. F Similarly I Botany precedes J Agriculture. This internal arrangement is by the principle of dependency first put forth by Auguste Comte (1798-1857). Unlike Dewey, Ranganathan preferred to collocate theory and practice of a subject. Indeed the Library of Congress classification earlier followed this principle. In humanities which spreads over to the main classes N/S, the arrangement is in the order of increasing richness of subject contents.

N Fine arts

O/P Literature, and Linguistics

Q Religion

R Philosophy

S Psychology

The order in the social sciences denoted by the main classes, T/Z is of increasing artificiality of the contents:

T Education

U Geography

V History

W Political Science

X Economics

Y Sociology

Z Law

One may find many faults with the arrangement of social sciences. Economic and social laws are not artificial – these are based on human nature. R S Parkhi (1901-1968) in an article published prior to the release of CC (1933) commended the arrangement of main classes as logical and evolutionary[13]. Elucidating his viewpoint he described Generalia class as complete microscopic view of knowledge preceding entire knowledge. Physical sciences C/F, study the mater and forces which constitute this universe. B Mathematics pervades every science. G Biology is vital science. H/K are in evolutionary order of life on the earth. L/P classes are application subjects for the well being and prosperity of humankind. Q Religion to T Education are for the moral and mental development of individuals, which in fact depend upon the correct application of L/P classes, which in turn feed upon classes A/K. Class U/Z study the geographical and social sciences–latest areas of knowledge to engage the human minds. Here W Politics (and Government) precedes the wealth creation and distribution X (Economics), and Y Sociology. Z Law keeps the society intact and going.

Later Ranganathan added a very unique main class Δ Spiritual experience and mysticism [denoted by the Greek alphabet Δ (Delta)]. Its position between sciences on one side and humanities and social sciences on the other is quite significant. Diagrammatically the arrangement of main classes may be represented as

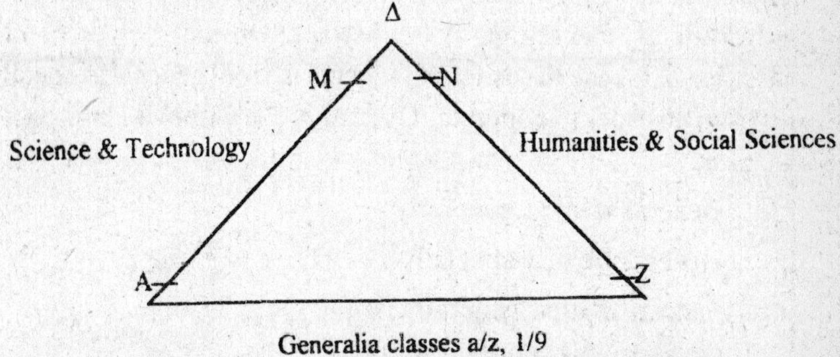

Generalia classes a/z, 1/9

Δ is on the confluence of these two different streams of sciences and humanities– the two different cultures of C P Snow (1905-1980). Ranganathan treats spiritual experience as the fountain head of all knowledge and thus refutes Snow's theory. This division has been influenced by Vedic system that is responsible for the spread out of the subjects into two halves as understood today. As we move from the end of each half to the middle, the subjects of each half culminate in the central subject Δ spiritual experience and mysticism[14].

The great classification philosopher and classificationist H E Bliss (1870-1955) endeavoured to discover a permanent main class order based upon scientific and educational consensus. This consensus can never be permanent, even if it exists. Ranganathan based his order on some concrete and objectively stated principles. These principles are helpful in placing newly emerging main classes at their logical places in the area of main classes. In CC-7 the number of basic subjects has been raised to about eight hundred without any problem of assigning them their right place in the array of basic subjects.

Principle of Inversion

The CC follows the Principle of Inversion which was first used by the UDC. In Ranganathan's famous PMEST formula

(i. e., the citation order) the categories have been arranged in the order of their decreasing concreteness. [P] Personality is the most concrete and [T] Time is the most abstract. [E] Energy lying midway is as concrete as it is abstract. On the shelves or in a classified database the order of subjects is from general to specific i.e. from abstract to concrete. Overall order within a class comes out to be:

General treated generally

General treated specially

Special treated generally

Special treated specially

This order has been achieved by ingeniously fixing the value of the indicator digits.

Syntax of Facets

In the facet formula a category may manifest itself in more than one facet. This phenomena has been accounted for by his postulate of rounds and levels. For example, in O Literature the category [P] personality occurs four times in what is called four levels. In "treatment of human diseases", diseases and treatment both are manifestation of energy described as first and second rounds of energy respectively. These rounds and levels of facets are usually arranged by the dependency principle named as Wall-Picture principle. Since there cannot be any mural without a wall, so wall will be the first facet. The master Wall-Picture principle has various corollaries formulated in the following axiomatically worded principles.

Whole-Organ principle	(Whole-part relation)
Cow-Calf principle	(Principle of Appurtenance)

A complex assimilating the above principles is

Actand-Action-Actor-Tool Principle.

It can be obtained by repeated applications of the Wall-Picture principle[15].

Absolute Syntax

In his spirited quest for discovering some natural order of facets, Ranganathan mooted the idea of "absolute syntax of facets". He wanted to discover what he called "hidden roots of classification". He was enormously enamored by a harmonious order of facets that "yields a sequence of subjects giving satisfaction to majority of readers"[16] He was of the opinion that to establish an enduring and helpful classification a vast team of experts of epistemology, Psychology, linguistics, statistics and library science be constituted to discuss the ways the human intellect works today. By the absolute syntax he meant a sequence in which component facets of a subject "arrange themselves in the minds of majority of person."[17] It may be different from the linguistic syntax. He conjectured that absolute syntax may be the "same for a large majority of persons irrespective of their mother tongue"[18]. He further believed that it is the syntax which comes closer to his own PMEST citation order arrived at by rigorous postulates and principles. Yet there is no empirical evidence. The basic question is whether there exists any such absolute syntax of ideas in the minds of the majority of adults free from the incessant impact of the mother tongue grammar impressed in the minds since infancy in human beings? There is no evidence that it exists at all. Nevertheless, Iyer asserts that "If a particular way of structuring a subject can be easily understood in translation to another language, regardless of the linguistic variations of individual tongues, then an absolute syntax may exist at some level."[19] Maltby truly points outs that Ranganathan believed in synthesis of knowledge than in its mere division for mapping and information retrieval.[20] This makes the search for the absolute syntax of ideas worth the pursuit.

Bond Strength

In 1965 at the time of Rutgers University Seminar on the Intellectual Organization of Information, Ranganathan mooted an idea of the "Bond strength" between facets (analogous to the molecular bond strength)[21]. The purpose seemed to quantify the force of cohesion between facets to study the structure for subjects in practical applications in information retrieval. He postulated that the bond strength between basic facet and [P] facet is the greatest and goes on weakening as we move towards [T]. The bond strength between components of a complex class is the least; and bond strength of a fissioned subject is more than a compound (laminated subject). Bond strength of the (ACIs) is more than the (PCIs). The facets with weaker bond strength are need of the minority specialists only.[22] It also follows the principle of inversion. Though interesting in itself. Ranganathan was not sure whether it will lead to new results[23].

APUPA Pattern

Ranganathan was not content with this broader though thoroughly formalised order. Within a given specific class he arranged documents on the shelves or their surrogates in, what is now termed by a famous acronym APUPA pattern. These initials stand for different pockets of subject in a given class as we move along the shelves. A is alien or related subject zone; P is Penumbral region; U is the Umbral region having core documents on the subjects. The terms have obviously been borrowed from astronomy. General Apupa pattern has been achieved by postulating two kinds of common auxiliaries (called common isolates in the CC):

Anteriorising Common Isolates (ACIs)

Posteriorising Common Isolates (PCIs)

Common isolates are like standard sub-divisions or common auxiliaries attachable to any class irrespective of its specificity. Documents fitted with (ACIs) are not the subject proper but approaches to reach or learn a subject. ACIs include bibliographies, synopses, histories, statistics on the subject. These are filed anterior to the subject proper. This forms the penumbral region i.e. having less of the subjects proper. Then follows the subject proper with all its sub-divisions. This could be the basic and compound subjects constituting the umbral region in the pattern. It is then followed by another penumbral region formed by fitting documents (of the Umbral region) with PCIs. Documents fitted with PCIs file in the posterior position to the umbral region. These are documents about the subject and are supposed to be read after the core subject by advance students or researcher. These include documents such as educational and research institutes on the subject, critical reviews and recent advances in the subject. Thus umbral region is surrounded by two different penumbral regions on both the sides which in turn are sandwiched between two different alien regions. APUPAPUPAP.

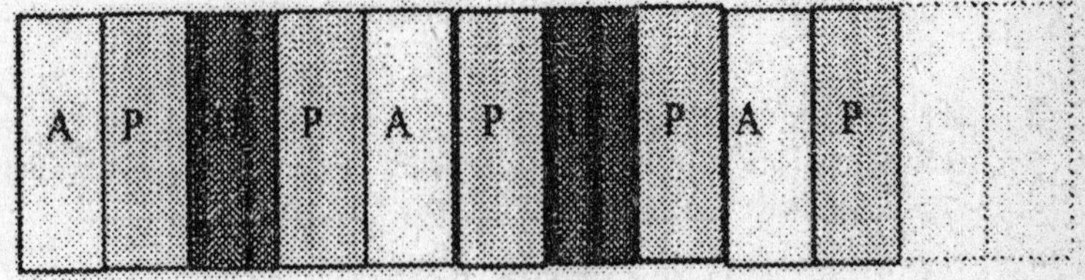

Going beyond this Ranganathan albeits that arrangement is "everywhere -APUPA."[24] It depends upon the reader's interest. Core documents of immediate interest to a reader anywhere on the shelf form the Umbral region which will invariably be surrounded by documents of lesser interest forming Penumbral region. On the left of the left Penumbral and right of the right Penumbral regions in turn will form Alien areas. This arrangements is of course automatically set forth by the arrangement of general to specific. So in the CC, Apupa prevails at every point.

Apupa pattern is one of the finely logical and pedagogically useful arrangement of documents on the shelves in an open access library.[25] It beautifully and uniformly weaves a useful pattern of the documents on the shelves or their surrogates in a bibliography. The arrangement is so impeccable that it is apt to say that to browse a CC classified library is itself an education. This has been achieved by investigating deeply the structures of knowledge and arranging its components in a way most useful to most of the users. For this he evolved apt principles and tools. It is fit to conclude with Fran Miksa that Ranganathan "treated library classification as a single unified structure of ideas which followed from a cohesive set of basic principles."[26]

REFERENCES

1. Francis Miksa. The DDC, the Universe of knowledge and the post modern library. (Albany, N. Y. : Forest Press/OCLC, 1998), p. 67
2. S.R. Ranganathan. Prolegomena to library classification, 3rd ed. (Bombay : Asia, Sec, Cr3.)
3. S. R. Ranganathan. Colon Classification, 7th ed. edited by M A Gopinath. (Bangalore: Sarada Ranganathan Endowment, 1987) p. 66-68.
4. Ibid, Sec.De71, p. 67.
5. S.R. Ranganathan. A descriptive account of the Colon Classification. (Bombay : Asia, Sec. K01 1965) p-96.
6. S.R. Ranganathan, Op cit. cap Dp, p 106.
7. D.W. Langridge, ed. Universe of knowledge. (University of Maryland, 1969 p, 2.).
8. S.R. Ranganathan (1967). Op cit. Sec. pa 3.
9. M.P. Satija. "Anatomy of the evolution and growth of knowledge." *Lucknow Librarian* 24(2) April, 1992. p. 49-57.
10. Hemalata Iyer. Classificatory structures, concepts, relations and representations (Frankfurt a/m : Indeks verlag, 1995) p. 19.
11. Iyer, Hemalata. Ibid, p.20.
12. S. R. Ranganathan (1987) Op cit. Sec. DB2, p. 52.
13. R. S. Parkhi, "Colon Scheme of Library Classification." *Modern Libn.* 3(2) : 87,
14. Ibid. Sec. DB 2, p. 52.
15. S. R. Ranganathan Op cit. Sec. Rn3.
16. Ibid. Sec. XJI.
17. Ibid. Sec. XJ3.
18. Ibid. Sec. XJ3.
19. Hemalata. Iyer Op cit. sec 11.4. p. 184

20. Matltby, Arthur. Sayers manual of classification for librarians. 5th ed. London : Andress Deutsch, 1975. p. 273.

21. S.R. Ranganathan. Op cit. Chap.V.

22. S. R. Ranganathan. Op cit Sec. WB 32.

23. Ibid, Sec RQ3.

24. S.R. Ranganathan. Classification and communication (Bangalore : Sarada Ranganathan Endowment, 1981), p. 228.

25. M.P. Satija. Colon classification, 7th ed: a practical introduction, (New Delhi : Ess Ess 1989), 57.

26. Miksa, Francis L. op cit 67.

IV : 4
Hierarchical Retrieval and Classification

V. Vishwa Mohan
J. Yadagiri Reddy

The superiority of library classification in document organization and retrieval was indisputable. Achieving perfect collocation of documents with the help of class numbers is well demonstrated by Ranganathan. His demonstration also proved how alphabetical arrangement causes scatter among the books belonging to the same class with different names and also books belonging to a chain and array of classes. Since books are arranged under classified order, in order to help retrieve books with other approaches, viz., author, title and subject (word) approaches, library catalogues played a key role. But still card catalogues as retrieval tools had their own limitations. However, machine retrieval provided many more retrieval options and capabilities. Retrieval became easy with search strategies such as Boolean logic searching, truncated searching, free-text searching, etc. However, information retrieval with key words or subject headings or key words with weightages, combination of key words have got their own limitations. Of late, hierarchical searching has been identified as one of the key issues in cataloguing/indexing systems. Perreault states, "Searching such a database as PsycInfo in DIALOG can be frustrating in that hierarchical search is not available. Documents headed Neuroleptic drugs (till recently Antipsychotic drugs) will only be documents bearing that general heading and a search under that heading will not necessarily retrieve those headed chlorpromazine, chlorprothixene, etc. There are 14 drug names in the 1974 edition of the *American Psychological Association Thesaurus* that are narrower terms subsumed under Neuroleptic drugs, with two more in the not wholly coterminous list subsumed under Antipsychotic drugs there. In order to be sure of retrieving all that is available on the *general* concept, at least sixteen *specific* drug names must be searched on as well." This being the kind of frustration Perreault expresses, imagine the case of searching with hundred and odd names under a general concept. For instance, the general concept "Diseases" has several specific disease names. *The Sears List of Subject Headings* presents the following under the subject heading 'Diseases'.

Sears List of Subject Headings 16 Edition*		*DDC 20th Ed. Nos.*
Diseases		**614.4; 616**
UF	Illness	
	Sickness	
SA	names of animals, classes of persons, and parts of the body with the subdivision *Diseases*, types of diseases, and names of Specific diseases, to be added as needed	
NT	**AIDS (Disease)**	**616.979 2**
	Animals—Diseases	**591.2**
	Arthritis	**616.722**
	Blood—Diseases	**616.15**
	Brain—Diseases	**616.8**
	Cancer	**616.994**
	Chickenpox	**616.914**
	Children—Diseases	**618.92**
	Cold (Disease)	**616.205**
	Communicable diseases	**616.9**
	Diphtheria	**616.9313**
	Elderly—Diseases	**618.97**
	Epidemics	**616.9**
	Heart diseases	**616.12**

Sears List of Subject Headings 16 Edition*	*DDC 20th Ed. Nos.*
Hyperactivity	616.858 9
Infants—Diseases	618.92
Influenza	616.203
Lungs—Diseases	616.24
Lyme disease	616.92
Men—Diseases	
Mental illness	616.89
Nervous system—Diseases	616.8
Occupational diseases	616.980 3
Plant diseases	581.2
Poliomyelitis	616.835
Rheumatism	616.723
Skin—Diseases	616.5
Teeth—Diseases	617.63
Typhoid fever	616.927 2
Women—Diseases	618.1
RT Health	
Medicine	
Pathology	
Sick	

The above list of subject headings is not an exhaustive one. Since there are names of several specific diseases and parts of the body with the subdivision 'Diseases', the above list is only an illustrative one. Hence, searching for all the divisions under the broader class 'Diseases' will be laborious, time consuming and certainly frustrating. Enabling hierarchical searching with key words or subject headings would be a Herculean task because the key words/subject headings lack the nature, quality and structure of hierarchy. It is the notation which is used for library classification that has hierarchical notation. Therefore, it has hierarchical quality. As a result, library classification provides a better solution for hierarchical retrieval even in the age of machine retrieval (through bibliographic databases) besides facilitating mechanized arrangement of documents in hierarchical order on the shelves.

It is well known that alphabetical sequences give rise to scatter among the related classes, particularly the classes which belong to the chain of classes whereas the classified number sequence ensures collocation of coordinate, subordinate and all related classes. This proved to be an advantage for collocation of documents on the shelves in a library. But, document retrieval with the help of conventional catalogues proved to have certain limitations with regard to maximum recall value as there was also a limitation to the cross-reference entries because no catalogue would be in a position to provide all possible cross-reference entries. Even if a catalogue provides exhaustive number of cross-reference entries for Narrow Terms, which stand for the subdivisions of a class, the amount of time taken to retrieve all the classes in chain of classes would be considerably more. Machine retrieval of bibliographic information from the bibliographic databases proved to have ensured more recall value and retrieval efficiency taking very less time. But, machine searching also turned out to be laborious and time consuming for hierarchical retrieval with the help of subject headings or key words, in spite of having truncated search facility, for the simple reason that the truncated letter or combination of letters or words may not form the subdivisions part of the subject headings which belong to a chain of classes. For instance, from the list of subject headings presented earlier, when we truncate the term 'Diseases' viz. Diseases* (* for truncation symbol) there may not be retrieval of any entries because, the *Sears List of Subject Headings* has no other subject headings following the heading 'Diseases' with any other extensions of the heading/word. Therefore, there is no chance of retrieval of entries on AIDS, Arthritis, Blood— Diseases, etc. though they are the subdivisions of the class 'Diseases'. Of course, ultimately the retrieval efficiency depends on the type of indexing language or system used. Because the very nature and form of the subject headings is not hierarchical, hierarchical retrieval will not be possible with the help of subject headings even if it is machine searching. Hierarchical retrieval would be very easy and effective when class numbers form the access points in the bibliographic databases. When we truncate the class number 616* and make the search, we will be in a position to retrieve all the subdivisions of the class 616, in other words, all the entries bearing the class numbers with the subdivisions of 616 class viz. 616.979 2; 616.15; 616.8; etc.

The capabilities of library classification for hierarchical retrieval are immense even with the conventional card catalogues, in other words, manual retrieval is also effective with the help of library classification. Ranganathan demonstrated the same through his classified part of the classified catalogue. Class numbers as the access points or indexing language provide high rate of recall value, especially with machine retrieval, because, when a class number is truncated all the extensions of that number can be retrieved resulting in exhaustive retrieval of all the subordinate classes. To ensure precision value, retrieval with the specific class number would prove to be the best. Therefore, document classification does not only facilitate arrangement of documents in a filiatory helpful sequence on the shelves, it also acts as better indexing language and thereby a better retrieval system/language. When class numbers form one of the bibliographic data elements in MARC records, hierarchical retrieval of these databases will not be a problem at all.

BIBLIOGRAPHY

1. Classified Catalogue Code : with additional rules for Dictionary Catalogue Code/S. R. Ranganathan -5 ed.- Bangalore : Sarada Ranganathan Endowment for Library Science. 1988 (Reprint)
2. Dewey Decimal Classification and Relative Index / devised by Melvil Dewey . - 20"h ed. / edited by John P. Comaromi ... [et al] . - New York : Forest Press. 1989.
3. Prolegomena to library classification / S. R. Ranganathan -3' ed.- Bombay : Asia Publishing House. 1967.

4. Sears List of Subject Headings. - 16th ed / edited by Joseph Miller. - New York : The Wilson Co., 1997.

5. Some perils of the "User - friendly" attitude in cataloguing / Jean M. Perreault. *Advances in Librarianship* edited by Wesley Simonton. - Orlando : Academic Press, 1986. P. 285-303.

V : 1

Microforms and Their Impact on Five Laws of Library Science

P. Venkataramana
L.S.R.C.V. Ramesh

INTRODUCTION

Library is the repository of information. The volume of information being generated around the world is increasing exponentially, doubling in something between three and seven years. Libraries receiving enormous quantity of documents have to process and organize them efficiently in order to provide relevant documents and need-based information to users effectively and instantly. The magnitude of information generated and its proliferation into many forms have created problems of storage, processing, retrieval and dissemination. Libraries are trying to overcome these problems by adopting modern technologies like microforms, computerization, CD-ROMs, networks, etc. Libraries use microfilming technology to preserve information materials and to protect the fragile originals from excessive use and consequently from damage. Documents in poor condition are consulted only on microfilm. Microfilm is an economic storage medium that meets not only the high demands of scientific research regarding quality of reproduction but also the strict durability requirements of a conservation strategy. Miniaturization of documents can probably be found in the microforms field where filming of documents resulted in tremendous reduction in filing and storage area needs. In addition to excellent space utilization, microforms provide efficient storage, fast retrieval, archival quality, durability and security as well as other benefits.

Libraries in the western countries have large collections of millions of books and other media documents. The space problem in their libraries is very acute because of their large acquisition programs. USA is at the top, making innovations and exploring new avenues in information storage and retrieval.

Microform literature is a small portion of the vast field of published knowledge. However, it is a significant segment of it. In India the problem of space is not so acute as in Western countries but at the same time the profession feels that it should not be complacent over the matter and should embark upon to make a beginning to avoid future space problems in libraries as well as to provide better services to readers by providing reading materials in microforms.

OVERVIEW OF MICROFORM DEVELOPMENTS

It is ascribed that micro writing was known to the ancients. Excavation at Ninevah is said to have recorded clay cylinders containing minute inscriptions. Robert Hooke (1665) discusses the application of miniatured handwriting for transmitting secret messages. In 1839 John Benjamin Dancer of Manchester, England, installed a microscope lens in a camera and created the first microphotograph.

The conversion of document images to microfilm began in the 1920's and this technology is now well developed. In 1929 the League of Nations Committee of Library Experts investigated the suitability of microfilms for documentation. During the late 1930's libraries began making microfilm copies of rare documents, newspaper files, etc., as a means of conserving storage space and preservation as the paper copies generally has a rapid decomposition rate. By the 1959s there was a widespread realization that microfilm could be used not only for the preservation of oversized or rare documents but as an integral part of active information systems. During 1960s introduction of large scale improvements in equipment and materials, and availability of less expensive reader printers contributed to the increased application of microforms in libraries. The most important development during this decade was that the micrographics technology and Electronic Data Processing (EDP) which were combined to permit direct recording on microforms the results of computer manipulated data. This was the beginning of Computer Output Microfilm (COM). During early 1970s, standardization of microforms and portable microform readers enabled us in handling of microform documents. By 1972, micropublishing has received unprecedented emphasis with more than 50 million worth of microforms being produced annually in the United States. A considerable number of books, journals and newspapers are now available in microforms. Today microforms are widely used in industry, government and education.

TYPES OF MICROFORMS

* Roll film
* Micro card
* Microfiche
* Ultrafiche
* Aperture cards
* Ultrastrips
* Chips
* Jackets.

AREAS OF APPLICATION

1 Microforms are used where information cannot be produced in the book in an economical way.

2 For acquiring copies of documents whose originals cannot be obtained, for preservation purposes, when documents are in fragile condition.

3 Where the information would not be generally available except for the use of microforms.

4 Where documents are constituted of materials which deteriorate rapidly such as newspapers, etc.,

5 Where time can be saved, for example, foreign reports and theses can be acquired in microfiche which can be rapidly flown.

6 For production of multiple copies of documents.

ADVANTAGES OF MICROFORMS IN LIBRARIES

1 Decreasing pressure on space as records on microfilm need only 4 percent of the space occupied by the same records on paper.

2 Microform materials need no binding.

3 Replacement of a lost volume is possible with least cost.

4 Reduction of considerable floor weight loading.

5 Substantial reduction in inter- library loan costs.

6 Theft and mutilation can be overcome.

7 Reduction in building and maintenance costs.

8 Time can be saved by acquiring reports and theses in microformats cheaply and rapidly by air mail.

9 Duplicate microfilm files can be prepared at nominal cost.

10 Records on microfilm are in a fixed sequence thereby guarding against misfiling, mislaying, alteration or loss.

11 Access to complete back sets of periodicals.

12 Easy to handle, use and store information.

13 Attractive packaging and durability.

14 Easy to obtain hard copy with the help of reader and printer.

15 Microfilm will provide an archival record of historical significance to future researchers.

DISADVANTAGES

1 It cannot be read with naked eye.

2 Access to information conditioned by mechanical equipment.

3 Staff time required for assistance in proper use of the equipment.

4 Continuous exposure to light causes eye strain.

5 Equipment cost is not within the reach of users for personal ownership.

6 Like books, microforms are not amenable for note making and inserting book marks.

7 File integrity problems for fiche formats may require closed access stack service.

8 Cost of services may increase as air-conditioning the microform collection is essential.

9 Automated microfilm readers are noisy and take-up considerable space themselves.

IMPACT OF MICROFORMS ON FIVE LAWS OF LIBRARY SCIENCE

The changes in the physical forms of document have a bearing on the Five Laws of Library Science.

Books are for Use

Microforms definitely help to observe this Law in a limited sphere. There are valuable documents which by their age and physical deterioration are likely to be preserved rather than used. These documents in course of time become ornamental and later wither away. By implication, "Books are for use" means only books which are in sound condition are meant for use.

Microforms can step in such cases to rejuvenate the document and activise its use. With modern equipment, most of it is semi-automatic. Large quantities of endangered documents can be recorded on film relatively in a short time. In this way, the microfilming of unique historic documents helps not only to protect the originals but also to improve accessibility and use for researchers/users.

Every Reader His/Her Document

Here again microforms help the users. The modern libraries have rejected the theory of self-sufficiency of resources in terms of individual libraries. This is an inevitable outcome owing to financial limitation. However, user needs should be satisfied. Library cooperation at various levels is the answer. But there are many hurdles that come in the way of promoting library cooperation especially with regard to inter library lending. One of the prerequisites of inter library lending is the availability of multiple copies. In case the document is in single copy or the physical condition is alarming the chances of procuring the document is altogether ruled out.

Another factor that has to be taken into account in inter-library loans is that the document should be procured with speed and least cost. It is here the microforms enable the libraries to get the required materials speedily at the least cost.

Every Book its Reader

To increase the chances of user getting the right document, many practices are common between conventional documents and microforms. But the real problems appear in the matter of open access system. In an open access situation, the users can browse in the process of selection of a document The users, of course, experience frustrating moments, but sometimes come across many "Eurekas" when they discover a document better than what they are searching for. There is a sense of personal freedom enjoyed by the user when he moves from rack to rack or room to room. This is another major limitation of the microforms.

Save the Time of the User/Staff

In support of this law, a distinction is made between subjective objective time. In library situations the user is mostly swayed by the subjective time. The thirst for information is short-lived. In serving the user to save the time he should be helped in the first instance (1) to locate the document, (2) to use it and (3) to take it out if he desires to do so. In all he should not feel that he is wasting his time. In the first approach there is not much of difference between the conventional document and microforms. With regard to the second one, more time is lost in reading the microforms, because straight away they cannot be used without the help of the machine. User's time can be saved by acquiring reports and theses in microformats cheaply and speedily by air-mail.

Library is a Growing Organism

The protagonists of microforms find fertile logic under Fifth Law "Library is a growing organism" The growth of library is organic and multidimensional. There is growth in the size of the readers, documents and physical facilities like buildings. The increased users and document demand more space. But physical facilities generally do not grow correspondingly. While allowing the growth, space should be saved in order to store more documents. The answer is found in microforms. If you are thinking of a complete microform library, the stacks will look like an island and the working rooms look more predominant. Now our stock rooms stand out mostly full of books and all other things exist in order to serve them.

THE FUTURE OF MICROFORMS

Microforms still retain their place despite the appearance of new digital media. Interfacing of microforms with other technologies is of more recent origin. The future of microforms depends on the developments that are taking place in related technologies to evolve absolute compatibility for interfacing. Digital information transmission through word processors, COM, CAR, etc., has succeeded in facsimile transmission of information records across distances linked by telephone cables. Updatable microfilm has been successfully developed for handling information records requiring frequent revision changes. This holds a great promise for the development of many micrographic systems. The future is for high technology micro-electronics and communication in technology in the arena of information management in modern libraries. The greatest advantage of microfilming technology over digital imaging technology (computers, optical disc) is that microfilm images are basically photographic images. Hence they will not get affected or destroyed accidentally due to system failure/electrical/magnetic field disturbances, etc. The only case necessary to preserve the microfilm document is to store them in air-conditioned atmosphere to keep humidity, dust and temperature under control. Microfilms can be preserved safely for long periods as long as they are stored in air-conditioned rooms. In principle microfilm systems are not likely to undergo any basic technical change and are compatible with the new digital systems. So in an information society despite rapid changes in technology, microfilm is the ideal upwardly compatible storage medium for the long-term needs.

MICROFORMS CANNOT BE SUBSTITUTE FOR BOOKS

The value of microforms has to be judged from the angle of economic advantages and not to be treated as a substitute for book. Nobody likes microforms except as a matter of necessity. To quote "Teague" in this context, the impersonal unlovely microfilm, requiring effort to read as a specially manufactured piece of equipment, will never compete with the sensuous feel of a book, nor will it ever view with the aesthetic reward in reading fine type beautifully imprinted on well-made paper. Which in itself adds to the transfer of information, positive reading enjoyment.

CONCLUSION

It is finally concluded that indiscriminate buying of all microforms should be stopped. The criterion of purchase should be based on the assessment of the demand. The material which is in constant demand should be bought in book form and less used may be bought in microform. The microforms are not to be treated as substitutes for books. They are complementary to books. For long time to come, the book is bound to be predominate factor in the communication process. In some libraries, the existence and use of both are necessary. In the composition of the documents what should be the ratio of each type of documents is very difficult to judge. This is linked with the type of library we are referring to. In Indian context, the use of microforms will be confined to university libraries and a few special libraries. In many libraries where the economic conditions have been steadily deteriorating, microforms are the only viable alternative since the relative inconvenience of utilizing microforms is preferable to doing without. The microform image will definitely move from the innovation stage to a condition of acceptance and widespread adoption. As Kleukens and Goebel predicted more than forty years ago, we have entered a third technological era in communication dominated by film and electronic media, and thus the chronicled history of microforms is but one page in an ongoing epoch. Microforms are useful for both library and information management. Microfilms provide great advantage of space saving and archival preservation of valuable documents in the libraries. Microfilm documents can be used for inter-library loans. Mailing microforms is far more cheaper than paper documents. Microfilm duplication is inexpensive; any number of copies can be made and distributed by air-mail. Thus, microforms offer a new dimension for better information management in modern libraries.

REFERENCES

1. Ashby, P (1979). Microform Publishing. London, Butterworths.
2. Avedon, D M (1979). Microforms as library tools. *Library Trends*. Vol 30, p 253-265.
3. Claridge, P R P (1969). Microfiching of periodicals from users point of view. *Aslib Proceedings*. V 21, p 306.
4. Diaz Albert Jams, *ed* (1975). Microforms in Libraries-a reader. London. Mansell.
5. Fussler, Herman H (1976). Microfilm and libraries. *In* Studies micropublishing. Ed A B Veaner, London Mansel Information.
6. Gabriel, Michael R and Ladd, Durathy P (1980). The Microform revolution in libraries. Connecticut. Jai Press.

7. Gaddy, D (1974). Microform handbook. *Maryland*. National Microfilm Association.
8. Lewis. R W. Users reaction to microfiche - a preliminary study. *College and Research Libraries*. V31. July 1920, p. 260-68.
9. Luther, M (1959). Microfilm: A history. Maryland National Microfilm Association.
10. Mehlan, Indervir (1978). Microfilms: their uses, abuses and user survey. *IASLIC Bulletin* V3. No.1.
11. Sridhar, M. S. (1982). "Prospects and problems of microforms in Libraries". *Journal of Library and Information Sciences* Vol 6. p 1-15.
12. Stevenson Rolland E. The microfilm revolution. *Library Trends*. Jan 1971. p. 379-349.
13. Teague, S J. (1977). Microfilm librarianship. London, Butterworths. chaps 1 and 2.
14. Williams, B J S. Microform in special libraries. *In* Handbook of special libraries. Ed W E Baten. London, ASLIB 1975.

V : 2
Preservation of Non-Book Materials

J. Vijaya Kumari

INTRODUCTION

Libraries are the store houses of knowledge and information. As such preservation of knowledge contained in various forms of documents, need to be cared, maintained properly to fulfil the knowledge thirst of future generations. Therefore, it is one of the primary task of the libraries to adopt adequate preventive measures to save the library documents from early decay.

NON-BOOK MATERIALS

Publications other than printed books or conventional documents are called non-book materials. They by virtue of their nature, scope, purpose, and structure require special treatment over books and periodicals in a library.

Harrod's Librarians Glossary refers them as "those library materials, which do not come within the definition of a book, periodical or pamphlet and which require special handling. Example: A/V material, microforms etc."

The term non-book material is closely associated with terms such as the new media, multimedia, non-print, special materials, etc.

Reasons for the Use of Non-book Materials

These are now used for several purposes.

(i) Space problem can be solved. For example a CD-ROM 4.72" in diameter, can store up to 2,50,000 pages of text and a microfiche can store a minimum of 98 pages of textual information.

(ii) Money savings i.e. cheaper than conventional documents.

For example:

	Normal price	*CD ROM price*
International Dictionary of Medicine and Biology	$ 395	$195
Groliers Encyclopaedia	$ 850	$ 299

Majority of the titles (5,325) on CD-ROM available at a cost range of US $ 1 to 500.

(iii) To preserve information which has been printed on poor quality and perishable paper.

(iv) To protect valuable information against loss. For example:

(a) one of the products of UMI is research collections in microform. They comprise old and rare books, periodicals, journals and other archival materials,

(b) UMI also produces more than 18,000 serial titles in microform.

(c) Since 1957, Inter Documentation Company, Switzerland has been building up an extensive collection of old and rare out-of-print titles of research material on microfiche.

(d) State Archives of Andhra Pradesh have also made a number of microfilm copies acquired from various sources including the India Office Library, London and the Saraswathi Mahal Library, Tanjavur in addition to old issues of newspapers. Important among the microfilms preserved are Saraswati Mahal Library collections, Sir Thomas Munro's Diary, Sri Gurazada

Appa Rao's diaries, Sadhanapatrika, Krishna Patrika, Andhra Patrika etc.

(v) To restore out of print books in print status. For example: Over 1,00,000 books are available as reprints through UMI's out of print books publishing service. The out of print books collection includes all earliest printed books of the 15th century as well as more than 20,000 upto-date books very recently declared out of print. (Some titles are also available on microfilm).

(vi) To replace large, bulky volumes (such as newspapers, encyclopaedias, etc.) with a compact form that is easier to handle and to use, etc. For example: Since 1965, Chemical Abstracts, published by American Chemical Society, has been available on microfilm. Now most of the information sources are available on CD-ROM form.

Types of non-Book Materials

These can be broadly divided into seven categories. They are:

(i) Still projection materials: Film strips, Slides, transparencies, projected opaque materials,

(ii) Motion projection materials: 33mm, 16 mm, standard 8 mm, super 8 mm films, video tapes, video discs.

(iii) Microforms: Microfilms, Microfiche, Microopaques.

(iv) Audio materials: Gramaphone records, audio tapes, audio cassettes, audio discs,

(v) Flat graphic materials: art and study prints, charts, map, pictures, photographs,

(vi) Three dimensional materials: globes, kits, models, realia.

(vii) Programmed materials.

Preservation of Non-Book Materials: General Considerations

There are certain basic considerations which are applicable to all non-book materials, and there are some well established principles from the preservation point of view. These are concerned with physical environment; security; circulation policy; maintenance and upkeep of equipments; storing; and handling.

Physical Environment

(i) **Temperature :** When dealing with various media forms, no single temperature can be prescribed, because the composition of each of the material is different from the other. The highest temperature recommended by various authorities for media forms is 75° F for videotapes and cassettes; for magnetic tapes the range is between 65° F and 68° F; while floppy disks can accommodate a range between 50° F and 125° F; for optical disks the range is between 5-50 degree Celsius not exceeding 70° F for microforms. Ideally, the temperature should be somewhere around 60° F as an optimum temperature, the whole range of media forms and for human comfort.

Whatever temperature is decided upon, it is important that it remains as constant as possible. Any fluctuations of more than a few degrees can harm materials. For this reason, the following precautions are needed:

(a) The collection should not be stored close to the doorways or windows;

(b) Where materials are removed for use from long storage, it will invariably cause temperature variation of more than a few degrees. Therefore, the material should not be put to use immediately. A process of 'staging' is required. It enables the item to adjust itself to the changed environment temperature in gradual steps.

(ii) **Relative Humidity :** Relative humidity is an expression of the moisture content of the atmospheric air. These non-book materials, like all book-materials, are sensitive to this factor. Here again, as in the case of temperature, there is no single relative humidity prescribed for all materials. However, a range of 45% + 5% relative humidity is considered suitable, with 47% as the optimum. For example in the case of microforms, above 60% relative humidity should be avoided, why because 60% relative humidity can completely destroy the image and below 40% can cause film to curl. High humidity encourages bacterial and fungal growth in discs and photographic emulsions and causes dampness to form between the layers of magnetic tape and the tape layers tend to stick together.

(iii) **Dust and other atmospheric pollutants:** No environment is completely dust and pollution free. Measures can be taken to minimise the effect. Dust can cause scratching, both on film and on disc. The fumes of either Hydrogen Sulphide or Sulphur Dioxide (these fumes may be hidden in air) can cause slow deterioration and gradual image fading of records. The air should be filtered, cleared, cleaned of injurious gases and circulated under slight positive pressure.

Air conditioning (which is the only means to control temperature and relative humidity) with filtration systems are beneficial.

Films, tapes should be stored in dust free containers. The polyester base attracts dust, which damages the film surface. Microforms should be stored in closed housings, in drawer type cabinets. They should not be stacked horizontally but shelved in the upright, vertical position to prevent wrappage. The microform enclosures should be made of acid free paper or plastic. Magnetic tapes should be enclosed in polyethylene bags and audio and video cassettes, optical disks should be kept in plastic containers. For removing dust from the disks, a soft, lint-free cloth should be used and wiping must be done in a circular motion from the centre to outer edges.

(iv) **Light :** Another environmental consideration concerns sunlight and excessive fluorescent lighting. These factors can damage all types of materials, for example: in case of film based materials it can cause fading of the images. Excessive heat, whether the sun or central heating, can cause disc to wrap, film to deteriorate, slides will turn dull and brown or yellow, so they should be stored at least one meter away from any other source of heat, and should be kept away from fluorescent lighting and also kept away from windows. Use of window curtains is also an effective option.

(v) **Magnetic Fields :** Many materials such as audiotapes, sound tracks of various media, video tapes etc. are on magnetic tapes or housed in electro-magnetic storage devices. The main problems with these magnetic recordings are undesirable erasing of the magnetic signals, separation of the emulsion from the base material, print through and tape breakage.

Audio and video tapes placed within any magnetic field will either be erased or will develop static charge. So they should be kept 3 to 4 metres away from magnetic fields and electric motors. In storing rewritable optical disks, magnets should not be allowed in the storage area.

Security

The preservation and conservation measures are designed to protect the materials from natural erosion, but security focuses on protection against human problems such as vandalism and pilferage. Therefore, the storage procedures should give serious attention to the security aspect.

It will be necessary to store materials in such a location and manner that these cannot be accessed without assistance from some members of the staff, and they are to be used only under their supervision. This is a basic difference between book and non-book access.

Original materials should not be accessed. There should always be at least 2 copies of the same document, one master and the other working copy. Master copies are seldom used or referred to. They are only used for duplicating purpose.

For cassette tapes it is preferable to display only the case with its leaflet, filing the cassette in a duplicate container, and accessible only to the staff, to prevent accidental erasure. Inspection of microform records should be undertaken approximately for every five years and copies are made if any deterioration has occurred.

Circulation Policy

In order to arrive at a common ground a balance between security and service has to be evolved This necessitates a well-thought-out circulation policy. In the process of evolving a judicious circulation policy, the fundamental consideration should be among others:

a. Whether or not a particular item should be permitted to be issued out from the library without involving any risk;

b. Are proper facilities available in the library for consultation of all non-book materials in-house;

c. The number of hours the collection is open for consultation;

d. Is it possible to identify some items which can be allowed to circulate outside, while keeping the others for in-house consultation only;

e. Has the library adequate staff to supervise in-house consultation of all non-book materials;

f. Has the particular user, who intends borrowing an item, the required equipment in perfect shape in his personal possession.

A strict in-house circulation policy has certain in-built advantages: but if such a policy is entirely guided by strict security and preservation considerations, it can be considered to be out of tune with the fundamental concept of libraries as user-oriented institutions

Maintenance and Upkeep of Equipments

Most of the non-book materials require additional equipments/Readers for their usage. These are too expensive also. For example: The microfilm reader costs Rs. 20,000 to Rs. 50,000/- depending upon the size, type and design. A reader printer costs Rs. 2 lakhs and above. In India, Hindustan Reprographic Ltd. is manufacturing the reader printer which costs about Rs. 2.50 lakhs. These items are all susceptible to damage caused by improperly maintained hardwares. Readers/equipments drives should be kept clean and in efficient working order.

Storing

It is now generally agreed that non-book materials like phonograph records, tapes, films etc. should be stored in a vertical position. Vertical storage will prevent wrapping of phonograph records, help protect tapes and films which are generally damaged by the excess weight on their edges when laid horizontally, slides and photographs are also best stored vertically. For materials specially like slides and prints, use of individual containers is very important. For photographs the use of acid-free envelopes made of plastic material is a convenient method of storing. Plastic resists moisture and will not grow misty with age. Interleaved acid-free black paper can help protect them from excessive light.

Cabinets are useful for housing slides, prints, negatives and other materials. The cabinets should be so designed as to ensure easy filing and access.

The photo duplication service of the LC is advising on the proper storage of non-book materials specially archival microforms.

Handling

Proper handling of non-book materials, which are mostly delicate, is extremely important. Handling involves both the user and the librarian. The user must know the correct handling procedure imparted to him by the librarian. Before educating the user, it is important that the librarian himself is fully aware of the proper handling of materials as well as of the hardware used. For this, proper training for them should be designed. For the users, it will be worthwhile to include maintenance brochures along with the materials for their guidance. While handling microforms, it is suggested that clean white cotton gloves have to be used.

The Department of Teaching Aids functioning under the NCERT is concerned with developing new instructional materials, providing training in theory, preparation and utilisation of A/V materials to teachers, information officers co-ordinators of extension education service departments, social workers, etc. and functioning as a clearing house for information relating to the A/V education. While handling films or magnetic tapes they should not be dropped. This may produce scratches on them. Never finger the film surface but always hold them by the edges and should not be twisted. Only qualified staff should be allowed to handle the media and the equipments.

CONCLUSION

It is the primary task of the libraries to pay proper attention in preservation of library reading materials so that the academic society could make the best use of the mankind's intellectual contribution. Baggs & Thompson have rightly observed that "these new services must be seen as an integral part of the library's role and adequate and continuing finance must be provided for them. Otherwise, as observed by the futurologists, the world in general will bypass those libraries which are not giving emphasis to non-book materials.

REFERENCES

1. Fothergill, Richard and Butchart, Ian, *Non-book materials in libraries: A practical guide*, 3rd ed (London: Clive Bingley, 1990.)
2. Weih, Jean et. al. *Non-book materials: The organisation of integrated collection*, 2nd ed. (Canadian Library Association, 1979.)

3. Teague, S. J. *Microforms, Video and Electronic Media Librarianship.* (London: Butterworths, 1985.)

4. B. P. Chakrabarty, et. al. "Measuring the quality of audio-visual services with particular reference to the storage of microforms in Indian Libraries", *ILA Bulletin*, 23(1&2), 42-51, (1987.)

V : 3

Non-Book Materials Among College Libraries in Karnataka State

B.S. Maheswarappa
P.G. Tadasad

INTRODUCTION

Education is recognized as the most important prerequisite for achieving economic, social, technological progress of a nation. It has three essential roles to play viz., providing information, providing skills for changing the behavior and attitude [1]. Libraries have a pivotal role in enhancing the qualitative dimensions of these roles, perhaps more so in respect of providing information. Information is considered as a national resource. Therefore, the libraries that aid in providing information go a long way in contributing to the development of a nation. But the information is available in various forms. Books, non-book materials, non-print materials, electronic, digital, non-book materials have much potential for library use because of the storage and retrieval capacity. Hence, an attempt is made in this article to discuss the availability of non-book materials based on the information collected from 571 college libraries in Karnataka state.

RESULTS AND DISCUSSION

About three-fourth of college libraries (72.15% ~N=412) do not have non-book materials in their collections. The collection of non-book materials was less than thousand in more than one-fourth of college libraries (26.79% ~N=153) and it ranged between 1001-2000 and more than two thousand in case of three college libraries each (0.53% ~N=3) (vide table-1).

Non-book materials were not found in half of the college libraries that have been established before 1900 (50% ~N =1) four-fifth of libraries that have been set up during 1901-1925 (80% ~N=4), more than three fifth of libraries established between 1926-1950 (61.54% ~N=16) and 1951-1975 (65.89% ~N=114), three-fourth of college libraries set up after 1975(75.89% ~N=277). Half of the college libraries estabishes before 1900 (~N = 1), more than one third establishe between 1926-1950 (38.46%, ~N = 10), less than one third set up during 1951-1975 (31.79%, ~N = 55). Non-book materials ranging between 1001-2000 were found in a small proportion of college libraries established during 1951-1975 (1.16% ~N=2) and after 1975 (0.25% ~N=1). One fifth of college libraries set up during 1901-1925 (20% ~N=1) and a small proportion of college libraries (1.16% ~N=2) established during 1951-1975 have more than 2000 non-book materials (vide Table-1).

Table-2 provides university-wise information about the strength of non-book materials in college libraries. Nearly three fifth of libraries of colleges affiliated to Mysore (59.65% ~N=34), more than four fifth of libraries of colleges affiliated to Karnataka (80.89% ~N=12), less than three fourth affiliated to Bangalore (73.26% ~N=96), more than three fifth affiliated to Mangalore (61.54% ~N-45), less than three fourth affiliated to Gulbarga (70.51% ~N=55), and Kuvempu (74.29% ~N=52) Universities do not have non-book materials in their collection, while it was less than thousand in more than one third of libraries of colleges of Mysore (36.84% ~N=21), less than one fifth of Karnataka (18.95% ~N=29), more than one fourth of Bangalore (26.72% ~N=35), more than one third of Mangalore (37.18% ~N=29), more than one fourth of Gulbarga (28.21% ~N=22), and nearly one fourth of Kuvempu (24.29% ~N=17) University's. A very few libraries of colleges affiliated to Mysore (1.75% ~N=1), Mangalore (1.28% ~N=1); and Gulbarga (1.28% ~N=1) Universities have non-book materials ranging between 1001-2000 in their collection, while still fewer libraries of colleges affiliated to Mysore (1.75% ~N=1) Karnataka (0.64% ~N=1) and Kuvempu (1.42% ~N=1) have more than 2000 non-book materials in their collection.

More than three fifth of libraries of colleges offering PU and UG courses (63.33 ~N=95), more than three fourth offering UG courses (77.71% ~N=258), less than three fourth offering UG and PG (71.25% ~N=57), and more than one fifth offering PU, UG and PG courses (22.22% ~N=2) do not have non-book materials, while it was less than thousand in more than one third (36.67% ~N=55), more than one fifth (21.69% ~N=72) less than one fourth (23.75% ~N=19) and more than three fourth (77.78% ~N=7) of libraries of colleges offering PU and UG; UG; UG and PU, UG and PG courses respectively. A small proportion of libraries of colleges running UG (0.31% ~ N=1) and UG and PG (2.5% ~ N=2) courses, have 1001-2000 non-book materials, while more than 2000 non-book materials were found in a small number of libraries of colleges offering UG (0.31% ~N=1) and UG (2.5% ~N=2) courses (vide Table-3).

Non-book materials were not found in more than two third of first grade (67.34% ~N=233), more than three fifth of education (62.5% ~N=25), a larger majority of law (97.06% ~N=33), more than three fifth of engineering (62.16% ~N=23), and more than four fifth of health sciences (85.96% ~N=98) college libraries, while its number was less than one thousand in less than one third of first grade (32.66% ~N=113), education (32.5% ~N=13), engineering (32.43% ~N=12), more than one tenth of health sciences (12.28% ~N=14) and a very small percentage of law (2.94% ~ N=1) college libraries. More than 5% of engineering (N=2) and 2.5% of education (N=1) college libraries have a collection of 1001-2000 non-book materials, while more than two thousand non-book materials were found in 2.5% of education (2.5% ~N=1) and 1.75% of health science (N=2) college libraries (vide Table-4)

More than three fifth of government (63.75% ~N=51),

more than four fifth of semi-government (85.71% ~N=12) and less than three fourth of private (73.16% ~N=349) college libraries do not have non-book materials in their collection, while a collection of less than one thousand was found in slightly more than one third of government (33.75% ~N=27), more than one tenth of semi-government (14.29% ~N=2) and more than one fourth of private (26% ~N=124) college libraries. A very small proportion of government (1.25% ~N=1) and private (0.42% ~N=2) college libraries have 1001-2000 non-book materials, while 1.25% of government (N=1) and 0.42% of private (N=2) college libraries have more than two thousand non-book materials (vide table-5).

Non-book materials were not found in more than two third of rural (70% ~N=154) and less than three fourth of urban (73.5% ~N=258) college libraries, while more than one fourth of rural (29.09% ~N=64) and one-fourth of urban (25.36% ~N=89) have less than one thousand non-book materials. Less than one percent of rural (0.45% ~N=1) and urban (0.57% ~N=2) college libraries have more than two thousand non-book materials (vide Table - 6).

More than two third of libraries of colleges headed by full time professionals (71.49% ~N=351) teaching staff (70.73% ~N=29) and more than four fifth headed by clerks (82.05% ~N=32) do not have non-book materials, while less than thousand non-book materials were found in more than one fourth of libraries headed by full time professionals (27.29% ~N=12) and less than one fifth headed by clerks (17.95% ~N=7). 1001-2000 and more than 2000 non-book materials were found in each of 0.61% of libraries of colleges headed by full time professionals (vide Table-7).

CONCLUSION

Slightly less than three-fourth of libraries do not have non-book materials in their collection, while less than thousand non-book materials were found in more than one-fourth of libraries only. This indicates the poor collection of non-book materials among college libraries in Karnataka State. Further, irrespective of their year of establishment, university affiliation, level of courses offered, category of the college, type of management–private or public, location–urban or rural, headed by full time professional or non-professional staff, the collection of non-book materials among college libraries is very poor. Therefore, it is interesting to study further the reasons for non-availability of non-book materials among the college libraries in Karnataka state in particular and the availability of NBM in Indian libraries in general. Some of the reasons may be: the lack of awareness and knowledge of non-book materials among library staff; non-availability of non-book materials relevant to the curricular and extra-curricular needs of the colleges; sheer neglect of non-book materials by the library staff, financial constraints, etc. The reasons could be any one or all of them but what is important is that the library staff need to give attention to non-book materials in development of collection required to meet the present and the future needs of the colleges.

REFERENCE

1. E Photograph Menon, " World education-need of the 21st century," *Indian Express*. 29.4.97, p. 11, col. 2.

Table-1 : Strength of non-book materials in college libraries of Karnataka : Year of Establishment

Range	*<1900*	*1901-1925*	*1926-1950*	*1951-1975*	*1976-*	*Total*
Nil	1 (50)	4 (80)	16 (61.54)	114 (65.89)	277 (75.89)	412 (72.15)
1-1000	1 (50)	-	10 (38.46)	55 (31.79)	87 (23.84)	153 (26.79)
1001-2000	-	-	-	2 (1.16)	1 (0.27)	3 (0.53)
2001>	-	1 (20)	-	2 (1.16)	-	3 (0.53)
Total	2	5	26	173	365	571

Table-2 : Strength of non-book materials in college libraries of Karnataka: University-wise

Range	*Mysore*	*Karnataka*	*Bangalore*	*Mangalore*	*Gulbarga*	*Kuvempu*	*Total*
Nil	34	127	96	48	55	52	412
	(59.65)	(80.89)	(73.28)	(61.54)	(70.51)	(74.29)	(72.15)
1-1000	21	29	35	29	22	17	153
	(36.84)	(18.47)	(26.72)	(37.18)	(28.21)	(24.29)	(26.79)
1001-2000	1	-	-	1	1	-	3
	(1.75)			(1.28)	(1.28)		(0.53)
2001>	1	1	-	-	-	1	3
	(1.75)	(0.64)				(1.42)	(0.53)
Total	57	157	131	78	78	70	571

Table-3 : Strength of non-book materials in college libraries of Karnataka: Level of courses

Range	*PUC+UG*	*UG*	*UG+PG*	*PUC+UG+PG*	*Total*
Nil	95	258	57	2	412
	(63.33)	(77.71)	(71.25)	(22.22)	(72.15)
1-1000	55	72	19	7	153
	(36.67)	(21.69)	(23.75)	(77.78)	(26.79)
1001-2000	-	1	2	-	3
		(0.30)	(2.50)		(0.53)
2001>	-	1	2	-	3
		(0.30)	(2.50)		(0.53)
Total	150	332	80	9	571

Table-4 : Strength of non-book materials in college libraries of Karnataka: Category-wise

Range	*First Grade*	*Educa-ation*	*Law*	*Engi-neering*	*Health science*	*Total*
Nil	233	25	33	23	98	412
	(67.34)	(62.50)	(97.06)	(62.16)	(85.96)	(72.15)
1-1000	113	13	1	12	14	153
	(32.66)	(32.50)	(2.94)	(32.43)	(12.28)	(26.79)
1001-2000	-	1	-	2	-	3
		(2.50)		(5.41)		(0.53)
2001>	-	1	-	-	2	3
		(2.50)			(1.75)	(0.53)
Total	346	40	34	37	114	571

Table-5 : Strength of non-book materials in college Libraries of Karnataka : Type of Management

Range	*Govt*	*Semi-Govt*	*Private*	*Total*
Nil	51	12	349	412
	(63.75)	(85.71)	(73.16)	(72.15)
1-1000	27	2	124	153
	(33.75)	(14.29)	(26.00)	(26.79)
1001-2000	1	-	2	3
	(1.25)		(0.42)	(0.53)
2001>	1	-	2	3
	(1.25)		(0.42)	(0.53)
Total	80	14	477	571

Table-6 : Strength of non-book materials in college libraries of Karnataka: Location

Range	*Rural*	*Urban*	*Total*
Nil	154	258	412
	(70)	(73.50)	(72.15)
1-1000	64	89	153
	(29.09)	(25.36)	(26.79)
1001-2000	1	2	3
	(0.45)	(0.57)	(0.53)
2001>	1	2	3
	(0.45)	(0.57)	(0.53)
Total	220	351	571

Table-7 : Strength of non-book materials in college libraries of Karnataka: Incharge of Library

Range	*Full time Profe-ssional*	*Full time Non-pro-fessional*	*Teaching staff*	*Clerk*	*Total*
Nil	351	-	29	32	412
	(71.49)		(70.73)	(82.05)	(72.15)
1-1000	134	-	12	7	153
	(27.29)		(29.27)	(17.95)	(26.79)
1001-2000	3	-	-	-	3
	(0.61)				(0.53)
2001>	3	-	-	-	3
	(0.61)				(0.53)
Total	491		41	39	571

VI-1
TQM in Library and Information Centres : A Conceptual Framework

Urmila A. Thaker

Alvin Tofler has warned in his book "The Third Wave", "Things are going to happen much faster in the future and only those companies who will keep up with the fast-pace will stay alive in the 21st century".

It is also true for Library and Information Systems/Centres (LISCs). All organisations everywhere are now in search of excellence in their diverse activities. The pressure of circumstances and the newly emerging challenges in socio-economic scenario are promoting them to do so. The LISCs are not an exception.

Today the Indian LISCs are entering into a new era of competition and globalisation through resource sharing and networking. The network of the library information systems is based on give and take policy. Only those LISCs which are quality conscious and cost competitive can survive and thrive in this new emerging environment.

What we need today are the quality LISCs not only quality librarians or quality information officers. If that be so, all the types of LISCs such as public, academic, special and research, need to be streamlined and all the sections of the systems centres have to work in a concerted and cohesive manner. Top management through its commitment to quality and suitable quality policy has to provide appropriate leadership for the LISCs. The challenge for top management, therefore, is to build and develop quality LISCs.

There has been a significant breakthrough in quality concept in recent decades. Today the emphasis has shifted from number of volumes to quality reading material or qualitative databases, from number of services to quality services, from number of techniques to accurate retrieval techniques, from number of users to users' satisfaction, from number of staff to skilled manpower and their participation and their satisfaction, from amount of budget to resource sharing and networking as well as timeliness, accuracy, speed, etc.

TQM is the real answer for this challenge. Now let us know what is TQM.

Total	100%	
	All are as	
	All activities	= Space
	Everybody	
	All ways.	
Quality	Users' Satisfaction	= Limit
	Users' delight	
Management	Structure	
	systems	
	process	= Time
	continuous	
	improvement	

The term 'quality' is an abstract term. Crosby opines that "Quality is the conformance to requirements". Quality essentially means conformance to users' requirements. Today the new thrust is on macro aspect that is the quality in its totality. It begins at the starting point of the process and is carried out through to finishing stage and beyond.

TQM means making or doing right things right the first time and every time. Regarding the LISCs, to provide the right information to the right user at the right time and every time in the right form. Dr. Ranganathan has not used the word TQM but he also believed in TQM. He has given stress on users' satisfaction.

Gradually, the focus has shifted to involvement of all sections of the LISCs under TQM.

The whole systems have to work in a cohesive manner to introduce TQM. In order to comprehend the importance of TQM, it is necessary to have clear perception as to what quality is all about.

Total Quality is now defined as "users' satisfaction at competitive cost". Quality has to be perceived through users' eyes. Quality should not be positioned as the absence of problems as defined by us. It should be positioned as the presence of value as defined by users.

Who are the users of the LISCs? There are two types of users. One internal users and the other external users. There are internal users in every LISCs the internal users who work with charging and discharging methods, retrieval techniques, periodical registration methods, classification and cataloguing methods, readers' services, Information technology etc. They must be satisfied. They should have 100% satisfaction.

There are also external users of the LISCs such as users of databases and information services and products of the LISCs. They should also have 100% satisfaction. TQM is users' driven, both internal and external users of the LISCs. To maintain quality is the job of everyone. TQM requires the management's commitment. It requires employees' involvement. It is necessary to ensure that each individual in the LISCs produces quality work.

RESPONSIBILITY FOR TQM

Top management has to play a crucial role for making Total

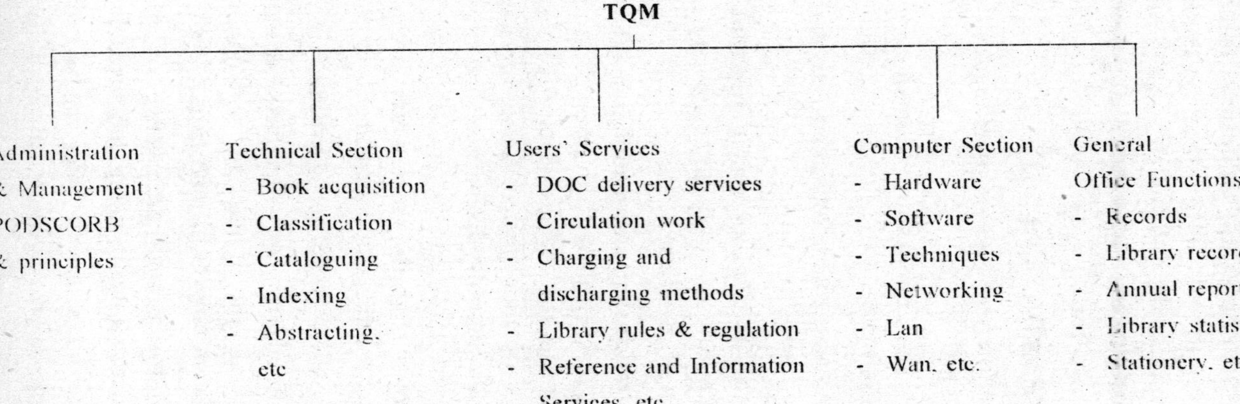
TQM
Administration
& Management
PODSCORB
& principles
Technical Section
- Book acquisition
- Classification
- Cataloguing
- Indexing
- Abstracting.
etc
Users' Services
- DOC delivery services
- Circulation work
- Charging and
discharging methods
- Library rules & regulation
- Reference and Information
Services, etc.
Computer Section
- Hardware
- Software
- Techniques
- Networking
- Lan
- Wan, etc.
General
Office Functions
- Records
- Library records
- Annual report
- Library statistics
- Stationery, etc.

Quality a part of the organisational culture. The main responsibility of top management is to build quality culture within the LISCs. It is the key to make TQM stands on the right foot and continue the activities in the right direction. The management has to provide the institutional environment for quality work from top to bottom.

INNOVATIVE STEPS FOR TQM

1 To generate continuous pursuit of ultimate perfection, harmony and value.

The TQM shifts the responsibility from single individual to the whole LISC.

2 All the decisions should be based on analysis of facts and figures.

Decision making is the important function of the management. It must be based on authentic hard facts, not on intuition or past experience.

Before taking any decision, information should be received from the lowest level of the employees, who are working in the present situation to highest level of LISCs that is, management. If top management wants to change any retrieval technique, charging-discharging method, indexing technique, or start new services, etc., first they should collect information from the persons who are presently working with the techniques or methods.

3 There should be policy-based management.

Emphasis should be given on value-based thoughts and policies which should synthesize the opinion and aspirations of the employees of the LISCs.

4 There is need for proper observance of planning, developing an effective team, doing and checking.

Management has to review it from time to time and evaluate the results obtained. After analysis of the results, further action has to be taken for standardisation of procedure.

5 There is a need for education and training of human resources.

Under the TQM philosophy, employees are recognised as the most important resource for the LISCs. Education and training are the tools to obtain a desired response from these living and dynamic resources for improved performance.

Training programmes arranged on decision making, problems solving, time management, leadership, information technology, information communication techniques, etc., certainly help TQM in LISCs. Skill development and technology training are the needs that must be fulfilled.

6 To create concern for all round growth of the LISCs coordinated with the individual and national growth.

7 To satisfy the users and employees through their requirements. TQM means users' satisfaction first time and everytime with respect to library and information services, products, timeliness, etc.

8 To encourage, involve and motivate all employees to think about the LISCs. TQM is innovation, involvement and responsiveness of all the employees from top to bottom.

9 The concern for environment. It needs organisational culture to create a positive attitude towards the entire environment.

10 To improve intangible qualities, one should accent on the intangible qualities like sincerity, cordiality, courtesy, harmony, mutual trust, better human relations, etc.

TQM is a continuous process and can be achieved by creating an organisational culture. It can be achieved only when the employees feel involved in the responsibility of library and information system towards stake holders. Hence, the top management has to create an environment for attitudinal change in employees.

ELEMENTS OF TQM

TQM is a philosophy, an attitude of mind. It is a journey not a destination. It means building quality into everything in every area: designing, purchasing, processing, classification, cataloguing, charging, discharging, reference and information service, information products, users' relations, users' satisfaction, development of human resources and productivity.

The philosophy of total quality management means not only an idea to achieve quality information service/product/ databases but also improving the capabilities of employees who are working in the LISCs thereby achieving improved quality services, products, better performance and user satisfaction. In fact, the process of TQM is a continuous process. It can be achieved by creating an organisational environment. To achieve quality and high performance, human resource motivation is needed. TQM is a team work. It develops commitment in people for quality service, quality information products and more productivity.

TQM is a very wide concept. The essential elements of TQM are :

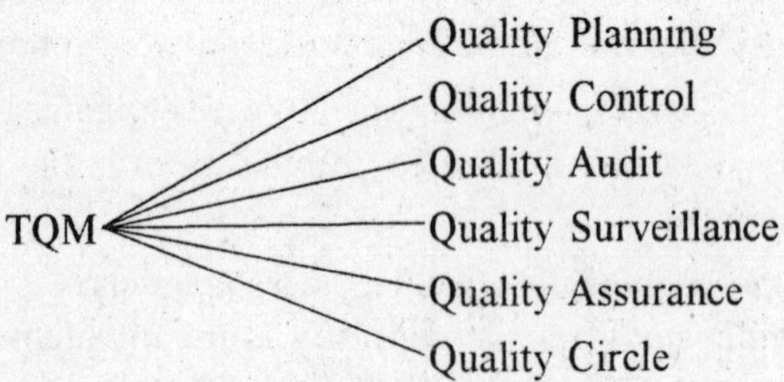

TQM concept means that the quality should be a way of life for all the employees of the LISCs. Therefore there is need for organisatinal environment. Quality circle creates that organisatinal environment.

QUALITY CIRCLE

Quality Circle is participative management system in which employees make suggestions and improvements for the betterment of the LISCs.

To fulfil the goals of the LISCs and to implement TQM, problems must be recognised and resolved through the employees participation. The employees participation is most important because they are working in the present situation in particular section. They know their own problems and their solution. They know their external users.

There are various types of problems in different sections. The employees know their problems as well as alternative solutions and hard facts such as

1) What type of information the users will need?
2) What type of documents the users will need?
3) How the users can use information themselves?
4) How to provide maximum access of information to the users?
5) What is depth of analysis of information or data?
6) How the information will be kept usable for a longer period?
7) How to make information use more efficient and effective?
8) Who are users of the system/centre?

The aim of the Quality Circle is to maintain quality in each and every function and service through employee participation. To maintain quality is the responsibility of everyone.

DEFINITION

"Quality Circle is a small group of employees in the same work area or doing similar type of work who voluntarily meet regularly for about an hour every week to identify, analyse and resolve work related problems, leading to improvement in their performance and enrichment of their work life. This concept originated in Japan."

CHARACTERISTICS OF QUALITY CIRCLE

1) Small group of employees

   Number of persons is generally between 3 to 12 or 5 to 15. There should be active participation by everyone. The discussion should be purposeful.

2) In the same work area or doing similar type of work.

   A Quality Circle is a homogeneous group.

   Members participating in Quality Circle activities must be on the same wavelength. Discussions taking place at the meeting should be intelligible to each one of the members. This is possible only if the composition of the Quality Circle includes employees working in the same work area engaged in a similar type of work. Designations of members need not necessary be equal but the work in which they all are engaged should be common.

   For example, persons who work in technical section, persons who work in book selection and acquisition section, circulation section, periodical section, reference section, account section, computer section etc. can decide to form a circle.

3) Voluntarily

   Quality Circle is a voluntary process and there is no force on employee to join in it.

4) Meeting regularly for about an hour every week

   Once the concept of Quality Circle has been accepted by the library management and employees, Quality Circle members should meet regularly for about an hour every week.

5) To identify, analyse and resolve work related problems.

   This is based on proven theory that the employees who work in any area day after day know best what problems are hindering achievement of good quality, productivity and optimum performance as also how they can be remedied.

There are number of functions and service in the LISCs There may be problems of automated retrieval techniques, charging & discharging method, technical processes, reference & information service, etc.

6) Leading to improvement in their total performance.

   As a result of quality circle resolving work related problems relating to quality, productivity, cost reduction, techniques, methods, services, etc., total performance of the work area naturally improves, resulting in both quantifiable as well as intangible gains to the whole LISCs.

7) Enrichment of their work life.

   The spin off benefits of Quality Circle to the whole LISCs include enrichment of the worklife of employees apart from attitudinal changes, cohesive team culture, etc.

The quality of worklife of any individual is said to be good only if he is enjoying the work that he is engaged in, is happy in the environment and finds his work place meaningful.

IMAPCT OF QC

1) It promotes participative culture.
2) It increases job interest
3) It encourages group activities or team work.
4) It reduces defects and improves quality of functions, services and products.
5) It improves housekeeping cost effectiveness, safety, etc.
6) It improves productivity.
7) It increases problem solving capacity.

STRUCTURE OF QUALITY CIRCLE

The structure of Quality Circle is governed by the unique conditions in different countries and organisations.

1 Co-ordinator

The LISC is itself the co-ordinating agency. It organises the activities of the quality circle.

2 Steering committee

Chief executive of the LISC as the chairman. For the successful implementation of quality circles, the top management support must be made available.

3 Departmental Committee

Individual section level.

4 Facilitator

Senior person of the section

5 Leader–Deputy leader

A healthy approach is for the members deciding to have rotation of leaders and deputy leaders.

6 Members

Any one from the same work area.

7 Non-member

Who are not members, but interested in the activities. Various types are LISCs public, academic, special and research information centres appear to be different, but they are similar to a greater or lesser degree as they are all involved in very similar activities. They can constitute Quality Circles.

QUALITY CIRCLE OPERATION

The concept of Quality Circle is one segment of TQM. Every section and work area should have the responsibility to make the operation of Quality Circle a success.

Quality Circle members meet at the appointed place and time regularly. In the first meeting they discuss their problems. They identify the problems through brain storming effort and suggestions. Quality Circle compiles a list of problems. It classifies and prioritises alternative solutions. Quality Circle develops one solution for particular problem. Then they present it to the top management and after the approval of the management, they implement the solution.

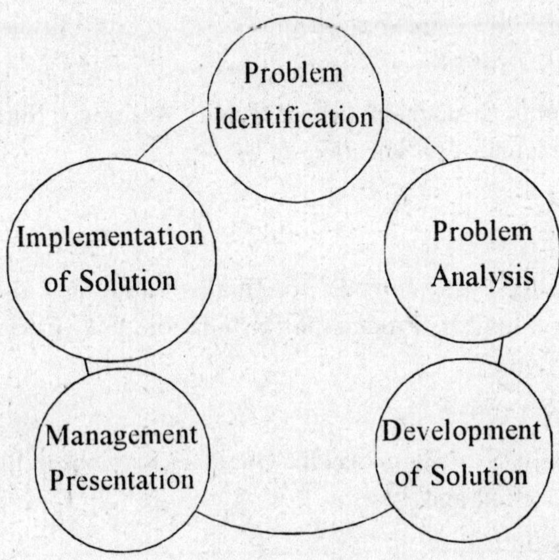

Problem Solving Cycle

Thus the problem solving cycle for each problem taken up by Quality Circle proceedes.

TQM AND ISO 9000

The Technical Committee 176 of the International Standards Organisation formulated the norms (ISO 9000) for ensuring quality standards for products and services in international trade. BS-5750 and BIS-14000 are similar standards set by the British Standards Organisation and Bureau of Indian Standards respectively for their national trade and activities. They resemble closely ISO 9000.

TQM focuses on continuous improvement while ISO 9000

provides a quality framework to guarantee consistency of operation. ISO 9000 is a subset of the TQM philosophy. It aims to promote standardization of products and services.

* ISO series consists of five documents:

  ISO-9000

  (BIS-14000)

  Quality Systems-model for Quality Assurance Standards : Guidelines for Selection & Use

* ISO-9001

  (BIS-14001)

  Quality Systems-model for Quality Assurance in Design/ Development, Production, Installation, and Servicing

* ISO-9002

  (BIS-14002)

  Quality Systems-model for Quality Assurance in Financial Inspection and Test.

* ISO-9003

  (BIS-14003)

  Quality Systems-model for Quality Assurance in Financial Inspection and Test.

* ISO-9004

  (BIS-14004)

  Quality Management and Quality System Elements Guidelines.

REFERENCES

1. Anand, K. K. Quality management handbook.edn. 2.New Delhi : Vikas, 1993.
2. Bittel, Lester Robert. ed Encyclopedia of professional management. New York : McGraw-Hill, 1978.
3. Ellis, Debbie and Norton, Bob. Implementing B55750-ISO9000 in Libraries. London : Aslib, 1993.

4. Feigenbaum, Arm and V. Total quality control. New York : McGraw-Hill. 1986.
5. IGNOU. Management of library and information centres. MLIS-05: BLOC-3
6. Maheshulari, B. L. ed. Quality circle. New Delhi: Oxford. 1987.
7. Sweeney Patrick. J TQM for Engineering : Quality Resources. London : CCIA. 1992.

VI : 2

Quality of Library and Information Services in the Changing Information Technology Environment : An Evaluation

T. R. B. Sarma
S. Sudarshan Rao

> Quality is the total composite product and service characteristics of marketing, engineering, manufacture, and maintenance through which the product and service in use will meet the expectation of the customer."
>
> - Feigenbaum (1983)

INTRODUCTION

Quality is a standard of an organisation according to which its products and services are produced for the satisfaction of its customers/consumers. All organisations, may be production, business or service organisations, have definite objectives to achieve. The success or failure of these organisations depends on the fact that how effectively they accomplished their tasks in achieving their set objectives. Thus, quality of an organisation is an indicator and a measure of its performance. It is also used as a tool to adopt corrective measures in the course of action of the organisation for improving its performance.

Evaluating the quality of a library and its services is important especially in the present context when huge investments are made on libraries in acquiring documents, journals as well as Information Technology (IT) tools. At the same time, the intelligent reader community is always demanding quality services for the satisfaction of its general and research needs. In this context, evaluation of library services occupies an important place in finding out the existing library's efficiency and also for offering suitable guidelines for improving its efficiency in providing better services to the users. Library being a service oriented and non-profit organisation, the evaluation of its quality can be categorised as intangible and it is very difficult to evaluate the quality in concrete terms. However, the quality of library can be evaluated in terms of the investment made in the library for acquiring different information sources vis-a-vis the quality of services offered and user satisfaction obtained.

In the present information society, most of the special and academic libraries are interested to provide information services through the latest Information Technology (IT) tools like CD-ROMs, computerized online databases, electronic networks, internet, etc. In the Indian context, the establishment of CD-ROM work-stations, collection of different CD-ROMs, creating a database of online searching of databases of other countries and formation of Internet workstations are expensive activities. In this context, evaluation of quality of library services provides appropriate feedback about the library's effectiveness in satisfying the needs of the users. It helps the parent organisation to make further plans for improving the quality of the library services.

Information Technology (IT) Tools in Library Environment

Applying Technology in information science or Information management to acquire better results is called Information Technology. The introduction of computerisation is having considerable impact on information technology. In the present decade utmost effort has been made to exploit technology for maximising information storage and retrieval procedure. New technology has had its impact on the manipulation of library functions and has led to automated systems, network technology, database management, computerised catalogue production, information retrieval packages and several on-line systems. Finally, now the library is adopting Information Technology in all its modules for providing maximum services to the users in less time.

Need to Evaluate the Quality of Information Technology (IT) Toois in Library and Information Centres

1. The allocation of the financial resources to the library are gradually decreasing.
2. The prices of IT tools both domestic and international are gradually increasing.
3. The usage of Information Technology (IT) tools by the library is not proportionate to the expenditure incurred on them.
4. Most of the users are not getting satisfied results, even after using the available IT tools in library.
5. IT tools developed by foreign countries are biased to their countries.

STANDARDS FOR QUALITY ASSESSMENT

The library and information science professionals have developed many sets of standards, usually through their professional bodies, over the years. One of the good examples is "IFLA's Standards for University Libraries" (1986). It was an internationally agreed document prepared by a committee of librarians to provide the standards for assessing the quality of libraries and offer guidance for improvement of the facilities in the library.

The IFLA Standards

1. Purpose of the parent institution
2. Organisation and administration structure of the library

3. Offering Services
4. Collection details
5. Staff details
6. Physical facilities (Quality and attractiveness of building and their layout)
7. Library Budget and Finance
8. Technology (Electronic data processing and Telecommunication systems)
9. Preservation and conservation policies
10. Co-operation (Resource Sharing, Union Catalogues, Collection development and co-operative activity in preservation and conservation of materials)

The IFLA recognised information technology is an important standard and grouped it as one of the major components under the above ten headings to evaluate the quality of the library.

CRITERIA FOR EVALUATING THE LIBRARY AND INFORMATION SERVICES

A regular feedback in library towards its services is necessary for achieving maximum utilisation of the users. The utilisation of the library can be assessed by measuring the effectiveness of facilities provided and services rendered by the library to the user community. The following type of information is helpful to evaluate a library and its services providing to the users.

1. Utilisation of documents, periodicals, newspapers, CD-ROMs and Internet facilities.
2. Rate of Information sources satisfying the user needs.
3. Rate of Accessibility of available Information Sources.
4. Collection of the library on subject areas of interest.
5. Facilities and Environment for using the library resources.
6. Range of borrowing entitlement
7. Rate of Reference Service satisfaction

8. User education effectiveness
9. Working hours of the library
10. Responsibilities of the library staff

USE OF INFORMATION TECHNOLOGY TOOLS IN LIBRARIES:

For improving the quality library services, the library professionals shall be acquiring the following types of IT tools for providing quick services to the readers.

1. Latest version computers with a powerful library package for quick retrieval of journal articles as well as documents or their references. Ready to use computer-controlled video discs, high speed printers or similar technology for providing quick reproduction of individual articles from serials in the collection.
2. Internet/intranet facility for retrieving information from world wide webs and disseminating the same to different faculties/departments of the parent organisation.
3. Facsimile transmission technology by both sending and receiving network member libraries.
4. Inter Library Loan (ILL) system or a similar system to request loans and photocopies by electronic means, not by mail. Requests for books and journal articles and other materials could be sent within the network system to any of the member libraries.

STEPS TO BE TAKEN BY THE LIBRARY ADMINISTRATION BEFORE ACQUIRING IT TOOLS

1. The appropriate IT tools which the library actually require
2. The assessed needs of the library and its clientele
3. The cost consciousness of the library's administration (Financial resources position)

Besides the above precautions, the library manager should conduct needs assessment survey to collect the actual ideas of readers for purchasing the appropriate available IT tools in the market. This information should be collected by conducting interviews, questionnaires, work manuals and onsite observation etc., techniques. The following information we can collect through the needs assessment survey:

1. Readers' existing needs.
2. Readers' future requirements.
3. Readers' existing thoughts and ideas on various available IT tools.

PROBLEMS IN COLLECTING THE LATEST IT INFRASTRUCTURE

The following are the two major problems being faced by the libraries in collecting the latest IT infrastructure especially in developing countries.

1. **Finance :** Financial constraints, especially foreign exchange, as well as strict foreign exchange controls, limit the amount of material or information to be bought or used.
2. **Manpower :** In most developing countries, there exists shortage of professionally trained staff who can organize effective information systems and who can impress the readers as well as higher management.

Qualities to be Improved by Library Professionals

1. A clear conception of the system in which he/she operates
2. Knowledge about:
   a. Subjects of interest of the organisation
   b. Use of computers for information retrieval and dissemination
   c. Adequate communication skills–both written and oral
   d. Sources of information–documentary, institutional and human
3. Public/human relations skill.

Training Needs

To meet the present day challenges, a broad based education with updated curricula is necessary for the present day Information Scientist. A developing country like India should take care of manpower training which is crucial to the success of development efforts. The Library & Information professional cannot satisfy the information requirements of his present day clientele unless he is well versed in modern information handling methods. To develop the knowledge and skills among Library Professionals, the Library & Information Science schools should give more emphasis on :

- Use of computers for information processing including systems analysis and programming
- Management techniques
- Written and oral communication skills
- Documentation standards and technical writing
- Information analysis, consolidation and repackaging
- Information sources and communication media

CONCLUSION

Modern computer and communication technology have an enormous impact on man's capacity to gather, organise, store, retrieve and disseminate vast quantities of information. The techniques and technologies in library and information science have been substantiated, strengthened and refined over the decades. These technologies offer great promise and even more efficient and effective delivery of information in future library and information centres. Through a combination of dynamic handling of information technology tools with quality management, the library professionals can provide advanced services to the library users. As the information technology products are playing a dominant role in the present libraries, the librarian himself should convert as a technical expert and extract services by using computer, telecommunication, reprographic and micrographic technologies, for providing effective and quick services to the users. At the same time, the user community should also improve their enthusiasm to learn some thing about the information technology tools used in the library and to co-operate with library staff in obtaining better services from the library.

REFERENCES

1. Quality Management for Information and Library Managers. By Peter Brophy and Kate Coulling. Jaico Publishing House. Mumbai. 1997. 196 p.
2. Library Techniques and Technologies : Perspectives in Multimedia Library Development (Volume 1). By S.N. Paruthi (Ed). Kanishka Publishers, New Delhi, 1997, 221 p.
3. User-oriented Evaluation of Information System and Services By David Bawden, Gower. UK, 1990. 209 p.
4. Computers in Library and Information Science : Need and Importance for Next Millennium By Chander Parkash, Mangal Deep Publications, Jaipur, 2000. 157 p.

VI : 3
Joy Committee and Quality Aspects of College Librarianship

R. Raman Nair

INTRODUCTION

In modern India the importance of library in higher education was emphasised by many educationists and expert committees. The Calcutta University Commission appointed in 1917 by the Government of India under chairmanship of Sir Michael Saddler pointed out that the weakness of the existing higher education system is the extraordinarily unimportant part played by the library.

University Education Commission (1949) chaired by Dr. S. Radhakrishnan, Ranganathan Committee (1958) appointed by UGC, and Education Commission (1966) chaired by D. S. Kothari pointed out the same factor and suggested measures for improving the situation. Sen Committee and Mehrotra Committee of UGC examined the matter in detail and gave specific recommendations for attracting and retaining qualified library professionals to maintain quality services by college libraries. Even though many enquiries by national level committees have vindicated the hindrances that existed against the need-based development of library and information system in colleges and put forward suggestions for improving the situation. serious attempt for reform was initiated. We could not even prepare standards for college libraries which would have served as guidelines for the development of 9000 and more colleges in the country. Another hindrance for reform is education being a State subject technically Union government will not be able to do anything more than giving some suggestions. When viewed in this perspective the initiative of Government of Kerala in appointing an Expert Committee on College Libraries in 1993 under the chairmanship of V. P. Joy, IAS, assumes great importance. It is the first of such attempts by any state government. The detailed report of Joy committee submitted in 1994 covering all facets of college library development has influenced many library modernization programmes over India. Various seminars and conferences discussed the report in detail, appreciated its recommendations and requested other States also to adopt the recommendations. His recommendations are based on an understanding of the correct position of library and information system in college, the role of library information science professionals in improving the quality of higher education and the nature of the profession.

Educational Role

In the teaching learning process expected in higher education, teachers and librarians have to play roles of equal importance. Both have to actively engage students in using library as a kind of laboratory for learning how to manage their own education. Teachers should know that library is an extension of the classroom and should make the students use it intelligently in preparation for discussions in class, seminars and other programmes. For this there must be a two-way flow of information between teachers and librarians and both have to contribute.

Ranganathan Committee has reported in detail librarian's duties to teachers and students. Mehrotra Committee of UGC has also stated that it should be the constant endeavor of librarian in a college to widen and update his range of knowledge so that he can extend valuable guidance to teachers as well as students. It accepted that librarian although not a formal member of the teaching faculty performs academic functions, and sustains and enriches the academic process. Joy Committee considers it essential that college library staff should keep abreast of current developments in every subject and should support teachers and students in their information search. The Committee considered it the duty of librarians to promote individual and motivated learning at all levels by providing the information sources required for that.

College Librarian

The functionalism of the library building and space, the relevance of the collection, the efficiency of its organization and services depend on the character and ability of the college librarian.

The head of the college library should be a successful administrator, a wise counsellor in the use of information sources and a force in shaping library policy. These requirements insist that the college librarian must be a person of imagination and initiative. That he must have a sound understanding of library administration and that he must know how to relate the use of library to the educational programmes of the college. If he is to be a leader in the college community, he must be a person of character, integrity and professional idealism.

Management Capabilities

The college librarian should have the qualities of a good administrator. He has to assume a large measure of administrative responsibility, including the supervision of the staff and the proper budgeting and expenditure of library funds. These functions require frequent consultation and close relationships with the principal, administrative officers and heads of subject departments as the librarian must impress them all with his sound judgement. He must also hold the confidence of the library staff by his ability to develop a systematic organization of library work, to conduct the many types of transactions involving the administration and faculty, and administer budgets and service in a satisfactory manner.

To attain even to an approximation of qualities required for these functions, the librarian must understand thoroughly the objectives of the library in a particular college and the problems and needs of teachers and students.

Scholarly Interests

It is important that college librarian be personally acquainted with his teacher colleagues and with their characteristic methods of operation. Likewise, it is important that he be kept minutely posted on the current curricular and administrative policies so that he may have a sharp conception of the special areas in which library support may be helpful. If he is not consulted and kept informed about curricular matters and administrative policy, his help in these matters will of course be negligible.

There is no need that the college librarian should be a scholar in the sense of an eminent specialist or researcher. But he should be familiar with the methods of research, have a through knowledge of bibliography and be competent to assist teachers and students in their search for information. He should also be widely read and well informed about the collections to be able to assist in their development.

ABILITY TO PLAN

In these days of increasing enrollment, rapid technological developments and frequent self examination of the educational programme, it is important also for the librarian to be something of a planner and to be able to convey to his colleagues and staff a sense of the direction in which library is moving. The quality of library service is to be maintained in face of increasing enrollments, professional staff shortage and limited resources. The new technological developments that offer opportunities for improving the library services should be utilised. The library has to secure resources to move ahead. It is the responsibility of the chief librarian of the college to devise plans for all these. If he fails in these areas, library will be forced to drift along in directions never consciously considered

Qualifications

The duties and responsibilities of the college librarian enumerated above show that his academic qualifications should be at par with those of senior teachers. Only simple logic is required to understand that the qualification of any librarian in the college should in no way be lower than the highest level course offered in the college as the librarians are expected to guide the students attending those courses in their information search and support their learning. Their qualification should be equal to that of the teachers because it is the librarian who is to give teachers the information support required for their teaching and updating of their knowledge.

Present day colleges demand higher qualifications for their librarians. The need for highly qualified librarians in universities and colleges was first pointed out by Saddler. Radhakrishnan has stated that libraries should be manned by adequate and well qualified staff. He recommended that at the top of a library there should be a man of the calibre of a professor who is specialised in library science after having done post graduation in a subject and he should have sufficient experience and capacity for organizing and managing such a department.

Ranganathan and Kothari clearly identified the functions of library staff. They stated that the librarian and his staff in the colleges have the responsibility to define and understand the purpose of the library in relation to the aims of the college, to become personally acquainted with their faculty colleagues and to know their teaching methods. They should know as to what is going on in curriculum matters and should have a clear conception of the specific ways in which library support is desirable and possible. It is implied that qualification of the librarian should enable them for fulfilling these duties.

Joy committee stated that college librarianship is a highly complex profession warranting specialised and technical knowledge of various sorts like personal administration, financial management and different bibliographical techniques. The successful performance of the college librarian demand a clear understanding of academic objective. A significant level of academic expertise and working partnership with heads of teaching departments, proper direction of policies and resources of the college libraries towards needs of teaching-learning process demands a chief librarian with high academic qualifications and knowledge of objectives and practices of education. Joy recommended that only those with qualifications and experience prescribed by UGC should be appointed as Chief Librarian in a college.

All that has been said above with respect to the qualification of the chief librarian is in varying degrees applicable to other library staff also. For most students the staff at the public desks signifies the library. Hence it is obvious that sympathetic relation between students and the library staff are of crucial importance in making the college library a real service library and not just a storage house.

College library staff who support the chief librarian must be capable of giving the students the kind of assistance they need in order to use the library intelligently and efficiently and they must have a clear idea of what the library is trying to do. This sense of guiding purpose, translates itself into the daily operations of the library and determines what activities shall be undertaken and how they shall be carried out.

These supporting staff should have a breadth of knowledge and a critical capacity based on habits of constant and discriminative reading. By their intellectual interests and their skill in human relations, they should help to convey the impression that librarians are persons whose opinions are important. It is interesting to find in many States including Kerala, the staff librarians do not even possess SSLC qualification and are designated as 'Attenders' or 'Library Assistants' they are posted as supporting staff in college as per existing staff pattern. Even in post-graduate departments the staff pattern allows only for an Attender to look after its library. By chance if he is a literate studied upto SSLC it will be a luck to that post-graduate department. But how can such staff attend the information services required to be provided for the post-graduate students and teachers specialising in a subject.

According to Ranganathan, the academic qualification of the library staff should be at par with those of the professors, the readers and the lecturers. Apart from general academic qualification of high order, the librarian and his professional staff should also have professional qualification of an equally high order. The Committee recommended M. Lib. Sc. or MA and first class BLISc as the minimum qualification required for a college librarian.

UGC appointed two committees under the Chairmanship of Dr. S. N. Sen, and R. C. Mehrotra in 1974 and 1987 to consider the scales of pay and qualifications of library staff. Both recommended the qualifications equal to that are required for college and university teachers for entry cadre librarians.

Joy Committee has also recommended that all library professionals posted in college libraries should have the minimum academic qualification that can give them a broad acquaintance with all subjects taught in the college so that they will be capable of interacting with degree and post-graduate students and teachers to support them and guide them in their information needs. Joy Committee stressed the need for implementing the recommendations of UGC on the qualifications of librarians.

Academic Status

Academic status to the college librarians mean that the college should regard the professional library staff as members of the instruction staff instead of administrative or clerical staffs. This status may be defined as the formal recognition in writing by an institution's authorities of librarians as members of the academic staff. The recognition may take the form of assigned faculty ranks and titles with faculty privileges of tenure, academic freedom, equitable salaries, etc.

The academic status carries with it certain definite obligations for librarian. The first requirement is for intellectual activity including a keen interest in the academic life of the campus. The librarian must accept the responsibility for independent learning, continuous intellectual growth and educational statesmanship. Status also implies the highest level of professionalism in performance of his duties.

In educationally advanced countries, librarians were given full academic status with most of the rights and privileges of faculty members from nineteen to twenties. This helped to create the best kind of library service to students and teachers and contributed to quality improvements in education in those countries. In India, it was Calcutta University Commission (1917) which for the first time recognised the importance of academic status to the librarians. Radhakrishnan Commission (1949) also pointed out the need for staff with calibre and qualification of a professor to head the libraries.

Ranganathan advised that status and salary scale of the library staff should be the same as that of teaching and research staff. The Committee has recommended Reader's scale and status for chief librarians of large colleges and Lecturer's scale for his supporting professional staff and also for the chief librarian's of large colleges and Lecture's scale for his supporting professional staff and also for the chief librarians of small colleges. Mehrotra Committee (1987) also accepted the academic role of librarians and recommended academic status to them. According to the Committee it is undeniable that a librarian, although not a formal member of the teaching faculty, performs academic functions, and sustains and enriches the academic process. While a teacher may be specialized in a particular branch, the librarian is required to have a wide and overall acquaintance with various disciplines in order to be able to bring the scholars to obtain knowledge from diverse areas. The student contact with the librarian is exhilarating and educative. The librarians interactions with members of the faculty should be of mutual benefit. The

Committee expressed the view that the emoluments of the duly qualified librarians should match those of the teachers and that they should have about the same promotional opportunities as have been recommended for the teachers. Based on its recommendations, Government of India has implemented parity in matters of scales of pay.

Career Advancement and other aspects between college teachers and college librarians. qualifications for the posts of college librarians were also fixed in accordance with this.

CONCLUSION

Very important suggestions with regard to the status of college librarians are contained in Joy Committee report. The committee considered it desirable to give the college librarians academic status and bring librarian also under the definition of teacher. The Committee recommended that the college librarian should be given the status and rank as recommended by the UGC, subject to satisfying the qualifications and other conditions prescribed by UGC. The Committee recommended full membership for the college librarian in the College Council. The committee also recommended that librarian should function as the Secretary of the Library Advisory Committee constituted in the college to advise and recommend on all matters related to organization and services of the college library. Implementation of the recommendations of Joy Committee Report can give new image to college librarianship and goes a long way in improving the quality of higher education in the country.

REFERENCES

1. India, Calcutta University Commission, 1917 (Chairman : Michael Saddler) (Calcutta: Government Press. 1919).
2. India, University Education Commission, 1948 (Chairman : S. Radhakrishnan.) (New Delhi. : Government Press. 1949).
3. University Grants Commission, Library Committee, 1958. (Chairman : S. R. Ranganathan.) (New Delhi : Government Press. 1959).
4. India. Education Commission. 1964 (Chairman : D. S. Kothari) Report (New Delhi : Government Press. 1916).

5. University Grants Commission, Expert Committee on Minimum Qualifications, work load etc. of Librarians.... 1983 (Chairman : R. C. Mehrotra). Report (New Delhi : the Author. 1987).

6. Kerala. Expert Committee on College Libraries. 1994 (Convener : V. P. Joy) Report (Trivendrum : the author. 1994).

7. Raman Nair. College Library Development (New Delhi : Ess Ess, 1996).

8. Raman Nair. "Role and Status of College Librarians : Comparative Analysis of Ranganathan. Mehrotra and Joy Committee Reports." Proceedings of the National Seminar : Preparing Libraries for 21st Century. Goa. University of Goa (1994.).

VI : 4

Human Resource Planning For Academic Libraries of Orissa

S. K. Satpathy
R. K. Rout

INTRODUCTION

Generally libraries are social institutions. But the libraries associated with the academic institutions (called academic libraries) are more complex organisations within their parent organisation, since they require a wide range of specialised skills in their employees in order to provide various library services to their target users of various status. Therefore, proper planning of human resource of these libraries becomes necessary.

Planning basically relates to the future. Planning means it is deliberate direction by persons in charge of large resources, of an activity towards choosen end. Human resource planning is synonymous to manpower planning. It is a process which involves systematic mobilisation and channelisation of human resources to meet the future challenges of the organisation. Thus human resource planning of academic libraries is a strategy for the acquisition, utilisation, improvement and retention of human resource to achieve the library's defined aim.

EXISTING SCENARIO IN ORISSA

The educational development in Orissa with comparison to other States was too late. Prior to the establishment of university in Orissa, it was under the jurisdiction of Calcutta University. Presently there are five universities and one council in orissa. These are:

i) **Utkal University :** It is the oldest university of Orissa and was established in 1943 as an examination cum affiliating university at Revenshaw College, Cuttack. The new campus at Bhubaneswar started from 1963.

   Presently there are 312 degree colleges, 45 professional colleges and 2 constituent colleges affiliated to the university.

ii) **Sambalpur University :** It has started functioning from 1967 as an affiliating cum examining body with its territorial jurisdiction over the Western Orissa. Presently there are 119 colleges (including professional colleges) affiliated to it.

iii) **Berhampur University :** It was established in 1967 as an affiliating cum examining body. Presently there are 65 affiliated colleges (including professional colleges) under it.

iv) **Sri Jagannath Sanskrit Viswa Vidyalaya :** It was established in 1981 and imparts higher education in Sanskrit and Oriental languages and literatures.

v) **Orissa University of Agriculture and Technology :** It has started functioning from 1962 to promote higher study and research exclusive in the field of Agricultural Sciences, Fishery, Animal husbandry and allied areas for the whole of the State.

vi) **Council of Higher Secondary Education :** It has started functioning from 1982 as per the Orissa Higher Secondary Education Act. It is an examination cum affiliation Council for +2 colleges. Presently there are 786 +2 colleges affiliated to it.

The above study reveals that there are 5 Universities, 543 degree colleges and 786 +2 colleges in Orissa, which are too much in comparision to other states. Accordingly there are same number of academic libraries (excluding school libraries) in Orissa. But these libraries are worst in its type. It can be said that in Orissa, the academic libraries are much in numbers with a wide collection of different subjects but without proper manpower. As a result, library organisation and services are very poor. No staffing pattern is also followed in any academic library of Orissa.

NEED FOR HUMAN RESOURCE PLANNING

The efficiency of academic libraries largely depends on the academic and professional competency of the library staff, their working environment and the facilities provided to them. Besides documents and financial support, the next most important element of academic library is the human resource. Without this resource, other resources cannot be utilized properly. Therefore proper human resource planning for academic libraries is highly needed. In the opinion of Edwards and Silver "the need to establish recruitment levels and number of promotions, anticipate redundancies and avoid unnecessary dismissals, allow for proper training and development and provide for the organisational infrastructure, argues well for manpower planning to enable the organisation to make best use of one of its most valuable resources in accordance with its goals".

The following points also highlight the need of human resource planning in academic libraries.

i) Ensures that adequate human resource is available in accordance with the demand.

ii) Facilitates better understanding between the library staff.

iii) Provides good working environment to the library staff.

iv) Ensures maximum utilisation of library materials.

v) Indicates the potential trouble spots of the library.

Factors Effecting Human Resource Planning:

The following factors effect in the planning of human resource in academic libraries.

i) Types and characteristics of users.

ii) Subject areas, inputs (documents and data) to the system and information needs to the users.

iii) Output/services of the library.

iv) Structure of the organisation and its functions for the services envisaged.

v) Financial resources.

vi) Attitude of the organisation's authority towards library.

HUMAN RESOURCE PLANNING PROCESS

The human resource planning process is likely to provide exact forecast of the existing and anticipated human resource of the library in accordance with the organisation's structure and function. This process is not a one time exercise but is a continuous process since the human resource of a library need to be constantly evaluated and updated. The flowchart on next page summarises the human resource planning process.

Human resource planning process begins with forecast of the human resource or manpower needs. This is first done by studying three types of forecasts i.e. financial or economic forecast, library service forecast and the availability of trained staff forecast. Such a forecast results in the library's plan and programs. A comparision of these two, namely, the forecast and plan can result in anticipating the human resource need. In terms of human resource needs, the staffing functions has to be done. This involves recruitment and selection which may be done from outside sources or could include promotions and transfers from within the library to jobs for which the existing personnel are more suitable. To provide an appropriate working environment is also important from the view point of performance likely to emanate from the personnel concerned. This includes consideration of adequate leadership quality and motivation with which the question of wage and salary administration is connected. Proper communications are also essential to create

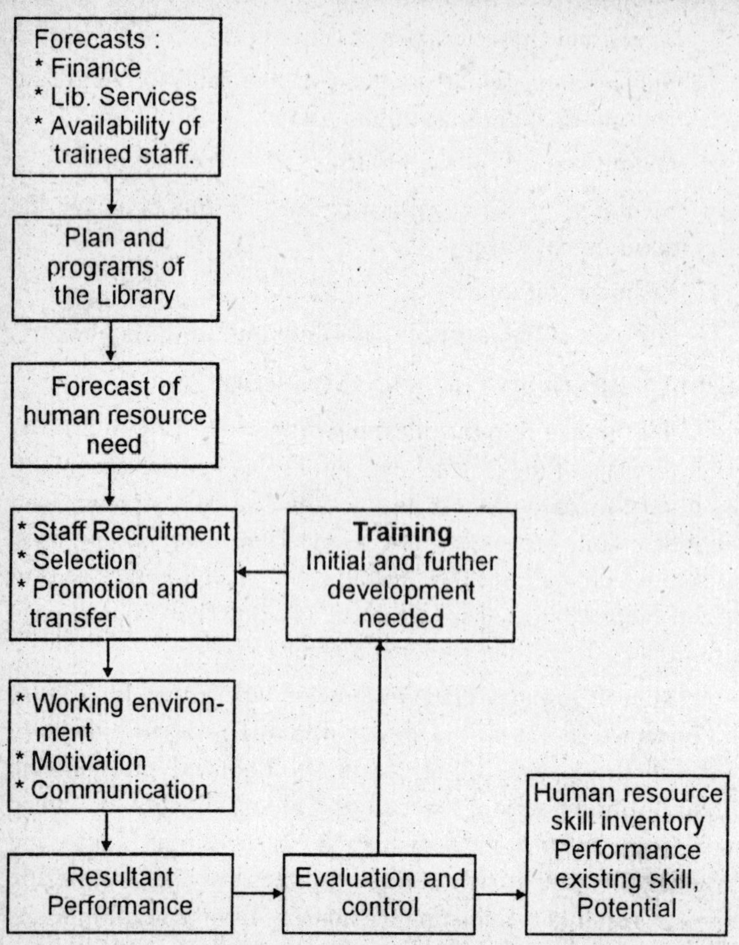

right working environment for maximum and effective service. Then the resultant performance must be evaluated. Such an evaluation would suggest changes required in the library set up as well as the future training required for the existing library staff to get them ready for future positions so that the library is aware of the types of skills already existing in terms of performance. Adequate development facilities should also be provided to prepare the staff for the higher positions and also to meet the new challenges of the library.

Thus, the human resource planning mainly involves the following steps:

i) Forecast of library requirements.

ii) Anticipating the manpower needs according to the library plan and programme.

iii) Recruitment of staff.

iv) Evaluation of resultant performance.

v) Training library staff according to the changing library environment.

THE STAFFING STRUCTURE OF ACADEMIC LIBRARIES

Dr. S. R. Ranganathan had formulated a staffing pattern for the university libraries of India. It was later on recommended by the University Grants Commission and was incorporated in the recommendation of the U.G.C. Committee. On the basis of this staff formula, manpower estimate can be made for any library system and it helps in the proper planning of human resource of academic libraries. But the academic libraries, its organisational structure, users and their demands, availability of library facilities differ from State to State. However it is also not always practicable to follow Ranganathan's or U.G.C. staffing pattern exactly especially in a State like Orissa where academic institutions and also academic libraries are passing through a great financial constraint. Therefore, according to the academic library structure, its users and their demands, finance etc., a suitable staffing pattern should be formulated separately for university, degree college and +2 college libraries. Besides this, the academic libraries should follow a hierarchical staff structure which can effectively organise and strengthen its human resource in order to lead it towards the fulfillment of the library's objectives. The staff structure of different types of academic libraries should be as follows:

University library	*Degree college library*	*+2College library*
Chief Librarian	Librarian	Librarian
↓	↓	↓
Deputy Librarian	Assistant Librarian	Asst.Librarian
↓	↓	↓
Asst.Librarian	Tech. Assistant	Professional Asst.
↓	↓	↓
Senior Technical Assistant.	Professional asst. Ministerial staff.	Library attendant
↓	↓	↓
Technical asst.	Library attendant	Other minial staff
↓	↓	
Professional asst/ Ministerial staff	Other minial staff	
↓		
Library attendant		
↓		
Other minial staff.		

CONCLUSION

Academic library environment is a dynamically changing environment with regard to its types of collection, structure, users and their demands, etc. Besides this the introduction of information technology, electronic media and different library networking systems have made it more dynamic and challenging unit in an academic set up. Therefore for the effective functioning of the academic libraries, proper human resource planning is highly necessary, because without this no library will be able to provide efficient service. For this purpose, the present conditions of the academic Libraries of Orissa should be examined and a staffing pattern should be formulated according to the present and future needs of the library to satisfy its users. The State Government should also take initiative to formulate and implement a staffing pattern for academic libraries so that proper planning and utilisation of human resources can be done which will ultimately enhance the quality of academic library services in Orissa.

REFERENCES

1. J. Edwards and M. Silver, "Introduction – the art of designing a manpower strategy" *Manpower Planning*. Ed. by Edwards & Others (New York : John Wiley & Sons, 1983).
2. S.K. Kapoor and Chatterjee. *Ed*. Manpower planning in library and information system in India. (Calcutta : IASLIC, 1989).
3. P.P. Mathur "Staffing in university libraries in India with reference to U.P. Libraries, *ILA Bulletin*. 24; 3; 1988; p45-51.
4. C.V. Penna. "Planning library services", *UNESCO Bulletin for Libraries*. 21 (1967): p 60-92.
5. J.S. Sharma, Library Organisation, (New Delhi: Vikas, 1978).
6. Seva Singh "Planning of library and information services in university libraries in India". *ILA Bulletin*. 23. (1987) 1-2, p 15-12.

VI : 5
What and How of Information Management?

S. Seetharama

INTRODUCTION

The importance of information as a vital source in today's society hardly needs emphasis as information brings people and thoughts together. It is the exchange of ideas, news and data that make a society what it is. In the Post-Industrial Society, it has been said that what counts is not raw muscle power or energy but information, and indeed the advanced economics of the world have already become information intensive. As a matter of fact, information is now called the fourth resource, the other three being people, money and physical resources. From the economic point of view, it has been recognised and realised that value is created by the interaction of these four resources. As David Best puts it "If this claim needs justification, consider the effects of lack of information on the financial markets on 'Black Wednesday', or the havoc caused by insider dealing when some individuals have information on adverse drug reactions not being available when needed or not being managed in a way which enabled early warning to patients is another case in point". In other words, he has emphasised on the necessity of taking charge of information (i.e. information management) in the same way that we actively manage money, people and equipment. (Best, 1996).

DEFINITIONAL ANALYSIS

In attempting to discuss the subject of Information Management, it would be helpful to define and delimit the use of the terms and consider some of the resulting implications. This is especially because the meaning of terms depend on the context in which they are used. Therefore, for any purposeful discussion which will ensure some degree of success, defining of terms becomes desirable, if not essential.

Information

Some meaningful message recorded in conventional or non conventional media and stored and processed by systems and services with a view to provide more or less permanent memory of the messages and their dissemination to users.

It (information) is a diffused resource, that enters into all the activities of business and forms a component of all products and services that are sold. As McPherson puts its, "Information permeates all organizations, it is the raw material of cognitive activity .... the means whereby the organisation obtains its window on the world". It also has the paradoxical quality of being usable for measuring the value of other things, but not of itself."

BS-3527, Part 1, 1976 defines information as "The meaning that a human assigns to data by means of conventions used in their presentation". In other words, information is data that has been given shape. It may be considered as processed data. Thus, information is data plus the meaning which has to be a result of human action.

An unconventional definition states that information is :

* What we take in from outside to feed our knowledge so that we can function successfully and achieve our aims.
* What is necessary and what is available in a given situation for this purpose.

Information as a resource

This concept can, perhaps, be explained by quoting more

or less verbatim Forest Woody Horton's excellent definition, which says that treating information as a resource means treating it as

* Something of fundamental value, like money, capital goods, labour or raw materials;
* Something with specifiable and measurable characteristics, such as method of collection, utilities and uses, a life cycle pattern with different attributes at each stage, and interchangeability with other resources;
* An input, which can be transferred into useful outputs that are beneficial to achieving the organization's goals;
* Something that can be capitalized, depending on management's purposes;
* An expense for which standard costs can be developed and cost accounting techniques can be used to monitor and control;
* Something that presents to top management a variety of development choices, e.g. making trade-off decisions between information-intensive and manpower-intensive investment; between teleprocessing and manual processing activities; or between maintaining an information product or service inhouse, or buying from an external source (Horton, 1982).

Management

Management has been defined by the American Management Association as the guiding of human and physical resources into dynamic organization units that attain their objectives to the satisfaction of those served, and with a high degree of morale and sense of attainment on the part of those rendering the service. Perhaps, a simpler definition would be "Getting results through people".

Generally speaking, management would include planning, organizing, staffing, directing, coordinating, reporting and budgeting ... POSDCORB, for short. Marketing, of course, forms part of managerial activities.

Information Management

While the terms 'Information' and 'Management' have been defined, there does not seem to be one view in regard to the couplet "Information Management" both in academic and professional circles. Consequently, it has been described as chameleonic in character or nature or to be more charitable as McGee and Prusat (1996) put it "Information Management (IM) is an emergent field of interest". Whatever it is, IM is one of the buzz terms of the present age of librarianship / information science /archives and records management. It is a term that has come to significance as a consequence of the greatly increased interest in Information Technology (IT). The following are some of the definitions/explanations found in literature :

1. According to Martin White "IM is at least two thousand years old, and has been masquerading under the name 'Military Intelligence". As a working definition, she cites "The efficient and effective coordination of information from internal and external sources (Cronin 1985). She goes on to identify three components of IM ;
   a) Information resources include the identification, assessment and use of both internal and external resources.
   b) Technology, covering methods of inputting, storing, retrieving and distributing information on both a local and remote basis.
   c) Management, involving strategic and business planning, human resource management, inter-personal communication, accounting, budgeting and marketing.
2. Marchard notes "IM includes two dimensions :
   a) Managing the information process, and
   b) Managing the data (information) resources of the organization.

3. According to Tom Wilson (1987), "IM has no standard definition, but the basis of the idea can be found in one of Peter Drucker's works : "The systematic and purposeful acquisition of information and its systematic and purposeful application are emerging as the new foundations for work, productivity and effort throughout the world". Wilson then goes on to comment "That notion that the economics of the future world depend 'upon the purposeful acquisition' of information is at the root of the IM idea. Also at root is the idea that the systematic and purposeful application of information will depend increasingly upon the application of IT.. Two ideas, therefore, come together in the concept of IM: information as an important economic resource and IT as a tool for its effective management."

Wilson's contention is that IM curriculum should be composed of:

i. The idea of the emergent "information society" and the need for information policies and IT policies in societies and organizations;
ii. The notion of systems and "systems thinking" and the exploration of these ideas in the design and development of computer based information systems and services;
iii. Information technology: Hardware, Software, and Telecommunications. Including such matters as the evaluation of software packages, and some exposure to computer programming,
iv. The Economics of Information: costs, value, pricing policies, information as a public good and information as a product, budgeting information systems and services;
v. The Evaluation of Information Systems and Services from the perspectives of efficiency and effectiveness;
vi. The identification of users' needs for information or as it is generally expressed in the IT management literature, "User requirements studies".

Concluding, he remarks that "The idea of IM as an integrating concept is that it will lead to the definition of a specilization within the information professions which can be applied to any organization, including libraries, archives, and the myriadic organizations which have needs for the organization and handling of information".

4. The introduction to the conference proceeding "IM in engineering education" (Lehigh University, USA, 1966) provides a practical and useful definition of IM. IM can be defined as that engineering sub-discipline designed to acquaint the engineering student with principles, theory and the use of information as an adjunct to his learning process and the practice of engineering. Specifically included are: the nature of engineering information, its sources, dimension, growth and scope, the manipulation of engineering information including storage, retrieval, transfer and application, available resources, including variety, number and location; methods and cost of use, the use of engineering information in directed study, free reading, problem solving and professional engineering application. The mechanisms, processes, benefits, costs, history, current use and possible future applications of IM and systems are implicit in this definition... The concept of IM is attractive because it provides a single concept in place of the several in "Information Sources, Media and Systems", thereby offering simplification in thought and discussion.

5. Lynda Woodman comments that "IM is all about getting the right information, in the right form, to the right person, at the right cost, at the right time, in the right place, to take the right action". This sounds quite familiar – a re-enunciation or implication of Ranganathan's Five Laws of Library Science!

6. Based on the Touche Ross survey (1994), Best (1996) defines IM "as the effective production, storage, retrieval

and dissemination of information in any format and on any medium to support (institutional) business objectives".

From the above, one can infer that IM covers the whole spectrum of information handling activities, technology and its role in information handling as well as various management activities practised in institutions.

TOOLS AND TECHNIQUES FOR IM

While the need for effective IM within an institution is not new, two major trends, however, have come together to create an unprecedental awareness of the importance of information. Firstly, the growing complexity of organizational structures and operations, and secondly the impact of computing and communications technologies (collectively called IT) on work functions and patterns. Consequently, the managerial spotlight is now on information processing and information resources handling within the organizational framework (Lewis, 1985).

The question then is not What IM but How IM ? The answer lies in the various tools and techniques available to the library and information profession, some of which are discussed below.

Information Technology

The field of librarianship and information science has undergone a sea change during the past three decades, due to the impact of information technology on the generation, processing, storage, retrieval and dissemination / transmission of information. At this juncture, it may be useful to remember that the four interrelated trends of IT... Multiple IT, Dispersing IT, Accelerating IT, and Pervasive IT have altered, for example,

* Objectives and strategies, the nature of sources and services
* Operational /organizational structures, the ways in which service(s) is delivered.

In addition, the advantages of IT which include : accommodation of increased workload, achievement of greater efficiency, ability for generation of new services, facilitating cooperation etc. can stand in good stead in the quest for quality and productivity of L & I sources (collection) and services.

This newly introduced technology essentially based on electronics seems to be gradually replacing the conventional tools (See table below) in information activities as it is amenable to integration unlike the latter. In other words, IT facilitates both manipulation and synthesis of information.

Information Activity	*Conventional Technology*	*New Information Technology*
ORIGINATE	Writing/Shorthand Typing- retyping (correction fluid) Carbon copies Typesetting	Word processing (Spelling checkers), Integral printing/ typesetting, character/voice recognition
PRESERVE	Filing cabinets In/Out trays Microfilm	Electronic Filing, Databases, Magnetic storage, Video Storage, Holography
RETRIEVE	Card index, Edge punched cards Body punched cards Abstracts index	Information Retrieval (IR) DBMS software WP/office automation software
MANIPULATE/ SYNTHESIZE	Diary centralised data processing Slide rule Calculator Manual graphing	Distributed/local processing/Micrographic IR statistical/what if/ modelling/scheduler/diary software
COMMUNICATE	Internal/external Postal service, Telephone Courier Telex Personal contact	Electronic mail computer/ WP communication Computer conferencing Facsimile. View data
DESTROY	Shredding Burning medium destroyed	Magnetic erasure Photo erasure Reusable media

Fig. 1. Information Activities and Technology (After Bob Wiggins)

Nevertheless, integration has not been achievable in many cases due to incompatibilities in system hardware and software design and associated standards.

At this juncture, perhaps, a listing of advances / key technologies which the market has identified as the necessary foundations on which to build an information revolution will be in order.

INFORMATION TECHNOLOGY COMPONENTS OF THE NEW INFORMATION AGE

- Invention of the **Mainframe Computers** acting as the first information repositories
- Invention of the **Minicomputer**
- **Word Processor** which appeared as a special hardware quickly disappeared to be embodied in PC software for **Word Processing** and **Desktop Publishing**
- **Personal Computer (PC)**
- Development **of Computer Network** and linking of PCs and Workstations to a central machine
- Development of LAN, linking individual groups of PCs together often with a minicomputer as a shared repository.
- Development of WAN via satellite or landline, linking users in one network with information stored on a remote machine or with users on that network.
- Creation of **Optical Storage Device** capable of mass storage of text and document images (Portable on-line libraries)
- Creation of **Document Scanning Technology** (Electronic Microfilm)
- Invention of **CD-ROM** which is becoming the dominant distribution medium for all documents / information for a wide audience
- Invention of **OCR** and **Intelligent Character Recognition** for converting older and incoming documents into a medium which can be understood and indexed by computers.
- Invention **of Optical Juke Box** for storing vast image and document libraries.

- Emergence of **Relational Databases** making separation of data and program a reality and making classes of information 'stored once' reusable in many applications.
- Creation of **Client Server Computing** making separation of the interface from the central information repository encouraging shared data and collaboration
- Evolution of Massive **Parallel Processing**
- Invention of **Text Retrieval techniques/methods** opening up the potential for content based searching of unstructured information the key to unlocking the value of documents.
- Creation of **Electronic Mail Systems** for providing much more than messages between people and for moving information around efficiently.
- Creation of **Electronic Workflow and Document Routing,** removing the need for serial processing of documents and freeing us from the wait state which reliance on paper imposes.
- Creation of Electronic **Document** Viewing **Technology** (the means by which one could eliminate paper from the equation much of the time).
- Emergence of UNIX **& Windows** NT (possibly the nearest we shall ever get to a universal operating system)
- Emergence and domination **of MICROSOFT Windows** as a generic PC-based user interface.
- Invention of Object Databases and Document Markup Standards.
- **Speech Recognition Technology** to make data input just a matter of speaking into a machine, the end of the keyboard eventually.

From the above, one can recognize the role of IT as a tool in IM. Further, comprehensive treatment of the application of IT for various library house keeping operations such as acquisitions, classification, cataloging, circulation, stock taking, serials control, etc. can be found in library literature and hence not discussed here. The role of networks, especially the arrival on the scene of INTERNET, has completely revolutionised the entire gamut of activities that constitute library and IM, be it Collection Management, Information Services Management, Document Delivery Services (electronic), etc. (IASLIC conference 1997, Chaudhary 1996, Seetharama 1996). However, some of the crucial issues that need to be addressed in a network environment include copyright management, standardization, training and education as these would facilitate effective utilization of valuable resources and power tools available on networks.

STANDARDS

Standards may be considered as important tools in IM. For example, Indian Standards Institution (now called Bureau of Indian Standards) has developed and published a number of Indian standards for documentation pertaining to bibliographical reference, book binding, books and periodicals, cataloguing, classification, library and archives building, furniture, lighting, microfilms, proof corrections, typography, etc. In addition, a number of institutions and individuals have formulated library standards, both official and non-official, useful in the planning and management of libraries and information centres. Similarly, British, European and International Standards for quality systems have been developed and if implemented successfully would lead to improved quality, reduced production cost, and enhanced ability to demonstrate credibility to the potential customers.

On the other hand, advent of computer communication facilities and their use in development of bibliographical databases has raised the hope of developing an Universal Bibliographic System through the cooperation of several national and international organizations. Consequently, standardized machine readable bibliographic formats like USMARC, UKMARC, UNIMARC, CCF, and ISO-2709, the international standard format for bibliographic information interchange on magnetic tape were developed. The CCF record structure as a basis for exchange format is also being used in its logical aspects for formatting of bibliographic data sent online and stored on other media such as floppies and CD-ROM.

System Analysis

System Analysis (SA), a tool for IM, has proved invaluable in analyzing complex organizations and solving problems resulting from organizations in conflict with an environment dominated by change and the uncertainty that inevitably accompanies change. But its use in library and information environments has been limited. Increasingly, however, in recent times, libraries are becoming aware of its potential usefulness to analyze and help solve their problems.

Bibliometrics–A Tool/Technique for Information Management

While British Standards Institution has defined Bibliometrics as "the study of the use of documents and patterns of publication in which mathematical and statistical methods have been applied", Sengupta defines it as "the organization, classification and quantitative evaluation of publication patterns of all macro and micro communication along with their authorships by mathematical and statistical calculus". It is a quantitative science and is divided into Descriptive bibliometrics (productivity count) and Evaluative bibliometrics (literature usage count). The techniques of bibliometrics have extensive applications equally in sociological studies of science, information management, librarianship, history of science including science policy, study of science and scientists, etc.

Work Analysis Techniques

In managerial work, it is essential to analyze operations step-by-step as this would facilitate efficiency and effectiveness of the operations. Several standard techniques have been developed to aid this type of work analysis. Some of the techniques of work analysis which will be useful for IM situations are **Block Diagram, Flow Diagram, Flow Process Chart, Decision Flow Chart, Operations Analysis, Form Analysis, Man-Machine Charts,** Other techniques of work analysis include **Multiple Activity or GANTT, Chart, Micromotion,** etc.

Monitoring Techniques And Controlling

While controlling usually refers to checking, verifying, testing, reputating, exercising restrain or directing influence in order to successfully carry out a management process, monitoring involves looking for faults, performing of duty, giving advice and instruction and exercising caution.

A monitoring technique is a time negotiated procedure on how allowed resources will be committed in achieving objectives. It is a guideline, a tool or an aid. The best techniques are those that are not rigid as they have provisions for adjustments as future events become known. These include:

Operations Research (OR), Management Information System (MIS), Management By Objectives (MBO), Network Analysis, other Monitoring Techniques, etc..

Evaluation Techniques

Evaluation of any service, process or activity in management usually refers to "determining its worth" or "assessment, valuation, appraisal, criticism, review, calculation, measurement" or need to know closely the utility. Evaluation thus is a matter of comparison of actual results, not only with anticipated results, but also with external standards, in the light of existing institutional realities which may be relevant to evaluating the future trajectory of the program or service and provide an objective basis for decision making. Some of the basic techniques which are applicable for evaluation process are :

* Performance measurement—helps us to decide how well the information system, service or resource is operating, compared with some theoretical maximum. Some of the performance measures are cost benefit analysis measures, decision analysis, etc. Two measures of great importance

to ascertain the effectiveness of information retrieval are : Recall and Precision.

* Performance Evaluation—is an assessment of how well a system or service is working, according to some previously decided measure. Two sorts of measures can be used for performance evaluation—INPUT measures investigate from the viewpoint of its operators and look at the resources invested and how they are deployed, OUTPUT measures try to look at customer satisfaction and the extent to which the service is succeeding in its objectives.
* Cost-Effectiveness Analysis—is the relationship between the level of performance (effectiveness) and the costs involved in achieving this level.
* Cost-Benefit Analysis—refers to the relationship between the benefits of a particular product or service and the costs of providing it.
* Bibliometrics—is the application of various statistical analyses to study patterns of authorship, publication and literature use. Bibliometric techniques can be used for various purposes in libraries. They can be applied successfully as evaluation techniques. For example, to evaluate journal collection, evaluate productivity of institutions and individuals, etc.

Conventional Techniques

It may not be out of place to mention that librarians were the first people to bring some discipline and order to IM with their classification and cataloging schemes (Cronin 1985). However, sometimes it is argued that with automation of information retrieval it is possible to dispense with traditional methodologies/techniques for organizing information, in particular classification. The strongest counter argument to this is that classification underlies all thinking; thus it would be prima facie surprising if it found no place in online systems of the future. Svenonius (1983, 1991) has identified some uses of classification in online retrieval systems:

However, classification has such an important place in online systems that we should prepare for a resurgence of interest in both its theory and practice. A similar line of thinking can be seen in the work of Stephen Walker (1991), Liu and Svenanius (1991), Nohr (1991), Watanabe (1994) who have used classification techniques in the context of OPAC searching.

Similarly, Library of Congress Subject Headings List, Rules for Subject Cataloging, Thesaurus, Keyword Indexing have been used for subject search and retrieval in OPACs.

To state that classification has a role in information management would be to state the obvious. It may be in relation to the users interest profile construction, document profile construction, arrangement and presentation of information, database creation, etc. Neelameghan (1992) has shown how Normative Principles of Classification are useful in designing of a database. According to him, they are useful in all the three planes of work.

In other words, in the preparation of the Field Definition Table (FDT), a pre-requisite for database creation, classificatory principles have a role to play.

Further, in studying the information needs of the potential users, classification is of great help in the case of specialists belonging to a particular discipline. But, in the case of planners and decision makers, it is rendered difficult as the information needs are not structured according to subjects in the usual sense of the term, but are essentially function or task-oriented. Therefore, an alternative approach–a Model or Reference Framework, according to which planning and decision making programmes are conceptually analysed into different phases, sub-tasks, activities, etc. and the information support needed for each are identified. When this is done (which is nothing but classification in one sense), it would be possible to select / extract relevant data and information from different sources / databases and repackage them into relevant subsets for convenient use at the different stages of planning work.

It has also been shown by Seetharama (1992) that

classification has a role in the generation of information services and products, especially in the arrangement of ideas in information consolidation products.

In the context of bibliographic description (cataloging) of documents, the role played by AACR and CCC in the development of machine readable bibliographic record formats — US MARC, UK MARC, UNIMARC, CCF, etc. – is well known.

CONCLUSION

Whatever Information Management is, perhaps it is concerned with obtaining the best possible value for money from an organization's information resources. In other words, the buzz words in this context would be economy, efficiency and effectiveness in relation to the information or record life cycle— creation, communication, use, storage and disposal of information. To achieve the 3 Es, numerous tools and techniques, both conventional and non conventional, have been developed. These include tools and techniques, such as: Information Technology, Standards, System Analysis, Work Analysis Techniques, Monitoring Techniques, Evaluation Techniques, Conventional Techniques of Classification, Cataloguing, etc. As a matter of fact, the entire lot of Management Techniques (See Appendix) seem to be applicable to Information Management. Since these techniques have been widely discussed in library and information science literature and are well known to information professionals, details of these have not been given.

While IT may be able to handle some of the problems within the present systems development paradigm presently, a time may come when it would be difficult to find solutions leading to major breakdowns in information systems. Hence, there is a need for research in the area of information management, particularly in the area of innovations including: Use of Artificial Intelligence; Improved methods of data storage and retrieval behaviours (Holtham, 1996). In this context, Holtham's observation that "Information is more critical to success than IT, but IT gets most of the attention and the great bulk of the investment in managerial time, financial investment, and media attention.... Continuation of this imbalance (between information and technology) will be the heart of failure to achieve the full benefits from information systems" is worthwhile recalling.

To conclude, as Best puts it "The field of Information Management has never been more exciting than it is today; our pressing needs, the technologies (and techniques) available to us, and the demands of our business, governments and society as a whole present a challenge to us to find ways of satisfying demands for ever more relevant, up-to-date and accurate information at an economic cost. Whether we succeed or fail is up to us".

REFERENCES

1. David P, BEST Ed, *The Fourth Resource : Information and its management* (Cower, Hanshive : ASLIB, 1996).
2. Blaise CRONIN, Ed, *Information management: From strategies to Action* (London : ASLIB, 1985).
3. P, DRUCKER, The *age of discontinuity* (London : Heinmann, 1969).
4. S. LIU and E SEVENONIUS, DORS : *DDC Online Retrieval System" Lib Res Tech Serv* 35; (1991) 359-75.
5. D.A MARCHAND, *Information management in public organizations : Defining a new resource management function* (The Bureaucrat 7; 1978) 4-10.
6. A, Neelmeghan, Use of S.R. Ranganathan's Normative Principles of Postulates in designing non-bibliographic specialized databases. Libri (1992)
7. H. Nohr, Classification as the basis of a subject cataloging component in an OPAC, demands on elements and structure, Bibliotheksdients 25; (1991) 664-70.
8. S. Seetharama, Role of classification in information services generation Library Science 29; (1992) 109-118.
9. S. Waker, Views on classification as a search tool on a computer. In Computers in libraries international'91 Proceedings of 5th Annual Conference (London, Feb. 1991) p. 130-139.
10. T. Watanabe. An experimental OPAC system using NDC 8 to improve subject access Toshokan Kai, The library world 46; (1994) 164-176.
11. T. Wilson. Information management : A new focus Paper 56- TRAIN - 2 - E. 53rd IFLA Council and General conference, Brighton, UK, 16-21, Aug. 1987.

APPENDIX

MANAGEMENT TECHNIQUES : AREAS OF APPLICATION

A: *TECHNIQUES APPLICABLE TO THE SYSTEM AS A WHOLE*

1 System Analysis:

Planning and designing of systems

Determining requirements of a new system

Formulation of objectives/goals

Prelude to library automation

Decision making in general

To study library system

To solve systems problems

To improve system performance

2 Problem Classification, Logic Tree, Critical Examination:

Designing, developing and operating information services

B: TECHNIQUES APPLICABLE TO LIBRARY OPERATIONS AND SERVICES

OR Techniques in General

Long term planning

Assisting library management

Resource allocation

Decision making in general

Decision making in regard to investment in new facilities

Policies for acquisition of stock

Loan policy

Planning of information services

Designing, developing and operating of information services

Implementation of information services

To improve information services

Advertising and marketing library services

Weeding policy

Library location

Decision Theory Model

Decision making in regard to information retrieval problem

Evaluation of retrieval system

Evaluation of information services

Graph Theory Models

PERT

Planning of information services

CPM

Planning of information services

Queuing Theory

To analyze the problem of congestion at card and book catalogues

Queuing Network Model

Decision rules for inter borrowing

Queuing and Markov Model

Staff schedule determination

M/M/S Queue Model & Dynamic Programming

Resource allocation

Queuing Theory & Dynamic Programming

Resource allocation

Stochastic Shelf Reading Model

Shelf reading policy

Linear programming

Resource allocation

Linear Programming Model

Journal selection

Non Linear Programming Model

Resource allocation

Dynamic Programming

Allocation of funds

Loan policy

Computer Simulation

Evaluation of retrieval system

Evaluation of information services

Monte-Carlo Simulation

To simulate variable loan and duplication policy

Mathematical Model

To estimate measures of effectiveness

Journal selection

To determine acquisition rates

Acquisition of Book

Decision of rules for inter borrowing

To predict a library's circulation

Evaluation of information services

Book Budget Model

Allocating book budget

Cost Effectiveness Model

To compare the cost of manual and mechanized circulation services

Network Flow Model

Determine the optimum shelf heights to effect economy

Computer Programme Model

To improve directory performance

Shelf Reading Model

Shelf reading policy

WORK ANALYSIS TECHNIQUES

Analysis and evaluation of current library procedure

Flow Charts

Multiple activity charts

Decision flow charts

Forms control programme

Work sampling

Cost analysis

STATISTICAL TECHNIQUES

General Statistical Model

Projection of the number of data bank users

Graphic Techniques

To evaluate library and information functions

Graphic Models

Designing, developing and operating information services.

Time Series Analysis & Multiple Regression Techniques

To forecast library growth

Regression Techniques

To predict, evaluate and control the performance of bibliographic search procedures

SURVEY TECHNIQUE

Survey Techniques in General

Decision making in regard to investment in new facilities.

Data for a cost benefit study of manually produced Current Awareness Bulletins

Data on library performance & operations

Data on user failure in the periodical section

Users' studies

Use Survey

Decision making in regard to :

Establish a new branch library

Users' studies

Diary Survey

To plan staffing

Management Survey

Costing service and functions

Failure Survey

Data on stock failures

Users' studies

User Frustration Survey

Data on user frustration

Performance of acquisition policy

Circulation policy

User studies.

Journal Usage Survey

To determine trends in journal usage

User studies

Users' Opinion

To determine trends in journal usage

User studies

Questionnaire Survey

To determine trends in journal usage

User studies

Statistical Survey

To determine trends in journal usage

User studies

Document Delivery Test

Evaluation of Information Services (Providing Documents)

Standard Sampling Theory

To study library book losses

MRAP (Management Review & Analysis Programme)

To examine the operational decision making process

To conduct a management self study

Internal evaluation of library management policies

To improve the management of research and university libraries.

To view and analyse the current management policies and problems

C. TECHNIQUES FOR PERSONNEL MANAGEMENT

MBO

Formulation of objectives/goals

Planning library operations

Improve administration

To plan staffing

Staff management and staff participation

Participative decision making

Training & development of personnel

Evaluation of performance

To solve management problems

Planning of information services

Evaluation of information services

Participative Management

Staff participation in decision making

Consultative Management

Staff participation in decision making

Job Analysis, Job Evaluation, Job Descriptive Index Staff Assessment, In-House Supervisory Programme

Personnel selection, motivation, job satisfaction,

Professional development, employee communication and implementing personal policy

D. TECHNIQUES FOR FINANCIAL MANAGEMENT

PPBS

Resource allocation

To view library costs in new ways

To present budgetary information in new ways

Allocation of funds

To cost an expenditure programme for demonstrating cost effectiveness

Costing a local abstracting service

Analytical evaluation of existing and proposed programme with quantitative measures of performance

Programmed Budgeting

To establish library priorities

Formula Budgeting

Allocation of funds

Serials Budget Formula

To measure cost effectiveness of periodicals

Brooks's Theoretical Model

To effect economics in periodical holdings

Randall's Rationalised Ratios

Allocation of Funds

Unit Cost–Study Programming

For costing library activities

Building Block Costing System

For collection of rational cost data

Cost Benefit Analysis

For determining the cost value of an electronic security system

Break Even Analysis

To determine economy.

VI : 6

Sustainable Manpower Development In Library and Information Centres

Amrit Pal

INTRODUCTION

The World Commission on Environment and Development, 'WCED' (popularly known as the Brundtland Commission) 1987'[1] defined sustainable development as "meeting the needs of the present generation without compromising the needs of future generations".

SUSTAINABLE LIBRARIANSHIP

As far as sustainable librarianship is concerned this can be interpreted to mean a continuous process of change in which the library resources and technological advancements are utilized for storage, retrieval and communication of information to satisfy the needs of the present as well as future generations.

SUSTAINABLE LIBRARY AND INFORMATION MANPOWER DEVELOPMENT

To have continuous existence and growth, Library and Information Science (LIS) education must adapt itself to the changing environment. However, in its attempt to assimilate the "new", it must not forget its 'cultural legacy'. It means LIS education must preserve current programmes but without sacrificing its knowledge base, approaches, values, practices and tools that must be applied to new problem areas. In the light of this we can say that LIS education programmes must be so designed as to (i) ensure the development of such personnel as are able to handle the present information environment and at the same time (ii) Provide necessary specializations which can be helpful to develop the libraries on modern lines during the foreseeable future.

At present, LIS education is operating in an extremely dynamic and competitive environment. The growing importance of information, developments in information technology and the information environment, all are necessitating LIS education to adapt itself to the change.

THE INFORMATION ENVIRONMENT

Due to increased technological advancements the information environment today witnesses a severe change in it. Information has become the axis of the whole development activity. LIS education's focus on libraries has been challenged by a "fundamental shift from a Ptolemaic information universe with the library at its centre to a dynamic Copernican universe with information at its centre and with libraries playing a significant but not necessarily central role."[2] The change has been due to (i) the fusion of computing and telecommunications, producing a geographically distributed environment for creating, storing, manipulating and sharing information and (ii) increased abundance and complexity of information through globally accessible networks and multi and hypermedia information structures.[3] Assessing the situation, some futurists even go to the extent of saying that by the turn of this century, many big libraries will lose their character as repository of books, journals and other paper based materials, and serve only as access points to world information. Some even talk of the possibility of emergence of 'private-space libraries and decline of public space libraries'. In such a situation, it is feared that LIS programmes, if they do not adapt themselves to the changing environment, will become automatically extinct.

However, a situation identical to this has not still emerged in India even though the use of computer, CD-ROM and other devices has just begun in many of the Indian libraries. As a consequence, they are beginning to experience a transitional phase and these have still been slow to react to developments in computer technology. This is probably due to the lack of overall computer environment in the country and technically trained staff.

In recent years, some favourable developments have taken place with the emphasis laid down on modernization in the Seventh Plan. The working group on Modernization of Library Services and Information of the Planning Commission made significant recommendations on the application of computers in libraries and information area. Recently the UGC has embarked on an ambitious library and information system known as INFLIBNET. This system aims at developing a mechanism to link libraries and information centres in universities, colleges, deemed universities, UGC information centres, institutions of national importance, R & D institutions, etc. The main objective of INFLIBNET is to make infomation accessible to all institutions engaged in higher learning, research and development. Undoubtedly, this is a major programme towards modernization of libraries and information centres with the application of computer and communication technologies.

Besides, due to the development of modern telecommunication facilities for the use of Indian telecom subscribers, general data networks and specialized networks have been developed. The NICNET, a Govt. data network of NIC and INDONET, the public data network of CMC, are two pioneer general data networks aiming at sharing the resources. Local networks such as BONET, CALIBNET, DELNET, MALIBNET have been installed. Many of the libraries/information centres such as BARC, TIFR, NAL, DESIDOC, INSDOC (NISCAIR), ICRISAT etc. have installed facilities for on-line search of information from international data-bases.

The above developments suggest that by the turn of the

century, India's transition to information based economy will be faster. To keep pace with the changing scenario, it will become imperative that information manpower required for the present and future libraries and information centres be developed with a good deal of forethought, care and planning.

LIBRARY EDUCATION IN INDIA

The present day library and information science education in India which aims at training general purpose librarians fails to develop knowledge and skills in information professionals necessary for handling the new information technology. Even libraries of some university and special libraries which are on the forefront of the new technologies complain that "the Library and Information Science schools in India have become irrelevant as they do not impart students that education and develop in them those skills which make them employable and useful to take up new challenging jobs–automated cataloguing, indexing, reference and information services, database searching, databases designing, etc."[4] The reason for this is that many of the library schools still persist in teaching traditional subjects like classification, cataloguing, reference service, book selection, acquisition, etc. The methods of information handling, storage and retrieval are not given their due share in the present curricula. There are some library schools which have deviated slightly from this pattern and introduced partially the subjects of information retrieval science and technology, but even these provide only theoretical knowledge without imparting practical training in advanced information technology. Hence, the traditional library science programmes offered at library schools do not always even accomplish the basic function of "turning out embryo librarians capable of functioning in a variety of operational environments"[5] and hardly ever manage to "achieve the degree of flexibility necessary to ensure that they reflect current professional requirements, trends and practices"[6].

No doubt INSDOC and DRTC are awarding associateship programmes with a greater emphasis on IT and practical work and also run several short term programmes on library automation and IT related topics for practising librarians, but even these have not produced the desired results and have failed to produce sufficient number of information professionals who can handle information technology. The result is that even UGC's efforts to modernize libraries have not been sufficiently fruitful.

CHANGE: THE NEED OF THE HOUR

As information world is undergoing a fundamental change due to developments in information technology, LIS profession/ education must respond to this change by assimilating the requisite characteristics of the 'evolving information professions' in its programmes, otherwise it will become "obsolete and die a slow painful death."[7]

NON-TRADITIONAL JOB MARKETS

Beyond the traditional job market, there are more avenues open for library and information personnel in the information society. They can work as system analysts, database designers, programmers, telecommunication experts, information resource managers and marketing information specialists. Library personnel with their basic knowledge of classification, indexing and abstracting coupled with the knowledge of information technology can work better on these jobs than the information professionals only with the knowledge of computer technology. But the irony is that due to lack of technological education to the library personnel, even the information centres and networks are preferring to employ personnel having the M.Sc. degree in computer science. If it goes on like this, then the library personnel will soon be "outnumbered, outmaneuvered and rendered marginal".[8]

TIPS FOR SUSTAINABLE LIS MANPOWER DEVELOPMENT

Preserving the Best From the Past and Assimilating the New

Library and Information Science schools must design and

implement a curricula which should prepare graduates to cope up effectively with each emerging situation.

It should retain only that part of the existing syllabi that can be adapted to the current programmes. Besides some of the topics required for a basic education in traditional library and information work, the topics which are now rapidly gaining importance should be incorporated in the curricula both at BLISc and MLISc levels. At BLISc level, the following two papers should be introduced:

i. Introduction to Information Technology and

ii. Computer Application in Libraries.

At MLIS level, the following topics should be incorporated.

- Information use and users.
- Information sources and communication media.
- Use of computers for information processing including systems analysis and programming.
- Information analysis, consolidation and repackaging.
- Database design and file structuring
- Electronic document delivery
- Intelligent Knowledge based systems/Expert systems.
- Online searches
- Telecommunications and networks.
- Economics and marketing of information

Emphasis on Specialization in LIS Education

Besides the core curriculum, sufficient options for specialization should be provided. Specialization in LIS could have several benefits. It will help the LIS personnel to move into new information functions. The curriculum could be better tailored to specific student and employer needs.

Also there should be a provision for advanced professional course of one year for those who wish to specialize in a particular area in Library & Information Science, and also to offer training in modern information technology. The topics covered can be:

- A-V technologies, CD-ROM, e-mail, teleconferencing, telecommunication,
- Use of DBMS packages
- On-line searches
- Statistical analysis and bibliometrics
- Information systems analysis, design and evaluation,
- Technical writing and information analysis.

Symbiosis between Theory & Practice

Theory and practice should find equal share in the course curricula. For providing practical training, the departments of library and information science should be provided with microcomputer to simulate information retrieval processes and telecommunication facilities on a laboratory scale.

Also provision for field work should be provided to the students. The libraries of universities and information centres where the courses are offered can act as laboratory cum workshop for the students. Most of the university libraries and information centres in some way are in the process of automation and it is hoped that by the year 2002 these institutions will be exploiting information technology to the maximum. Thus these libraries can be best utilized to offer practical training to students in library and information science. Students should be registered with the library at the beginning of the academic year and it should be expected that every student spends a minimum of four hours a week gaining experience in a modern library. This type of weekly training done continuously during the academic year will be more beneficial, because it will enable the students to perceive theory and practice in context. Information technology innovations such as planning for automation, feasibility studies, systems design, testing, implementation and evaluation will enable the students to see the whole operation in its totality.

Students who may be interested in joining special libraries/ information centres should be sent to the special libraries/ information centres for a short period of internship to have practical experience of the working of these libraries. The special libraries and information centres should also co-operate with the LIS schools in accepting interns and trainees.

Dynamic Methods of Teaching

The teaching of LIS can be made more effective by including such methods as discussion, demonstration, dialogue, tutorials, study groups, talks, assignments, case studies to the traditional expository method (classroom lecture). These methods of teaching not only keep the students' mind active but also help in the development of ideas in the subject field. Due emphasis should also be given to the teaching teaching techniques like the holding of seminars, role-paying exercises simulations, creativity etc. as these develop a self-analytical attitude and initiation capabilities which are essential for adopting dynamic approaches to the management of information services. Also extensive use of audio-visual aids such as microfilm readers, overhead projectors, films and filmstrips, slides, transparencies, tapes, disks, television, video, computer simulation presentation, CD-ROM etc. should be made to make the practical sessions more effective,

Quality Staff

To introduce the necessary innovations in LIS education programmes, nothing proves more effective than the quality of the teaching staff. Because of the specialized topics to be covered in the LIS curricula, the LIS schools must be provided with the staff best equipped to deal with the challenge of new information technology. The effort should be to appoint teachers with the specialized knowledge and skills. If the requisite talent does not exist in-house, then it should be possible for some time at least to draw on the expertise of staff in other academic departments e.g. system analysts, computer scientists, management experts or to rely on guest lectures. However, no matter how useful or desirable it may be to take the help of outside experts, it would always be desirable for the departments of library and information science to equip themselves with the specialized staff.

Continuing Education Programmes

Continuing education programmes i.e. short term courses in application of information technology, refresher courses, workshops, seminars and symposia should be organized on regular basis for LIS teachers and practitioners to enable them to gain the necessary knowledge in the practical application of the new technology and its social implication. This will assist the continual change in librarianship and adaptation to the new practices.

Emphasis on Quality and not on Quantity

Emphasis should not be on establishing new and more library schools. Sometimes this trend results in the over supply of the LIS personnel with no jobs. This creates frustration among the personnel with no jobs and sometimes proves fatal to the existence of the profession. Hence, our focus should be on quality education as quality is the key to both competition and cooperation. LIS programmes must be first perceived as being of good quality in terms of the specific values and second, must be able to bring a clearly articulated, unique knowledge base to both teaching and research.

Flexibility: the Hallmark of Sustainability

Rapid change and adaptability require flexibility. LIS education programme need to be able to experiment with new programmes, courses and specialities, dispense with the unsuccessful ones and move on. This requires flexibility in faculties and courses, possible strategies include innovative delivery mechanisms, and flexibility in student admissions, schedules and the like.

The Integrated Approach

'Librarianship' and 'Information science' are largely overlapping fields, and the overlap represents the common areas of study for education in librarianship and information science. They include human communication, management and systems science, computer science, reprography, information retrieval, user studies and information sources. It is conceived that an integrated approach is not only feasible but essential for education in librarianship and information science. T. Matsumura rightly observes:

> "The practical and applied aspects of information science which are concerned with information systems, services and networks, and information use and users are certainly of common interest to librarianship. The concern with the application of information technology in information which characterizes the field of information science is what librarians have to look to for more effective library operations. And information science as a theory concerning the theories and experimentation in communication, information systems and processes has particular relevance to librarianship in providing theoretical base for this discipline."[9]

National Policy for LIS Education

The national policy for LIS education should be formulated in close co-operation with LIS schools, professional organizations and the U.G.C., keeping in view the changing role of library in society and developments of information technology. It should be designed within the framework of national education policy. It should provide guidelines for planned and co-ordinated growth and development of LIS education so as to meet the needs of Indian libraries/documentation centres/information systems/ library schools adequately for the present as well as for the future.

CONCLUSION

In order for LIS personnel to assume a central position in the information society, the schools of LIS need to broaden their perspectives by assimilating the characteristics of the 'evolving information professions'. These should not direct their energies exclusively to traditional current library needs and practices. They must, in addition, play a role of an "innovator by proposing new developments, investigating the old, re-examining the accepted, experimenting with the untried and in sum serve as leaders in the field".[10] They should take best ideas from the past, shed the redundant and assimilate the new ones. The LIS education programmes must be revised from time to time so as to be responsive to the needs of the society for today and tomorrow. Such a modernization of the LIS programmes will help in the sustained growth of LIS manpower and will ensure the continuous growth and development of the profession.

REFERENCES

1. World Commission on Environment and Development, Our Common Future, (New York : United Nations, 1987)
2. N. V. House and S. A. Satton, "The Panda Syndrome : An Ecology of LIS Education", *Journal of Education for Library and Information Science*. Vol. 37, No. 2, (1996), 134.
3. Ibid.134 p.
4. K. Navlani," Library and Information Science Education in India", *CLIS Observer*. Vol. 13, no. 3-4, (1996), p. 6.
5. M.T.R. Martinelli, "Education and Training for Agricultural information Work" *Journal of Library and Information Science*. Vol. 8. no. 2. (1983) 116.
6. Ibid, 116.
7. D. O. Connor, and J.P. Mulvaney, "LIS Faculty Research and Expectations of the Academic culture Versus the Needs of the Practitioner". *Journal of Education for Library and Information Science*. Vol. 37, no. 4, (1996) p. 313.
8. House and Sutton. op. cit., p. 145.
9. J. Matsumura. "The Integrated Approach:Library and Information Studies". Library Education Programmes in Developing Countries with

Special Reference to Asia Ed. Russel Bowden. (London; the Library Association) pp. 124-125.

10. P. B. Mangla. "The levels of courses? : The place of Library schools in educational Institutions and Teaching staff Requirements". Library Education Programmes in Developing Countries with Special Reference to Asia, op. cit., 133.

VII : 1

Electronic Information Sources in The Digital Library Environment

B. Ramesh Babu

INTRODUCTION

The society is experiencing the phenomena of information explosion which in turn has revolutionised the thinking and outlook of the librarians during the recent years. This phenomena has triggered a series of changes posing corresponding challenges necessitating the reexamination of technical policies of library and information centres. As the information seeking behaviour is changing day by day, the corresponding changes have been expected from the LICs (Library and information centers) in areas of collection development and collection building policies.

Information revolution has led to a vast expansion in our ability to access and communicate. The new technologies have abundantly provided a wide range of electronic media of information sources. Till recently the print media was the prominent source for communicating information. The use of components of Information Technology (IT) has revolutionised the storage and dissemination of massive volumes of information in the media other than print media. A majority of the primary, secondary and tertiary sources hither to issued in print are now made available in the electronic form which are accessible via on-line hosts. These sources are forming the collection of the virtual library or electronic library or digital library.

DIGITAL LIBRARY

A digital library is a global virtual library, which provides access to a very large information collection. It includes the collections of electronic sources in addition to books and journals, such as :

* Cartographic materials
* Sound recordings
* Film strips
* Computer files
* Microforms
* Motion pictures
* Video recordings
* Graphic Materials

Characteristics of Digital Library

* Information is stored in electronic form.
* Provides access to a very large information source
* Supports multimedia content.
* Offers network accessibility.
* Provides user friendly interface.
* Provides access to more information than possible to physically acquire and maintain.
* Delivers information in a variety of formats.
* Offers advanced information storage and search and retrieval.
* Opens unique referencing of digital object.

What is an electronic information source?

Information stored in electronic form can be accessed in any remote corner of the world with the help of new emerging information technology. It is a convergence of computer and communication technologies with the publishing of information sources, to mean that a source published in electronic (machine readable) form. This would include sources distributed on magnetic tape and such media as videodiscs etc., but also accessible like databases. These are in machine readable forms like:

* Bibliographic databases
* Education software
* Electronic textbooks. Knowledge based multi media
* Full text of journals (Electronic journals)
* Clinical decision aids
* Factual databases like directories, encyclopaedias

Lancaster forecasted that by 1990, 25% of information sources will be in electronic form. Further he says by 2000, 50% of the existing indexing and abstracting sources will be in the electronic form. The first electronic book was published from Germany in the year 1985. Since then there has been a steady growth in the electronic publishing.

WHAT IS AN ELECTRONIC JOURNAL?

Electronic journal is one which is available in electronic form and can be accessed using computer and communication facilities.

NATURE OF ELECTRONIC SOURCES

Broadly speaking three kinds are recognised through which the information sources in electronic forms are stored, namely, Visual, Audio and Audio-visual.

PRODUCERS OF ELECTRONIC SOURCES

1. Commercial agencies like UMI, DIALOG, etc.
2. Information institutions like American Chemical Society, Institution of Electrical Engineers, etc.
3. Information networks at local, national and international levels.
4. Library and information centres.
5. Journal publishers and book publishers.

AN OVERVIEW OF VARIOUS ELECTRONIC INFORMATION SOURCES

IEEE / IEE Electronic Library

- Joint venture by Institute of Electrical and Electronics Engineers (USA) & Institute of Electrical Engineers (UK).
- Covers records from INSPEC database.
- Covers IEEE/IEE Journals, conference proceedings, standards etc.
- Adds 25,000 (approx.) records per year.
- Fields covered: Electrical Engineering, Electronics, IT, Computer Science, Applied Physics and related areas.
- Subscribers will get monthly updates.

American Chemical Society

First professional association to bring electronic form of its 18 periodicals in full text over Bibliographical Retrieval Service (BRS) in 1983.

By 1993, there were 6998 online and CD ROM databases.

Elsevier's 'TULIP' Project

* The University License Project (TULIP) provides access to Elsevier's journal.

Association of Computing Machinery [ACM]

* Its Electronic Publication Plan provides access to its publications.

Compendex on Silver Platter

* Only interdisciplinary Engineering absuacts index.
* Covers 2,600 Engineering journals, reports, conference proceedings, etc.,
* Areas Covered : Mechanical, Electrical, Civil, Environmental, Structural Engineering, Materials Science, Bio Engineering, Solid State and Super Conductivity, Energy, Chemical, Optics, Air, Water Pollution, Road Transportation.

Adonis (Advanced Document Over Network Information Services)

* Covers about 650 journals from 40 publishers.
* Covers Biomedicine, Bioengineering, Biochemistry, Biotechnology.
* Supplies weekly new CD ROM to the subscribers of this service, which covers all articles in the fields covered.

The Core Project

* Chemical Online Retrieval Experiment [CORE] at Cornell University Mann's Library.
* Started by American Chemical Society with OCLC.
* Provides access via electronically to all the Journals of ACS .

Dialog Knight-Ridder Information Services Inc.,

* Serving since 1972.
* Covers 400 databases.
* One stop service for all the information needs.
* Areas Covered: Agriculture, Food and Nutrition-Chemistry
  Bio-Sciences and Technology, Engineering
  Business News and Information
  Company Information and Financial Data
  Computers and Software, Physical Science
  Energy and Environment, Industry Analysis
  Govt. and Public Affairs, Travel
  Medicine, Health Care and Drug Information
  Patents, Books and Consumer News
  Social Sciences and Humanities

Products of DIALOG

* DIALOG Business Connection (DBC):
* DIALMAIL

* DIALOG ALERT
* DIALORDER
* DIALINDEX
* ONE SEARCH
* DIALOG ON DISC
* DIALOG LINK

Silver Platter (Database vendor, London)

Covers about 180 database

Coverage:

Education	Business
Food and Agriculture	Humanities
Social Sciences	Environment
Science & Technology	Reference Sources
Health Science	

Provides world-wide access to Electronic Information Sources.

Proquest Databases (Universal Microfilm International) (UMI)

Coverage:

Business
Scientific
Technical
Humanities
General Reference

Products:

Abstract and Index Databases
Full Text Databases
Full Image Databases

UMI Document Delivery Services:

Supply of article reprints

Supply of reprints of theses

OCLC Electronic Journal On-line (EJO)

* Started in July 1992.
* Offers peer-reviewed journals on-line.
* Offers journals on CD ROM for yearly subscription.
* 1995 onwards Institution of Electrical and Electronic Engineers Conference Proceedings are available from EJO.

INFORMATION SOURCES ON INTERNET

* Electronic Journals
* Electronic Discussion Lists/Forums
* Usenet News
* Data and Software Archives
* E-mail based Information Services
* Campus Wide Information Systems (CWIS)
* Library Catalogues
* Online Databases
* Guides to Information Sources

Most of these sources are accessible through INTERNET Navigation Tools like Gopher, Web and FTP

ADVANTAGES OF ELECTRONIC INFORMATION SOURCES

* Minimum access time and cost-effective
* Streamlines update process and promotes availability of accurate documents instantaneously
* Reduces distribution and storage overhead costs
* Allows media enhancement of existing reference materials with sound, video and animation
* Increases user effectiveness and productivity
* Results in error reduction in the production process
* Allows rapid information retrieval

DISADVANTAGES OF ELECTRONIC INFORMATION SOURCES

* High initial costs to the publishers as well as library and information centres
* Usage of different retrieval software by different publishers
* Ease of use not possible i.e., reading at a convenient time and place
* Needs necessary training for the users/subscribers to handle electronic sources

MAJOR IMPEDIMENTS IN THE USE OF ELECTRONIC INFORMATION SOURCES

* Lack of knowledge about the availability of the electronic information sources
* Lack of information and facilities on how to use the resources in Internet
* Lack of knowledge on how to utilise the electronic sources of information
* Lack of financial resources to acquire these sources
* Psychological barriers

CONCLUSION

Information sources are many and increasing exponentially and the access mechanisms are also diversified. Electronic sources have come to stay as a storage and dissemination media. As we approach 21st century, the digital medium will increasingly become the medium of choice for information seeking pattern by the society at large. In the Indian context, it is not an utopian concept. It will certainly gain sufficient momentum in the near future and slowly substitute to a large extent the print based information sources.

VII : 2
Growth Pattern of Literature in the Field of Demography

S. L. Sangam
Bharari Tubachi

INTRODUCTION

Growth of publications and citations is a common feature among different branches of knowledge. The changes in the size of the literature over a specific period may be termed as growth of literature. Many studies have been made on the growth of literature, Price (1) has predicated the annual growth rate and suggested a nearly exponential growth curve over a long period of time. Teague et. al., (2) have discussed in detail the theoretical aspects of exponential growth and instead of an exponential pattern, rather suggested a logistic pattern. One of the most developed theoretical model of literature growth on a specific scientific topic is that of epidemic growth and it has been first propounded by Goffman (3). Mahapatra (4) has suggested a new theory of growth measurement by means of calculating the relative growth rates and doubling time of literature for better assessment of growth literature.

OBJECTIVES OF STUDY

The primary objective of the study is to identify the growth pattern of literature in demography. Specifically, the objectives of the study are to identify the:

$$Dt\ (C) = \frac{\text{Log } e^2}{\bar{R}(C)} = \frac{0.693}{\bar{R}(C)}$$

Here. Dt(P) and Dt(C) are the average doubling time of articles and citations respectively.

RESULTS OF THE STUDY

The RGR were calculated for both publications and citations separately. The Dt against each year of study was also determined. The values of RGR and Dt for publications are represented in table 1 and the values of citations are shown in table 2.

It can be seen in table 1 that the value of average relative growth rate of articles $\bar{R}(P)$ decreased gradually from 0.62 to 0.23.

Similarly, in case of citations (Table 2) the value of average relative growth rate of citations $\bar{R}$ (C) decreased from 0.64 to 0.26.

The value of doubling time of publications Dt (P) increased from 1.11 to 3.01.

In citations the corresponding values of doubling time of citations Dt(C) increased from 1.08 to 2.67.

The mean relative growth $\bar{R}(P)$ for the 5 years showed a growth rate of 0.35.

The corresponding mean doubling time Dt(P) for the period is 2.29.

In case of citations the mean relative growth rate $\bar{R}(P)$ was 0.38 and doubling time Dt(C) for 1989-1993 was 2.08.

The values of RGR and Dt sufficiently indicated that the linear growth curve would be more appropriate. To find out the specific trend of growth, the linear growth equation was applied and expected values were plotted on the graph (Fig. 1).

To get the specific trend of growth of citations the equation for linear growth curve was applied and expected values were plotted on a graph (Fig.2.).

Table 1 : RGR and DT for publications in demography journal during 1989-1993.

Year	No. of articles	Cumulative no.	$\log_e 1^P$	$\log_e 2^P$	$\bar{R}(P)$	Mean $\bar{R}(P)$	Dt (P)	Mean Dt (P)
1989	54	54	-	3.99	-		-	
1990	46	100	3.99	4.61	0.62		1.11	
1991	38	138	4.61	4.93	0.32	0.35	2.16	2.29
1992	37	175	4.93	5.17	0.24		2.88	
1993	45	220	5.17	5.40	0.23		3.01	

Table 2 : RGR and Dt for citations in demography journal during 1889-1993.

Year	No. of citations	Cumulative no.	$\log_e 1^C$	$\log_e 2^C$	$\bar{R}(C)$	Mean $\bar{R}(C)$	Dt (C)	Mean Dt (C)
1989	1504	1504	-	7.33	-		-	
1990	1363	2867	7.33	7.97	0.64		1.08	
1991	1224	4091	7.97	8.32	0.35	0.38	1.98	2.08
1992	1214	5305	8.32	8.59	0.27		2.57	
1993	1586	6891	8.59	8.85	0.26		2.67	

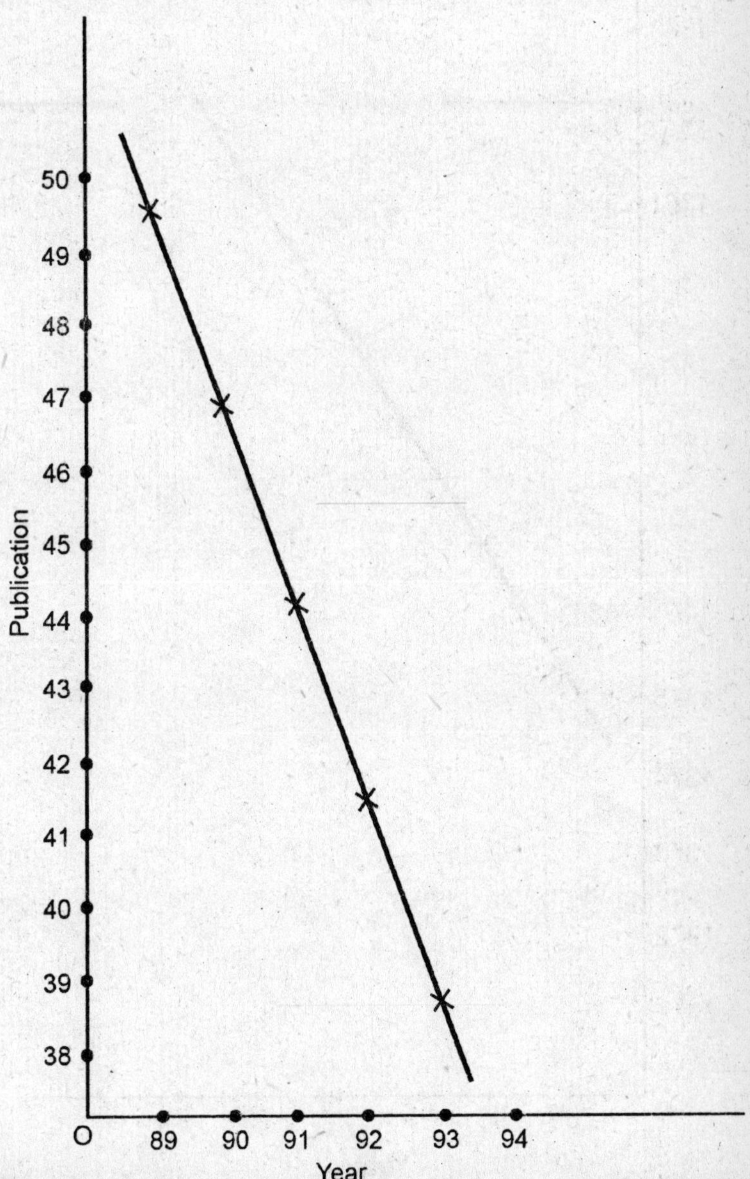

Fig. 1. Fitting of straight line (Linear growth curve) for publications

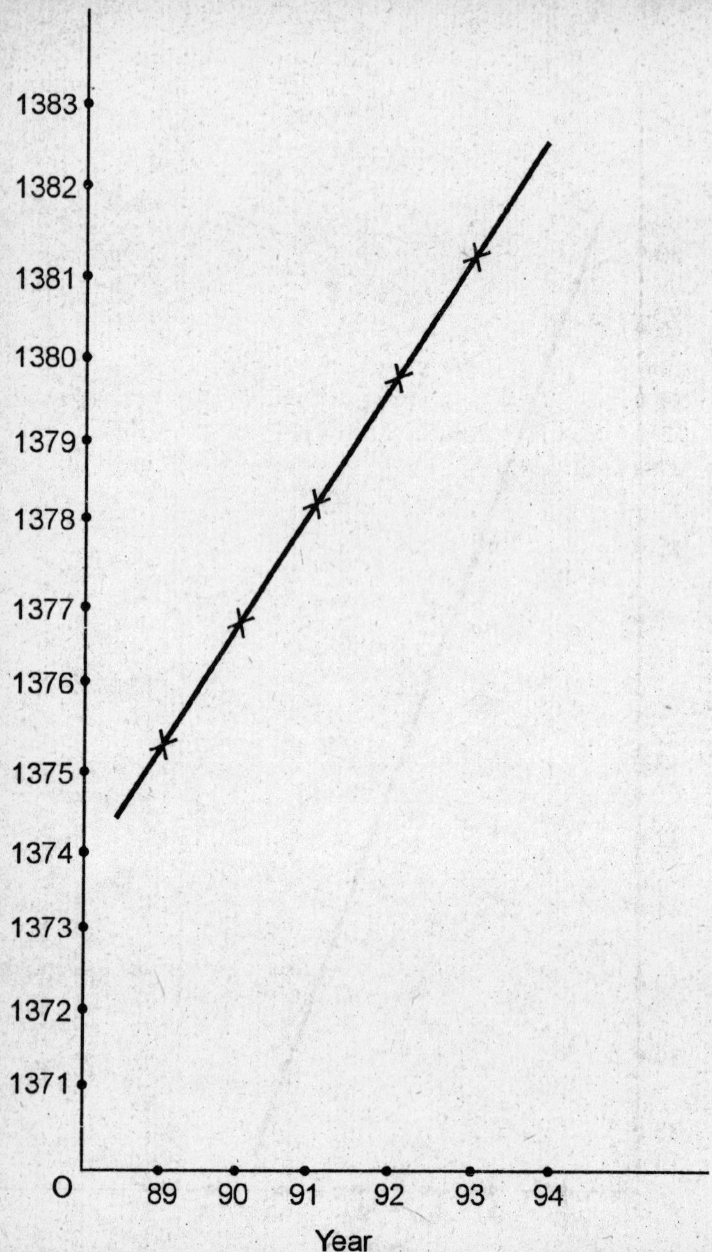

Fig. 2. Fitting of Straight line (Linear growth curve) for Citations

It was also noticed that the nature of growth to follow linear growth pattern.

CONCLUSION

The equal rate of RGR and Dt for both publications and citations indicates that probably with the increase of number of publications, the number of citations will also increase. Therefore, citations may be used as a yardstick to study the nature of growth of literature in a subject. The reducing trend of RGR and increasing rate of Dt in both publications and citations indicates that the growth is neither exponential nor logistic. The size of the literature was calculated by applying linear growth formula and the curve obtained is also linear.

REFERENCES

1. D. J. Desolla "The exponential curve of science". *Discovery*, 17 : (1956) pp 240-243.
2. J Teague, et. al. "The law of exponential growth evidence, implications and forecasts". *Lib. Trends*, 30. 1: (1981), 125-149.
3. W Gaffman Mathematical approach to the spread of scientific ideas - the history of mass cell research. W. Gaffman. T. Sarcevic Ed. (N. Y : Bowker, 1970) 65-68.
4. M Mahapatra "On the validity of the theory of exponential growth of scientific literature." IASLIC Calcutta conf. 15th ed. I. N. Sengupta and S. K. Kapoor. Calcutta : Iaslic: 61-70.
5. S. C. Gupta and (VK) Kapoor. Fundamentals of applied statistics (Reprinted). 1989. (New Delhi : Sultan Chand, 1989) 2.9-9.11.

VII : 3
Scientometric Portrait of L. L. Narayana

V. L. Kalyane

INTRODUCTION

Kuhn (1970) had urged that greater attention be paid to exemplars in science and to the social structure of science. Schubert and Glanzel (1992) expressed an evergrowing stress on scientometrists to publish data on individual scientists. We have studied individual scientists in the following disciplines: *Astrophysics* - S Chandrasekhar (Kademani, et. al. 1996 b); *Physics* - C.V. Raman, (Kademani, et. al. 1994 b), P. K. Iyengar (Kademani, et.al. 1994 a) K.S. Krishnan (Kademani, et.al. 1996 a), P. G. de Gennes (Kalyane and Sen, 1996); *Chemistry* - T. S. West (Kalyane and Munnolli 1995); *Crystallography* - R. Chidambaram (Kalyane and Kademar 1995, Kademani and Kalyane 1996); *Modern Biology* - P. M. Bhargava (Kalyane 1995), Barbara McClintock (Kalyane and Kademani 1997); *Medical Science* - Vinodini Reddy (Kalyane and Kalyane 1993); and *Agriculture* - M.S. Swaminathan (Kalyane 1992, Kalyane and Kalyane 1994), U. R. Murty (Kalyane and Kademani 1994), C.S. Venkata Ram (Kalyane and Devarai 1994), and K. Ramiah (Kalyane and Samanta 1995). The studies generated inquisitive responses from the historians of science, biographers of scientists, science policy makers, administrators of scientific establishment, R and D managers, scientometricians, educationists, young scientists, documents, information scientists, science journalists, etc. 'Scientometric portraits of individual scientists' has emerged as an interdisciplinary multi-disciplinary, and extra-disciplinary domain of research which has practical implication.

Present paper deals with quantitative facts about a renowned *botanist* L.L. Narayana whose pivotal role was recognised by publishing a commemorative volume of the *Indian Journal of Botany* (Sathyanarayana 1990).

RESULTS AND DISCUSSION

L. L. Narayana has published 26 single authored papers during 1955 to 1975 at his 25-45 years age. Multi-authored papers to his credit where 149. Out of 86 double authored papers, he was first published 44 triple authored papers during 1978-1990 in which he was first author in seven papers, second author in five papers, and third author in 32 papers. Four authored papers to his credit were 19 published during 1980-1990; wherein he was first author in three papers; second and third author in one each; and fourth author in 14 papers (Table 1). He was main author in 82 papers, and co- author only in 93 papers.

Publication productive life (the count from the year in which first paper by an author was published to the latest year of publication) of L.L. Narayana was 36 years (1955-1990). Noteworthy feature is that 46 years age onwards all of his papers were collaborative. Collaboration coefficient is the ratio of no. of Multi-authored papers to the total number of papers published in the same period. He had triple authored papers after 48 years age, and four authored papers after 50 years age.

Domainwise classification (Table 2) indicated the highest 57 papers in *Chemotaxonomy*, followed by *Floral Anatomy* (53), *Embryology* (37) and *Systematic Position* (15). His first paper in Chemotaxonomy appeared in 1977 at 47 years of age, land with collaborative pursuits resulted in maximum output of 12 papers in 1984. Domainwise growth curves of publications is shown in Fig. 1.

Fifty percentile age (the corresponding productivity year of 50 percent of all papers) was 27 at his 51 years age in 1981. It is interesting to document that second 50 percent of articles were published in just nine years (1982-1990) of latest professional life. Fifty percentile age is expected to accelerate the progress of a scientist resulting into high visibility and recognition. Productivity coefficient (the ratio of 50 percentile age to the total productivity age) was d 0.45. publication rate (the number of papers published per annum) was four. Papers published during first half of professional life (1955-1972) were 40, and second half of professional life (1973-1990) were 135. He has published 19 papers in 1984; 14 papers in 1978; and 11 papers each during 1989 and 1990.

Tables 3 and 4 document research group productivity of L. L. Narayana and associated. Total authoriships were 406 out of which multi-authorships were 380 establishing the fact that it was indeed an excellent team. M. Radhakrishnaiah collaborated during 1976-1990 in 60 papers with L.L. Narayana, followed by D. Rao (24) during 1965-1978, G. Nageswar (17) during 1983-190, K.T. Sundari (15) during 1977-1984, S.M.J. Anuradha (12), P.S. Narayana (10), and M. Satyavati (9), In all 35 collaborators (including 12 Ph. D. Students) received the benefit of mentorship by L.L. Narayana. Active researchers and active collaborators are delineated in Fig.2.

Mentors, Models, and a special companion or companions often play an essential role in the development of creativity which probably depends upon a nurturant and facilitating environment in the family, in the interpersonal network, and in society (Gedo 1996). Creativity is required at all stages (Bamfield 1996). Scientists have two sorts of offsprings: their contributions to the substantive content of science and, their scientific descendants. With respect to the first sort of offspring, Some scientists general numerous bright ideas and produce mass of publications, while others cherish every publication. With respect to the second sort of offspring, some scientists work very much in social isolation and discourage the advances made by other scientists to become their descendants, while others are extremely social, maintaining large number of graduate students and junior colleagues. The prevalence of one strategy over the other varies with respect to individual scientists, but it also varies with respect to fields of inquiry at particular times (Hull 1988).

Domainwise author productivity and distribution of authors and papers (Table 5) indicated 0.57 positive correlation coefficient between author productivity and areas of research interest.

As per 80/20 rule 20 percent of the authors (7.2) are supposed to get credit of 80 percent of the authorships (324). Since, here, we are considering only seven authors for calculation (as round figure), they are supposed to contribute 315 authorships but here observed value is 313. This clearly indicated that 80/20 rule is valid in the present case of research group of L.L.Narayana.

The journals (Table 6) wherein L.L. Narayana had published more than 10 papers were: *Current Science* (34): *Journal of Japanese Botany* (28); *Journal of Botanical Society* (21): and *Proceedings of Indian Academic of Sciences* (11). *Publication density* (the frequency of papers per journal) was 5.5. Publication concentration (the ratio in percentage of the number of journals possessing half of the papers published to the total number of journals used) was 12.5 percent. He has used 32 journals to publish his 175 papers. Bradford-Zipf bibliograph is depicted in Fig.3.

Average Bradford multiplier was 5.1 (Table 7). First zone had 52 published in two journals only. Second zone had 72 papers in three journals. Third zone had 51 papers scattered in 27 journals.

Familywise keywords (from titles of the articles) frequencies (Table 8) indicated maximum contributions to Linaceae (19), Pittosporaceae (15): and Humiriaceae eight only. Genuswise frequency for Sorghum was five: and for *Pittosporum* three: and for *Belanites, Bauhinia, Indigofera* and *Gisekia* it was two each. Tribe and species keywords frequencies are provided in Table 9. Above data clearly indicates divergent creativity of L.L. Narayana and his research group members.

CONCLUSION

Gaillard (1991) stated that of the developing countries lack local role models to motivate other contemporary scientists present paper refutes the statement with clear cut documentary evidence of the fact that there is no dearth of local role model scientists at least in India. However, organised efforts are necessary in the research on individual scientists.

REFERENCES

1. Bamfield, P. 1996. Creativity and innovation. In: Research and development management in the chemical industry. Weinheim: VCH: 93-109. (ISBN 3-527-28778-7)
2. Gaillard, J.E. 1996. Scientists in the Third World. Lexington, Ky. USA. (ISBN 1731 3).
3. Gedo, J.E. 1996. The Artist and the Emotional World: Creativity and personality. New York, Columbia University Press (ISBN 0-231-07853).
4. Hull, D.L. 1988. Science as a process: An Evolutionary Account of the social and conceptual Development of Science. Chicago, the University of Chicago Press. (ISBN 0-226-36050-4).
5. Kademani, B. S.; Kalyane, V.L. and Balakrishnan, M.R. 1994a. Scientometric portrait of
6. Iyengar, P.K.; Library Science with a slant to Documentation and information Studies, 31 (4): 155-176.
7. Kademani, B. S.; Kalyane, V.L. and Kademani A.B. 1994b. Scientometric portrait of Nobel laureate Dr. C.V.Raman, Indian Journal of Information, Library and society, 7(3-4):215-249.
8. Kademani, B.S. and Kalyane, V.L. 1996. Outstandingly cited and most significant publications of R. Chidambaram, a Nuclear Physicist. Malaysian journal of library and information science, 1(10: 21-36.
9. Kademani, B.S.; Kalyane V.L. and Kademani A.B. 1996a. Scientometric portrait of Sir K.S. Krishnan. Indian Journal of information, library and society. 9(1-2): 125-150.
10. Kademani, B.S.; Kalyane. V.L. and kademani. A.B. 1996b. Scientometric portrait of Nobel Laureate S. Chandrasekhar. *JISSI*: The international Journal of scientometrics and Informetrics. 2(2-3) 119-135.

11. Kalyane, V.L. 1992. Dr. M.S. Swaminathan-Biologist par excellence. Biology education, 9(3): 246-248.

12. Kalyane, V.L. and Kalyane, S.V. 1993. Scientometric portrait of Vinodini Reddy. Journal of Information Sciences, 4(1):25-47.

13. Kalyane, V.L. and Devarai, R.S. 1994 information C.S. Venkata Ram. In: New Horizons in library and information Science. ed. Vashishth, K C.P. et. al, T.R. Publications, Madras, pp. 475-478. (ISBN 81-8547-54-2)

14. Kalyane, V.L. and Kademani, B.S. 1994. Scientometric portrait of M.S. Swaminathan. Library Science with a slant to Documentation and information studies, 31(1): 31-46.

15. Kalyane, V.L. 1995. Scientometric portrait of P.M. Bhargava. Lucknow Librarian. 27 (1-4): 42-70.

16. Kalyane, V.L. and Kademani, B.S. 1995. Scientometric portrait of R. Chidambaram: A publication productivity analysis. Journal of information Science, 5(3): 101-140.

17. Kalyane, V.L. and Munnolli, S.S. 1995. Scientometric portrait of T.S. West. Scientometric, 33(2): 233-256.

18. Kalyane, V.L. and samanta, R.K. 1995. Information on K. Ramiah. In: New Vistas in Library and information Science, ed. Raju A.A.N. et. al. Vikas publishing House, Delhi, pp. 565-578. (ISBN 0-7069-9126-5).

19. Kalyane, V.L. and Sen, B.K. 1996. Scientometric portrait of Nobel Laureate Pierre-Gilles de gennes. Malaysian journal of library and information Science, 1(2): 13-26.

20. Kalyane, V.L. and Kademani B.S. 1979. Scientometric Portrait of Barbara McClintock : the Nobel laureate in physiology. Kelpro Bulletin. 1(1), pp 3-14.

21. Kuhn, T. S. The structure of scientific Revolutions. 2nd ed. (Chicago: University of Chicago press 1970)

22. Sathyanarayana, A. 1990. Indian Journal of Botany, Half-yearly Journal of Research. Professor L.L. Narayana Commemorative volume, 13. I-VIII. Hyderabad.

23. Schubert, A. and Glanzel, W. 1992. The 100 most frequent family names among science authors, 1981.-1985. *Psientometrics*, 60-3.

Table 1 : Yearwise authorship Pattern in Publications of L.L.Narayana with collaboration coefficients and age

Year	Single authored	Two authored		Three authored			Four authored				Total authorship	Collaboration Coefficient	Total publications		Age of L.L. Narayana
		I	II	I	II	III	I	II	III	IV			Main auth.	co. auth.	
1955	-	-	1	-	-	-	-	-	-	-	1	1.00	-	1	25
1957	2	-	1	-	-	-	-	-	-	-	3	0.33	2	1	27
1958	2	1	-	-	-	-	-	-	-	-	3	0.33	3	-	28
1959	3	1	-	-	-	-	-	-	-	-	4	0.25	4	-	29
1960	4	-	-	-	-	-	-	-	-	-	4	0.00	4	-	30
1962	1	-	-	-	-	-	-	-	-	-	1	0.00	1	-	32
1963	2	-	-	-	-	-	-	-	-	-	2	0.00	2	-	33
1964	2	-	-	-	-	-	-	-	-	-	2	0.00	2	-	34
1965	1	-	2	-	-	-	-	-	-	-	3	0.66	1	2	35
1966	1	1	1	-	-	-	-	-	-	-	3	0.66	2	1	36
1968	-	-	2	-	-	-	-	-	-	-	2	1.00	-	2	38

1969	-	2	2	-	-	-	-	-	-	-	4	1.00	2	2	39
1970	6	-	-	-	-	-	-	-	-	-	6	0.00	6	-	40
1971	-	11	1	-	-	-	-	-	-	-	2	1.00	1	1	41
1973	-	3	-	-	-	-	-	-	-	-	3	1.00	3	-	43
1974	1	2	-	-	-	-	-	-	-	-	3	0.66	3	-	44
1975	1	-	-	-	-	-	-	-	-	-	1	0.00	1	-	45
1976	-	5	1	-	-	-	-	-	-	-	6	1.00	5	1	46
1977	-	5	3	-	-	-	-	-	-	-	8	1.00	5	3	47
1978	-	7	5	-	2	-	-	-	-	-	14	1.00	7	7	48
1979	-	2	-	-	1	1	-	-	-	-	4	1.00	2	2	49
1980	-	3	1	-	-	1	-	-	1	-	6	1.00	3	3	50
1981	-	2	1	1	-	1	-	-	-	-	5	1.00	3	2	51
1982	-	2	2	1	1	2	-	-	-	-	8	1.00	3	5	52
1983	-	2	1	1	-	1	1	-	-	-	6	1.00	4	2	53
1984	-	6	1	1	-	8	-	1	-	2	19	1.00	7	12	54
1985	-	-	2	1	-	-	1	-	-	2	6	1.00	2	4	55
1986	-	-	2	1	-	3	1	-		1	8	1.00	2	6	56

1987	-	-	2	-	-	3	-	-	-	4	9	1.00	-	9	57
1988	-	1	2	-	-	3	-	-	-	1	7	1.00	1	6	58
1989	-	-	3	-	-	5	-	-	-	3	11	1.00	-	11	59
1990	-	-	4	1	1	4	-	-	-	1	11	1.00	1	10	60

I = First author, II = second author, III = Third author, IV = Fourth author

Table 2 : Domainwise publications of L.L. Narayana

Year	A	B	C	D	E	F	G	H	I	J	Total	Perc-entage	Cumulative
1955	-	-	-	-	-	-	-	-	1	-	1	0.57	0.57
1957	-	-	3	-	-	-	-	-	-	-	3	1.71	2.28
1958	-	2	-	-	1	-	-	-	-	-	3	1.71	3.99
1959	-	1	3	-	-	-	-	-	-	-	4	2.29	6.28
1960	-	-	1	3	-	-	-	-	-	-	4	2.29	8.57
1962	-	-	1	-	-	-	-	-	-	-	1	0.57	9.14
1963	-	-	2	-	-	-	-	-	-	-	2	1.14	10.28
1964	-	-	1	-	1	-	-	-	-	-	2	1.14	11.42
1965	-	-	2	-	-	-	1	-	-	-	3	1.71	13.13
1966	-	1	1	-	-	1	-	-	-	-	3	1.71	14.84
1968	-	-	1	-	1	-	-	-	-	-	2	1.14	15.98
1969	-	4	-	-	-	-	-	-	-	-	4	2.29	18.27
1970	-	-	6	-	-	-	-	-	-	-	6	3.43	21.70

1971	-	2	-	-	-	-	-	-	-	-	2	1.14	22.84
1973	-	3	-	-	-	-	-	-	-	-	3	1.71	24.55
1974	-	3	-	-	-	-	-	-	-	-	3	1.71	26.26
1975	-	-	-	-	1	-	-	-	-	-	1	0.57	26.83
1976	-	5	-	-	1	-	-	-	-	-	6	3.43	30.26
1977	1	5	2	-	-	-	-	-	-	-	8	4.57	34.83
1978	1	7	3	1	-	-	1	1	-	-	14	8.00	42.83
1979	-	1	3	-	-	-	-	-	-	-	4	2.29	45.12
1980	2	3	1	-	-	-	-	-	-	-	6	3.43	48.55
1981	2	2	1	-	-	-	-	-	-	-	5	2.86	51.41
1982	4	2	-	2	-	-	-	-	-	-	8	4.57	55.98
1983	3	2	1	-	-	-	-	-	-	-	6	3.43	59.41
1984	12	4	1	1	-	1	-	-	-	-	19	10.86	70.27
1985	3	-	2	1	-	-	-	-	-	-	6	3.43	73.70
1986	5	2	1	-	-	-	-	-	-	-	8	4.57	78.27
1987	8	1	-	-	-	-	-	-	-	-	9	5.14	83.41

1988	4	1	-	1	-	-	-	-	-	1	7	4.00	87.41
1989	8	1	-	2	-	-	-	-	-	-	11	6.29	93.70
1990	4	1	1	4	-	1	-	-	-	-	11	6.29	99.99

A = Chemotaxonomy, B = Floral anatomy, C= Embryology.
D = Systematic position, E = Floral anatomy and Embryology,
F = Floral morphology. G = Vascular anatomy,
H = Floral Morphology and Embryology, I = Life history.
J = In vitro germination

Table 3 : Research group of L.L. Narayana

Author	***S***	***Two***			***Three***				***Four***					*AGT*	*Year*
code	***I***	***I***	***II***	***T***	***I***	***II***	***III***	***T***	***I***	***II***	***III***	***IV***	***T***		*Fp-Lp*
NLL	26	46	40	86	7	5	32	44	3	1	1	14	19	175	`55-90
VJ	-	2	-	2	-	-	-	-	-	-	-	-	-	2	`55-77
SM	-	-	2	2	-	-	-	-	-	-	-	-	-	2	`58-59
RD*	-	2	22	24	-	-	-	-	-	-	-	-	-	24	`65-78
SR	-	1	-	1	-	-	-	-	-	-	-	-	-	1	`66-68
RNGP	-	1	-	1	1	-	3	4	-	-	-	-	-	5	`68-90
SK	-	6	-	6	-	-	-	-	-	-	-	-	-	6	`68-78
RM*	-	2	9	11	3	25	3	31	2	2	13	1	18	60	`76-90
SK.T*	-	1	6	7	2	3	1	6	-	-	1	1	2	15	`77-84
SVV.LN*	-	3	2	5	-	1	-	1	-	-	-	-	-	6	`77-90
DBSM	-	-	-	-	1	-	-	1	1	1	-	-	2	3	`78-84
PA*	-	3	2	5	-	-	2	2	-	-	-	-	-	7	`78-90
RRN*	-	-	-	-	1	2	1	3	-	-	-	-	-	3	`78-90
PPS	-	-	-	-	1	1	-	3	-	1	-	1	2	5	`79-86

KVL*	-	3	1	4	-	-	-	-	-	-	-	-	-	4	'80-84
RMI	-	-	-	-	-	-	-	-	1	-	-	-	1	1	'80-80
GRB	-	-	-	-	-	-	-	-	-	-	-	1	1	1	'80-80
SC	-	1	1	2	1	-	-	1	-	-	-	-	-	3	'81-84
RBB*	-	1	-	1	1	-	-	1	-	-	-	-	-	2	'82-82
NG	-	-	-	-	8	2	1	11	1	3	1	1	6	17	'83-90
RRV	-	-	-	-	1	-	-	1	-	-	-	-	-	1	'83-83
KK	-	-	-	-	2	-	-	2	3	2	-	-	5	7	'84-90
SM	-	-	-	-	7	1	-	8	-	1	-	-	1	9	'84-90
NPS*	-	6	-	6	-	2	-	2	-	2	-	-	2	10	'85-90
RVS	-	-	-	-	-	-	1	1	-	-	2	-	2	3	'85-86
SPR*	-	-	-	-	-	-	-	-	1	-	-	-	1	1	'85-85
ASMJ	-	-	-	-	5	-	-	5	5	2	-	-	7	12	'86-89
RTPS	-	1	-	1	-	-	-	-	-	-	-	-	-	1	'86-86
SDVL*	-	2	1	3	1	-	-	1	-	-	-	-	-	4	'86-88
PC	-	-	-	-	-	1	-	1	-	-	-	-	-	1	'86-86
VBK	-	-	-	-	-	-	-	-	-	2	-	-	2	2	'87-87

LK	-	1	-	1	-	-	-	-	-	-	-	-	-	1	'87-87
RAM	-	-	-	-	1	-	-	1	-	-	-	-	-	1	'88-88
KPB	-	-	-	-	-	1	-	1	-	-	-	-	-	1	'88-88
RMS	-	-	-	-	1	-	-	1	2	2	1	-	5	6	'88-90
RDD*	-	4	-	4	-	-	-	-	-	-	-	-	-	4	'89-90

* = Those who have completed Ph. D. under the guidence of L. L. Narayana.

I = First author, II =Second author, III = Third author,

IV =Fourth. T =Total, AGT = Authou ship grand total.

Fp = First Paper, Lp= Last Paper, S = Single authoured papers.

Two = Two authored Papers. Three = Three authored Papers. and

Four = Four authored Papers.

Table 4. Author Productivity

No. of Papers (a)	*Active associates (b)*	*Total No. of researchers*	*Total Papers (a.b)*	*Perce-ntage*	*Cumulative percentage*
1		10	10	2.46	2.46
3		4	8	1.97	4.43
4		3	9	2.22	6.65
5		4	16	3.94	10.59
6		3	15	3.69	14.28
7		2	12	2.96	17.24
2		14	3.45	20.69	
9	Satyavati, M.	1	9	2.22	22.91
10	Narayana, P. S.	1	10	2.46	25.37
12	Anuradha, S. M. J.	1	12	2.95	28.33
15	Sundari, K. T.	1	15	3.69	32.02
17	Nageswar, G.	1	17	4.19	36.21
24	Rao, D.	1	24	5.91	42.12
60	Radhakrishnaih, M.	1	60	14.78	56.90
175	L.L. Narayana	1	175	43.10	100.00

Table 5 : Author Productivity and distribution of authors and paper by number of subject catagories (domains)

NPP	Number of domains to which contributions belong and number of contributors										TNR
	A	B	C	D	E	F	G	H	I	J	
1	2	5	1	-	-	-	-	-	-	2	10
2	2	1	2	2	-	-	-	-	1	-	4
3	1	6	-	2	-	1	-	-	-	-	3
4	5	4	5	1	-	-	-	-	-	-	4
5	5	4	6	-	-	-	-	-	-	-	3
6	6	5	-	-	1	-	-	-	-	-	2
7	10	1	1	2	-	-	-	-	-	-	2
9	6	1	-	2	-	-	-	-	-	-	1
10	6	1	2	2	-	-	-	-	-	-	1
12	12	-	-	-	-	-	-	-	-	-	1
15	4	3	8	-	-	-	-	-	-	-	1
17	16	-	-	1	-	-	-	-	-	-	1

24	-	20	1	-	-	1	1	1	-	-	1
60	42	12	-	4	-	1	1	-	-	-	1
175	57	53	37	15	5	3	2	1	1	1	1
Total	174	115	63	31	6	6	4	2	2	3	36

A = Chemotaxonomy, B = Floral anatomy, C = Embryology.

D = Systematic Position, E = floral anatomy and Embryology, F = Floral morphology.

G = Vascular anatomy, H = Floral morphology and embryology.

I = Life history, J = In vitro germination,

NPP = Number of papersn productivity

TNR = Total number of researchers

Table 6: Journalwise scattering of papers of L. L. Narayana

Rank	Journal title	TP	Percentage	Cumu. (%)	PJU FP-LP	Total
1.	Curr. Sci.	34	19.43	19.43	'55-89	35
2.	J. Jap. Bot.	28	16.00	35.43	'65-81	17
3.	J. Indian Bot. Soc.	21	12.00	47.43	'58-90	33
4.	J. Econ. Tax. Bot.	12	6.86	54.29	'82-89	8
5.	Proc. Indian Acad. Sci. Sec. B.	11	6.29	60.58	'6090	31
6.	Fedders Report	10	5.71	66.29	'86-90	5
7.	J. Swamy Bot.Club	9	5.14	71.43	'84-88	5
8.	Bull.Indian Nation Sci. Academy	6	3.43	74.86	'70-70	1
9.	Indian J.Bot.	5	2.86	77.72	'78-87	10
10.	Nation. Acad. Sci. Letters	4	2.29	80.01	'78-90	13
11.	Phytomorphyology	4	2.29	82.30	'57-59	3
12.	Act. Bot.Indica	4	2.29	84.59	'78-84	7

13.	Phytochemistry and Taxonomy	3	1.71	86.30	'90-90	1
14	Sci. Cult	2	1.14	87.44	'52-59	8
15.	Life Sci. Adv.	2	1.14	88.58	82-82	1
16.	Plant and Nature	2	1.14	89.72	'83-831	1
17.	J.Pl.Anat.Morph.	2	1.14	90.86	'84-84	1
18.	Bangladesh J.Botany	2	1.14	92.00	'89-89	1
19.	Indian J.Genet.	1	0.57	92.57	'68-68	1
20.	Bull.Torrey Bot.Club	1	0.57	93.14	'69-69	1
21.	Caryologia	1	0.57	93.71	'78-78	1
22.	Phyta	1	0.57	94.28	'80-80	1
23.	Bot.Notiser	1	0.57	94.95	'80-80	1
24.	Can.J.Bot.	1	0.57	95.42	'82-82	1
25.	Trends Pl.Res.	1	0.57	95.99	'85-85	1
26.	Plant Syst Evol.	1	0.57	96.56	'86-86	1
27.	Proc.Nation.Acad. Sci.(B)	1	0.57	97.13	'87-87	1

28.	Ad.Plant Sci.	1	0.57	97.70	'88-88	1
29.	Indian J.Forestry	1	0.57	98.27	'89-89	1
30.	Plant Sci. Res.in India	1	0.57	98.84	'89-89	1
31.	Proc. Symp. Andhra University	1	0.57	99.41	'90-90	1
32.	Geophytology	1	0.57	99.98	'90-90	1

TP = Total Papers, FP = First Paper year, LP = Last Paper year

PJU = Pericd of Journal usage. Cumu. = Cumulative

Table 7 : Bradford's Zones for Research Papers of L. L. Narayana

Zones	*Number of Papers*	*Number of Journals*	*Bradford Multiplier*
First	52	2	-
Scond	72	3	1.5
Third	51	27	9.0
	Average Bradford Multiplier		5.1

Table 8 : Keywords frequencies for famil, and genus included in the articles published by L. L.Narayana

Family	*Frequency*	*Genus*	*Freaquency*
Linaceae	19	Sorghum	5
Pittosporaceae	15	Pittosporum	3
Humiriaceae	8	Belanites	2
Erythroxy Laceae	5	Bauhinia	2
Balsaminaceae	5	Indiagofera	2
Acanthaceae	5	Gisekia	2
Oxalidaceae	4	Staurogyne	1
Rubiaceae	4	Trapa	1
Geraniceae	3	Cuscuta	1
Bignon Caceae	3	Ceratophy llum	1
Stegnospermataceae	3	Moringa	1
Boraginaceae	3	Cassia	1
Simarou basceae	2	Hibiscus	1
Meliaceae	2	Pandanus	1
Burseraceae	2	Typha	1
Capparidaceae	2	Aesculus	1
Papilionaceae	2	Arachis	1
Moringaceae	2	Abrus	1

Corynocarpaceae	2	Clerodendron	1
Mimosaceae	2	Crotalaria	1
Lentibulaiaceae	2	Heylandia	1
Staphyleaceae	1	Cicer	1
Rutaceae	1	Acacia	1
Topaeolaceae	1	Ixora	1
Ochnaceaeae	1	Gardenia	1
Primulaceae	1	Jacaranda	1
Scrophulariaceae	1	Parmentiera	1
Pedaliaceae	1	Averrhoa	1
Annonaceae	1	Impatiens	1
Menispermaceae	1		
Averrhoaceae	1		
Malvaceae	1		
Tremandraceae	1		
Basellaceae	1		
Balanitaceae	1		
Viticeae	1		
Crescenatieae	1		
Melastomataceae	1		

Table 9 : Keyword frequenies for Tribes and Species included in the titles to the articles published by L. L. Narayana

Tribe	***Frequency***	***Species***	***Frequency***
Amhersticeae	2	Hydrocera triflora	2
Trifolieae	1	Stegnosperma halimifolium	2
Ruelieae	1	Garuga pinnata	1
Vicieae	1	Cipadessa baccifera	1
Bignonieae	1	Boswelia Serrata	1

Acantheae	1	Impatiens leschsenaultii	1
Nelsonieae	1	Biophtum intermedium	1
Cynometreae	1	Oxalis pubescens	1
Caesalpinionideae	1	Primula floribunda	1
Hedysareae	1	Utricularia caerea	1
Crescenteae	1	Utricularia stricticaulis	1
Eucesalpineae	1	Nepenthes Khasiana	1
		Pronaya elegans	1
		Marianthus bignonaceus	1
		Moringa concanensis	1
		Cuscuta chinensis	1
		Pittosporum floribundum	1
		Utricularia aurea	1
		Utiricularia exoleta	1
		Utricularia stellaria	1
		Emilia flammea	1
		Sesamum indicum	1
		Gyrocarpus americanus	1
		Phryma leptostachya	1
		Schizanthus wisetonensis	1
		Tetratheca efoliata	1
		Corynocarus laevigatus	1
		Tetratheca affinis	1
		Vigna trilobata	1
		Hydrocera triflora	1

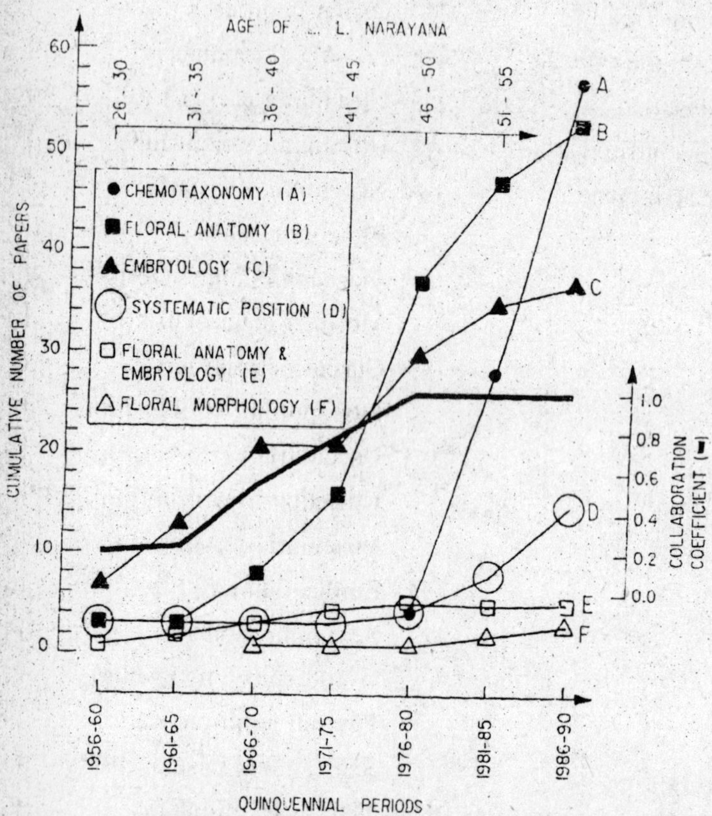

Fig. 1. Domainwise contributions of L.L. Narayana

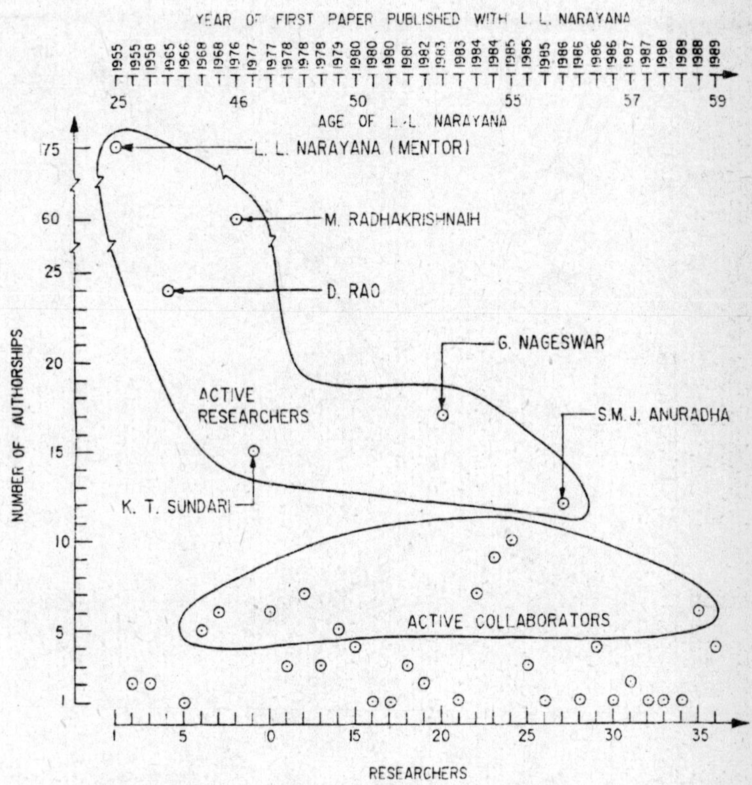

Fig. 2. Authorship credits to the researchers in chronological order

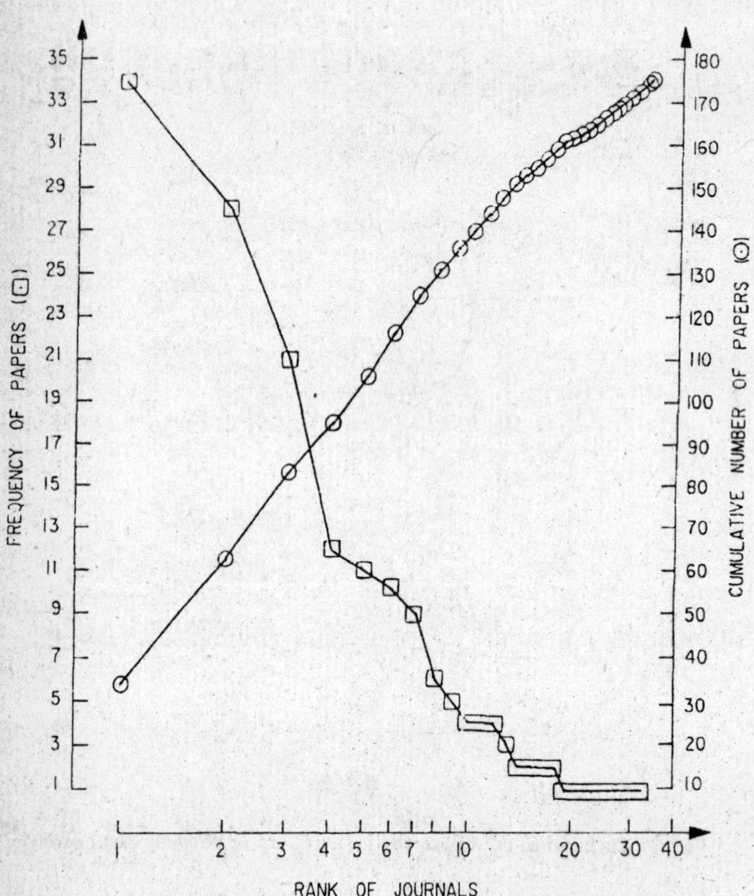

Fig. 3. Bradford - Zipf bibliograph on publications of L.L. Narayana

VIII : 1
Library Movement in Dakshina Kannada District of Karnataka State (India) Since Independence

A.K. Baradol

INTRODUCTION

The field of library movement is too broad for discussion. The present discussion is limited to the library movement in undivided Dakshina Kannada district of Karnataka State since Independence. In 1977 the Dakshina Kannada district was bifurcated in to two namely, Dakshina Kannada (D.K.) and Udupi. The Udupi district is in its formative stages. Hence the study includes the undivided D.K, district. The district is one of the very progressive districts in the fields of education, banking, industries and libraries. The district has literacy of 53.46% (1). The Karnataka State government has launched its adult education programme in the district. Due to this it has achieved 100% literacy. The district has produced many scholars including the Jnanapeetha award winner late shri K. Shivaram Karanth, a noted writer in Kannada literature. The district is lucky enough to have talented individuals who have made progress in the banking sector in the country. The district has a good number of education institutions. It was fortunate to have Bassel mission which established printing press in 1841. The district has exported good number of individuals to the gulf countries for employment in different sectors. With such a background the district has made progress in the establishment and maintenance of libraries and information centres. The library movement gained momentum after the independence of the country.

PUBLIC LIBRARIES

Due to the high percentage of literacy in the D.K. district, there was a demand for the library services. Hence, the public libraries were in existence to cater to the intellectual needs of the people since the beginning of the twentieth century. The district was part of Madras State till re-organisation of the states on the linguistic basis that is up to 1956. When it was a part of Madras State it was known as South Kanara district. In November 1956 the South Kanara district was united with the Karnataka State. The Madras Public Libraries act. 1948, was in force in the district upto November 1956. The local library authority was constituted for the Dakshina Kannada district, the then called South Kanara district. In August 1950, as per the provisions of the Madras Public Libraries Act, the district administration has established the branch public libraries to serve the public in the towns. In accordance with the Madras Public Libraries Act, the Karna Sadashiva Rao municipal library, Mangalore, was taken over in 1951, at present, it serves as city central library. The Karnataka government enacted the Public Libraries Act in 1965, The Act made the provisions for the maintenance of the existing public libraries. As per the provisions of the Act the district library authority is maintaining public libraries all over the district. As on today the district has, the following libraries under the district library authority: 18 branch libraries 25 Mandal libraries, 36 book delivery stations and a reading room.

The Mangalore city has the following libraries under the city library authority: one city central library. seven branch libraries one reading room and a mobile library. The mobile library covers thirty four points per week. The reading room provides the facilities for the reading of the news papers and popular magazines, namely weeklies, fortnightlies and monthlies , and not the books. The Book Delivery Stations (BDSs) are mainly in rural areas. They do not have full-time professionally qualified staff. The BDSs have small collections of books and few magazines and news-papers. The public library services in the district are satisfactory.

Village Information Centres

The village information centers are established in some villages in the district by Manipal Industrial Trust, Manipal, a voluntary organisation. These centres are useful for the continuing education of the neo-literates in the district. They provide the information required for the rural development namely, Agriculture, Dairy, Poultry, Piggery, etc. in the udupi taluk of Dakshina Kannada district, these information centres have been established. These centres were established in 1989 on an experimental basis. To quote rao, "the objectives of the village information centers are:

* To collect the information required for formulating rural development programmes, and to provide them to the rural community as and when required.
* To make use of different types of media for the purpose of providing information.
* To develop programmes for the neo-literates so as to enable them to continue their education.
* To organise periodical training for the functionaries of local organisations such as Mahila Mandals and Yuvak Mandals so that they can provide information service to the rural community on a continuing basis."[2]

The village information centers are function as per the objectives. Although the project was initially started on an experimental basis it is now continued further.

Presently, it is financed by the International Development Research Center (IDRC) Ottawa, Canade, an international organisation. These centres serve the information needs of the public in the district to some extent.

ACADEMIC LIBRARIES

The D. K. district has large number of academic institutions which include schools, junior college, con-professional college, professional colleges and an University. The district has 99 colleges affiliated to Mangalore University 3 and 5 colleges affiliated to Manipal Academy of Higher Education (MAHE), manipal, a deemed university. Apart from these, the district has a college exclusively devoted for fisheries. In all, the district has 105 colleges.

Mangalore University Library, Mangalagangotri

The Mangalore University Library was started as a library of the university of Mysore, Post Graduate (P.G.) Centre, Mangalore in 1968. The Mangalore University was started in September 1980. The University of Mysore P.G. Centre became a part of Mangalore University, Mangalagangotri in 1980. Consequently, the library also became part of the Mangalore University. It is housed in the newly constructed spacious building. The university library has over one lakh books and bound volumes of periodicals on its shelves. It is a very well-equipped library with all modern facilities and equipment. It caters to the needs of the students and staff of the 21 P.G. departments of the university. Whenever required the library also caters to the needs of neighouring institutions and colleges affiliated to the Mangalore University. It is using computers for some house-keeping operations and services.

College of Fisheries Library, Mangalore

The College of Fisheries, Mangalore, is a constituent college of the University of Agricultural Sciences, Bangalore. The college has a well-equipped library. This serves the under graduate students. Post graduate students, research scholars. Teaching staff and field staff of the college. The library is covered by the Overseas Development Administration (ODA) with assistance of the British Council.

Non-Professional Colleges

The D. K. district has 59 non-professional colleges. These include both private and government colleges. The library of an old college namely, St. Aloysius College which was established in 1887 has a very rich collection which includes some rare books. The university college, the earstwhile Government College. Mangalore, is one of the oldest colleges in the whole of South India. This was established in 1866. This college also has rare books printed in the second half of nineteenth century. A special mention has to be made of the St. Agnes College which was the first women's college managed by private management in India. Few government colleges which are recently established are yet to develop their libraries. Except these few colleges, all the government colleges have libraries and are serving the information needs of the students and staff of the respective colleges.

Professional College Libraries

A number of professional colleges namely, the colleges of hotel management. The colleges of nursing. The colleges of physiotherapy and the colleges of dental sciences have been established in the district. The district has a deemed university namely, Manipal Academy of Higher Education (MAHE), Manipal, which has five professional colleges. As it is compulsory for every college to have a library, there are libraries attached to all the professional colleges. The district has the 45 professional colleges. They include 2 medical colleges (allopathic) affiliated to MAHE, deemed university, one ayurvedic college. One homeopathic medical college, one naturopathy college. Five dental colleges two pharmacy colleges. Seven nursing colleges and seven colleges of physiotherapy. All these medical and paramedical colleges which were affiliated to Mangalore University till 1996 have been now affiliated to the newly established Rajeev Gandhi Medical University. Apart from these, there are seven colleges of hotel management, three education colleges, five law colleges and four engineering colleges.

All these professional colleges have contributed to the library movement of district. The library movement is possible because of the factors, namely the interest of the concerned people at large and the necessary financial input. The financial input is visible in the institutions, namely Karnatka Regional Engineering College. Surathkal, Kasturba Medical College, Manipal, Kasturba Medical College, Mangalore, Manipal Institute of Technology, Manipal, A. B. Shetty Memorial College of Dental Sciences and a few other colleges. These institutions have invested a large amount of money in procuring the necessary computers. CD-ROM drives, CD-ROM data bases etc. this shows the interest of the administration in making the library movement more successful.

SPECIAL LIBRARIES

Mangalore Chemicals and Fertilisers (MCF) Ltd. Mangalore

Mangalore Chemicals and Fertilisers (MCF) Ltd. Mangalore, is a major fertiliser industry. This has got a library. It caters to the needs of the research and development section staff of MCF Ltd. It has added to the library movement in the district.

Libraries Attached to Jain Maths

The district has a few libraries attached to the Jain Maths. One of these is located at Moodabidri town. It has a good collection of books on Jainism and related subject. The books on jainism and related aspects are also found in the library attached to Shri Dharmasthala Manjunatheswara Trust at Dharmasthala.

LIBRARY AND INFORMATION MANPOWER DEVELOPMENT

To develop the Library & information science manpower. the educational institutions are conducting various courses. Government Polytechnic for Women, Mangalore & Mangalore University, Mangalagangotri, are the two institutions in the district engaged in library and information manpower development.

Government Polytechnic for Women

The Government Polytechnic for Women, Mangalore, has started the Diploma course in Library & Information Science in 1975. In the beginning, the intake of students was 30, now the intake has been increased to 44 students. Many institutions in the district have employed the persons trained in the polytechnic.

Mangalore University

The Department of Library and Information Science was established at Mangalore University in 1982. In the beginning it conducted only the Bachelor's programme In 1985 the name or the department was changed as department or library and information science. Accordingly, the nomenclature of the Bachelor's course was also changed as BL/Sc the department of Library and information science was expanded in 1990 to conduct the master's (MLISc) programme and the research programme[5]. accordingly. the MLISC course & Ph.D course were started from 1990. The mangalore University has started the two-year MLISc. Programme combining the two different courses, namely one year BLISc course and one year MLSc course in 1996.

The research activities in the Library and information science in the district are mainly conducted as the doctoral programme in the mangalore university. Two scholars have successfully completed research in Library and information science. Research is being conducted on different areas of Library and Information science. namely academic library system, public library system, special library system, information processing, etc.

CONTINUING EDUCATION PROGRAMMING

Since 1950s, Workshops and seminars are being conducted in the district. The District Central Library organised the workshops to create awareness among the public regarding the library services. To quote Hoskote, "In May 1958 a library week was inaugurated by Dr. Ranganathan to give full and wide publicity to the library services rendered by the autority".[4] The public library set up in the district has been conducting such programmes even now. The district central library, Mangalore, organised a book week and library exhibition in November 1990 to create an awareness about the library services among the people of the district. Lectures by Library and information science professionals were organised during the observance of the book week. A two-day training programme was organised for the benefit of the working library staff by the district central Library. Mangalore, in September 1993. On this occasion, Lectures and group discussions were organised.

At Karnataka Regional Engineering College (KREC). Surathkal, a work-shop was conducted on collection development of libraries and use of engineering literature in science and technical institutions in January 1986. It was sponsored by the Department or science and Technology, Minister of science and Technology, Institutions, Government of India. Over 25 papers were discussed in different sessions. The workshop was attended by librarians of engineering colleges in the Karnataka State. The KREC organised another workshop in August 1995.

In January 1987, Kasturba medical College (KMC). Manipal, organised the 'Third National seminar on Health / Literature. For all by 1990' under the suspicious or medical Library Association of India (MLAI) and the National medical Library. The seminar discussed number of issues pertaining to the medical information. The KMC organised a week-long workshop on Information Technology in November 1996.

In January 1990 the Department of Library and Information Science, Mangalore University. Organised a seminar on 'women and library service'. The seminar was sponsored by the Department of Women and Child Development, Ministry of Human Resource Development, Government of India. Sixteen papers were discussed on the issues concerning women and library services.

INFORMATION TECHNOLOGY (IT)

Information Technology (IT) includes the use of computers. CD-ROM discs. Fax, Internet. E-mail, etc. This helps the libraries to render library and information services in an efficient manner. This satisfies the readers in a better manner. The libraries in Dakshina Kannada district have been using IT The Mangalore University Library, Mangalagangotri, Kasturba Medical College (KMC) Library, Manipal, the Manipal Institute of Technology Library, Manipal, the Karnataka Regional Engineering College Library (KREC), Surthkal, the NMAM Institute of Technology Library, Nitt, the ABSM College of Dental Sciences (ABSMCDS) Library, Mangalore use computers for library services. CD-ROM discs are used by Mangalore University Library, Mangalagangotri, Manipal ABSMCDS, Mangalore and Fr. Muller's Homeopathic Medical College, Mangalore. The use of IT has contributed to the library movement.

CONCLUSION

The Dakshina Kannada district has been a centre of learning and other related activities since the last two centuries. To quote Gulvadi, "A fortnightly titled as 'Mangalore Samachar' was being published from Mangalore since July Ist, 1843. It was the first periodical in Kannada Language."5 The district has been progressing at a very fast rate since Independence. the district has 100% literacy. Hence every citizen of the district wishes to be well-informed. Because of the demand by the public. the district and city local authorities have to provide the library facilities properly. The district has required number of branch and mandal libraries. The academic community of the district namely, the students and teachers working in different educational institutions want to be up to date. Hence, the administrators of the academic institutions have to provide better library facilities and information services. The library-centered education is found in the university, colleges and schools in the district. Because of the excellent library facilities, the graduates of the Dakshina Kannada district are of good quality graduates who can compete with the graduates of other districts in the State. The libraries attached to the educational institutions and the district library authority have conducted the continuing education programmes namely workshops. Seminars and conferences. The religious institutions like Jain Maths have kept their libraries open for the needy persons. All these factors have made library movement in the Dakshina Kannada district a success story.

REFERENCES

1. Das, B. K. Census of India, 1981, Series 9 Karnataka: paper 1 of 1983, Final population tables. Director of census operations Karnataka, 1983, P. 21.
2. Rao, P. V. Case study on the village Information centres (India) Project, Manipal. Mimeographed paper p.5.
3. Mangalor University. Annual Report, 1994-95, p. 115.
4. Hoskote, Vasanti N. "Library movement in south Kanara : Historical survey" *Timeless Fellowship* Vol 3&4. 1966-67, p.174.
5. Gulvadi, Santosh Kumar. "Antaranga Bahiranga" *Taranga* 20 January, 1989. p. 6.

VIII : 2
The State of Public Library Services in India : Achievements And Failures

L. S. Ramiah

PROLEGOMENA

We had adopted democratic form of government. For democracy the two important props are education and access to information to the people. As far as education is concerned, the country could achieve only 52 percent of literacy. It is estimated according to a survey that there will be 200 million illiterates in this country at the beginning of the 21st century. The country has failed to provide education, at least primary education, to all. With regard to access to information to the people which is the another prop of our democracy, our constitution couldn't provide the right to information. In the absence of such right, one of the important channels to provide access to information to the people is the public library. The UNESCO manifesto clearly stated that the public library is the local center of information, making all kinds of knowledge and information readily available to its users in the community regardless of race, colour, age, sex, nationality, language, status or level of educational attainment. Now let us see the growth and development of the public library in our country during the last fifty years including the achievements, failures and the future prospects. The academic libraries and the special libraries are left out from the purview of this article.

OUR POPULATION AND OUR PUBLIC LIBRARIES

India is the second largest populous country in the world covering an area of 32, 87, 263 sq. Kms with a population of 943.9 millions. The country consists of 24 states and 6 Union territories, about 500 districts, 12 big cities, 3949 towns and 5,75,937, villages. Eighty percent of the people live in the villages.

All the states and the union Territories in the country except Sikkim and Lakshadweep have set up state central Libraries. Out of 500 districts, only about 400 districts have district central libraries. According to the *Report of the Working Group of the Planning Commission on Modernization of Library Services and Informatics for the Seventh Five year Plan 1985-90*, it was estimated that out of the total 5,75,937 villages only 41,828 villages have libraries. Dr. Pande S.K. Sharma in his book, *Public Libraries in India*, estimated that there are 40,107, public libraries. RRRLF data shows that there are around 21,906 public libraries in the country. Dr. Velga Venkatappaiah in his article *Need for Library Legislation in south Asian Countries* (1997) estimated that there might be 44,205 public libraries in the country. Whereas Dr. H.K. Kaul hinted in his article, *Networking of public libraries in south Asia* (1997) that there are approximately 60,000 public libraries in the country. No definite statistics about the total or statewise break-up of the public libraries are available. Even when we work out an average between the number of libraries given by the working Group of the Planning Commission and Dr. H.K. Kaul, the public libraries in the country may be around 50,000. Hence hardly 12 percent of our villages have public libraries. Further if we evaluate the functioning of these libraries with some internationally accepted standards very few of them will come up to the standards of real public libraries.

The subject 'public libraries' is part of the 'State List' under our Constitution. The central government as per the present constitutional position cannot do much in the case of public libraries except regarding the National Library and few other libraries like The Asiatic Society Library, Rampur Library etc. Fifty years, though a short period in a nation's life, is an appropriate and sizeable period for a retrospective introspection about the efforts of The Central and State Governments for the development of the public libraries in India.

CENTRAL GOVERNMENT AND THE PUBLIC LIBRARIES

Inspite of the limited obligations under the provisions of the constitution, the Government has done considerable amount of effort for the growth and development of the public libraries in India. These are shown below in chronological order:

1948 The Imperial Library (Change of Name) Act.

1954 Delivery of Books and Newspapers Act.

1956 Amendment to the Delivery of Books and Newspapers Act.

1957 Appointment of the Advisory Committee for Libraries.

1957 Indian Copyright Act, 1957.

1958 Starting of the Publication of the Indian National Bibliography.

1963 Model Public Libraries Bill (MOE, Govt. of India; drafted by Dr. M.D. Sen)

1965 Model Public Library Bill (Planning Commission under the chairmanship of Dr. VKRV Rao)

1969 Khudabaksh Oriental Public Library Act.

1972 Establishment of the Raja Ram Mohan Roy Library Foundation

1975 The Rampur Raja Library Act

1976 The National Library of India Act

1983 Appointment of the Working Group of the Planning Commission on Modernisation of Library Service and Information for the Seventh Five Year plan (1985-1990).

1984 The Asiatic Society Act.

1985 Appointment of the Committee on National Policy on Library and Information System.

Whatever that was done by the Central Government is commendable but there still remains a lot to be done.

DEVELOPMENT OF LIBRARY ACTS IN THE STATES

Libraries are in the 'State List' under the constitution of India. The growth and development of public libraries is, therefore, the responsibility of the State Governments. As stated in the UNESCO manifesto of public libraries (1989,1972,1994) the public libraries can be placed on firm footing only when their establishment and growth is ensured by a mandate of law and public finance. Among the 26 Indian states and 6 Union Territories, the public library legislation enacted so far is given below in a chronological order.

1945 The Kolhapur Public Libraries Act

1948 The Madras Public Libraries Act

1955 The Hyderabad Public Libraries Act

1960 The Andhra Pradesh Public Libraries Act

1965 The Karnataka Public Libraries act

1967 The Maharashtra Public Libraries Act

1979 The West Bengal Public Libraries Act

1988 The Manipur Public Libraries act

1989 The Kerala Public Libraries Act

1989 The Haryana Public Libraries act

1993 The Mizoram Public Libraries Act

1994 The Goa Public Libraries Act.

Out of the above 12 public library Acts, the Kolhapur Act, 1945 which was enacted before Indian Independence and the Hyderabad Public Library Act, 1955 have lapsed after the reorganisation of states on linguistic basis. See the figure given The states and the union Territories and their population who have the benefit of library legislation and those who don't have the same are shown in figure. There are still 16 states, some of them very big states and the six Union Territories with a total population of 483,653,881 which don't have library legislation, whereas there are 10 states with a population of 363,558,807 who have the benefits of the library legislation. Even after 50 years of Independence, the State Governments, more than half of them, are not able to enact library legislation. The progress in this direction is at snail's pace. At this rate it would take a minimum another 25-30 years to enact library legislation in all the states. It is a long period in this Information age. Enactment of library legislation is one thing and the insurance of the growth and development of public libraries providing access to books and information to the, rural people is yet another thing. The purpose of the argument here is to show that we don't have today in the country the minimest of the minimum in the provision of the public library services. Both the central land state governments are showing the least importance for development of the information facilities.

The country has made tremendous progress during the last fifty years on the fronts of agriculture, food, housing, industry, health, defence etc. In order to carry this development to the people at the grass root level, the channels of information, among which the public library is the richest and the most economical source of information, should be cared and strengthened at the national level. The central government and the state governments should work together hand-in-hand in this important sector.

Though the retrospective glance at the development of the public library services in India did not reveal an impressive picture, let us hope that the future perspective would be brighter.

Outer Circle without Library Legislation

State and their people who do not have the benefit of Literary Legislation

Uttar Pradesh	139,112,287	Manipur	1,837,149
Bihar	86,374,465	Meghalya	1.774,778
Madhya Pradesh	66,181,170	Nagaland	1,209,546
Rajahthan	44,005,990	Arunachal Pradesh	864,558
Gujrat	41,309,582	Chandigarh	642,015
Assam	22,414,322	Sikkim	406,457
Punjab	20,281,969	A and N Islands	220,661
Delhi	9,420,644	Dadra and Nagar Haveli	138,447
J and K	7,718,700	Daman and Diu	101,586
Arunachal Pradesh	5,170,877	Lakshdweep	51,707
Tripura	2,757,205	Total	483,653,831

Inner Circle with Library Legislation states and their people who enjoy literary legislation in modern India

Maharashtra	78,937,187
WestBengal	68,077,965
A.p.	66,508,008
Tamil Nadu	55,558,946
Karnataka	44,977,201
Keral	29,098,518
Haryana	16,463,648
Goa	16,463,648
Pondicherry	807,785
Mizoram	689,756
Orissa	31,659,736
Total	362,598,807

Fig.: Population served by library legislation

AN AGENDA FOR THE 21ST CENTURY

The 21st century is the century of information domination. Information is knowledge and knowledge is power. The foretaste of the information dominance of the coming century is already seen in the form of information markets, information superhighways and global internet. Less informed will be swallowed up by more informed. Nations which are less informationally developed will be subservient and dumping grounds of goods and other technologies for the nations that are informationally more developed. We may have the threat of loosing our independence once again in a different way. The nation should develop an agenda of action not only to meet the challenges out even to achieve progress on the information front. This brooks no further delay. The central and state Governments should have a Common Minimum Programme (CMP). Some suggestions in this direction are provided below:

Constitutional Amendment

Public libraries are as on today under the constitution of India, in List III, Which is the 'State List' of subjects. It is one of the arguments put forward by the central authorities for their inaction and inability to take progressive steps in the matter of public libraries. Earlier education was also in the 'State List' of subjects. Government of India through the 42nd Constitutional Amendment in 1976 brought education into list II, called the Concurrent List of subjects. Thus it established throughout the country, Residential schools and Navodaya schools for the great improvement of educational standards at the primary and secondary levels. In the same way the Central Government through an amendment of the constitution should bring the subject of public libraries into the Concurrent List. In the absence of such amendment, the State Governments may take another 25 years or 50 years to enact library legislation in their States. Public libraries, being the important channels of information, are as important as the defence establishment of India. Hence the Government of India should act in this direction. The Central Government can take as model the US Federal Public Library Services and Construction Act of 1956 and 1964.

Public Finances

The mandate of the State alone is not sufficient. There should be stable and continuous finances. At present library cess is levied in most of the States where library legislation was enacted. This is insufficient and inadequate. As finances are provided in the national and state budgets for agriculture, health, industries, defence etc. there should be regular budgetary provision for the development of public library and information centers. At least 5% in the Central budget and 10% States budget finance may be provided for the establishment, maintenance, modernistation and improvement of the public libraries and community information centers.

Model Libraries

The Central Government should take a lead role and establish Model Libraries one in each district throughout the country. There are already district libraries in 400 districts at the district headquarters established by the State Governments. The Model Libraries should be located at a central point in the district but not at the district headquarters. They will be reference libraries and provide information to the people. They also should set standards in the professional activities.

Public Library Network (PUBLIBNET)

In a democratic set up, people are rulers. In order to enable their rights and to discharge their duties they should have access to information. A reading nation is a leading nation. Information should be taken to the doorsteps of the people. Modern information technology makes it possible. Our public libraries should be computerised for resource sharing. On the model of various networks abroad and the INFLIBNET in India, there should be a Public Library Network (PUBLIBNET) connecting all public libraries, from the National Library down to the village libraries. This should be planned and achieved in different phases. In the first instance there is an immediate need to connect all the State Libraries with the National Library. Later District Libraries and still later the village libraries can be integrated into the PUBLIBNET.

National Library

The National Library and the other deposit libraries are to be further strengthened. They should not be lending libraries but only reference libraries. They should completely computerise their collections. They should be able to prepare CD-ROMs for special collections for use locally and abroad. The National Bibliography which is the main tool of bibliographical reference and control should come on time in better getup. The Delivery of Books Act should be amended to incorporate penal clauses in case books are not deposited after publication by the publishers. The national Library should not only publish bibliographical tools itself, but it should also encourage other agencies to publish subject bibliographies. It should act as the actual leader of the profession.

RRRLF

The RRRLF has creditably discharged its assigned role since 1972. It should be further strengthened by the Central Government in manpower as well as in its programmes. It is the bridge between the Central and State Governments in the field of public libraries: 1) It should conduct on regular basis short-term courses in IT for the working public librarians, 2) It also in consultation with the National Library and professional Associations in the country should develop a National Policy for the Public Libraries. 3) It should conduct and encourage research in the matters concerning library management, library standards, user studies, resource sharing, etc. 4) It should create reading awareness among the public. 5) It should publish a list of best books published in the constitutionally recognised languages of India for the benefit of young readers and scholars.

Backward Areas and Disadvantaged Groups

In our country there are certain areas which are backward and there are also large groups of people who are facing different

VIII : 3
Developing Rural Libraries As Rural Information Centers

Velaga Venkatappaiah

INTRODUCTION

It is Universally agreed that the development of a community is linked with knowledge and information it acquires. The knowledge and information can be had from documents available in libraries. In rural development, libraries play a greater role. It is true that 80% of the Indian population live in rural areas, thus justifying the fact that India lives in villages. Conceptually a Rural library or Village Library is meant for the economic development of the rural folk located in villages or a cluster of villages, or hamlets or settlements or thanas in Rajasthan. In the past, there were subscription libraries, but not rural libraries. Rural Libraries found their place in the pre-independence days. The only objective of the rural libraries in those days was the attainment of Independence. After 1947, the objective of a rural library is changed to Rural Reconstruction and social elevation of the rural masses.

The objectives of a public library as envisaged in the revised UNESCO Public Library Manifesto (1994) are as follows:

Center for Education

The UNESCO manifesto proclaims, that a public Library is a practical demonstration of democracy's faith in universal education as a continuing and life long process, in appreciation of the achievement of humanity in knowledge and culture. The rural library will serve as a centre for informal self-education. It opens its doors for all sections of the community at all levels.

Center for Information

A rural library should supply all types of information to the community success on culture, agriculture, education for rural development and for individual benefit. It should also serve as a referral point, for any specialized information, if any needed by an individual. The rural library thus should provide accurate information to a group or individual quickly.

Center for Recreation

The rural library should play a vital role in positive use of leisure of the rural folk. It is concerned with the refreshment of man's spirit, by providing books and other reading materials for relaxation and pleasure.

Center for Culture

A rural library should act as a center for cultural activities and promote keener participation, enjoyment, appreciation and information creative talents of rural art. It should provide equal opportunity to all sections of the community to exhibit their talent. It should arrange discussions, lectures, musical performances, stage plays and playlets, exhibit films, videos and slides for children youth and adults of the village. A rural library should also be developed as a center for folk arts, dance and music.

GUIDELINES FOR A RURAL LIBRARY

1 A rural library must be readily accessible and its doors must be kept open for free and equal use of all members of the village, regardless of race, colour, age, sex, religion, language, backwardness, economic or educational attainment.

2 A rural library should be opened and maintained under clear mandate of law. It should have a separate public

libraries act, or a provision in the laws of local bodies such as municipal corporations, municipalities or panchayats.

3 It should wholly be maintained by public funds and no direct charge or any fee should be collected for any service unless it is a specialised one like photocopying, typing etc.

FUNCTIONS OF A RURAL LIBRARY

The functions of a rural library should be suitable to the need of the hour.

1 Basically, it should serve as a traditional library with books, news papers and periodicals, The rural libraries should be kept open for proper use.

2 A rural library should closely follow the activities of *Jana Shikshana Nilayams*, sponsored by Department of Adult Education, Ministry of H R D, Govt. of India. A modern rural library must have -

1 Evening class for upgradation of literacy and numeracy skills.

2 A 'charcha mandal' for discussion on common problems.

3 A Training center-for simple and short duration courses relating to health, public health, family welfare, new developments in agriculture, animal husbandry, conservation of energy, improvization of crops, etc., and other vocational programmes.

4 Center for rural games and competitions.

5 Center for recreational and cultural activities.

6 An information window for securing information on various developmental programmes. The infirmation and material suitable for the rural people should be procured from the concerned agencies.

7 It is a community center with a community radio, video-audio, tape recorder, TV set, etc.

TARGETS OF A RURAL LIBRARY

A rural library, how small it may be it must have the following :

1 Collecting suitable literature according to the needs of the locality and organising them for effective use.

2 Providing reading room or other suitable place for reading books, magazines and newspapers, etc., for information, education and recreation.

3 Providing books and other reading materials for home reading.

4 Feeding rural organizations with helpful literature.

5 Arranging exhibitions, book displays and using audio-visual aids.

6 Providing a forum for group discussions on topics of interest and holding group activities.

7 Collection of information for the use of all sections of the community.

Based on the areas and the present conditions, library services in rural areas should be improved qualitatively and quantitatively

PROVISION FOR RURAL LIBRARIES

Many States in India have a great history of rural libraries managed by voluntary organisations. But of late, it is evident that the N.G.O.s are unable to maintain libraries, may be due to steep rise of prices of reading materials and gradual down fall of donation. There may be very few exception, but they cannot be generalized. However, experience warrants us to have a system with a statutory base, to provide a perennial source of income for running these libraries.

According to 42nd Amendment of the Constitution of India, which came into force on 3rd January, 1977, libraries form the part of Concurrent list. Therefore the Central Government has no role to play in respect of Libraries, the State Governments have power to make laws on the subject. Accordingly, public libraries acts were enacted in the States of Tamil Nadu (1948), Karnataka (1963), Maharashtra (1963) W. Bangal (1979), Andhra Pradesh (1960), Manipur (1988), Kerala and Haryana (1989), Mizoram (1993) and Goa (1994).

As per the public libraries act, the district library Authorities will establish and maintain public libraries in major cities, towns and villages somehow, even forty years after library legislation, it has not been possible to cover even 20% of the Gram panchayats with the public libraries or rendering some kind or library services. On the other hand, it is rather a pity that the library cess is collected from even illiterates and neo-literates in the villages and most of it is being spent for literates living in towns and cities. Not even a single pie of library cess was spent for illiterates during the last four decades or more. This is a social injustice. This is to be considered by administrators and planners to rectify this social injustice.

Some how, the Government of India came into the picture and amended the constitution (73rd Amendment) (Bill No. 158) of 1992 for establishment of panchayats with statutory powers and obligations. As per Article 243 G. (Eleventh Schedule-20) the Gram panchayat has to establish and maintain a public library for the inhabitants of the village. Its expenditure shall be met from the consolidated fund of the panchayat. The Philosophy behind the amendment is "that the state should take steps to organise Gram Panchayats and endow them to function as units of self-government".

THRUST ON RURAL LIBRARIES

The committee on National Policy on Library and Information System (NAPLIS) headed by Prof. D.P. Chattopadhyaya, former Chairman Raja Ram Mohan Library Foundation in its final report submitted to the Government of India in May 1986, recommended that the 'main thrust in this area should go to Rural Public Library'. A village or village cluster with adequate population should have a community library which will serve as an information center. Resources of different agencies engaged in the work of public health, adult education, local self-Government, and such others may be pooled to build up this composite center. "The empowered committee's recommendation on this area is that the Rural library service should be made available in each village under minimum needs programme by 2000 A.D.

RURAL LIBRARY SCHEME OF THE HRD

In this regard, the Human Resources Development Department of the Government of India released a press note in the last week of August 1994, which reads as follows- "The Government plans to set up village libraries to make up for the dearth of reading material for neo-literates. As sum of Rs. 1 crore has been earmarked for about 500 libraries which will be started in the same year on a pilot basis. The cost of each library, to be located in selected middle and high schools, is expected to be around Rs. 20,000."

The decision was announced by the Human Resource Development Minister at a meeting of the Parliament Consultative Committee. There has been a substantial growth in literacy in rural India. But in the absence of public libraries or book shops, neo-literates have little access to to reading material. The Government is of the opinion that under such circumstances villages are prone to watch the electronic media programmes. The Libraries under the scheme will have a modest collection of 300 to 400 books, three or four literary Journals and one local newspaper. The Minister said depending on the success of the pilot project, the scheme would be extended to include libraries in each village panchayat. It was also stated that however, educationists are skeptical about the success of the scheme. They observe that even in a high literate state like Kerala, local libraries are in a pitiable state. There are no new books. The Government's proposal that one of the school teachers be made the librarian is also regarded skeptically. Many are of the opinion that given the high rates of absenteeism among school teachers. the suggestion may not work out well."

To work out the details for organisation of these Rural Libraries, the Raja Rammohun Roy Library Foundation (RRRLF) appointed a committee at the and of 1994. As one of the members of the committee, the author of this paper prepared an exhaustive report and it is pending with the RRRLF.

COMMUNITY CENTERS OF RURAL DEVELOPMENT

It is also known that the Union Ministry of Rural Development has chalked out a very ambitious plan to establish 1,00,000 (one lakh) community centers under panchayats during Eighth Five Year Plan. This Plan, has taken the assistance from the Department of Social Welfare, National Library Mission (NLM), Education for all (EFA) etc. who have common welfare programme. The NAPLIS has also recommended that a community library should also cater to the needs of the children, and adult education and provide adequate audio-visual aids to attract more and illiterate villagers. This scheme is yet to take the shape for implementation.

WAY AHEAD

Observing various attempts explained above it appears that the Gram panchayat is only the appropriate organisation to establish a rural library. An impression should be given to the panchayat authorities, that it is the statutory obligation of the panchayat to open and run a rural library, naturally, the authorities will be obliged to open a library.

FINANCES OF THE LIBRARY

Where there is a commitment among the managing authorities, finance is not a big problem. Any small unit shall have the following minimum expenditure per year.

1.	Honorarium for the part-time librarian Rs.500/- month	Rs. 6,000-00
2	Books, Newspapers and periodicals	Rs.5,000-00
3	Stationary, lighting and other miscellaneous expenditure	Rs.1,000-00
		Total Rs.12,000-00

The expenditure mentioned above is tentative and may be revised atleast once in three years according to the local needs. The panchayat should provide accommodation in its office or school building or in a community center.

INCOME SOURCES OF A RURAL LIBRARY

To meet the day-today expenditure and maintenance of the library it must have a perennial income source from the following avenues.

1. A possible allocation of fund for library service in a village in the budget of the Gram Panchayat.
2. A panchayat must have a provision to levy library cess, as surcharge on property tax and house tax, entertainment tax, octroi, or on any reasonable items in the their jurisdiction.
3. If the library cess is being collected as per the public libraries Act, which is in force, the library cess collected in a village should not be remitted to the district library. Authority concerned, but will be spent for the library functioning in the area.
4. Donations from the local industries, banks and philanthropists. Membership fee or any fee for utilising the library service should not be charged from the rural people. This is quite against the manifesto of library service.
5. The expenditure for the library service in a panchayat area is worked out to Rs. 12,000 per year. The state Government

from its consolidated fund or sources of minimum needs programme, or any development programmes should substitute the balance amount derived from the areas mentioned in points 2 to 4, as above.

Then only there is possibility for opening and organising rural libraries in the villages properly. There is no agency in the rural area than a Gram panchayat which has the statutory authority and more with an embodiment to the Constitution of India, authorized to open a library. It is also to be noted that the Rural library, which are developed in book stock, readership, equipment and assets, should gradually merge with the district Library Authorities to maintain it more systematically with certain standards. This is the first phase of Rural Libraries.

RURAL LIBRARIES AS COMMUNITY INFORMATION CENTERS

In the second phase, the Rural Libraries should be developed as community information centers to act as resource centers to the community to cater not only to the needs of panchayats' Functionaries at various levels, but also to the general public. In this connection, we should make use of the well structured National Information Center of the Planning Commission, Government of India. Which has the following centers under it:

1 Mother Earth station at New Delhi

2 Regional Centers at Pune, Bhubaneswar and Hyderabad

3 State systems at all the district Head quarters

4 District systems at all the district Head quarter

5 Block system at all block Head Quarter and lower levels. (This proposal is pending with the Govt.)

DISTRICT INFORMATIC CENTERS

The satellite based communication Net-work (NICNET) covering all district head quarters, for the present.

District Information System Programmes (DISNIC). It had the following objectives:

1 Develop necessary information system/data-bases in various sectors of the economy for planning and decision making at the district level.

2 Promote information culture at district level.

3 Develop modelling and forecasting techniques that are required for decision making for socio-economic development.

The DISNIC thus paves the way for collection, completion and dissemination of qualitative information at all possible levels like District, Taluk, Block (Manda), Panchayat and village. One of the components of DISNIC in the General information service Terminal of the National information center (GISTNIC). The GISTNIC is designed with an objective to make general information available about India. This will-

1 Offer on line general information database services to common public by deriving useful information from various existing databases and other information sources.

2 To act NICNET based communication channel for the Government to assist in dissemination of important development information to common public.

3 To popularise information culture into the life style of common public for improving quality of life.

GISTNIC is available throughout the country through NICNET or at specially designed GISTNIC booths that are strategically located at State secretariats, Legislative Assemblies, Libraries, Airports, Hostels etc.

GISTNIC offers the following on line information services.

1 Statistical profile of India

2 District Level Economic Indicators

3 District profiles

4 University Education Guide of India

5 Tourist Guide of India
6 All India Railway Time-Table
7 Hotel Guide of India
8 General Information Guide
9 All India Hospital Directory
10 Country Profiles
11 World Economy Tables
12 Industrial Directory of India
13 Employment Guide
14 Investment Guide

DATA BASE ON TRADITIONAL SCIENCES

The NIC has expanded the area of information to traditional sciences and rural technology of India.

It also appears that there is a proposal to translate the data-bases in the regional languages and keep them available to the rural people. We can also impress them to increase their data base, based on the requirement of the villages.

RURAL BOOK TRUST, INDIA

Today the existing Rural libraries are purchasing books available in the market which may or may not be useful for them in real sense. Secondly, books useful exclusively for rural people are very few in number in regional languages. To do justice to rural people, there is a need to impress on the National Book Trust, India to establish a Rural wing in the NBT or request the Government of India to start Rural Book Trust, India, to publish books exclusively useful for rural masses. The Center on Rural Development (CORD) should organise orientation courses for the personnel working in these libraries, and should prepare a MANUAL on the management of Rural Libraries in English and the publication of language versions may be entrusted to State Governments. In this connection the attention of the CORD is drawn to similar publications brought by the Commonwealth

STAGES OF DEVELOPMENT

Beside on the past experience, and the social and economic conditions of the rural areas in the states workable proposals are suggested as follows:

1 To start with Gram panchayats should organise Rural libraries or at least reading rooms particularly where the Literacy programme is completed. This should also be treated as a part of post-Literacy programme continuing education programme.

2 Develop reading habits in rural people by innovative activities, programmes may be taken up for personality development of rural people.

3 Create awareness in the rural people about the need for education knowledge and information which will help them for better living.

4 Necessary educational inputs may be given to the rural folk about the need to support and develop the local institutions.

5 To depend or make use of the existing systems such as District Library Authorities, District Literacy Mission, Gram Panchayats, Religious endowments, National Information Centers which have a network and jurisdiction on rural areas.

6. NBT may be requested to short rural wing or the Govt. of India may be requested to start.

REFERENCES

1 Vashisht, C. P., *ed.* Libraries as rural community Resources centres, Delhi: B R Publishing Corporation, 1994.

2 Sarada K. Rural Library services in India. New Delhi: Ess Ess Publications, 1986.

3 Venkatappaiah Velaga in collaboration with P K Jayaswal, A comprehensive plan for rural libraries in India, calcutta: RRRLF, 1995 (Unpublished Report).

4 National Policy for Library and Information System Final report, May, 1985.

5 District Information system of national Information center, New Delhi: Planning Commission, 1988.

VIII : 4

Humanities Collections in Select Public Libraries In India

M. Kanakachary

INTRODUCTION

All the nations of the world are slowly shifting towards an information oriented society. Our country is not an exception. To this to have control over the growing information, the advanced countries like USA, UK, USSR, Germany and Japan are introducing new Information (IT) so that they are repackaging the information to disseminate it to right persons at right time. This revolution in the IT in the Western countries have its impact directly or indirectly on developing countries like India. No doubt, information is our national asset. But how to cope with this stupendous growth of information in different forms, on different subjects, in different languages from different places, in different times. It is really a heart-beating aspect for all of us. To have bibliographic control over this mess-mass production of varied types of information in our country is a very big task.

Library and information centers are one section of the information controllers, in relation to acquisition, storage and dissemination of information. There are several types of organisations in India in various fields functioning towards improvement of knowledge and societal and national development, striving towards the socio-economic, cultural and scientific and technological development of the nation. These organisations require information of all types and at all levels in order to achieve their ultimate target of improving the quality of life of every citizen of the country. They must purely rely on and have the support of libraries and information centers and adequate access to the right information at the right time through effective communication channels and consolidation and repackaging of data, in the form of various information services.

Therefore, the Government of India has established several special libraries to cater to the different needs of the people. These libraries include Indian Institute of Chemical Technology, Bhaba Atomic Research Center, National Geophysical Research Institute, Indian Institute of Science, National Dairy Research Institute, Central Drug Research Institute, Central Food Technological Research Institute, for example. The information required by any scholar or scientist or any body can fall into any one of the broad divisions of 'universe' of information, i.e., science information, social science information and the humanities information. The Government of India has given top priority to the field of science and technology, industrial sectors, research and development institutions as catalysts to development, and a little importance was given to the field of social sciences, but not much importance was given to the field of the humanities though they are as important as science and technology and social sciences for the development of country. This sector is badly neglected and there by the scholars working in this field are forced to depend upon the public libraries. Hence, this paper discusses how far the public libraries can provide services to the humanities scholars.

That the public libraries which constitute an isolated sector, have been suffering due to lack of adequate infrastructural facilities in terms of funds, manpower, physical facilities, computerisation etc. is a known fact. Though many professionals and professional organisations of libraries as well as those other than libraries are demanding from time to time, the development of public libraries in India, but not much attention has been paid by the governments (both Central and State).

There are about 75000 public libraries including those run by the governments (Central and State), private and voluntary organisations (social and philanthropic) in India. This figure seems to be a very large, one. Further, there is a very big question before us: Why don't we have bibliographic control over the literature that has already published and over the literature which is being produced now? A modest attempt in this regard is made in the present paper with the following objectives so that we could find out the ways and means in achieving the goal:

OBJECTIVES

Following were the main objectives of the study on which this paper is based:

i) to assess the existing resources and facilities available in the public libraries in India for information access in humanities;

ii) to provide a useful background study on the basis of a survey to the government agencies so that they could take appropriate steps for the improvement of the situation; and

iii) to suggest an ideal networking for the public libraries so that resource-sharing is possible for the purpose of exchanging humanities information.

METHODOLOGY OF THE STUDY

The study is based on an all-India survey which includes questionnaire technique and personal interviews with the librarians. Besides these methods, the relevant data has also been collected through the handbooks, annual reports, information brochures, etc. For this purpose, the following institutional libraries were selected as sample for the survey covering fair geographical area of the country and a fair coverage of administrative control of the governments (Central and State) and private people over these libraries. The author of this paper has made personal visits to each of these libraries during 1993 and held discussions with the librarians or the Incharges of the libraries.

	Library	Region
1.	Abul Kalam Azad Oriental Research Institute and Library (AKAORIL), Hyderabad	Southern Region
2.	Tanjore Maharajah Serfoji's Sarasvati Mahal Library (TMSSML), Tanjavur	
3.	National Academy of Letters (Sahitya Akademi) (NAL), New Delhi	Northan Region
4.	National Academy of Fine Arts (Lalit Kala Akademi) (NAFA), New Delhi	
5.	Bangiya Sahitya Parisad (BSP), Calcutta	Eastern Region
6.	Indian Languages Division (ILD), Calcutta	
7.	National center for performing Arts (NCPA), Bombay	Western Region
8.	Bhandarkar oriental Research Institute (BORI), Pune	

DATA ANALYSIS

The data collected from the above institutional libraries has been tabulated and anaysed in terms of the following variables:

Book Stock of the Libraries

The overall total collection of the eight libraries for 1990-91 was 6,09,985 which includes books, back volumes of periodicals, research dissertations, government publications, pamphlets/ handbooks, maps/atlases, manuscripts and non-book materials. The institution-wise (including region-wise) collection and the type of collection are given in Appendix. In additions to these stock, the libraries have some more materials like bound newspapers, coins, clay tablets and special collections such as old and rare books. Books form the major portion of these library collection. The TMSSML and BORI have very good collection of manuscripts. It was also found that the manuscripts at BORI were being microfilmed by Indira Gandhi National Center for the Arts, New Delhi. By this time, all the manuscripts are microfilmed and must have been preserved in IGNCA.

Subject Coverage of the Collection

The majority of the book stocks in these libraries are available in the following subject: Philosophy, Religion, Literature, Linguistics, Fine Arts, Arts History, Oriental Studies, Indology, Tantra, Jyouthisa and Journalism. There are also some books on other subjects of science and technology and social sciences.

Language Coverage of the Collection

The book stocks in these libraries are in English and other Indian languages such as Assamese, Bengali, Gujarati, Hindi, Kannada, Malayalam, Marathi, Oriya, Panjabi, Sanskrit, Tamil, Telugu and Urdu. A major part of books are in English. A few of the libraries have books in some foreign languages also. National Academy of Letters has books in Dogri, Kashmiri, Nepali, Rajasthani, Sindhi, Manipuri and Maithili in addition to other regional languages of India, while Bhandarkar Oriental Research Institute has documents in the Korean language.

Periodical Collection

For the year 1990-91, the total number of periodicals (both Indian and Foreign) published in English and other regional languages, subscribed by these libraries (except BSP and ILD which did not give details) were 438 and the total number of magazines and newspapers in English and other regional languages, subscribed by these libraries (except NCPL) which did not give the details were 409.

Membership

It was found from the records that in all the libraries there are nearly 10 thousand members, when all the categories of library members are pooled together. The category of the library members were teachers, research scholars, students, administrative staff and general public those who were using these libraries.

Services Provided

The libraries covered for the survey are providing the following services: Photocopying; Translation; Information; Bibliographic; Newspaper Clipping; Translation; Indexing and Audio-Visual services. No library is providing a all these services. In fact, some libraries do not have photocopying and translation services, but they are arranging these services with the help of other organisations. It was also observed that the translations provided by few of these libraries are only from English to their respective regional languages, that too of small articles of 4 to 5 pages.

Open/Closed Access System

It was found from the survey that 'open access system' is available in four libraries, namely TMSSML, NAL, NAFA and NCPA and 'closed Access system' in the remaining libraries.

Daily Usage

During 1990-91, daily on an average, 470 users visited these libraries, 195 books were borrowed from those libraries, 635 exposures were zeroxed from these libraries and 103 reference queries were answered by these libraries. Of course, these statistics appear to be very meagre because of several factors.

Technical Processing

Of these libraries, five libraries namely, AKAORIL, BSP, ILD, NAL, NAFA, are following DDC for classifying the books. Only one library, i.e. TMSSML is following CC Scheme. May be the reason for this is that Tanjavur district is the birth place of Dr. Ranganathan who designed the scheme. BORI is following its own classification system and ILD has not started any classification system and their books are shelved according to the subjects (at the time of survey).

All the libraries (except two libraries, namely TMSSML and BORI) are following AACR for the purpose of cataloguing of the books. TMSSML is following CCC of Dr. Ranganathan where as BORI is following its own cataloguing system. Several libraries, out of the above eight have adopted card catalogue and AKAORIL has adopted Register system for indexing the books.

Preservation Techniques

Since these libraries have many rare and old documents in their book stocks, their preservation methodology has been studied. Of these eight libraries, National Academy of Fine Arts and National Center for Performing Arts have A.C. facility. Abul Kalam Azad Oriental Research Institute and Library, Bhandarkar Oriental Research Institute, Tanjore, and Maharajah Serfoji's Sarasvati Mahal library are following fumigation methods for preserving the old and rare manuscripts and books. TMSSML has also adopted mending and dedication methods. Some other methods like using of napthelane balls, gammexane powder are also found in some of these libraries. In some libraries, the old and rare books are being xeroxed and bound. It was found at BORI, the manuscripts are being microfilmed by a Bombay company with the financial expenditure of IGNCA.

Computer Applications

No library has introduced computers for library services (At the time of survey). However, only National Academy of Letters is using the software (CDS/ISIS) with its PC-AT for the purpose of cataloguing the books. NCPA has also acquired the computer and the work is on the way.

From the personal interviews, it was found that due to lack of financial resources, and trained manpower, the librarians are not able to automate their libraries. Acquiring hardware and software is also costly for these libraries. The training which is being given to the professionals by some of the organisations like INSDOC and DRTC and some other institutes is also not adequate. Therefore, at present, computer facilities available are not geared up to form the basis for an information network. When all the public libraries are equipped with computers, it will be possible to form a network which could provide satisfactory services to the public including the humanities scholars.

Problems

All the eight libraries indicated some problems or the other related to collection, funds, staff, space, management support, etc. Lack of funds was the major problem faced by all the libraries and this caused some other consequential problems. Some librarians said in the personal interviews that there are staff in their libraries, but most of them are only unskilled/untrained and, as a result, they are not able to take up technical processing of the documents. If sufficient funds are provided, most of the problems could be solved.

Librarians Opinions

When the author of this paper had asked the librarians about their opinions for improvement of their library systems, they expressed the following keeping in their mind, the management attitude and the needs and demands of their library users:

i) Books on national integration and language problems in English should be translated into all regional languages and supplied to the libraries by the government in interest of national integration and dissemination of knowledge.

ii) A seminar of all the public librarians should be organised exclusively on the theme "computerisation of public libraries" since resource-sharing is essential and it is possible only through computerisation of all the public libraries.

iii) An agreement should be made among the public librarians so as to exchange in-house publications and sending of books on inter-library loan facility for mutual benefit.

iv) The pay scales and service rules of all the members of the staff in the public libraries should be made uniform so as to avoid frustration which will affect the services in the libraries.

v) The governments (central and state) should sanction adequate funds for creating information infrastructure for providing qualitative services to the users.

SUGGESTIONS

On the basis of the findings, the following suggestions are made:

a) in some libraries, the photocopiers are not available, but they are providing photocopying service with the help of other institutions. First, they are collecting the charges toward tick-marked material to be xeroxed and sending one of the library staff to get it outside. This is causing lot of delay for the users. Hence, all the libraries should be given photocopiers:

b) the translation services offered in some of these libraries are very few, that too of small articles of four to five pages and it was only from English to other regional languages. These services may be strengthened by appointing a panel of translators in different languages (to be identified from the universities/Research Organisations). They may preferably be recently retired a cademicians and they may be contacted whenever needed on adequate payment. The translations should be from English to other regional languages and vice-versa:

c) due to inadequate budgets, the libraries are not able to meet the information requirements of the users. The books are inadequate. Sufficient space is not there for the buildings itself and also for reading halls and facilities are very meagre. Due to lack of promotions, good pay scales, incentives, some of the library staff are frustrated. Books are in disorder and the services are poor.

For all these above lapses the lack of funds is the primary reason. Hence, the government should provide adequate funds for the development of public libraries in India to meet the research needs of the scholars, researchers, students and others who are interested in the field of the Humanities.

ACKNOWLEDGMENTS

The author of the paper extends thanks to Dr. Kuppa Srinivasa Sastry of the Department of English, Osmania University for making language corrections.

Annexture: (Library Collections in Humanities 1990-91)

Name of the Institutional Library	*Books including Ref. books*	*Back Volumes of Period-cals*	*Research Reports/ Dissert-ations*	*Govt/ Offcial Publica-tion*	*Pamph-lets/ Hand-books*	*Maps/ Atlases*	*Conf. Procs.*	*Mss. palm-leaves*	*Non-book mate-rials*	*Total*
1. AKAORIL (Hyderabad)	12,500	3,000	—	—	—	25	100	127	—	15.752
2. TMSSML (Tanjore)	43,732	909	—	—	—	368	—	44,316	295	89.611
3. NAL (New Delhi)	93,000	1,500	—	—	—	—	100	—	—	94.600
4. NAFA (New Delhi)	6,500	1,000	—	—	10,000	—	50	—	—	17,550
5. BSP (Calcutta)	2,10,000	25,000	—	3,000	—	100	—	9,000	—	2,47,100
6. ILD (Calcutta)	18,000	50	—	20	—	—	—	—	—	18,070
7. NCPA (Bombay)	11,352	—	—	—	—	—	—	—	—	11,352
8. BORI (Pune)	72,500	10,000	250	—	—	200	1,000	30,000	2,000	1,15,950
Total	4,67,575	41,459	250	3,020	10,000	693	1,250	83,443	2,295	6,09,985

It has to impart education to its students more effectively so that after receiving the education, they can teach other students properly and can be good teachers. But imparting education by the teachers to their students in the class room does not come to an end. Effective teaching and learning bring harmony to teacher's training college education where library plays an important role, teachers, scholars, and students seek information regarding their educational and vocational guidance where library whole heartedly serves to get acquainted with the sources of knowledge and broaden the horizon of knowledge these libraries act as the nerve centre of all academic and intellectual activities. Therefore to meet the basic purposes of teacher's training colleges, a good and well organised library is very much needed in every college and this can not be ignored.

EXISTING SCENE OF TEACHER'S TRAINING COLLEGE LIBRARIES

In the realisation of the objectives of the teachers' training colleges, libraries with its organisation, services and administration plays an important role, but peeping into the working of these libraries of Orissa, one can see gloomy and depressing picture. The existing condition of these libraries can be briefly summarised as follows:

(a) Library Building

Almost all libraries have no independent library building and are located in one room of the college main building. Some colleges have also no separate room for the library. Besides this there are no lighting ventilation and electrification facilities, more accurately, these can be compared as store rooms for books and other documents.

(b) Library Collection

Most of the libraries are stocked with old text books. Reference books such as encyclopaedias, thesauri year books, etc. are still a dream for maximum colleges the prevailing practice of book purchase is that book-sellers often contact the principal or H.O.D. and try to push rarely used or unwanted books ignoring the student's interest, as a result old and low quality unused books enter into the library and college librarians are totally helpless to find a suitable solution to this problem.

(c) Library Organisation

There is no library organisation so as to say, most libraries are poorly equipped with a few almirahs or booksellers, where books are kept in more than one row. Consequent retrieving of books becomes more difficult. In maximum college libraries, classification and cataloguing of books is considered a luxury on the ground of economy. Therefore, these libraries follows their own local classification and cataloguing system without adopting any standard scheme as a result identification and detailed information about a book is not available

(d) Library Service

In true sense no library service is provided by these libraries Due to lack of library space and inadequate staff, maximum number of libraries follow closed access system. Further books are issued to users on weekly basis denying students the privilege of borrowing books during the whole week. Reference tools and services are still a dream for these libraries.

(e) Library Staff

The staff position of teacher's training colleges is that of a one man show some times the college authorities dispute one of the office attendants to work in the library temporalties still consider library as an administrative accessory and librarian as the store keeper of books in most cases, the librarian has no authority to take independent action and frame policies for the library.

The probable reason for this poor state of affairs is that we have failed to consider the aim of education which is to educate and train students, to stimulate research and build up their character. The aim of our educational system is to get a passport for job and to earn bread without any values. Moreover, poor conception of college authorities regarding the library, poor financial conditions and inadequate qualified staff are the major factors for the depressing condition of the teacher's training college librarians.

SOME SUGGESTIONS FOR IMPROVEMENT

Some suggestions for the improvement of teacher's training college libraries are as follows.

(a) Library Building

The library should be established in a separate building or in case it occupies a portion of the college building, it should be provided with a separate hall with adequate lighting and ventilation facilities. Further it should be equipped properly for their maximum use.

(b) Library Finance

Finance is the primary factor for the effective functioning of any organisation and library being a service unit must be financed properly. In 1948, Ranganathan Education Commission had recommended that 6.5% of the total budget of the university/ college should be allotted to the library. Therefore, it is essential that a fixed percentage, atleast 5% of annual college budget should be allotted to the library for its proper functioning.

(c) Library Collection

Libraries should be stocked with course oriented text books, reference books, general reference books such as encyclopadias, directories and year books to meet the requirements of the users, there must be a book selection committee consisting of principal, senior teachers and librarian the suggestions of the librarian must be taken into consideration because he/she is the only person who can know the actual requirements of both the students and the teachers. Further, books must be purchased on a regular basis.

(d) Library Organisation

Every college must follow standard schemes of classification and cataloguing. The college authority should supply necessary tools and equipment. This is because without proper organisation of library books their maximum use can not be ensured.

(e) Library Services

The libraries should follow open access system, provided there is an adequate number of library staff, and necessary arrangements to check the loss of books. Regular issue and return of the books should be made in the libraries. There must be provision for a general reading room in every library. It provides an opportunity to consult a number of reserved and reference books and created reading habit among users. For this purpose, library should regularly procure newspapers, popular magazines, journals on different subjects, etc.

(f) Library Staff

It is the most important factor of the library because without library staff no library facilities can be provided. In every college, there must be qualified library staff only. Further, there must be one circulation section and one general reading room in every teacher's training college library. Accordingly, there must be one Librarian (for overall functions of the library). Two assistant librarians (one for circulation section and one for reading room) and two library attendants (one for circulation section and one for reading room). Since the effectiveness of the library services mainly depends upon the librarian, he should be provided with good working environment. Librarian should also be treated as teaching staff and should be given authority to take independent decisions and frame policies for library on academic lines.

CONCLUSION

The importance of library in teacher's training college can hardly be overstated. The library plays vital role in helping teachers, staff and students to meet their information needs. No teacher's training college can produce good and potential teachers without having a well stocked, well-staffed and up-to-date library. Therefore, it is essential that the college authorities, state government and also librarians should give special emphasis on library so that the aim of teacher's training education can be fulfilled.

REFERENCES

1. Girja Kumar. Academic status for university and college librarians. *ILA Bulletin* : 12:1, 1976 : p 5-14.
2. Krishan Kumar. Library administration and management. 1994. Vikas : New Delhi.
3. Mittal (R L), Library administration: Theory and practice. 1969. Metropolitan : New Delhi.
4. Mukherjee (A K) Librarianship: its philosophy and history. 1966. Asia publishing House: Bombay. p25-30.
5. Ranganathan (S R) Academic library system: Fourth plan period. Library science : 2: 4: 1965: p 227-328.
6. Wood (D N) Users studies. *ASLIB proceedings* : 23: 1: 1970: p 11-23.

IX : 2
Challenges Before the University Libraries in the New Economic Environment

Dinesh K. Gupta

INTRODUCTION

Since 1991, there has been a drastic change in the functioning of private and public sectors. Due to changed economic scenario of the country under the economic reforms there has been an emphasis on deregulation, liberalization, privatization and globalization of the economy. The changes in macro-economic policy of the country led to the changes in operational mechanism of enterprises of the different sectors which are transforming and restructuring their strategies and have become more concerned with efficiency and competitive edge. "Even previously restricted areas of public sector such as health, Public transportation, education, libraries, etc. have also been affected with the direction and pace of the economic changes. It has become, therefore, imperative for service providers to recognise as sharply as clearly the overall character of the changed environment and set their mind set for future directions" [1]. In this paper, an attempt has been made to:

(a) Highlight the key indicators of the changed economic environment:

(b) Analyse the likely changes / consequences of privatization on higher education and libraries:

(c) Suggest the appropriate measures to face the challenges of privatization of higher education on library and information services.

NEW ECONOMIC ENVIRONMENT

India has been following a policy of mixed economy since 1951, in which there are vector of sectors, wherein public sector, Private sector, joint sector and cooperative sector co-exist. The importance given to different sectors depended upon the situations prevailing at the particular point of time. Since the beginning of the planned era, the role of public sector was enlarged so that it may occupy the 'commanding heights' in the economy. But, from 1980's the private sector began to receive greater importance aiming at greater increasing productivity reducing costs and improving quality. In recent years, there has been phenomenal increase in the popularity of the concept and policy of privatization and the government with social commitments is enchanting the mantras of privatization and free market policies for solution of all evils and problems. The economic environment of the country has undergone a sea change since the launching of the new economic reforms in 1991. The following are some of the key indicators of the changed economic environment:

(a) There has been a shift in the state support to deregulation, delicencing, and depermitting;

(b) There has been a shift in the state control on output, supply, and price to free market competition;

(c) There has been a shift from nationalization to privatization;

(d) There has been a shift from social objective of public sector enterprises to economic viability and self sustaining policies;

(e) There has been a shift from bureaucratic style of management to professional style of management;

(f) There has been a shift in labour – intensive technique of production to capital – intensive techniques of production, particularly high technology and sophisticated technology: and

(g) There has been an overall emphasis on competition, efficiency and profitability.

PRIVATIZATION AND HIGHER EDUCATION

The changing economic environment has thrown open the gates of competition, not only in those involved in the trade and commerce, but also to professionals engaged in service sector. The dictum "Survival of the fittest" could have been never experienced ever before than now.

The process of changed economic environment has also posed a number of challenges before the economy. They have their political, administrative, social, cultural and educational implications. The role of State has shifted from Social Welfare to *laissez fair*. The man is being gradually replaced by technological factors from the center of development process. The social and cultural activities are under great stress. The domain of higher education which continued to be state responsibility is being opened for private sector [2]. Though there have been hardly any debate, during the fifty years of independence, as to whether state control or privatization is better as higher education is concerned. Even the New Education Policy (1986) stated that the role and responsibility of the state in regards to education would remain unchanged. But, the winds of change in favor of privatization blowing strongly over the economic scene in the county. Previously restricted areas for public sector like public health, public, transportation, is being opened for private sector, and the higher education may not escape for too long.

The privatization of higher education is mainly based on two grounds. [3]

(a) The strain on public resources had made funding of

subsidised higher education increasingly difficult and the higher education bid fare to lose government support, and

(b) Operations of universities left much to be desired, they did not fulfil the test of competitive efficiency mainly due to bureaucratic set-up and political interference.

The impact of privatization policies is taking shape in the field of higher education. The Govt. Has brought out private-University Bill, 1995. There has been increasing emphasis on university-industry interaction for resource mobilisation. Many of the Universities have started self-financing courses; they are making seats reserved for NRIs and have revised their fee structure upward substantially. Consequently, there has been discussion on learner-focused education; accountability of administration; performance appraisal to respond to new challenges.

CHALLENGES FOR UNIVERSITY LIBRARIES

Changes caused by new economic thinking are manifold and deeper. Public sector enterprises involved in health, insurance, banking, telecommunication, public transport, university and libraries are under threat and the government now prefer as a matter of social as well as economic policies to put almost anything in private sector. Challenges of change in academic libraries are in no matter different from others, as "the present day Indian library and information centers are unable to maintain their acquisition and services at previous level with the finances made available by state agencies, which has cut down or remained static for the last few years. A major portion of the State grants goes for staff salary and it has become difficult for L and I Centers to cope up with the growth of literature which resulted in great pressures on acquisition. Similarly, there has been a great necessity of funds for the acquisition of newer technologies to enhance services and products. There is also a threat from competitors to maintain quality services, as in market economy, public funded institutions and commercial organizations co-exist for making free flow of information. Commercial organizations engaged in production of information and its organization and retrieval would also charge for services [4] "Thus, the main challenges before the university libraries are:

(a) To exploit resources properly and use them efficiently.

(b) To mobilise resources to meet the financial demand;

(c) To make service and products qualitative and competitive through accountability;

IMPROVING EFFICIENCY

Information professionals working in Universities consider the collection of their libraries as inherently desirable to the user and the role of non-use or low use of books is placed on users who are treated sometimes as inefficient information seekers. This has been caused mainly due to 'free service' philosophy of the library services. Although there is nothing like free service', but the burden in money terms in most of the University libraries does not go to users, but borne by someone else in the form of taxes, levies, etc. But, the 'free service' philosophy has been a hindrance in the delivery of efficient services in University libraries. This approach is certain to be changed if there is any fear of competition among libraries, particularly with the private sector. It is an understatement that when of public and private sectors are compared in terms of cost of producing similar output, it is argued that the private sector has a competitive advantage over the public sector in terms of efficiency" [5]. Thus, there will be a pressure on university libraries to improve their efficiency, if they fail to attain it, there might be some danger for such libraries.

RESOURCE MOBILISATION

One condition that seems certain to occur and recur in the foreseeable future is that libraries will continue to feel the efforts of periodic downfall in the economy in a number of ways their financial support is curtailed. The time has come when the state cannot alone bear the total financial burden of financing higher education and libraries. Additional resources are to be mobilised to share the cost. If universities have to manage their financial resource more professionally, they will require to find ways and means of raising additional resources without government intervention. Thus, the implication for libraries is to take up measures for resource mobilisation through:

(a) Finding out ways to deliver their services while holding the line on budget increase e.g. Collection development policies will have to be even more carefully formulated to permit the libraries to continue to acquire the basic reference sources and text books in their collection. There will be much more pressure on collection development staff to acquire the most appropriate material available with the limited amount of funding.

(b) Participating in resource sharing arrangements, as University libraries have to rely on resource sharing arrangements with the libraries particularly for more specialised and costly serials, as a means of containing costs and optimal use of resources. Liberal use of technology can play a vital role in effective resource sharing through networking of libraries.

(c) Earning some money by selling services and products of libraries thorough charges from members of the other organisations, and / or libraries can charge for services from the users or other departments of the institution.

ACCOUNTABILITY TO USERS

A major thrust of privatisation policies on higher education is to promote the culture of enterprise and accountability. "Accountability is, in a way, a guide post to excellence. Lack of accountability breeds, irrelevance and mediocracy. An assessment of the performance of the Universities and institutions of higher learning must be made against the objectives set forth for them.

Excellence and accountability would go together. If an institution is intrinsically committed to excellence, it automatically wishes to be accountable. Accountability is a moral enforcement which the society has a right to exert upon a University or a institution of higher learning. Therefore, conscious attempt should be made to introduce accountability in the University system as a measure of reform. [6] The consequence for library professionals is the need to be more accountable to users of the services who are becoming highly discerning and critical. They are expecting library services who are becoming highly discerning and critical. They are expecting library services, Which traditionally are free at the point of use, To demonstrate the same efficiency and quality of their operations as commercial enterprises.

CONCLUSION

Private sector is being given a larger space to operate in the spheres of higher education in which the public sector will have to compete private sector, even though the public sector may continue to play the dominant role. What is needed is the improvement in the functioning of the University system–public and private, both. There is nothing in the new economic policies which takes away the role of University and their libraries, except that they need to improve their efficiency and productivity, and generate resources of their own. It is only the efficient system that can enable Universities to meet their social obligation.

REFERENCES

1. Dinesh Kumar Gupta and S. L. Jain. "Library and Information Centers in new economic era: An overview." *Herald of Library Science*. 35 (1-2). Jun -April. (1996) 41-47.
2. Mehata. Amit Kumar Shrikantbhi "Liberalisation of economic policy." *Globalisation of Indian Economy*. ed. Ramakant and Sugan Chand Jain. (Jaipur pointer : 1996.) 65
3. P. R. Bubhashi. "Privatization of higher education". *University News* 35 (26): June 30. (1997) 1-4.
4. Denesh Kumar Gupta and S.L. Jain. " Making a charge for library and information services." ***In**. library Database management; working papers of the CALIBER - 96* (Ahmedabad: Inflibnet 1996.)
5 Shridhar Pandey. "Economics and politics of privatization". ***In***

Economics of Privatization, ed. D.S. Avasthi (Kanpur. Bodh : 1995.) 40.

6. D. Swaminathan. "Higher education reforms: financing, freedom and accountability", ***Journal of Higher Education***, 18 (2). Summer (1995J 343-349.

IX : 3
Library Support Services to Distance Learners in India

M. Anjaiah

INTRODUCTION

Industrialization has made a great impact on human civilization and the world culture and it has generated basic changes in all spheres of human existence including education. It is not an exaggeration that "Correspondence Education" has been prevalent since the middle of nineteenth century. But it could develop only when the requisite conditions of fast, regular and cheaper postal and transport services were available. In fact, the first railway lines and the first correspondence schools were established around the same time. Similarly, with the development of modern communication and information technologies a new and innovative education concept namely 'Distance Education' or 'Open Education' came into existence.

'Distance Education' (DE) has emerged out of the needs of a 'knowledge-intensive society' which gives prominence to 'self-acquired learning throughout the life span. To keep pace with the accelerating change and to withstand 'Explosion of knowledge' individuals have had to embark upon a programme of learning which is a 'continuous process from birth-to-death. The concept of life long learning has caused an upsurge of adult learners who desire to enrich their knowledge and skills by choosing to study through the distance mode in order to circumvent the constraints of the conventional system. However, DE is a very specialized kind of non-traditional approach that requires learner adaptation to an entirely new mode of voluntary, creative learning with the help of a set of self-instructional materials of the class room without the direct supervision of the teacher or regular contact with peers. Such an isolated pedagogue situation poses several problems. Also, the different need projections of a vast majority of the heterogeneous learner clientele call for a provision of additional support which is made available through various Student Support Services (SSS) in Distance Education. The need of the hope is to revolutionize student support services by incorporating multi-media approach (MMA) which helps in organizing and conduction the educational transaction to the benefit of multitudes of learners. Multi-media approach can enlarge the scope and expand the reach of student support services.

Student support services play a very significant role in distance education system. In fact, the qualitative and quantitative improvement of distance education over the last two and a half decades is due to the provision of strong and varied support services to distance learners. The provision of library and information services is as much of vital importance to the distance learners as it is to their counter parts in conventional universities. Distance Education being essentially learner oriented self-study, library support is indispensable to distance learners in pursuing their studies independently.

Library facilities to distance learners vary from country to country depending upon the policy decisions taken by distance teaching institutions and availabiity of information technologies for retrieval as well as dissemination of information. A few multi-media communication technologies to provide access to 'dial-a-book' or provide information either on the spot through networking and teleconferencing or within a few hours through telefacsimile services using communication and electronic devices such as telephone, telex, facsimile and electronic mail whereas, in developing countries, it takes days to receive communication by post.

LIBRARY SERVICES TO DISTANCE LEARNERS

In India there are 57 Correspondence Directorates and eight open Universities but the library services to the distance learners of these institutions are meager. Very few libraries of the Correspondence Directorates provide borrowing facilities to students on depositing prescribed security money which is refundable when a student completes the course and ceases to be a member at the Library. Refund is made within one year after expiry of validity of membership. The library at the study centres have some facilities such as library books, audio lectures, video lectures, printed course materials and question papers of the previous years. But, most of these libraries have books and cassettes for reference and not for sale or lending.

The open Universities in India operate through two or three tier system where either study centers are directly under the control of the university or are linked through regional centers to the University. They have a Central Library for the University staff and libraries at Regional and Study Centers for supporting staff as well as counsellors and students. They provide reading and reference services, facilities to listen to audio cassettes, to view video cassettes and general information service. The central Library at the main campus combines the features and functions of both, an academic library as well as a special library. This dual characteristic increases the complexities of library policies regarding the development of collections and provision of library and information services and responsibility of building collections for the main as well as branch libraries. The collection for each category of the libraries has been developed considering the needs of the users. But even then, it is not possible to satisfy their demands and expectations entirely.

Acquisition management being a centralized process, the central library has the responsibility of building collections for the main as well as branch libraries. The collection for each category of the libraries has been developed considering the needs of the users. But it is not possible to satisfy their demands and expectations entirely.

REQUIREMENTS OF DISTANCE LEARNERS

Distance Education Leaners are heterogeneous in nature. The characteristics of distance learners are:

a) They come from different social and economic backgrounds.

b) Their qualifications are not same, and

c) Their aspirations are different. As such they require some student support services.

In distance education, the 'Learning Environment' plays a significant role since the process of learning is a challenging task for the distant learner. Unlike the conventional face-to-face learners, adult learners in Distance Education system have to carry on their studies amidst of responsibilities, occupations and other social pressures.

Here 'Learning Environment' denote the conditions of learning or the habit or domain of learning. It also constitutes, the educational inputs support services given by the open Universities, Distance Education Institutes and the conditions prevailing at the study centres and home. In short it encompasses all the communication and support from the institution, learning inputs, human element at the study centers and home.

Distance Education being a learner-oriented self-study system, library support is indispensable for distance learners to pursue their studies independently. The self-Instructional materials (SIMS) supplied to them is not self-sufficient at all levels. Students of certificate and undergraduate programmes can write assignments and prepare for term-end examination by reading self-instructional materials, whereas students of post-graduate diploma and degree programmes need to refer to text books. reference books and journal articles listed as suggested readings at the end of each block/unit in order to write assignments and prepare for term- end examinations. They are also required to submit project reports or dissertations. Some of them need to do practical work for completing the course. They need library facilities to accomplish their tasks. The research students of M.Phil and Ph. D must have an access not only to the library of the parent institution but also to the collections of other leading academic and special libraries of the country through inter library loan.

The requirements of the distance learners are varied as they belong to different categories, pursue studies in courses of various levels, progress diverse characteristics due to diversity in terms of caste, class, religion, social and cultural practices, age, socio-economic, educational and linguistic backgrounds of various regions of the vast country like India. These factors increase the complexities in satisfying their demands. They are mature and motivated adults, no doubt, keen on pursuing their studies independently, but they do expect appropriate student support services to justify and complete their courses.

IMPORTANCE OF LIBRARY SUPPORT SERVICES IN DISTANCE EDUCATION

In view of the fact that in Distance Education mode of education the learner is an isolated individual, the Library support services occupy a significant place and can almost be a substitute for a teacher. But, unfortunately the LSS a highly neglected area of students support service (SSS) in India. The importance of library support service in distance education may be summedup in the following words:

1. A learner needs supporting material and reference material to supplement the reading material. In the absence of an effective Library Support Services (LSS) the learner becomes handicapped.
2. Good library support services are needed for the learner in

providing Audio/Visual aids and such Hi-tech facilities, so as to enable the learners who constitutes the heterogeneous group to acquire necessary information and knowledge quickly and with minimal cost.

3. The library support services also become important for a learner as they inculcate reading habits among the learners.
4. Dissemination of information including the information pertaining to career development, personality development and the knowledge of environment is yet another important function the library support services could render to the learners.
5. The other area where the Library support services could support the learner is lending of books to the learners which benefits the learners in having economic viability and wider accessibility to wide choice of books.
6. The Library support services also have an important role to play in providing sufficient reading material, as often the conventional course material provided to the learner happens to be inadequate and limited.
7. In a competitive world it is a must for the leaner to keep update with the knowledge on the subject and the Library support services have an important role to play in updating knowledge on the subject through current journals, etc.
8. More often the course material provided to the learner covers the information upto past date of printing and rarely the new ideas are incorporated into them.

REFERENCES

Articles

1. Neela Jagannathan. "Taking stock of Library services to distant Learners," *Kakatiya Journal of Open Learning* (Hyderabad : Society vol .2 No. 2. 1996.
2. V. Vishwa Mohan. "Library services for Distance Learners in library and Information science : Some observation". Paper presented at National seminar on "From the Learner to the Learner: Developing

Improved Strategies towards Better student Support services" Held at BR Ambedkar Open University, Hyderabad : 1996.

3. S. Sudarshan Rao, : "Towards improvement of Library services in Distance education system : Impressions of a Learner-cum-Counsellor". Paper presented at National seminar on 'Student support services' held at BRAOU, 1996.

4. Anjaiah, M : "Library services to distance Learners - A study of SDLCE" paper presented at national seminar on 'Student Support Services' held at BRAOU, Hyderabad, 1996.

5. M. A. Prodhani. and J. N. Gautham, : "Library services in the Universities in North-East India", *IASLIC Bulletin* 42 (4), (1997), 165-174.

6. D. R. Kalia, : "A New approach to Library services in Asia", *CLIS Observer*, vol. XIV, No 3 and 4, July-Dec, (1997)117-120.

7. Neelam Sinha : "Student Support Services: A perspective from the National open school" *IJOL*, vol. 4 No. 1, (1945) 22-25.

8. Pravakar Rath, : "LIS Service to Distance Learners", Paper presented at National seminar on 'student support services' held at BRAOU, Hyderabad, 1996.

BOOKS

1. K. Murli Manohar, Distance Education in India (Warangal: Kakatiya University, 1993)

2. G. Ram Reddy.: Readings in Distance Education, (New Delhi : Ashish Publications 1987.)

3. R. Sweet,: "Perspectives on Distance Education - student Support services : Towards more responsive system", (Vancouver : 1993.)

X : 1

Designing Curriculum for Handling Archival Documents in University Libraries

S. S. Pal

INTRODUCTION

The necessity of education and training (E & T) of personnel for the management of university archives in India the documents which are produced for the multi-dimensional functions of universities involving teaching, research, administration and preservation of knowledge, and which have academic, historical and evidential long-term value-has arisen due to the growing concern for preserving academic records, especially because the University Grants Commission would also support it. The Universities therefore, need professionals who acquire perception and the needed skill to supplement their Library Science qualifications. There is another dimension of the situation, that is, the universities are not only expected to recruit professionals for the management of their archival material but also prepare manpower for handling the academic archives. This requires designing an E & T programme taking note of principles, techniques and methodologies applicable to archival material and the new information technologies including reprographics, microforms and the electronic storage.

HISTORICAL PERSPECTIVE

The issue as to what should be the qualifications of an academic archivist in a university environment is debatable. There has been difference of opinion as to who should be entrusted with the responsibility of imparting archival training in the universities: the university Department of History or the Department of Library and Information Science or any other institutional set up.

In world context, before the beginning of the 1980s, the holding of a master's degree in History and training in historical methodology was generally considered sufficient for the management of archival material. The historical background of an archivist's education was more in common than archivits with library training and experience. Brichford' survey [1] supported this view and so the notion that person with historical background are best equipped to understand the scholars' need of archives has been in practice for long, though the emphasis on it varied. The formal education of archivists in France, Germany, Great Britain and the United States usually has been History with specialization in auxiliary science, language and archival administration. The formal archival education in the United states has been divided between History and Library Science with a "strong reliance on special post-appointment training programmes[2]". The UNESCO has played a significant role for the development of archival education and training, especially under its General Information Programme (PGI).

The archival E & T is now imparted by various agencies including professional institutions, library schools, History departments, professional societies and through the media of workshops conferences and seminars at the state, national and international levels.

E&T IN U.S.A.

In the United States there are several institutions such as the Archives Institute, Atlanta, Modern Archives Institute,

Washington. D.C., the North Carolina Department of Archives, Raleigh, and universities such as Alberta, Case Western Reserve, Catholic, Columbia, Denver, Emory, Florida State, Illinois, Maryland, Michigan, Minnesota, Missouri, North Carolina, North Dakota State, Rhode Island, Washington, Wayne State, Wisconsin, Wright State, etc., which run archival study programmes. While Denver, Florida State, Minnesota, Missouri, North Carolina, North Dakota State offered courses in their History departments, such courses were available in the library schools of the universities of Alberta, Catholic, Illinois, etc. The master's level programme in historical archives was offered by universities such as Case Western Reserve, Wisconsin, Maryland, etc. The Maryland had programme for advanced studies in archives, manuscripts and historical collection. The courses were taught both in the History department and the college of Library and information services. The two-year curriculum led to MLS and MA in History.

Course Contents

A representative example is the University of Denver program for (1) Dual degree in history and Archival studies and Librarianship and Information Management, and (2) Master's Degree in History and Archival Studies. The former programme consists of History Requirement (20 credit hours) and Archival requirement (15 credit hours). The archival requirement comprised courses on introduction to archives, records administration and management, historical and contemporary manuscripts and archival document. Another ten hours were given to any of the three options: the archival option, curatorial option, and Art and the Architectural option. The Archival option comprised courses designated as readings in archival studies seminar, independent studies in archives, conservation of archival material, and image as document. The curatorial option provided for studies on local history, historical editing, oral history, and introduction to museum methods. The Art and Architectural option included courses on history and aesthetics of photography, photography for art anthropology and museology, history of prints, history of architecture, twentieth century architecture, and historic preservation [3].

E&T IN INDIA

The National Archives of India, New Delhi, has a School of Archival Studies which provides both regular and short term archival training courses. Its one year diploma course is open to candidates holding a second class master's degree in History with an optional paper in modern Indian History post- 1600 period.

Course Contents

The diploma course covers five papers incorporating archival theory and practice, including administration, records management, conservation, administrative history, archival libraries, documentation and information systems, and a dissertation on an archival topic. Most of these papers have theoretical and practical divisions. The reading in Archives Administration covers: definitions: acquisition of archives; arrangement; description of archives; publication programme, and programmes for exploitation of archives; archival legislation; access to archives; search-room practices; special types of archives, and private papers. The courses in Records management covered: introduction; office organization and management; documentation practices; filing procedures; mechanics of a file; departmental record rooms; records centres; appraisal, retirement and storage of archives; and records management in India. The conservation and Reprographics included readings on the introduction of the concepts of conservation and reprographics included readings on the introduction of the concepts of conservation and reprographics. The conservation part dealt with the constituent materials, housing of manuscripts and records, buildings, enemies of records and control measures, restoration, and requirements of a conservation unit. The reprographics part covered course on reprography systems (copying and duplication methods), photography, microphotography, preservation of microfilms, and planning and organization of a reprographic system. The paper on Administrative History covered the mechanics of a government, Central Secretariat, Ministry of Home Affairs, Ministry of External Affairs and the Ministry of Finance.

There is also an exclusive paper dealing with archival libraries, documentation and information covering readings on archival library, documentation concept, function, structure, organization and information systems and services.

The school of archival studies also runs various eight-week certificate courses on archives administration, records. management, reprography, care and conservation of books, manuscripts and archives, and servicing and repair of records. The courses are open to graduates from public and private agencies, however, the course on reprography requires the additional study of physics and chemistry at the Higher secondary level or intermediate level or intermediate level. Likewise, for the course on care and conservation, the candidates should have Chemistry at the Higher secondary or intermediate level. The course on servicing and repair of records is open to persons with elementary knowledge of English or Hindi.

INSTITUTIONAL GUIDELINES

Society of American Archivists

Thompson [4] refers to the society of American Archivists' recommendations identifying the following basic courses for all branches of the profession: Records management, microforms, introduction to Archives, manuscripts and Historical Archives, Conservation, Introduction to Museology, Introduction to Historic preservation, and Introduction to Graphics.

Indian Historical Records Commission

The commission has emphasized the introduction of teaching of archival studies in Indian universities as a separate paper at the post-graduate level. The Commission vide its resolution VIII of its proceedings dated may 19-20, 1981 had recommended to the universities to introduce archival science as one of the optional papers at the post-graduate level, and practicals in archival administration to be conducted by archival repositories in their respective areas.

University Grants Commission

The UGC [5] too favoured instituting a diploma course in archival studies and provided the following guidelines regarding the duration, courses of reading, eligibility and the location of the teaching programe:

"The duration of the diploma course may be one year. The syllabus should be on the same pattern as in the school of archival studies. The course should be offered under the auspices of the History department but on an interdisciplinary basis involving the Department of Library and information science, University library and visiting lecturers from the National Archives/State Archives and other institutions. The diploma course should be open to those with M.A. in History, Economics, political science, sociology or M.Sc. in physics or chemistry or any other relevant subject."

UNIVERSITY ARCHIVAL EDUCATION

The new development in the information world have also included the archival profession. The courses for the education and training of archivists should, therefore, reflect the new trends in the preservation and use of archival resources particularly the effect of new information technologies, and also seek synthesis with other information processing areas. This assumes significance, especially in universities where the archives/archival cells are to be a part of the university library or the university information systems.

LEVELS

The universities can devise archival education at three levels:

Level I

A regular diploma course with specialization in university archives may be conducted in collaboration with the faculty of the department of History, Library and Information Science, and experts from the national and state archives.

The Diploma course in the universities should cover the syllabi of the School of Archival Studies of the National Archives except the paper on administrative history which may be substituted with a paper on university archives covering the following subjects:

1. Development of Universities in India.
2. Structure of a University.
3. University information system.
4. Nature and kind of university archives and records.

The history and the working of the National Archives of India, the Indian Historical Records Commission, and one or two state archives should also be incorporated in the diploma course. Such a course in a university department should be open to persons holding a Master's degree in one of the subjects of Social Science such as Political Science, Economic, Public Administration, Education, Sociology, and Library and Information Science. The course should be introduced only at such universities which have archives/archival cells so that facilities for practical work exist. Alternatively, an understanding should be arrived with the National Archives or some state archives for providing practical training to their trainees.

Level II

An optional paper at the Master's level may be introduced in the subjects of History/Library and Information Science in respective departments. The paper can be divided into:

1. Theory and
2. Practicals.

Theory

The theory Part should include the following courses:

Archives Administration and Management

Definition, Identification and Appraisal of university records; Acquisition and processing; Arrangement and description; Restoration; Storage; Indexing and publication; Access to archives and reference service; Microphotography and reprographic services.

Practicals

For practicals, two weeks training in handling of archival material and equipment at the National/ State Archives should be arranged. The candidates should record the methods and techniques used in the archives visited by them.

Level III

Short-term courses for librarians may be introduced to acquaint them with archival practices and handling of the university archives. These courses may be organized by the Departments of Library Science in cooperation with the national and state archives.

REFERENCES

1. Brichford. M.J. Archives and manuscripts: appraisal and accessing. Chicago : Society of American Archivists. 1977. p. 13.
2. *Ibid*. P.12.
3. University of Denver (U.S.A.). Education programme for the dual degree in history and archival studies and librarianship and information management, and Master's degree in history and archival studies.
4. Thompson. Enid T. Commentary on the archival management and special libraries. ***Special Libraries*** 69 (Dec 1978) : 491-492.
5. University Grants Commission (India). Communication no. F. 22-2/81 (Hr. H/IIR) dated 7th February, 1983 to the universities.

X : 2

Continuing Education Programmes (CEPs) For Agricultural Librarians

T. Rajagopal
K. Veeranjaneyulu

INTRODUCTION

The Library and Information professionals of agricultural information systems who have completed their formal library education years ago and who have not subsequently participated in informative educational activities are a dead wood to the agricultural librarianship unless they update themselves. It is essential to organise refresher/ in-service training courses for them both at local and national levels.

Concept of Continuing Education Programme

Continuing education is based on the philosophy of life long education. It is applicable to all persons irrespective of their age, sex, location and occupation. Paul Lengrand in his introduction to life-long education has mentioned some factors which have created the need for continuing education. They are: Acceleration of change, demographic expansions, Evolution of scientific knowledge and technology and threat of technology unemployment. The above factors are applicable to the agricultural librarianship. In this age of knowledge and information explosion one has to acquaint himself with the latest information and techniques by CEP in one or the other way. The agricultural librarians like the agricultural scientists are supposed to continue the education in their respective fields in order to keep themselves aware of he latest information and knowledge to increase their professional competence.

Continuing Education Programmes And Agricultural Information Professionals

Continuing education is essential for agricultural librarianship and can take many forms – which may or may not lead to degrees. Attending professional meetings and annual conferences of professional organizations, Attending short term workshops, Visiting other libraries and education institutions are some of the CEPs for agricultural libraries. Such CEPs help them to keep abreast of all information in era of knowledge explosion. The following CEPs for agricultural information system may be offered.

FORMAL EDUCATION

a) **Formal Courses:** Library schools will take responsibilities in offering formal courses. They aim as:
   1. Guiding for research
   2. To enable the librarians to hold administrative posts

b) **Extension Courses:** Summer schools run by Indian Universities offer extension courses. They provide practical demonstration of different works in library.

c) **Refresher Courses:** Library schools and national library associations which provide refresher courses are meant:
   1. To brush up all and recall acquired Knowledge.
   2. Increasing of work efficiency.

d) **In Service Training:** Agricultural information systems organise in-service training programmes to improve knowledge and to increase Job efficiency.

Informal Education Obtained Through:

a) Reading, writing and editing.

b) Attending lectures, professional meetings, conferences and workshops.

NEED FOR CEPS FOR AGRICULTURAL LIBRARIANS

The new developments are of a highly technical nature and librarians trained in the conventional library schools are not trained in the know-how of the latest technology and its application to libraries. Hence in addition to formal library education, there is an urgent need to provide in service training for library and information science professionals on the new concepts, skills and technologies.

Objectives of Continuing Education

The objectives of the CEP may be the following:

1. To help the library professionals to keep abreast of the new developments in the field.
2. To help them to be fit and competent in the ever changing technology field.
3. To help them to improve their career prospects.
4. To help them in dissemination of new ideas and concepts.
5. To help them to render user-oriented services.
6. To update professional knowledge.

Constraints

The success of CEPs for agricultural librarians depends on availability of highly trained man-power and adequate financial resources.

a) Manpower

Teachers from Library and Information Science would have to be drawn to implement the programme. Since they may have expertise in specific areas. This may include reprography, computer software, A/V materials, indexing methods etc. If necessary the teachers from other disciplines are to be selected for conducting CEP for eg. Operation Research Models, Statistical Methods, System Analysis, Information Technology etc.

b) Financial Resources

Adequate financial support from national and international organizations become necessary to conduct CEPs effectively. UGC, ICAR, DST should take up the responsibilities in providing funds for CEPs.

For offering continuing education programmes at international level. The international organisations such as UNESCO, FAO, IFLA, FID, etc. should take up the responsibilities in providing funds. The State Government and Central Government should draw the plan for implementation of CEPs for agricultural librarians. Apart from that the agricultural universities should develop their own financial resources to finance the CEPs for agricultural college libraries.

CURRICULUM FOR CEPs FOR AGRICULTURAL LIBRARIANS

A specific curricula should be framed for the CEP for the agricultural librarians.

1. Fundamentals of Agricultural Science Subjects.
2. Agricultural Library terminology.
3. Agricultural Library management.
4. Agricultural Information Processing and Retrieval.
5. Introduction to Agricultural Information science Resource Sharing and Networking.
6. Micro Computer, Programming, Database Management and Agricultural literature search & retrieval (CD-ROM search)
7. Introduction to Agricultural Information sources, reprographic services and Inter-Library Exchange Programmes.
8. Agricultural Information Research Methodology and Biostatistics.
9. Practicals on:

a) Micro Computer Operation-Database Management

b) CABI, AGRIS

c) E-Mail, Internet

d) Desk Top Publishing

CONCLUSION

It may be said that library profession is fast changing. Continuing education of library professionals has become a necessity in view of new developments. The professionals themselves must be alert and keep with the changing time lest they become irrelevant and incapable of providing services to the seekers of information. The parent bodies, employers of library professionals must adopt a liberal attitude towards the professionals so that they may update their professional knowledge and skills through continuing education.

REFERENCES

1. B. Guha, "Continuing education of library and information Specialists". *Lib. Sc. Doc.* 15, (1978.).
2. M.E.D. Koenig, " Education for information management: competition or cooperation?" *Library Trends*, Spring (1986.).
3. P.B. Mangla "Library and information Science Education in India for the 21st Century: Trends and Issues". Information and society, ed. L.S. Ramaiah, et al.. (New Delhi: Ess Ess publication, 1997.)
4. P. B. Mangla, Manpower development for information handling. *J. Lib. Info.* Sc. 4, (1979.).
5. S. Seetharama, and M.A. Gopinath, "Continuing education for librarians: Its needs and methods: *DRTC annual seminar* 10, (1972.).
6. M. K. Srivastava, "Role of Library Associations in continuing. Education to Libraries." *Lib. Her.* 23, (1984.).
7. Steig, Margaret F. "Change and Challenges in Library and Information Science Education." (Chicago: American Library Associations, 1992.)

X : 3

Specialisation in LIS Education : Changing Trends and Current Perspectives

R. S. R. Vara Lakshmi

INTRODUCTION

Library and Information Science (LIS) education is devoted to impart professional training in transferring the information from documents in the library/information centre to the memories of human beings. As such, the accelerating revolutionary process in libraries, a revolution driven by powerful economic and technological forces have a direct impact on LIS education. In other words, it becomes imperative for LIS educationists to consider how this translocation of information may be accomplished most expeditiously and to what extent the 'Specialisation' can serve additional purpose. Inspite of initial resistence and grudging to accept specialised education[1], the concept of specialisation for the first time was incorporated in LIS education In USA, in late 1950s, when the core curriculum had been supported by a 'follow-up sequence of courses devoted to specialisation'. Later, other countries have also adopted the idea but in India, the concept was established only in 1960s.

Specialisation involves adaptation of these aspects of education that are unique or are added to the regular curricular programme. The amount and kind of adaptation needed depends upon the rate of organisational growth, growth of users and their information needs and the extent and rapidity of technological change.

NEED FOR SPECIALISATION IN LIS EDUCATION

The primary value of specialisation lies in the capacity to anticipate the changes in information environment and fulfil its mission in new ways with extensive use of information technologies.

Guruswamy Naidu[2] has observed that the "need for specialisation is not the result of any break through, but it is in response to the failure of traditional methods to the ever growing user demands".

According to Deshpande[3] specialisation in LIS education is necessary (a) to provide in depth specialised knowledge (b) to lay more emphasis on recent trends in information services and (c) to attract intelligent and scholar students to the discipline.

Therefore, the need for specialisation in LIS education can be summarised as

1. The professional training requirements vary from one library to another i.e. the special library needs differ substantially from the traditional library;
2. To make the library instrumental in the Institution's policies, planning and functioning;
3. To develop a professional who can
   - coordinate library's strategic planning and development efforts;
   - establish new partnership roles for exchange of information within and outside the country ;
   - recognise the growing need for technological support and trained in handling them.
4. To produce specialist professionals keeping in view the changes in information environment; Changes at work and management; changes in financial situation which demands for cost-effectiveness in every performance; changes in information handling techniques.
5. To improve the employability/saleability of the graduates.

OBJECTIVES OF SPECIALISATION

The primary objectives of specialisation in LIS education are :

- to understand the nature, type, functions, users and their needs of specialised institutions.
- to know different information tools and services required to disseminate information in that field.
- to understand information management skills to provide global access to information in that field.
- to understand facets, potential and working of different information technology tools useful for storage and dissemination of information.
- to have basic know how of the specialised subject in terms of its structure, growth and its relation to the society.

SPECIALISATION IN LIS EDUCATION IN INDIA : THE CHANGING TRENDS

The LIS education, training and research are meant for producing adequately educated and trained librarians/information scientists and teachers. To fulfil this objective, the LIS schools in India have been responding to the changes in Library and information system and incorporating new specialisations, re-designing courses and progressing well to uplift the profession with qualitative improvement. The concept of specialisation in LIS education had been a phenomenon of 1960s and by 1990 it has reached a state of relative maturity. The developmental trends in 'Specialisation' can be briefly presented as follows :

1960s

The Report of the University Grants Commission (UGC) Review Committee (1965) on Library Science in Indian Universities under the chairmanship of Dr. S. R. Ranganathan, has listed the following optionals under the course contents.

Aligarh, Kerala, Madras and Rajasthan Universities used

to offer BLISc, out of which only Aligarh Muslim University had included optional papers of (1) Documentation (2) Oriental librarianship (3) Audio-visual library methods, (4) Universe of knowledge and world of books. The student can opt for any one among them.

At Diploma level, out of eleven universities, Banaras Hindu University had offered the optional papers - university, college and special libraries; Public libraries; and School and Children's library. It is evident that the concept of specialisation offered as optional/elective was in its infancy upto 1965.

All the subjects are treated with equi-importance and there was no special emphasis on particular branch of study. The establishment of INSDOC (1952) and DRTC (1962) served the purpose, which have offered specialised information science programmes.

1970s

There was a phenomenal growth in number of LIS schools and the courses offered during 1970s. Out of 33 schools, as listed by Bhattacharya[5] in IFLA compendium of courses in LIS (1981), that offered BLISc programme, Andhra, Lucknow, Mysore Universities included elective papers. The areas of specialisation, are very basic such as :

Public/National Library System

Academic Library System

Special Library System

Rural Library System

Archives and Manuscripts Library System.

However, the electives papers have a vital place in MLISc programme. Ten universities have introduced MLISc programmes and six of them have offered variety of specialisations as elective papers. The areas of specialisation includes :

1. Bibliography and Literature on Social Sciences/Natural Sciences/ Applied Sciences/ Humanities/ Medicine/ Agriculture/ Engineering and Technology/Law etc.

2. Information systems such as Public. Academic. Research, Health Science, Agriculture, Engineering and Technology. University of Delhi is unique by introducing the areas like Information Storage and Retrieval System, Reprography and Computer Applications. Infact, use of computers for library operations started 1960s. But: in India, it got a place in LIS curriculum in 1970s.

Thus, new areas of specialisation have been introduced by restructuring and redesigning of courses during 1970s, in addition to Public Academic and Special Librarianship. INSDOC and DRTC continued to offer more elective papers such as industrial Information System; Information System for R & D; Information Systems for Development and Planning; Management Information Systems, etc.

1980s

Master programmes in LIS have been started by many universities during 1980s. Further UGC (India) Panel on LIS Education has been started functioning. This makes recommendations to devise suitable LIS curricula. The impact of emerging technologies has been identified and attempts have been made to incorporate them in the syllabi. All these factors have contributed to significant changes in specialisation of LIS education in India. Offering of specialisation has become a common feature at MLISc level. UGC Panel (1978/82) suggested:

"a. Universe of Knowledge : Its development and structure

b. One of

   i. Information Storage and Retrieval

   ii. Depth classification

c. Information systems and programmes

d. Information and literature sources in any one of

i. Humanities	iv. Medical Sciences
ii. Social Sciences	v. Engineering and Technology
iii Science	vi. Agriculture Sciences, etc.

e. One of following :

i. Computer Applications

ii. Comparative Librarianship

iii. Library Systems Analysis

f. Any one of the following

i. Public library system

ii. Academic library system

iii. Technical library system

iv. Agricultural library system

v. Medical library system

vi. Engineering and Technological library system".

Thus the option to select a specialisation has become an integral part of core curriculum instead of an appendage to the core curriculum as was practised upto 1970s. Though the importance of IT has been realised, it has not taken a prime place in elective papers.

1990s

There has been revolutionary changes during the present decade, with regard to specialisation in LIS education.

IATLIS Seminar

The first contribution is by IATLIS by organising a Seminar on specialisation in LIS education during 17th-19th Jan. 1991 at Bangalore[7]. The facets of presentations Include: Need for specialisation. Areas of specialisation and Specialists. Nearly 15 papers have discussed about the need, means and methods to include Information Technology (IT) as a specialisation. It is apparent that there is significant change in LIS teachers thinking and wide recognition for courses on IT.

CDC Report

The second contribution has been Curriculum Development Committee (CDC) (UGC, India) Report published in 1993[8]. The Committee has suggested the following scheme of papers as Electives in BLISc programmes[9] :

"a. School and children's libraries
b. University and college libraries
c. Public library system
d. Government department libraries
e. Research and Development libraries
f. Archives Librarianship
g. Engineering and Technology Library and Information System
h. Medical Librarianship
i. Agricultural Library and Information System
j. Law Libraries
k. Music libraries
l. Industrial library and information system
m. Manuscriptology
n. Library Buildings, Fittings and Furniture
o. Local Studies Librarianship
p. Non-Book materials".

The committee has suggested six elective papers for MLISc[10] programmes :

a. Comparative and International librarianship
b. Higher Education and Academic Library System
c. Communication, Mass Media and Public Library
d. Bibliographic control
e. User Education and User Studies
f. Education for Library and Information Science".

The University departments, with due consideration to their local needs and demands have adopted some of these subjects and added few other areas. The IT component has been included as core paper by majority of universities and very few universities., have offered it under elective papers. A study conducted by A. A. N. Raju, revealed that "the impact of IT has been felt by the LIS departments in the country and it is evident that various aspects/areas of IT have been included in the syllabi of MLISc programmes either in the form of one paper or two papers". He has also observed that out of 15 universities he has analysed in the study only one university (University of Delhi) offers IT as elective paper.

Integrated MLISc Programmes

The third revolutionary change in 1990s is the starting of 2 Year integrated MLISc programmes by 14 Departments of LIS (upto 1998 June) instead of 1 + 1 stream of BLISc and MLISc. The curriculum for these programmes has been revamped and restructured pruning many of traditional courses and introducing new courses with emphasis on IT components.

Thus, under integrated programe, universities of Andhara, Bharathi Dasan, NEHU, Madras and Mysore have introduced a number of new courses under electives, though the other universities confined to the traditional library systems. It is evident from the above that the LIS schools in India have traveled a long way in the area of specialisation and are providing to the student an option to select from a variety of specialisations as per his/her interest and career development. They have responded positively to the changing trends in information environment and adopted courses of contemporary value. The other schools also must add new courses at a rate substantially greater than they appear to accomplish.

CURRENT PERSPECTIVES

The developmental trends of specialisation in LIS education programmes is apparent, but there are certain issues

Specialisation in 2 year Integrated MLISc Programmes

Name of the Univ.	*Semester/ Annual*	*Electives*
Andhra	Annual	1. Economics and marketing of information 2. Design of computer assisted information systems 3. Academic library and inormation systems 4. Public library system 5. Community and information services 6. Health and welfare library and information services 7. Industrial library and information system 8. Agricultural library and information system 9. Organisation and preservation of special materials.
Birla institute of Tech.. Ranchi.	Semester	No electives. 11 Courses on I.T. includig 4 practices under core courses.
Bishop Heber College. Tiruchinapalli	Semester	4th Semester 3 electives under Group A. B and C

Bharatidasan Univ.,		A. Bibliometrics, Academic Library and Information System, field work. B. Social science information system. Information system for R and D field work. C. Preservation ad conservation of Library materials. user education, field work.
Karnatak	Annual	Public library system Acadimic library system Special library system (in final year.)
Kuvempu	Annual	Public library system Academic library system Special library system (in final year.)
Mangalore	Annual	Public library system Academic library system Special library system(in final year)
NEHU	Semester	Electives in fourth semester I. Information and literature sources in any one of the following :

		a) Humanities b) Social Sciences c) Natural sciences 2. Information systems and services Management of Information systems
Sri venkateswara	Annual	No electives
University of Madras	Semester	Electives in 3rd and 4th semesters I. a. Inf. Sources and services in Humanities and social sciences b. Inf. Sources and Services in Science and Technology c. Legal aspects of information d. Book indexing II. e. Design of indexing language f. Academic libraries g. Public libraries h. Inf. System for R and D i. Inf. System for rural development III. j. Preservation and conservation of materials k. LIS Education

		I.	CDS/ISIS
		IV.	Marketing of Information
			Basic courses in statistics
			Advance courses in statistics
		V.	Introduction G.I.S.
			Computer application –social/earth sciences
			Management of information systems
University of Mysore	Annual		Agricultural libraries and information service
			Health and welfare library and information services
			Industrial libraries and information services
			Social science libraries and information services
			Dissertation.

which require attention of academicians and professionals. In other words, there is a need to identify and study the extent to which the specialisation courses are being implemented.

Pre-requisites for Specialised Courses

(a) Need for the course- a study through a survey has to be conducted to ascertain the demand for the course and of employment potential:

(b) Relevance of courses to the contemporary information society has to be analysed:

(c) Intake criteria- the number of candidates opt for the course and the cost – effectiveness have to be ascertained:

(d) Infrastructural facilities – specialisation requires a blend of traditional and I.T. Skills. The knowledge of information industry, publication industry, marketing techniques, consultacy techniques have to be taught in a specific area, which requires adequate infrastructural facilities to practically train for the high level professional capabilities:

(e) Teaching methods- traditional class room teaching is inadequate to train a specialist. Fieldwork or laboratory with simulated packages is essential:

(f) Variations in training – the specialist training varies from library to library e.g. Medical and Industrial libraries. Hence, the teacher should also be a specialist in that field.

Hence, adequate attention has to be paid to the above factors before starting a specialisation course. The LIS Schools have to give utmost priority to these aspects and the courses should not be introduced arbitrarily without any assessment.

Problems of Implementation

The LIS Schools are facing certain hiccups while implementing the specialisation courses.

a. **Regional language :** Of late some universities are allowing the students to take their examinations in regional languages due to pressures from student community. The specialisation courses are too advanced and the literature is not being available in regional languages.

b. **Duration:** The course is being offered as one paper or few credits and valued for 100 marks on par with other papers. Hence, 3 to 4 hours per week are allocated to teach specialisation. It is not possible develop a specialist within this short time. He may get knowledge but cannot acquire the required skills.

c. **Subject background of students:** The students may join the course either from Arts, Humanities or Science background. The Arts and Humanities subjects will not help them to study the sophisticated technologies. This become difficult for teacher as well as to the students. Further lots of difference exists between a fresher and candidates having work experience in that field of specialisation.

d. **Teachers, Specialisation and Training:** To impart a specialised course the teacher should be an expert in that field. But there is a dearth for such subject experts in various specialisations.

e. **Distance Education and Specialisation:** Nowadays, LIS education programs are being offered through distance education system. To educate and train a specialist through distance education programs is very difficult. Hence, the institutions offer only one theory based specialisation, which creates imbalance in LIS trainees.

Therefore, there is a need to find means and methods to overcome the problems for effective implementation of the specialisation programmes.

SUGGESTIONS

The following suggestions may help to produce a true specialist, with high caliber in a chosen field, who can meet the expectations of the employers.

a. **Postmaster certicficate:** Specialisation can be offered after Postgraduation in Library Science as in the case of medicine, law etc. For a period of one year so that ample training can be offered.

b. **Internship:** Apprenticeship in a related library atleast for a period of six months in addition to the theoretical aspects covered and dissertation / Project in that particular field should be made compulsory.

c. **Progressive Courses:** Library Schools need to develop and emphasize courses in the areas of information technology, information services to special groups and types.

d. **Study for demand:** There is a need to conduct surveys to ascertain the nature of the society to be served and the courses on demand. This satisfies the basic principle of supply and demand.

e. **Updation of in-service Candidates:** There is a need to introduce courses on specialisation for the in-service candidates, especially to those who have taken the course prior to the 'electronic era'.

f. **Role Of Professional Associations:** The National bodies / associations should conduct the training programs either before or after recruitment as are being offered by MLA (USA), SLA (USA), ASLIB (UK), etc.

g. **Involvement Of Experts:** The involvement of subject specialists and specialist librarians with the department in devising curriculum and for the special lectures, in a way helps to utilise the expertise.

h. **Selection of Students:** Though the student have the option to choose a particular specialisation, scrutiny must be made to assess the students aptitude, subject background, and communicative skills.

REFERENCE

1. Williams Robert V Zachery and Martha Jane K, "specialisation in library education: A Review of the trends and issues". *Journal of Education for Library and Information science.* 26 (1996): 215-233

2. N. Guruswamy Naidu, "Specialisation in Library Science problems and Prospects", *8th IATLIS National Seminar on Specialisation in LIS education.* Ed. by A. Tejomurthy. (Bangalore, 17th – 19th Jan. 1991) 23-29.

3. N. J. Deshpande, "Need for specialisation in Library science: An Analytical study," *8th IATLIS Seminar on specialisation in LIS Education,* ed. by A. Tejomurthy. (Bangalore, 17th –19th Jan. 1991) 1-7.

4. Library Science in Indian Universities. *Report of the UGC Review Committee* (Chairman, S. R. Ranganathan). (New Delhi : UGC, 1965.)

5. Bhattacharya, G. *Comp, IFLA Compendium of courses in LIS.* (The Hangue: IFLA, 1981.) 31-119.

6. UGC (India). *Report of the Curriculum Development Committee in library and information science.* (New Delhi: UGC, 1993.) 24.

7. IATLIS Report of *8th IATLIS National seminar on specialisation in LIS education* (Bangalore, 17th –19th Jan. 1991.)

8. UGC (India). *Report of the Curriculum Development Committee in Library and Information Science.* (New Delhi : UGC, 1993.)

9. Ibid. P. 55

10. Ibid. P. 92

11. A A N Raju. A study of I.T. Components in MLISc courses in India," *Information Technology and its impact on LIS Education and library management. Ed.* A. A. N. Raju, N. Lakshmana Rao, and S. Sudarsana Rao. (Hyderabad: Delta Publications, 1997.) 45-53.

X : 4
LIS Education and Research in West Bengal: An Overview

P. Barua

INTRODUCTION

The historical development of L and I S education in India dates back to 1911, when Mr. W. A. Borden American Librarian was invited by the Maharaja of Baroda to introduce library education in the State. He established the first Library Training school at the then Baroda State in 1911. Mr. Asa Don Dickinson, who was appointed as Librarian in Punjab University also started a library apprentice training programme of three months duration in 1915 in Punjab. Andhra Desa Library Association (ADLA) conducted training classes for the library workers in Andhra Pradesh in 1920 at Vijayawada. Mr. M. Visweswarayya, The then Dewan of Mysore initiated a Library Science Training course at Bangalore under the "Programme of library development". The Madras Library Association (MALA) conducted a summer school for college librarians in 1929. Later on Madras University took over the course in 1931, and converted it to a full-time course leading to the Diploma course in 1937. The Hooghly District Library Association organized an experimental librarianship camp training center at Bansberia in association with the Bengal Library Association (BLA) in West Bengal in 1934, and subsequently arranged a regular training programme in Certificate of Librarianship in 1937. In 1935, The Imperial Library (Now the National Library of India, Calcutta) also introduced a training course leading to a diploma in librarianship under the supervision of the then Librarian, Mr. K. M. Asadullah. The Training programme was continued till 1944, when the Calcutta University started a regular diploma course in librarianship in 1945. Since then a large number of Universities in different States and library associations have come forward to introduce a variety of courses in Library Science at different levels.

PRESENT SCENE

Today, about 80 Universities in the country are imparting L and IS education, Out of which more than 40 Universities are conducting M L I S Course, And about 30 University have been offering research programmes. Moreover, all State Associations and a few polytechnics are also imparting education in L and I S at lower level. West Bengal is no exception in this regard as it made mighty strides in this direction.

L AND IS EDUCATION IN WEST BENGAL

West Bengal has a glorious past in the field of education especially in the field of library development and library movement. The library movement which started during the freedom struggle has laid foundation not only for the development of different kinds of libraries, but also for the development of library science education in the State. Before and after independence, BLA, National Library of India and Calcutta University were the institutions mainly responsible for the development of L and I S education in West Bengal. At present the state has ten Universities including Netaji Open Universities, amongst these Universities seven (viz. Calcutta, Jadavpur, Burdwan, Vidyasagar, Rabindra Bharati, Kalyani and North Bengal) Universities offer L and I S course at post-graduate level and are awarding B. Lib. Sc. / BLIS degree. Again four Universities namely, Calcutta, Jadavapur, Burdwan and Vidyasagar have masters degree programme. Burdwan, Jadavpur, Vidyasagar and Calcutta also introduced research programme leading to a Ph. D. Degree. Rabindra Bharati and Kalyani Universities have already decided to start the MLIS Course in near future. In addition to these. L and I S programmes a specialized course in special librarianship and documentation was introduced and conducted by the IASLIC and IOL (Institute of Librarians) but the course was discontinued subsequently.

Apart from the establishment of various educational institutions for imparting L and I S education, a significant development in the history of library development in west Bengal was the enactment of W.B. Public Libraries Act, 1979. The Act enables to set up a public library network throughout the State which clearly testifies that the public libraries play a significant role in the promotion of library education, recreation and other activities. This demanded a need for a large number of professional and semi-professional manpower to provide better and effective library services. It gave an impetus for the development of L and I S education in the State.

EXISTING LEVELS OF L AND I S EDUCATION

At present the L and I S education and training programmes are offered at different levels by the different Universities in the State. They are as follows:

[a] Certificate Course

[b] Bachelor's Degree (i.e. B. Lib. Sc. /BLIS)

[c] Master's Degree (i.e. M. Lib. Sc./MLIS)

[d] Ph.D. Programmes.

Certificate Course

The course is designed to give elementary training to library workers and new entrants to the library profession in general library education in its basic principles, Organizational procedures. Skill and management. The main objective of the course is to train persons as semi-professionals to serve in the academic. Public and other libraries. The course is conducted by the Bengal Library Association (BLA). Calcutta; Rabindra

Bharathi Mission Boys' Home, Ratra, 25 Parganas (North); Janata College, Kalimphong (Darjeeling) (now closed); Banipur Library Science Training Center, 24-Parganas (North). The minimum qualification for admission into the course prescribed by all institutions is H.S. or Matriculate/School Final/Madhyamik or equivalent with five years practical experience in a recognized library as a full-time employee. The duration of the course is 6 months.

Bachelor Degree Course

At University level in West Bengal the first-degree course in L and I S education is either B. Lib. Sc. or BLIS. The course is offered by Calcutta, Jadavpur, Burdwan, Rabindra Bharati, Vidyasagar, Kalyani and North Bengal University. IGNOU also introduced BLIS programme at its Calcutta Center and Suri (Birbhum District) Center. To fulfil the demand of the professional manpower requirement in different libraries in the state and the enactment of W.B. Public Libraries Act in 1979, gave a new impetus to the Universities to introduce the BLIS programme. The overall objective of this course is to provide training at the post-graduate level to prepare trained professional staff for holding the different positions in libraries of various types and sizes. The duration of the course is one full academic year. The eligibility for admission into the course differs from one University to another.

Master's Degree Course

This stage of L and I S education has been designed as a post B.Lib Sc. or BLIS Course leading to M. Lib. Sc. or MLIS degree. It is imparted by Calcutta, Burdwan, Jadavpur and Vidyasagar Universities. It may be mentioned that Calcutta University was the pioneer in introducing the Diploma Course in Librarianship in 1945 for the first time in the country. Later on the course was transferred into the B. Lib. Sc. Course. Just to bring it at par with the other schools in the country. But there was a growing demand for the introduction of master Degree programme from all corners and considering the need for the initiation of programme, Calcutta University again took the lead and started two years M. Lib. Sc. Course in 1974 with an intake of 5 students (Gradually increased to 15). Which was the first of its kind in the whole of the country. The master's degree program in other universities is of usually one full academic year duration. The aim of this higher level is to train up persons to fill up the top posts in different library systems, viz. Special, Public academic, Industrial, R and D, Business libraries and information and documentation centers and make library system modern and more dynamic. The University of Burdwan started one year Master Degree course in 1979 with an intake of 8 students and the intake has been gradually increased to 15. Jadavpur University started offering MLIS degree course from 1984. The total seats in the beginning were 10. It has now been extended to 15-18.

Vidyasagar University introduced the MLIS programme in 1978 with an intake capacity of 10 students. The minimum requirement for admission to this course recommended by all the Universities is graduation having a degree in L and I S and a good academic back ground. The other criteria recommended by the Universities differ from one University to another. It is curious to note that no University in the state has come forward to initiate the M. Phil. Programme, though the programme has already been introduced and followed by other faculties at the Universities level. The reason is probably the dearth of suitable teaching staff and lack of minimum infrastructure in the existing department.

Research In L and I S

Research activities in L and I S have not progressed considerably, Though it has made mighty strides in other disciplines since independence. The various reasons that may be accounted for are lack of research tradition, proper methodology and techniques, lack of research-oriented teachers, motivation and above all adequate funds. Prof. Ranganathan started the research programme first in Delhi University. Since then there was a considerable gap in this respect. However, in the meantime the need for research in L and I S has been greatly accelerated due to the rapid advances in scientific, industrial and technological field generating increased information on all aspects. This demands development in information technology and information handling techniques, and urges new methods and techniques for effective processing and utilization of information and the services to be provided by the various libraries and documentation centers or information centers. All these provoked modern researchers in this field to take active interest in research projects and an aptitude for research has already been created. Today about 30 Universities have already introduced research programme and considerable number of candidates have come out successful with Ph. D. Degree in L and I S from these schools.

Ph. D. Program

Research programme leading to a Ph. D. Degree is conducted by the four Universities, namely, Calcutta, Burdwan, Jadavpur or Vidyasagar in West Bangal. The Burdwan University is the first one to offer a doctoral programme in the State and the present contributor of the paper took active initiative in this regard since the need for research is very much felt in this area and he is mainly responsible for initiating the programme for the first time in the University. 10 scholars have already been awarded Ph. D. Degree from the Burdwan University since 1989 and a number of scholars are pursuing their research studies. Jadavpur University and Vidyasagar University also awarded Ph. D. Degrees to 6 and 2 scholars respectively. But no research output has yet been made by the Calcutta University in the field. The objective of the Ph.D. programme is to extend the boundaries of the L and I S discipline, thereby creating new knowledge and make the knowledge more useful and meaningful to the community. The research programme follows the pattern of all other faculties in a University.

CONCLUSION

It is heartening to note that the L and I S education have been progressed considerably in our State since independence in comparison with the other States. It may be pointed out that the L and I S education at present are being influenced by the latest developments in the field of information technology. With this changing environment the L and I S education be restructured in order to reshape the L and I S education infrastructure based on information technology by the different library schools in the State. Therefore, a qualitative improvement is expected in library professionals to meet the manpower requirements of the different libraries, Document and information centers.

REFERENCES

1. P. B. Mangla, Ed. *Library and Information Science Education in India*, (Delhi: MacMillon, 1977)
2. P. N. Kaula *Library Education in perspective library Science Today*. Ed. By Kaula. (Bombay: Asia Publishing House, 1965. P. 541-52.
3. P. Barua, "Library and Information Science Education at higher level in West Bengal : Structural differences in their syllabi : A Comparative study." *Hundred years of Library Education and its Failure* – Ed. P.S.G. Kumar (ILA-IASLIC-GILA-IATLIS, Library Education Centenary Seminar) held at Nagpur 10-12 October, (1987).

X : 5

Library Science: A Subject As Well As A Profession

S. D. Vyas

INTRODUCTION

Oxford Advanced Learner's Dictionary defines profession as a "Paid occupation, especially one that requires advanced education and training". Thus any profession is a means of earning a livelihood. In making library science as a subject, there were two problems. One was to develop the subject as discipline and other was to develop it as a full fledged profession. In the development of library science the role of Melevil Dewey, Paul Otlet, Henry la Fontaine, Pierce Butler and S. R. Ranganathan is significant. W. C. Berwick Sayers says that prior to S. R. Ranganathan there was no library science. It was a mere craft like binding. It was S. R. Ranganathan who gave the principles and laws to the library science.(1) Many British and American library scientists contributed to library science, and it subjected to careful scrutiny. The arguments of Pierce Butler in providing a theory of library science is highly interesting. Butler says that library science is a newly emerging subject and the librarians have always been inclined to imitate the outward forms of the other professions before attaining the corresponding internal development. (2) Some argue that library science cannot become full fledged subject as it touches only fringes and not the core of culture.(3) But S. R. Ranganathan's overwhelming contribution to the subject and later research in library science refutes this opinion. It has now become a full subject. S. R. Ranganathan is still the most cited author of the library science world. Americans remember his five laws and their relevance.

HISTORY

While looking at the history from ancient times, we find that library science took different forms. In Vedic age, book conservation was the sole province of the purohits who allowed the use of books in the ashram itself. This occupation then developed as inherited profession. There was no need of any training and education as the number of books were limited. Gutenberg's invention of printing led to the information explosion which created a problem. We have come from simple mere book-keeper as a hereditary job to now a specialization for which we need high academic and professional qualifications as well as sound training. It is emphasized that education and training in library science should be for longer period of time so that one learns the basics of the profession. It would be hard to imagine that had there been no Melvil Dewey, Henry La Fontaine, Paul Otlet and S. R. Ranganathan, what would have been the scene of libraries? It was Melvil Dewey who organised library collection based on a sound scheme of classification. It revolutionised the use and form of libraries. It became the modern fashion to organise libraries on a scheme of classification.

It is realized that unless a vision is developed no principles and laws could be developed. In the beginning of any phenomena concepts originate. Concepts give birth to facts. Facts generate hypothesis and from hypothesis principles and theories develop. No profession develops without a vision. It has to be agreed that the above pioneers who were responsible for the making of the subject had a vision. Pierce Butler's *Introduction to Library Science* has discussed the issue of library science as a full subject long back in 1933. According to him many of us are not good at mathematics. He argues that if a coin is tossed at random, one can know the result whether it will fall head or tail. One simply has to find out the weight, shape, position, velocity and friction of the coin. Butler says "only few persons have mathematical ability to attain real understanding of those parts of modern science whose validity can be established solely by the mathematical theory of probability."(4) Butler's statement proves that any understanding of a problem could be better solved or understood with mathematical solutions.

PROBLEMS

According to Lester Asheim the following problems exist in the library profession.

(1) There is a difference in ideals and realities, but this difference exists in every profession.

(2) The duration of library science training is too short to learn any thing worth considerable.

(3) There is no internship in library science courses as well as written examination.

(4) Library professionals are not fully involved in the professional activities of the national association. At present hardly 5 to 10 percent of the professionals are members of Indian Library Association. There are 270,000 doctors in USA out of which 69% are members of the American Medical Association.

(5) According to Ralph M. Edwards lack of research in the library science is the main reason for it not becoming a full fledged subject.

(6) American Library Association has powers to accreditate any school of library science. Many schools have not been accredited by American Library Association. If we have similar system in our country, it will help us to eliminate mushroom growth of library science schools or at least categorise them either accredited or non-accredited.

(7) Women professionals out number men professionals. There is a low image of the women in the society. It does not

mean that the women are in any way less intelligent or hard working than the men. It is the stereotype attitude of the men towards the women as stated by the feminists:

STATUS

L. Carroll De Weese says that the following are the three strategies to be adopted by library professionals to improve occupational status:—

(1) Leave the profession and strive for higher profession.

(2) Increase his status within the profession.

(3) Improve the status of his occupation.

De Weese admits that the first two strategies are achievable by individuals. But third strategy is generalized and is the main concern of library profession.(5) Lester Asheim says that if a cup of tea is ordered, a waiter would serve the tea keeping in view status of the person. In addition to this, pay scales of professionls also matters. Unless a librarian is well paid, he will not be able to work with zeal. His psychology of getting low pay scales will loom large in his working style. He would resort to union activities which are against the objectives of the professional duties, rather than earning favours from the government.

The professional situation of librarians in India is different. Ours is a developing economy and hence a developing profession. We have different kinds of problems than American library professionals. Comparing the professional situation of these two countries would be of no use. At the time of announcement of the Fifth Pay Commission Report a large number of different professions were dissatisfied with its recommendations. Many of the groups went on strike to meet their demands. Thus a vocal group can pressurise the government to get more pay and facilities.

ISSUES RELATED TO LIBRARY OBJECTIVES

Ralph M. Edwards gives the following library objectives:

(1) Professional objectives, and

(2) Management objectives.

There is always a conflict between the above functions. Library profession has been given autonomy by the society because of its specialized training and expertise. It means no one knows better than librarians so far as library organization is concerned. Authority of subject expertise has also been given to them. Ralph M. Edwards says that professional functions should have sway over managerial functions. Librarians are engrossed more in routine than professional jobs.(6) Indian librarians have hardly any say in book selection. According to Ralph M. Edwards collection building and book selection are the professional jobs of the librarians. But how many librarians are involved in it, and how many of us are giving reference and documentation service to the users?

In library science, except classification, book selection and reference service. Other subjects are not challenging. In cataloguing once one masters the rules of cataloguing, there is hardly any academic challenge. These are the views of Ralph M. Edwards. Library science is still in a developing stage. It is influencing other subjects and is being influenced in return. Ralph M. Edwards is of the opinion that more research in the subject will offer the correct answers to the problems. The library profession is client oriented. Hence clients satisfaction will matter more to the success of the library professionals.

CHARACTERISTICS

According to Lester Ahseim, any profession should have the following characteristics:

(1) It has been already mentioned that it should have a national professional body.

(2) It should have an altruistic code, that is, it should help others.

(3) It should be a calling.

(4) It should not resort to unionism, but rather earn to meet their demands.

(5) Professionals should involve in research.(7) Library professional To achieve full status of profession, will have to work hard and correct the mistakes committed in the past. They have to discuss the matters of national importance. It was one of the objectives of the Indian Library Association to eradicate illiteracy through their meaningful role by spreading public library network. Today still 60 percent of the States are without public library acts particularly big States. S. R. Ranganathan's dream that the whole country will have 100 percent literacy by 20th century end is still a mirage. Could we achieve the target? Library profession has its uniqueness, but we have to strive for achieving objectives in an earnest manner.

CONCLUSION

The library profession should imbibe the characteristics of the well established profession. Moreover a few professionals should go for top class research in the subject so that we can get answers to the problems afflicting the profession. Rather than opening more schools of library science, we must give better training to our incoming professionals. Indian Library association should play a meaningful role. It is to be realized that one year duration of B. Lib. Sc. and M. Lib. Sc. is not enough to train library professionals. Moreover, internship training under the guidance of senior librarians should be encouraged to make them fully trained. It is recommended that library professionals involve more in professional work than managerial to play a meaningful role.

REFERENCES

1. S. R. Ranganathan. Five Laws of library science. Bombay. Asia. 1961. Foreword.
2. Pierce Butler. An Introduction to Library science. Chicago. University of Chicago Press. 1933. 115 p.

3. Lester Asheim. Library profession. *In* B. S. Panwar and S. D. Vyas. Library Management. Delhi. B. R. Publishing House. 1986.

4. Pierce Butler. An Introduction to Library Science. P. 16-17.

5. Lester Asheim. Library profession. p. 4.

6. Ralph M. Edwards. The management of libraries and the Professional Functions of librarians. *In* B.S. Pawar and S.D. Vyas. Library Management, Delhi, B. R. Publishing house, 1986. P. 39-40.

7. Lester Asheim. Library professionals. P. 1-37.

X : 6

Continuing Professional Education for the Staff in The Zilla Granthalaya Samsthas (ZGSs) In Andhra Pradesh

J. Yadagiri Reddy
B. Ramesh Babu
V. Vishwa Mohan

INTRODUCTION

A library is one of the effective repositories of our cultural heritage. The term Public Library is an amalgamation of two attributes, namely "Public" and "Library". The first one is an epithet dependent on and supplemented by a noun of common utility which means a collection of books and other reading material assembled for public use as against a collection assembled for sale, for display or for any other such purposes. A public library is the local gate-way to knowledge, it provides basic conditions for life-long learning and promotes cultural, social and individual development. The UNESCO Public Library Manifesto (1994)[1] proclaims Public Library as a "living force for education, culture and information and as an essential agent for the fostering of peace and spiritual welfare through the minds of men and women".

"Public Library" as understood in the West (meaning unfettered service to all, free of cost) has an altogether different connotation in India. It denotes any library which permits its material to be used by the public with or without paying a fee. There are libraries set up and sponsored and / or supported by the government, including local bodies. Private individuals and organisations have established libraries, some of which receive aid from the government.

A more competent and well trained library staff is required in order to achieve the desired goals of public libraries. According to the UNESCO Library Manifesto: - "Trained and competent staff in adequate numbers are vital to select and organise resources and assist users. Special training will be required for many activities such as work with children and handicapped, audio-visual materials and the organisation of cultural activities".

This statement emphasises the need for Continuing Professional Education (CE) for the library staff.

CONTINUING PROFESSIONAL EDUCATION (CE)

CE is a life long education in one's profession. There is an increasing concern about life-long learning (LLL) or education permanent which is otherwise known as "educational third dimension". A commitment to continuing education is one of the distinguished marks of a true profession. The library and information profession is not an exception to this phenomenon. CE is a process through which an individual updates his or her already acquired knowledge in any profession so as to improve efficiency in the respective profession. CE for library and information science professionals is of considerable current interest.

SCOPE OF THIS PAPER

This paper introduces the concept of public library and CE for librarians. Presents the structure of public library system in Andhra Pradesh and an over view of ZGS Libraries in A.P. analyses the staff opinions with regard to CE. For this purpose the staff in the cadres of Grade III to Secretaries were considered.

A sample of staff were administered a questionnaire and the data has been analysed and interpreted.

STRUCTURE OF THE PUBLIC LIBRARY SYSTEM IN A.P.

The present structure of the Public Library System in A.P. conforms to the structure suggested by the Advisory Committee for Libraries in India in the year 1958[2]. The present structure of the Public Library System is given in Chart 4.1.

ZGS LIBRARIES IN A.P.

In 1970, there were only 1040 ZGS libraries functioning in the state, which comprises DCL, CCL, Branch Libraries, Mobile Libraries, Village Libraries, Book Deposit Centres. By March 1996, the number of ZGS libraries increased more than two-fold and reached to 2405. However, there is three-fold increase in branch Libraries from 517 in 1970 to 1448 in 1996[3].

Libraries under ZGSs/CGS

1)	District Central Libraries	22
2)	City Central Library	1
3)	Branch Libraries	1448
4)	Mobile Libraries (Hyd.)	3
5)	Village Libraries	355
6)	Book Deposit centres	576
	Total	2405

Table 5.1 presents the trained professional staff working in ZGSs/CGS Libraries in A.P.

Table 5.2 presents the total professional staff (posts) in ZGSs/CGS as on 31-3-1996

ANALYSIS AND DISCUSSION

Distribution of Questionnaires and Responses

Table 6.1 presents the District-wise distribution of

Chart 4.1. Organisational Structure of PS in A.P.

Government of Andhra Pradesh

↓

Andhra Pradesh Granthalaya Parishad

↓

Department of Public Libraries

↓

Govt. Libraries	City Granthalaya Samastha/ Zilla Granthalaya Samastha/Libraries	Aided Libraries
↓	↓	↓
State Central Library	City Central Library & District Central Libraries	Managed by
↓	↓	↓
Regional Libraries	Branch Libraries	1 Voluntary Organisations
↓	↓	
Mobile Library	Mobile Libraries	2 Corporations
	↓	
	Village Libraries	3 Municipalities
	↓	
	Book Deposit Centres	4 Panchayats
		5 Co-op Societies

Table 5.1 : Trained Professionals in ZGSs/ CGS Libs. in A. P

S. No.	District	1970 Dip/ Deg	Cert.	Total	1980 Dip/ Deg	Cert.	Total	1990 Dip Deg	Cert.	Total	1996 Dep/ Deg	Cert.	Total
1.	Adilabad	1	5	6	2	16	18	6	26	32	6	37	43
2.	Anantapur	3	17	20	5	28	33	6	42	48	7	47	54
3.	Chittoor	7	15	22	7	17	24	11	50	61	15	44	59
4.	Cuddapah	1	16	17	5	23	28	4	32	36	3	26	29
5.	E. Godavari	5	21	26	7	59	66	12	65	77	9	67	76
6.	Guntur	14	41	55	10	52	62	18	69	87	25	56	81
7.	Hyderabad	24	31	55	11	44	55	21	89	110	34	73	107
8.	Karimnagar	1	6	7	2	18	20	17	21	38	24	26	50
9.	Khammam	2	3	5	2	6	8	9	30	39	11	30	41
10.	Krishna	5	49	54	14	74	88	18	84	102	18	75	93
11.	Kurnool	1	23	24	3	23	26	3	52	55	9	34	43
12.	Mahboobnagar	2	2	4	4	5	9	8	42	50	8	44	52
13.	Medak	1	6	7	4	13	17	2	30	32	6	25	31

14. Nalgonda	2	7	9	4	12	16	8	32	40	21	40	61
15. Nellore	3	16	19	5	25	30	9	40	49	9	40	49
16. Nizamabad	2	10	12	2	22	24	4	35	39	5	37	42
17. Prakasam	-	-	-	3	22	25	5	43	48	15	38	53
18. Rangareddy (Old Hyd.)	1	4	5	2	22	24	3	30	33	9	30	39
19. Srikakulam	1	4	5	2	10	12	2	29	31	6	27	33
20. Vijayanagaram	-	-	-	-	-	-	3	27	30	11	30	41
21. Visakhapatnam	9	27	36	9	31	40	6	46	52	6	46	52
22. Warangal	3	7	10	4	13	17	16	28	44	17	33	50
23. W. Godavari	7	19	26	7	28	35	11	57	68	17	49	66
Total	95	329	424	114	563	677	202	999	1201	291	954	1245

Dip / Deg = Diploma / Degree holders Cert. = Certificate holders

Table 5.2 : Professional Staff (Posts) in ZGSs / CGS as on 31-3-1996 according to designation

Sl. No.	District:	G. Librarian	Gr-I	Gr-II	Gr-III	Total
1.	Adilabad	1	1	6	42	50
2.	Anantapur	1	4	8	50	63
3.	Chittor	1	4	9	58	72
4.	Cuddapah	1	3	7	26	37
5.	East Godavari	1	6	11	47	65
6.	Guntur	1	7	12	59	79
7.	Hyderabad	1	6	19	77	103
8.	Karimnagar	1	1	4	47	53
9.	Khammam	1	2	1	43	47
10.	Krishna	1	8	20	58	87
11.	Kurnool	1	1	9	30	41
12.	Mahaboobnagar	1	2	1	53	57
13.	Medak	1	1	4	34	40
14.	Nalgonda	1	3	3	55	62
15.	Nellore	1	3	3	50	57

16.	Nizamabad	1	1	2	32	36
17.	Prakasham	1	2	4	46	53
18.	Ranga Reddy	1	1	4	30	36
19.	Srikakulam	1	1	1	33	36
20.	Vijayanagaram	1	1	4	30	36
21.	Visakhapatnam	1	6	8	41	56
22.	Warangal	1	2	5	47	55
23.	West Godavari	1	6	3	53	63
	Total	23	72	148	1041	1284

questionnaires and the responses received from the professionals working in the ZGS libraries.

Attendance to the CE Programmes

The need for CE exists in almost all the professions and LIS is not an exception to this. Table 6.2 presents the quantum of staff who have attended the CE programmes in their service.

Table 6.2 : Attendance to the CEPs

S. No.	*Description*	*ZGCs / CGS Libraries*
1	Yes	64 (34.0)
2	No	124 (66.0)
	Total	188 (100)

Reasons for Attending CEP

Table 6.3 Presents the reasons for attending the CEP with their rankings.

Since CEP adds to improve their knowledge which has been ranked as first followed four other reasons. The X value is 1.32

Reasons for not attending CEP

Table 6.4 presents the reasons for not attending the CEP with their rankings. Lack of awareness about the CEP has been cited by the respondents as the first rank and the X value is 3.06.

Attending CEP seems to be a rare exercise in Public Library System in A. P. since a majority of the respondents (66%) have not attended any CEP in their service.

Table 6.1 :District-Wise Distribution of Questionnaires And Responses Received From ZGSs CGS

S. No.	District	No. Of Questionnaires Distributed	Received
1.	Adilabad	8	7
2.	Anantapur	12	10
3.	Chittoor	12	11
4.	Cuddapah	10	7
5.	East-Godavari	5	-
6.	Guntur	15	13
7.	Hyderabad	35	33
8.	Karimnagar	5	4
9.	Khammam	10	8
10.	Krishna	18	15
11.	Kurnool	5	-
12.	Mahboobnagar	10	8
13.	Medak	12	11
14.	Nalgonda	10	8
15.	Nellore	5	-
16.	Nizamabad	8	-
17.	Prakasham	5	-
18.	Ranga Reddy	10	8
19.	Srikakulam	5	-
20.	Vijayanagaram	12	9
21.	Visakhapatnam	20	19
22.	Warangal	8	5
23.	West Godavari	10	7
	Total:	250	188 (75%)

Table 6.3 : Reasons for Attending CEPs by ZGSs / CGS Staff

S. No.	Description / Reason	Variable	RANK						$\overline{X}$	Rank
			1	2	3	4	5	Total		
1.	It is mandatory for Promotion	X 74	6 (9.4)	8 (12.5)	10 (15.6)	6 (9.4)	34 (53.1)	64	2.46	5
2.	Addition to my knowledge	X 75	32 (50.0)	8 (12.5)	12 (18.8)	12 (18.8)	-	64	1.32	1
3.	Enhances Professional competence	X 76	10 (15.6)	30 (46.9)	6 (9.4)	10 (15.6)	8 (12.5)	64	1.68	2
4.	Familiarity With fellow professionals	X 77	4 (6.25)	10 (15.6)	28 (43.8)	14 (21.9)	8 (12.5)	64	2.04	3
5.	Helps to keep abreast of latest trends	X 78	12 (18.8)	8 (12.5)	8 (12.5)	22 (34.3)	14 (21.9)	64	2.10	4
	Total		64	64	64	64	64			

Table 6.4 : Reasons for Not Attending CEPs by ZGSs / CGS Staff

S. No.	*Description / Reason*	*Variable*	*RANK*						$\bar{X}$	*Rank*
			1	*2*	*3*	*4*	*5*	*Total*		
1.	Lack of avenues	X 79	20 (16.1)	54 (43.5)	20 (16.1)	16 (12.9)	14 (11.3)	124	3.22	3
2.	Restricted to a particular grade	X 80	16 (12.9)	18 (6.45)	34 (27.4)	34 (27.4)	32 (25.8)	124	4.30	4
3.	Do not influence professional work	X 81	2 (1.61)	12 (9.7)	28 (22.6)	36 (29.0)	46 (37.0)	124	4.84	5
4.	Lack of awareness	X 82	40 (32.2)	30 (24.2)	24 (19.3)	16 (12.9)	14 (11.3)	124	3.06	1
5.	Lack of encouragement	X 83	46 (37.0)	20 (16.1)	18 (14.5)	22 (17.7)	18 (14.5)	124	3.18	2
	Total		124	124	124	124	124			

CONCLUSION

Necessary efforts are to be initiated and suitable avenues are to be provided to inculcate the staff of the PLS for undergoing CEP. The SILERT (a constitute organ of DPL) has to evolve a special training programme to conduct CEP in the form of refresher courses, in-service training, short term courses and to hold them periodically in consultation with the Departments of the Library and Information Science in the State.

REFERENCES

1. UNESCO Public Library Manifesto 1994. *UNISIST Newsletter*. 23 (1). 1995. P. 9.
2. India, Ministry of Education, Advisory Committee for Libraries, 1985. Report. Ed. 2. Delhi: Manager of publications, 1961.
3. Yadagiri Reddy, J. Personnel in the Public Library System in A. P.: A study of career development. Ph. D. Thesis submitted to Osmania University, 1997, P. 20.

Index